D1090420

**Humanistic
Education: An
Interpretation**

# Humanistic Education: An Interpretation

Elizabeth Léonie Simpson
*with*
A Comprehensive Annotated Bibliography of
Humanistic Education
*by*
Mary Anne Gray

A Report to the Ford Foundation

Ballinger Publishing Company • Cambridge, Massachusetts
*A Subsidiary of J.B. Lippincott Company*

Library
I.U.P.
Indiana, Pa

370.1    SL58L
c.l

 This book is printed on recycled paper.

Copyright © 1976 by The Ford Foundation. All rights reserved. No part of this publication may be reproduced, stored in a retrieval system, or transmitted in any form or by means, electronic, mechanical, photocopy, recording or otherwise, without the prior written consent of the publisher.

International Standard Book Number: 0-88410-168-1

Library of Congress Catalog Card Number: 76-15280

Printed in the United States of America


**Library of Congress Cataloging in Publication Data**

Simpson, Elizabeth Léonie.
   Humanistic education.

    1.  Education, Humanistic—United States.
2.  Education, Humanistic—United States—Bibliography.
I.  Title.
LC1011.S55                370.11'2'0973            76-15280
ISBN 0-88410-168-1

# Contents

# Preface

"Humanistic education" has attracted growing attention among educators, academicians, researchers, and the general public. A spate of texts and popular trade books has appeared, and a collection of readings in humanistic education has now come forth—a sure sign that the field has arrived academically (Read & Simon, 1975). Related social developments, such as the Human Potential Movement and "Third Force" Humanistic Psychology, also have gained widespread interest. The time has come for a bird's-eye interpretation of the state of the art of humanistic education in the United States today as part of an effort to place humanistic education in its historical and philsophical contexts. Thanks to the generosity of the Ford Foundation, I was able to spend two years trying to achieve such an interpretation. My results are presented in this report.

Chapter One attempts the most difficult of tasks: conceptual clarification. What is humanistic education? Whence sprang it? How is it distinct from other major educational movements and innovations? Chapters Two and Three examine humanistic education in practice and *in situ.* What do teachers who call themselves humanistic educators do in the classroom? How do these classrooms differ from others? What do those who train humanistic teachers do? What are the characteristics of humanistic teacher training and curriculum development? The appendices provide a brief description of principal informants, detailed slices of curriculum, and a pathfinder guide to the literature.

An extensive annotated bibliography prepared by Mary Anne Gray titled *A Comprehensive Bibliography in Humanistic Education* comprises Part II of this publication.

A final procedural note: All the footnotes are gathered together at the end of my report. Not only do they include the customary references and citations, but they also present detailed excursions into theories, elaborations of textual points, and such other academic arcana as might otherwise interfere with the flow of the argument in the text. The professional reader will probably want to use most of the footnotes; the interested layman may find them less useful.

The making of this report is itself an attempt at communication. Never before have I been made so aware of the invisible barriers which like-minded individuals and groups unwittingly maintain about the labors that engage them. The same urges that generate creative work act to preserve its distinctiveness. Apart from the two centers (at the University of California, Santa Barbara, and the University of Massachusetts) formerly funded by the Ford Foundation, few of the groups with whom I talked were aware of others already deeply committed to related work. Thousands of educators are engaged in this field—perhaps tens of thousands, counting all levels of formal education. Humanistic education is alive and well and more widespread than even some of its practitioners realize.

To anticipate several other major conclusions, I found that the clearest common denominator among humanistic educators as they ply their trade in classroom and university is the inclusion of the self-as-curriculum. Feeling and thought, affect and cognition are joined together in pursuit of knowledge about the self. Despite differences in vocabulary and in theory, almost all projects in humanistic education share a common developmental framework. Beneath the variations, within the matrix of an ideology still forming, humanistic educators share common purposes and beliefs about the nature of humanity and the process of learning. By example and by precept I hope to elucidate these commonalities in the pages that follow.

# Foreword

From the vantage point of 1976, it seems clear that the 1960s ushered in a new era of concern about the human condition. Dialogue and action on race, poverty, the disadvantaged, "identity," individualized instruction, open education, ethnic pride, along with new religious expressions, war protests, and environmental awareness—all marked a new kind of individualism, compounded of a sense of responsibility and respect for others' individuality and worth as well as for one's own self. Not least among the expressions of this reawakened individualism was the "human potential movement," which, like the civil rights movement and anti-poverty programs, left its mark on education. All were reminders of forgotten or neglected elements of the human condition. As it turned out, they converged in the Ford Foundation's involvement with what has come to be called humanistic education.

For sixteen years, from 1951 to 1967, the Foundation sponsored an agency for educational change, the Fund for the Advancement of Education. Although independent and guided by the policies of its own board of trustees, the Fund operated in a symbiotic relationship with the Foundation's own education division. Controversial throughout its lifetime, the Fund sought to inject new ideas into education, to test imaginative approaches, and to be an innovative force. As such, it was usually ahead of the times in the projects it financed. One of these was the Elementary School Teaching Project (ESTP), started in 1964.

At that time, the educational problems of the "disadvantaged" were a national preoccupation. The Elementary School Teaching Project began as an attempt to develop successful teaching practices and curriculum content for "disadvantaged" children—black youngsters from low-income, ghetto surroundings. It started with cognitive goals, but ended with affective strategies

—and with the conclusion that those strategies had implications for all learners. From it evolved a model that used pupils' personal concerns both as the starting point for selecting curriculum content ("relevance") and as legitimate learning content in their own right. The two project leaders, Gerald Weinstein and Mario D. Fantini wrote about the project's experience and product in *Toward Humanistic Education: A Curriculum of Affect* (Praeger, 1970).

By the end of ESTP, the stage was set for a direct encounter between educators and those practitioners in the human potential movement whose special territory was developing self-awareness. The Fund for the Advancement of Education again led the way, through a grant in 1967 to the Esalen Institute in California for a project that sought to invent and test affective teaching techniques and sample lessons to fit the conventional curriculum. Directed by Professor George Isaac Brown of the University of California (Santa Barbara), this project involved a dozen teachers and was one of the first conscious efforts to bring affect and cognition together in the classroom and to teach teachers how to integrate affective learning with cognitive learning.

Together, the Elementary School Teaching Project and the inaccurately tagged "Ford-Esalen" project laid the groundwork for substantial Ford Foundation support of humanistic education. In 1970 the Foundation made three-year grants for two new university-based programs: one, the Confluent Education Program at the University of California (Santa Barbara), directed by Professor Brown; the other, the Center for Humanistic Education at the University of Massachusetts, Amherst, directed by Professor Weinstein. Both were developmental—they concentrated on systematic research, curriculum building, and training, and both had at their core experienced, practicing public school teachers. Their accomplishments were sufficiently solid that both continue as integral parts of the graduate schools at their respective institutions.

As the Massachusetts and Santa Barbara grants drew to a close, Foundation staff thought it would be timely to take a look at humanistic education in a larger context of practice. By that name (or by one of the many others that had become current, e.g., affective education, confluent education, self-science, psychological education, and more) humanistic education seemed to have gained acceptance as a legitimate area for scholarship, training, and practice. But no one could say for sure how pervasive it might be or how well sanctioned by "the system." Nor was it clear what the distinctions might be among the different brands parading under the banner of humanistic education. We wanted to see how humanistic education fitted into the landscape of American education. To act as our eyes and ears and reporter, we called on Dr. Elizabeth Léonie Simpson, on the faculty at the University of Southern California. A former teacher and writer trained as a psychologist, Dr. Simpson had herself been active in the growth of humanistic education and had wide knowledge of people and projects in this field.

What follows is the report Dr. Simpson prepared from her travels, interviews, reading, and professional background. It is accompanied by the product of her research assistant's extensive labor—Mary Anne Gray's annotated bibliography of humanistic education in its different forms. Even before the study was completed, there were many requests for copies. Since scholars of education, writers, policy-makers, trainers, administrators, and teachers saw merit in having the report and bibliography publicly available, we were glad to arrange for publication of the two parts as a single reference volume.

Dr. Simpson's assignment was challenging. The subject defied clear definition, its shifting forms were hard to categorize, and its boundaries were hazy. That she so capably rose to the challenge and brought us to a better understanding of our own and others' efforts in the evolution of educational theory and practice puts us greatly in her debt. Her choice of Mary Anne Gray as research assistant to tackle a critical review of the copious literature in this field was a happy one. For advice in the planning stages of Dr. Simpson's study and for commentary on the final draft, credit must go to Paul Bohannan, Elliott Eisner, Paul Gump, Richard Jones, Floyd Matson, and Michael Scriven. At the Foundation, my colleagues Nancy Dennis, Richard Lacey, and Marjorie Martus contributed to the project immeasurably with their guidance, support, time, and caring. All concerned are grateful for the skilled editorial guidance of Daniel Stein.

Finally, special acknowledgement should be made for the cooperation of many persons and institutions consulted by Dr. Simpson in her field visits and information gathering. They welcomed her as a colleague, opened materials and classes to her, and demonstrated by example the meaning of humanistic education.

**Edward J. Meade, Jr.**
Officer in Charge,
Public Education
April, 1976

**Humanistic
Education: An
Interpretation**

 *Chapter 1*

# What Humanistic Education Is
# and How It Got That Way

## THE PROBLEM OF DEFINITION

Why "humanistic education"? Is another jargon phrase needed in a field already overflowing with a seemingly endless series of catchall phrases and vague terms? Already blessed with affective education, confluent education, psychological education, experiential education, compensatory education, value-free education, must education's vocabulary suffer yet another dubious accretion? Furthermore, is it not a travesty on the long and honorable traditions of the humanities, which go back to the beginnings of western civilization, to attach "humanistic" to what is a relatively recent and possibly faddish development?

Both questions are legitimate—and both are answered at length in the body of this report. By way of preliminaries, however, let me emphasize that I use the word "humanistic" partly because it is the currently popular word to refer to the areas I will discuss and partly because its very umbrellalike ambiguity seems to be valuable. I want to be inclusive, rather than exclusionary. I argue at length below that "humanistic" as a broad rubric includes such separate educational developments as confluent education, affective education, self-as-science, and psychological education.

I further argue that humanistic education as I construe it has deep roots in and affinities with the traditional humanities. Because some of the cherished values of the humanities find a reflection and embodiment in humanistic education, this is, in fact, the statement of a significant relationship.

My approach will be to use a series of successive approximations to focus gradually on the content of humanistic education. By thus inching to a definition, the contours and outlines of humanistic education will emerge and give

*1*

form to the examination in Chapters Two and Three of the substance of humanistic education in practice: in the classroom, in curriculum development, in teacher training, in research.

In this country's schools humanistic education has many forms. In my travels and reading I found variants in title: affective education; environmental studies; special education; school counseling, emotional education; self-science, values, drug, or sex education; human development; social studies; political or legal socialization; and psychological education. All of these variants and variations on the basic themes of humanistic education share a central focus on affect: on the incorporation, experiencing, and analyzing of feelings and emotions as part of the educational process.[1]

### Affect in Humanistic Education

Affect in humanistic education has three principal foci. The first focus is on the *feelings that grow out of the content of the curriculum itself* and the relevance of the issues it presents to the individual lives of students whose interests and motivations are taken seriously. Concern for these feelings is often manifest in attempts to present the curriculum and achieve cognitive learning goals in an exciting way—for example, through simulations, games of various kinds, and role playing of relationships or interaction patterns such as "slave and master."

The second focus is on the *preconditions of learning*—those feelings of acceptance and competence which help to determine the success of the student as a student. While many of these feelings have their origins beyond the school walls, the school environment may substantially shape them by increasing teacher awareness of unconscious rejection, by using a range of ways of coping with interpersonal issues, by building autonomy through the assignment of responsibility, and by rewarding competence not necessarily associated with verbal or mathematical skills. Thus, the broad context of learning becomes supportive of self-esteem. Individualized learning (when the student takes part in shaping the *goals* of the programs instead of simply proceeding at his own pace) is one method through which these positive feelings may be fostered.

The third focus is on *feelings as the content of curriculum*—the personal, emotional material that the student brings to class from, for example, his dreams, his reactions to people or situations, knowledge of fears, doubts, or joys derived from introspection. Direct work may be done with student feelings about themselves, alone, or as a group, using techniques of various kinds (encounter group, Gestalt, psychoanalysis of various forms, or, more commonly, low key group or individual processes which may also utilize a wide variety of creative arts).

### Cognitive Content in Humanistic Education

Cognitive content in humanistic education is built around concepts and processes from behavioral science, psychoanalysis, and clinical and counseling psychologies of varying genre. Data are drawn from both the available body of scientific research about the generalized self and the specific self of the learner as he experiences himself. They are also drawn from the study of groups from the dyad to the society, although curricular emphasis is strongly on the person and interpersonal relations. While theories have appeared to support the feelings-as-content curriculum, most programs in the field have either been loosely atheoretical in origin or eclectically based. Humanistic education at Santa Barbara, for example, draws on both Gestalt psychology and Psychosynthesis. The program at Amherst utilizes Gestalt and development psychology.

The range of systematic psychological thought which has been carved up and applied piecemeal and freehandedly to educational practice is almost as broad and as varied as that of the discipline of psychology itself: psychoanalytic theory (itself with many emphases); Gestalt; Transactional Analysis; Psychosynthesis; perceptual or phenomenological psychology; ego psychology; developmental psychology; and behaviorism, as well as less well known schools of thought. Some of these represent fairly minor differences—more of methodology than of substance. Others clearly derive from beliefs in differing models of humanity, our nature, and our capacities, which inevitably shape educational outcomes.

Made conspicuous by its absence or much vitiated presence, theory is needed —not for its own sake but to ward off the kind of "mindlessness" to which Silberman referred in *Crisis in the Classroom*. Theory is indispensable to create a context for the examination of the reasons behind the methodology and procedures. Over and over I asked teachers why they were doing what they did in the classroom and got a blank stare or the vaguest of generalizations in return. More than once I was told by heads of programs or participants that it was difficult enough for teachers to learn techniques without having to worry about reasons and objectives. It is hard to see how intelligent choice of objectives and methods can be pursued without consideration of the reasons for those choices in the light of desired outcomes.[2]

### Antihumanistic, Pseudohumanistic, and Authentic Humanistic Education

Contemporary teachers, like other mortals, are what they take for granted: beliefs about a model of humanness govern their behavior within the classroom as well as outside it. The nature of humanistic education—past and present —can be examined through those beliefs.

**Antihumanistic Education.** Actively antihumanistic education occurs when teachers believe that human purposes and goals are determined from without, from external authorities, whether groups, individuals, or personalized all-powerful forces, rather than from within the individual. It occurs when learning and the development of the person are rooted excessively in commemoration of the past or anticipation of the future, to the neglect of present experience. It occurs when human beings are perceived as animals driven by instincts that are socially evil, and society is perceived as that which checks the lunging beast and designs the competitive hierarchy within which these barely civilized creatures must relate. With these beliefs, the purpose of education becomes not the development of an adaptable community supportive of individual growth, but, rather, establishment of the secure rigidity of social groups maintained by pressures for conformity.

**Pseudohumanistic Education.** A pseudohumanistic education results from almost the opposite of this picture. It is a rejection of both past and future. Tradition and accumulated wisdom are abandoned as useless. Social groups are not seen as structures to facilitate intimacy and community, but as associations of other-rejecting anticonformists tied only by expediency. Interpersonal relations are essentially manipulations that are designed to satisfy personal needs while rejecting responsibility for responsiveness and commitment to others. Extreme individualism and autonomy are encouraged as evidence of achievement and are accompanied by high self-esteem, disregard for others, and a lack of guilt. In this model, humanness is defined by the capacity to *feel* (especially, to feel creative or powerful), while the use of the intellect is seen as alienation from the self.

**Authentic Humanistic Education.** What, then, are the assumptions that underlie authentic humanistic education? First, the process of learning is the active search and incorporation by the knower of the known. The learner controls his own life and values his own competence as actor in the world. Second, human beings as phenomena are whole and integrated; opposites do indeed coincide. Emotions, rationality, and will—intentionality—are all legitimate and inseparable aspects of humanness and are all engaged as learning occurs. Second, traditions, beliefs, and values are selectively retained, reshaped, and modified to present needs. Third, it is not enough to speak of emotion, the spirit or the soul, the intellectual power of rationality, consciousness, or of valuing. These are inseparable from, not merely encased in, the human body—palpable, solid, and real. Even the extrasensory is rooted in the physical. Auden's great insight, "... the kind/Gates of the body fly open/To its world beyond, the gates of the mind ...," has been surpassed, for we have found the tentative forms of new gates, yet shadowed, waiting: powers beyond feeling or thinking. Fourth, the individual's reality, grounded in present experience, extends both forward to the future and backward to the past from which the here and now have arisen. Fifth, autonomy may find high expression by yielding commitment to the social group. Creation and affirmation may find their application in the quest for the good life with others, as well as for the individual alone.

**Psychological Education As A Subset of
Humanistic Education**

The term "psychological education" has been defined by some as a distinctive form of humanistic education. Yet the similarities between psychological education and humanistic education as I construe it are striking. Both demand the integration of ideas, feelings, and behavior within the curriculum. Both demand relevance to the needs, wants, and interests of the individual student and demand that he accept responsibility for active participation in his own learning. Both imply the superordinate goal of human development toward the whole, autonomous, and differentiated person.

The principal difference is of occasional emphasis. Psychological education always makes explicit that the self and interpersonal and intergroup relationships are legitimate learning foci and that such learning is a precondition for future learning, both intellectual and emotional. Formalized psychological education embodies the substance, concepts, and principles of the discipline of psychology. To this are added by each student those materials produced by introspection, dreams, intuition, and the self-conscious reflexive examination of other personal experience. The learner is also the learned. Depending upon the stage of development of the learner, a special intensity may haunt the subject matter. (Roen, 1967) It is equally true that students may be bored as rapidly as in any course when the class structure rigidifies into a familiar litany of expected problems and solutions, however personal.

Psychological education is an ambiguous concept. It can refer to the professional education of teachers, scientists, scholars, counselors, or other members of helping professions, or to the specialized education of layment from the cradle to the grave. Such an undifferentiated term has little utility.

I propose now to examine two tap roots of humanistic education. First, I will explore its relationships to the great traditions of the humanities, which extend backward in time to the ancient Greeks and Romans, and are reflected in that uneasy amalgam of values and practices lumped together as the Judaeo-Christian heritage. Then I will go on to show how the mental health education movement that began four decades ago and continues to be influential today has become part of humanistic education.

## THE HUMANITIES AND HUMANISTIC EDUCATION[3]

"The humanities" is one of those broad rubrics that has come to mean many different things to many people. Behaviorists, scholars, and teachers alike group themselves under its banner, though they festoon it with different emblems and often march in different directions.[4] The claims of the humanities to be considered humanistic education are not to be casually dismissed, but neither are these disciplines to be automatically included. The substance of a classical humanities curriculum need not necessarily lead to a humanistic education, nor humanistic studies necessarily include the traditional humanities (defined by Act of Congress to be history; philosophy; literature; ethics and comparative religion; language; jurisprudence; archaeology; the history, theory, and practice of the arts; and the humanistic social sciences). In ancient Rome and Greece, the humanities were a creative frame of mind expressed through curiosity embedded in *logos* (word or speech, reason). Rejection of the mutual exclusion of opposites—thinking and feeling—was already in the literature but, in today's jargon, "underutilized." Education was based upon values of wholeness—of harmony and of balance, of integration and interconnectedness: mind *with* body, form *with* content, and theory *with* practice.

Humanistic education is not just the development of symbolic, cognitive capabilities or of evaluative or valuing competencies, or, indeed, of sensitivy or sensibility. It is all of these and more. It enters in where traditionalists have feared to go, or at least have avoided going. While utilizing some of the humanities, its total domain is different. What binds contemporary humanistic studies to the traditional humanities is concern not just with man's highest values, but also with those values as uniquely the product of passion as well as intellect, of emotion as well as reason.

The enduring object of both the humanities and of humanistic education is the enlargement of the human spirit, not merely the development of the capacity to think or to judge esthetically or morally. The humanities have traditionally been concerned with the person—the individual—and the eternal, existential questions of relationships among persons, universes, gods, and dreams. The questions addressed by these disciplines remain: What is life? What is humanness, justice, love, faith, community, and awe? It is the answers, or rather, some of the modes of searching for answers, that have changed.

The experiential bases of the traditional humanities must be broadened and the ordinary, the personal, included. Belief in the examined life must admit new routes to that examination: passion, sensuality, intuition, imagery—subjective truth invented by each participant and not inherited. The culture can provide the framework, but not its processes or its personal meaning. For the individual, cultural values as a traditional group of revered beliefs and objects are personal values privately arrived at, or they are nothing at all. It is not isolated ancient truths, inherited experience, belief, and values that make up the living humanities today, but these as the wellspring of an ever-broadening and deepening stream of personal consciousness centered on understanding the self and other human beings.

Humanistic education attends to bone, blood, and flesh, as well as the spirit. It has to do with people—their mundane lives and lesser values—as well as with dreams, beauty, aspirations, and ideals. It has to do with latent capacities, not of the "race," the species, or of the hero alone, but of the common person. It has to do with the will to understand these capacities in human, not stereotypic, terms and to utilize them. It dwells more in what *is, might* be, and *can* be, and less in what *ought* to be. It avoids the high-minded, guilt-producing, humanity-hating moralism rooted in the view that analysis and rejection are the means to goodness and idealism.

Traditionally, the humanities have sought to educate the imagination to empathize with objects of beauty and of value. But an increase in sensitivity and responsiveness is sterile if it is directed exclusively toward objects and nonhuman experience. This has been a failure of much of aesthetic education. So far as the humanities relate only to objects, whether natural or manmade, living or inert, and not to people and the context of those objects, they are invalid as humanistic studies. The circling eagle, the carved rock, the weaving of design—all are received in the experience of the perceiver and creator. That these artifacts and processes may exist in and of themselves is beside the point—our concern is with the nature of experience within the self.

The cultural heritage is not enough. Each generation and each individual must generate its own inheritance, and that from a profound understanding of the self and others. This is the clear message of authentic humanistic education wherever encountered, in whatever of its protean forms. Left to its classical proponents, until recently education in the humanities had diminished, becoming each year more of an evaporating lake, inaccessible, cold, and threatening, with a scabrous overlay of intellectuality and elitism. Are the humanities for all who are human or for the few? Are they—as content—to be the humanistic studies of today or the ornamentation of a small "cultured" class? Those are the questions that educators, not scholars, will decide. Either these studies will be adaptive in process and content, like self-renewing institutions, or the hide binding their scholarly traditions will serve as shroud.

Further, a humanistic education based on the humanities cannot remain solely in the private places of personal experience and reflection. It moves out, into public places, into the streets and structures where action—social, political, and economic—is carried out. The ethical purpose of the classical humanities was the amelioration of life through change in perception of reality. It remains so today as we articulate an ecology of survival values that are absorbed, internalized, and put to work in the service of the good life. The spirit, enlarged, finds its way into the body politic as well as the body social. While the purpose of humanistic education is the fullest use of their human capacities—physical, mental, and spiritual—by all human beings, that use is set within a social context of relationship and responsibility: independence within community and self-actualization within social responsibility.

## VALUES EDUCATION: THE HUMANITIES IN
## CONTEMPORARY HUMANISTIC EDUCATION

Whenever teaching occurs—be it formal or informal, at home or in school—the process is underlain by basic beliefs and values about what should be taught, to whom, and how. The process itself communicates values. The advice that comes from the Delphic Oracle "know thyself"—suggests that we must know not only what we *are* but what we *ought to be*. Knowing ourselves and what we value in other people and our environment have received a new emphasis and meaning in contemporary education.

Shoben (1965: 117–118) persuasively restates the classic argument for knowing oneself through the examination of one's values:

> The examined life is one in which values are constantly being made articulate, subjected to criticism, and revised in the light of experience and thought. At one level, this process is sophisticated and intellectual; at another, it may be naive and both unenlightened and unencumbered by a tradition of ideas. At all levels, however, it can be authentic. The constant defining and re-defining of one's self in relation to one's work and one's family, for example, entails nothing less than an ongoing appraisal of one's aspirations and obligations of the progress made by one human being in the human search for contentment and self-esteem. So presented, the examined life is as serious and as possible—even as necessary—for the plumber or the gardner as for the physicist or philosopher. Knowledge is deeply relevant to it, but a clarity about values and an ability to think of one's self in valuation terms is still more so.

How is the developing human organism to learn to examine his life in these terms? In the United States today, values education appears to have two principal thrusts, concerned both with informing the individual about his preferences and their strength and consistency and with attempting to influence his choice of action by using the increased self-awareness he acquires. Most widely used have been the approaches of Lawrence Kohlberg and Sidney Simon.[5]

Values education has assumed the proportions of a nationwide movement. The *New York Times* of April 30, 1975, enthusiastically devoted an entire page to it under the headline "New Techniques Help Pupils Develop Values." The *Times* article quoted an official of the New York State Education Department as approvingly estimating that 80 percent of the elementary and secondary schools in New York state "are doing something in this area." The unnamed official went on to say that the state education department has "put out a discussion guide on 'valuing' and acting upon a mandate from the Board of Regents and, with foundation support, is conducting research in six school districts on how to foster moral development." As the *Times* article proceeded to make evident, such developments are not unique to the state of New York.

### Lawrence Kohlberg: The Hierarchy of Moral Development

Kohlberg has written of his work (*Psychology Today*, September 1968, p. 25):

Inspired by Jean Piaget's pioneering effort to apply a structural approach to moral development, I have gradually elaborated over the years of my study a typological scheme describing general structures and forms of moral thought which can be defined independently of the specific content of particular moral decisions or actions.

The typology contains three distinct levels of moral thinking, and within each of these levels distinguishes two related stages. These levels and stages may be considered separate moral philosophies, distinct views of the socio-moral world.

We can speak of the child as having his own morality or series of moralities.

His hierarchy of three levels with six stages follows:

I.  Preconventional Moral Reasoning
    1.  Goodness defined in terms of the physical consequences.
    2.  Instrumental reciprocity ("I'll scratch your back if you'll scratch mine").

II.  Conventional Moral Reasoning
    3.  "Good Boy" orientation; goodness is defined by the approval of others.
    4.  "Law and Order" orientation; goodness is maintaining the social order.

III.  Postconventional Moral Reasoning
    5.  Morality based on "social contract"—agreement among individuals, which may be changed for reasons of social utility.
    6.  Morality based on principles of justice, equality, and reciprocity dependent on respect for the dignity of human beings; the autonomous functioning of conscience.

Lawrence Kohlberg's work on moral judgment rests on the premise that exposure to value issues through discussion and the cognitive dissonance that occurs internally when conflicts appear will cause the student to move upward on this hierarchy of moral development.

Kohlberg describes progression along the hierarchy as cognitive change, facilitated by socioenvironmental interaction and based on the developing capacity to reason and not on the acquisition of specific content. However, others disagree on several counts. (Simpson, 1974) Certain values are being taught as content and the process of moral judgment is by no means solely intellectual. However, the stage theory has proved interesting heuristically for theoreticians and scientists and provocative for curriculum developers. Its overtly rational basis lends it utility where the examination of values as both cognition- and affect-based would be threatening. Its content is built around concepts and principles associated with the humanities and the traditions of western civilization.

Two curriculum development efforts typify this approach. The first is film-strips for elementary school children produced by Guidance Associates (Harcourt, Brace, Jovanovich). The second is the incorporation of public issue dilemmas into the teacher training and published work of Edwin Fenton at the Carnegie Institute of Technology.

### Sidney Simon et al.: *Values Clarification* (1972)

The second approach to humanistic value education, values clarification, is, like Kohlberg's, organized around processes, but there the resemblance ends. Described by John Dewey and interpreted by Raths, Harmin, and Simon (1966), the processes are:

I.   *Prizing* one's beliefs and behaviors
    1. Prizing and cherishing
    2. Publicly affirming, when appropriate

II.  *Choosing* one's beliefs and behaviors
    3. Choosing from alternatives
    4. Choosing after consideration of consequences
    5. Choosing freely

III. *Acting* on one's beliefs
    6. Acting
    7. Acting with a pattern, consistency, and repetition

The proponents of values clarification, of whom the most visible is Sidney Simon, assert that their approach is value-free and that they have only developed a methodology which will enable each person to unearth his own "already formed beliefs and behavior patterns" and "those already emerging." (Simon, Howe, and Kirschenbaum, 1972: 20) The kinds of problems, their solution, and the range of alternatives utilized in the strategies are straightforwardly public and middle class. For these proponents, values are not real if privately, not publicly, affirmed in behavior.

Some anti-intellectualism is also implied. No doubt, for example, there *are* people who have wondered passionately about the leading products of Argentina, one of the many topics used to point out that nobody could care about learning anything substantive just for the sake of learning it. Many of the issues raised are trivial; frequently, they are presented as discrete items unattached to a conceptual whole, either of the individual's personality or his professional life. Empirically unsubstantiated claims do not increase the credibility of the proponents.[6]

For all the limitations, however, thousands of educators are finding elements of values clarification useful as a readily available technology which stimulates interest in the meaning of human behavior. A second short book (Harmin, Kirschenbaum, and Simon, 1973) points out the usefulness of attaching personal meaning to the concepts and facts taught through the use of the student "you" and, like the first cited above, provides some recipes for integrating values work with subject matter courses. (See Appendix B for an example of the curriculum.)

Both values education and values clarification show the contemporary vitality of the relationship between the traditional humanities and humanistic education. The "problem" of values was central to the Greek philosophers and, in a far less abstract form, to the biblical scribes and interpreters. It remains central today but has been given new interpretations and frameworks within the broad contexts of humanistic education. However limited and circumscribed by their assumptions, the proliferation of values education and clarification shows that the old questions have retained their centrality to educational principles and practices.

## THE MENTAL HEALTH MOVEMENT AND HUMANISTIC EDUCATION

Humanistic education can be traced directly back to another group of educational values that first appeared during the third decade of the twentieth century. In opposition to long-standing and conflicting traditions that affective learning was either properly the responsibility of church and home or would automatically result from knowledge of content matter learned in school, "mental hygiene" programs were initiated as part of an emphasis on character education.

These have ramified over time into various kinds of mental health approaches, such as the Loftus "activity program" in New York City (1948), human relations curricula based on the junior high work of Bullis (1941), and the intergroup education advocated by Hilda Taba (1950). Psychotherapists have persistently advocated public responsibility for the emotional education of youth. Like William James' (1958) *Talks to Teachers on Psychology,* Anna Freud's *Introduction to Psychoanalysis* (1931) remains lively and useful today alongside the work of many others using psychoanalytic insights for educational purposes.[7]

The ideology of psychoanalysis has spawned a wide variety of educational techniques that are used at varying levels of social structure: the individual, the group, the organization, or the community that assumes total environmental control. These include techniques providing short term, limited experiences (such as behavior modification for a single, specific educational purpose; role playing; and psychodrama) and techniques providing longer, developmental experiences (such as life within a total learning community, for example, Synanon). Psychoanalysis, however, based on pessimistic Freudian views about human nature and mental illness, has not contributed until recently to the development of the model of ideal functioning—that is, what constitutes mental *health*. Such a model was necessary before psychological training could become the education of healthy individuals for their own further growth and not therapy for those who were psychologically deficient.

### A Model of Mental Health

No all-inclusive definition of *mental health* exists, although many persons have attempted to describe "the mature personality" by degree of conformity and adjustment. After an extensive review of the literature, Jahoda (1958; 82–100) listed six categories of criteria for positive mental health:

1. Attitude of the individual toward himself, including accessibility to consciousness, correctness of self-concept, self-acceptance, and sense of identity;
2. Degree to which a person realizes his potentialities through action (self-actualization);
3. Integration, including balance of psychic forces, a unifying outlook on life and resistance to stress;
4. Autonomy in the sense of the individual's degree of independence of social influences;
5. Perception of reality, including freedom from need-distortion as well as empathy and social sensitivity; and
6. Degree of environmental mastery (ability to give and receive love, adequacy in daily activities and interpersonal relations, efficiency in meeting situations and in problem-solving, capacity for adaptation, etc.)

Whether tacit or explicit, these goals of positive mental health were by no means broadly accepted. However devoted its early proponents, widespread advocacy of any form of emotional education in the public schools in the United States was not easily forthcoming. How slowly its gains have been made may be measured by the number of today's educators (even those deeply involved in the field) who are unaware of programs that have already been in effect for a considerable span of time. At least three of these—the programs of Ojemann, of Combs, and of Biber—have lasted over twenty-five years and contributed important concepts to humanistic education.

### Programs in Mental Health Education: Ojemann, Combs, and Biber

Each of these long-lived programs presents an emphasis on one of the categories of tactics described by Alschuler (1973: 216–226) as elements in a typology of procedures for psychological education. These elements are:

1. A *congruent* curriculum which teaches "a well-defined, limited aspect of psychological growth," such as self-esteem, achievement motivation, or

"origins"—the self as the origin of control, rather than the pawn of external forces. These curricula may be either *lateral*—that is, designed to provide "new action and affective experiences that may be assimilated into one's repertoire with as little conflict as possible"—or *vertical*—the teaching of higher order capacities through conflicts intended to move the students upward on a developmental hierarchy. (Kohlberg's moral development strategies typify the vertical approach.)

2. *Confluence* courses use personally relevant subject matter in any field to facilitate psychological learning. These deal with the "here-and-now through the use of imagination, touching student feelings, and translating ideas into action." Courses in anything from English through behavioral science to mathematics or vocational training can be taught confluently.[8]

3. *Contextual* methods promote psychological growth by changing the demand characteristics of the educational situation. These characteristics—which constitute the classroom climate—are the "expectations, roles, rules, and cues in the situation" that "also determine in part students' thoughts, actions, and feelings." Climate mediates between such structural factors as class and school oganization and teacher leadership style and the psychological states of the students.

Each of these have been developed into programs in mental health education still influential today. The three described here are typical: the congruent curriculum in causal orientation developed by Ralph Ojemann; the confluent program in perceptual psychology and education of Arthur Combs; and the contextual method of education through the school atmosphere of Barbara Biber and her associates at the Bank Street College. In Chapter Two the classroom procedures that embody some of these programs will be described, along with others, and in Chapter Three some of their consequences for teacher training and curriculum development will be explored.

**A Congruent Curriculum in Causal Orientation: Ralph Ojemann.** Beginning at the University of Utah in 1941, and later continuing their work at the Educational Research Council in Cleveland, Ralph Ojemann and his associates have carried out a research and development program in human relations and mental health designed to teach children a "causal" orientation to the social environment. Ojemann defines this orientation as the understanding that dynamic, complex, and interacting forces operate in human behavior, that human behavior is caused, and that knowledge itself is probabilistic because its certainty is impossible to ascertain. Thus, the causal approach is characterized by the capacity to see things from the viewpoint of others and by a flexibility in the solution of personal and social problems.

Ojemann's work is intended neither to revamp the school curriculum by introducing new items nor simply to leave the old ways intact. Unlike some contemporary attempts to introduce behavioral science knowledge into the class-room by hacking out new space, it demonstrates his belief that the existing curriculum can be modified and restructured to attend to issues of human be-havior derived from the causal model. In doing so, it provides for lateral psy-chological growth—the opportunity to assimilate new but limited affective experiences with minimal conflict. (The description of classrooms in Mayfield, Ohio, in Chapter Two shows Ojemann's theories in practice.)

A **Confluent Program in Perceptual Psychology and Education: Arthur Combs.**  To many professional educators, Arthur Combs' work became known when it appeared in 1962 in the most popular book that the Association for Supervision and Curriculum Development ever published: the yearbook on *Perceiving, Behaving, and Becoming.* More widely known than either of the other two programs, until recently it existed more as theory derived from the concern of "Third Force" psychology for individual growth than as actual edu-cational practice. (See the section on the University of Florida in Chapter Three for an account of the developing practice.)

According to this theory, the clue to education is understanding the percep-tions of the individual and the personal meanings that situations have for him. All behavior of a person is the direct result of his field of perception at the moment of his behaving. Behavior, then, is the result of (1) how he sees him-self, (2) how he sees the situation in which he is involved, and (3) the inter-relations of these two. "To change another person's behavior it is necessary somehow to modify his beliefs or perceptions. When he sees things differently, he will behave differently." Most influential is the self-concept, for the in-dividual's self is the "center of his world, the point of origin for all behavior. What he believes about himself affects every aspect of his life." (Combs et al., 1974: 14–17)

Combs' approach, rooted in the human potential for development, contrasts markedly with the other two programs more closely associated with traditions of mental health education. The work of both Ojemann and Biber is based on the concept of *primary prevention,* that is, intervention without definite knowl-edge of causality that is made to keep something unfortunate from happening (in this case, mental illness or neurosis). Since the unwanted occurrence is a function of the interaction between environment and individual, the inter-vention may occur in either or both areas. A *congruent* curriculum, such as Ojemann's, attempts to shape the individual. *Contextual* methods modify the environment. Combs' *confluent* program attempts to restructure the environ-ment at the same time that the individual is educated emotionally, intellectual-ly, and behaviorally.

A **Contextual Method of Education Through the School Atmosphere: Bar-bara Biber.**  A quarter century old, the historic work of Barbara Biber and the group at Bank Street College in New York City looks strangely modern viewed against current work on school and classroom climates. In the teacher-training programs and in classrooms of the schools, concepts of individual growth and precepts drawn from the philosophy of humanism form a framework of educational objectives. Mental health aims are integrated with such goals of cognitive mastery and achievement as positive feelings toward the self; realistic perception of self and others; relatedness to people; relatedness to environment; independence, curiosity, and creativity; and recovery and coping strength (Biber, 1961). Cognitive and affective growth are seen as intricately interdependent. An atmosphere of positive staff-student relationships and flexibility of curriculum and evaluation permeate the schools.

### Mental Health Education in the Schools Today

Beginning as the belief that mental health programs in the school could *prevent* psychological problems and continuing as the potential of these programs for the *fostering* of healthy growth became apparent, mental health education had gained new acceptance by the time that emotional development was publicly added to cognitive growth as a valued goal of learning. The National Education Association mandate for the "Schools of the '70's" expressed clearly this shift in objectives:

> In addition to purely intellectual growth, the curriculum should regard emotions, attitudes, and ideals, ambitions, and values as legitimate areas of concern for the educational process, and should emphasize the student's need to develop a sense of respect for self and others.

Mental health education has found a place at the family table, although even in its contemporary adapted and evolved forms it is still somewhat mistrusted. Therapy—the treatment of malfunction—has never been seen as a proper function of schools, nor is it today except for marginal students usually placed in special education programs.

Today three branches stem from mental hygiene roots. The first of these, *prevention,* is still the major preoccupation of the emotional education proponents who conceptualize their goal as mental health. For many who think of themselves as actors and shapers of humanistic education today, the second branch, *concern for the development of affective competence*—the capacity to be aware, to love, to respond, to trust, to be an individual, and, above all, to choose for the good, the positive, the growth-producing, the valuable, and to enact these choices—has linked mental health education to the august traditions of the humanities. The search for values to be affirmed merges with the meaning of the self, the other, mystery, and awe.

Historically parallel to this concern for affective competence has been the third branch: the work of the *developmentalists* such as Piaget in childhood cognition and Erikson in life span psychosocial development. During the last decade a conception of human functioning has emerged from the work of Jane Loevinger which holds considerable promise as an educational paradigm. According to Loevinger, *ego development* is the central characteristic of human personality. Differentiating this process from maturation or psychosocial development, she has drawn on the work of other theorists including Piaget, Harry Stack Sullivan, Erik Erikson, and Lawrence Kohlberg to describe seven stages of normal development: presocial, impulse-ridden, opportunistic, conformist, conscientious, autonomous, and integrated.

Each of these stages has both cognitive and affective elements and carries value-motivational or behavioral implications. Loevinger's scheme, and the theory behind it, present an interesting possibility for future curriculum development that provides conceptual unity to the study and education of human beings over the life span, while at the same time incorporating the humanities' search for values and their integration into personality as the life work.[9]

The tributaries of the humanities and of the mental health movement flow respectively from the ancient wellsprings of western civilization and from our recent history to form the contextual values that give purpose and meaning to humanistic education. With this as background, let us now take a final loop inward in our spiraling effort to define humanistic education.

## WHAT IS HUMANISTIC EDUCATION?

Humanistic education is not just "good" education. All "good" education ("good" for what?) is not the result of conscious or unconscious commitment to equal or near equal priorities for cognitive, conative (willing or motivational), and affective aspects of human personality. As a universal and objective construct, unspecified and value-free, "humanistic education" would become meaningless. But as a value-invested, bounded construct, it can be extremely useful.

So used, the idea of humanistic education reminds us of the integrative traditions of the humanities from which this kind of education is descended— traditions of the search for the good life with harmony among mind, body, and soul and with balance among the experience of feeling, the explanations of reason, and the implementation of action. As a concept, humanistic education includes the philosophical and psychological forebears of the present movement: the existential notions of human freedom, personal choice, and self-actualization—commitment and fulfillment through behavior—as well as those values implied in the ego or personality integration expressed in the lively and accurate phrase, "getting it all together."

Emerging from the beginning stretch of tentative roots in the humanities and the mental health education movement, humanistic education is already under stress from the confirming forces of routinization and institutionalization. It appears far more viable than earlier movements—partly perhaps because of its ubiquitous and protean forms and partly because of the academic respectability of many of its proponents. May humanistic education be considered a social movement? Will it be subject to the rapid cyclic patterns of generation, decay, and incorporation to which such movements are prone? We do not yet know.

But if not a social movement, what, then, are we experiencing? *The irreversible emergence of a new area of conscious, enacted, legitimized concern for public education—a new aim for curricula and schooling—based on a substantial and accretive shift in values and beliefs.* Humanistic education came in in somewhat the way that vocational education did earlier—as a valued, new, albeit more widespread, emphasis in the general education of American youth.

Affect and cognition, feelings and intellect, emotions and behavior blend in an affirmative framework of values derived from the humanities and from positive conceptions of mental health. These are the hallmarks of humanistic education.

Now to the classroom, the school, the teacher-training curriculum, and the supporting groups and institutions that are humanistic education in America today. . . .

 *Chapter 2*

# Humanistic Education in Practice

### INTRODUCTION

What is actually occurring in the field? From both reading and word of mouth advice, my research assistant and I compiled a list of projects and programs whose work seemed to be strongly based upon the humanistic model of education. When we agreed that the work seemed innovative, we contacted the people in charge and arranged a visit. Examples of teacher training and curriculum were found in public schools; in private camps; in schools both secular and religious; in country centers and in the closeness of cities; in universities, colleges, and school districts; in the work of foundations, commercial ventures, and entrepreneurs whose offerings ranged from individual consulting to the maintenance of elaborate national matrixes to coordinate teams of trainers in various regions. (See Appendix A) I have tried to be intuitive and inferential in making this report, and to convey some of the feelings and flair of the projects where I observed, shared, and learned.

Out there, out in the classrooms, out in the field where humanistic education is being done (rather than philosophized about or deplored or lauded) much of the work is by individuals, sometimes identified with a recognizable educational philosophy or teacher-training school, sometimes not. This chapter, then, will be a report of people and of places, of sometimes disjointed ideas and of deeply felt impressions, of public and private schools.

### PHILADELPHIA, PENNSYLVANIA: THE
### AFFECTIVE EDUCATION PROGRAM (AEP)

Norman Newberg, director of the Affective Education Program, speaks of the need for a roadmap to learn about the topology of one's interior life and of his

belief that individuals can learn to map their own inner worlds. Like others committed to humanistic education (such as Terry Borton, who was directing AEP
when Newberg joined him in 1966; Eli Bower in Special Education at the University of California at Berkeley; and Richard Jones, the author of *Fantasy and
Feeling in Education*), he believes that feeling is not "real," not internalized,
and certainly not understood until it has been conceptualized and labeled. As
is often true of programs with the word "affective" in their titles, the Affective Education Program is misnamed because high level *cognitive* processes are
also used to identify feeling and to name what is felt.

### The AEP Curriculum

Curriculum materials developed for secondary and elementary grades incorporate these logical and psychological processes. The focus is less on specific
content than on how the student manipulates the material as he learns it. The
same processes (pretending, describing, distinguishing, questioning, analysis,
problem solving), once practiced and internalized, may be used to learn many
subjects.

Process and content, the curriculum, what actually happens in the classroom
are effectively learned only when directly connected to the basic concerns of
students. In the Philadelphia program, these concerns are identified as the
universal human needs for *identity* (positive self-concept), *connectedness* (meaningful relationships with others), and *power* (the sense of control over what
happens to oneself). Derived from Abraham Maslow's theory of motivation,
these concerns are discussed by Gerald Weinstein and Mario Fantini in their
book *Toward Humanistic Education: A Curriculum of Affect.*

This public school district may be the only one in the world that gives affective homework. For the primary grades, there is a highly successful work-
book written by a teacher. Nearly 2000 copies of the *Sharing Book* by Sonya
Shulkin have been published by the district and used to date. Like other AEP
curricula, the book is aimed at the development of psychomotor and cognitive
skills as much as at the development of affective skills. One assignment begins
at school with the child (alone or with the teacher's help) writing at the end of
the statement: "One thing I'm really proud of about myself is . . . . . ." It is
continued at home with statements to be completed by parents or siblings:
"One thing I am really proud of about you is . . . . . ." Such assignments, in a
small way, also help to build connections between school and home and to
minimize the chance that the child will consider the school a place in which
nothing *real* happens.

Three questions (*What? So What? Now What?*) form the framework of the
upper elementary curriculum, *The Living Classroom:* the *What?* of processes,
activities, and experiences; the *So What?* of analysis and integration in which
the student identifies the meaning of his behavior and his experiences; the
*Now What?* of the student's extension and application of what he has learned
to new areas of learning relevant to him.

At the secondary level, an Urban Affairs curriculum replaces the second year of American History and a Communications program replaces a year of English. Additional units designed to teach decisionmaking processes through poetry and such provocative novels as Golding's *Lord of the Flies* and Dickey's *Deliverance* are available. Each program is built about active participation and the understanding of the meaning of that experience. For example, the Communications curriculum utilizes role playing, dramatic fantasy, and gaming, which carry within them implicit, nonreflexive, non-self-conscious learning. These are followed, however, by analysis—by the attempt to make explicit, to bring to consciousness through conceptualization, the learning that has been accomplished.

### Theories Underlying AEP Process Curriculum

What theories underlie the specific classroom activities? Many theories are drawn from, although none is accepted as the most important. Usually a process curriculum, wherever encountered, is based on a mechanical model of the information-processing loop derived from the science of cybernetics. Three principal stages of "processing" are described: (1) *sensing* (What information is being given by my senses?); (2) *transforming* (What do the data mean to me?); and (3) *acting* (How can I put this understanding to use? Now what can I do?) Critical to this information-processing model of learning is the feedback loop. Feedback may occur in or out of classes. Wherever it occurs it is useful because it tells the actor whether or not his actions are congruent with his intentions—whether they are producing the result he wants.

A view of humans as information processors, using feedback to adjust communications—sensing, transforming symbolically, then acting—appears in AEP alongside both Piaget's views (that the learner processes information through assimilation and accommodation in different ways throughout his development) and group dynamics theory. AEP classrooms provide the experiences through which students learn how groups function, the roles people play in groups, and the roles available to them as members of groups. Virginia Satir's *Conjoint Family Therapy* is mentioned in the same breath with Polanyi's *Tacit Dimension*. The search for personal authenticity described by existential psychologists and philosophers, the need for individual adaptability hypothesized by Robert Lifton in his description of *Protean Man,* Erikson's delineation of the developmental life cycle—these and more underpin the program.

**The Psychomotor Aspect in AEP.** A recurring element in humanistic education is the psychomotor aspect of human personality. Much less emphasized than conative, cognitive, or affective aspects of human development, physical attributes nevertheless are manifestly integrated with those other elements through role playing, simulation, drama, and body movement and body language activities. Usually this is done without specific reference to theories that relate action to understanding, physical activities to words, movement to knowledge, or that refer to the early stages of life when activity is thinking. In Philadelphia, it is taken for granted that people know more than they can say and that even abstract concepts can be made physical through the body.

AEP has tried to explore possible types of physical relationships among people, for example, the "pulls" that individuals have on one another and how people can be asked to let their psychophysical crutches go. This type of demonstration can be simple and dramatic when subordinate-dominant or slave-master relationships are explored through symbolic role playing. When black or white, standing on a chair, places his foot on the back of the other who is kneeling on the floor, the response is immediate. The juxtaposition itself is revealing to the participants. When the subordinate-slave moves away from under the master's foot and the dominant-master falls off the chair, the change in relationship is felt instantly.

Through outside funding, AEP provides a number of full time services to administration and staff in two districts, as well as limited assistance to other schools on request. Such services include in-service teacher training (described below) and a teacher resource center, curriculum development to integrate subject areas and affective concerns, assistance in organizational change, and administrative and parent-training programs.

## AEP GOALS AND IN-SERVICE
## TEACHER TRAINING

The Affective Education Project has four main objectives. First, public knowledge (traditional subject matter), personal knowledge (student knowledge of himself), and interpersonal knowledge (the student in relation to others) are all within the domain of the affective teacher. Second, the teacher must be able to structure experiences so that students can make connections between their inner lives and the happenings of the classroom. Third, the teacher must be able to recognize and diagnose the concerns and affective needs of students and respond to them appropriately. Fourth, the teacher must be able to identify what is happening in the class at several levels and to "process" (focus on, describe, and analyze) behavior with the students through the cognitive work that program director Norman Newberg calls "the discipline of feeling." These four objectives are the structure of the in-service education program and of the relatively small program conducted for teachers in preparation.

Conditions for the successful achievement of these goals include:

1. Expert training in teaching (working with groups, curriculum development) and in relationship skills (awareness of own and student feelings, awareness of effects of own behavior);

2. Support that begins during the initial apprenticeship period and continues

through the development of self-sustaining peer groups that provide necessary help, feedback, and processing for their members and offer opportunities for the enlargement of positive feelings of identity, competence, and acceptance;

3. A theoretical framework that offers teachers a clear image of what they wish to achieve in the classroom and what decisions they must make about authority relationships, substantive material to be taught, outcomes to be sought and how to achieve them; and

4. The opportunity for personal and professional growth, although some teachers may prefer at least temporarily to limit these experiences to clearly professional concerns.

**The Three Phases of Training.** The training is divided into three phases which cover at least a year's time. During the first phase ("awareness-responsibility"), the teachers receive training through experiences and classroom assignments that connect deepened awareness of the feelings of self and others to their professional lives. They are taught consciously to use techniques that build rapport and to respond to students from a Rogerian "helping" rather than an authoritative role.

In the second phase, the teacher chooses a curriculum model such as the Confluent Model (Brown at the University of California at Santa Barbara), the Trumpet Model (Weinstein and Fantini), or the Affective Education Program Model (What? So What? Now What?) described above. (The Confluent and Trumpet models are discussed below.) Training consists of experiential and simulation techniques used as integral components of lessons based on the specific curriculum model and later field-tested in the classroom.

The final stage of training is devoted to practice in achieving balance between the personal, interpersonal, and public types of knowledge taught and between the dependent, interdependent, and independent kinds of experiences students need to integrate all three kinds of knowledge.[10] Teachers practice the skills needed to deal with the "life concerns" of power, relationships, and identity described by Weinstein and Fantini (1970), as well as day-to-day student concerns. They also practice the skills needed to cope with classroom procedure and the presentation of subject matter. All of these phases include training weekends, weekly or biweekly group meetings, and workshops centered around the acquisition of specific techniques. Skilled personnel provide observation and feedback.

Interestingly, Marc Levin of AEP, whose article on affective teacher preparation has been an important source for the above, reports that even teachers who are trained to teach what Alschuler calls "congruent" courses (restricted to a well-defined, limited aspect of psychological growth) as a separate body of subject matter find it very difficult to integrate this knowledge with traditional subject matter. Habit provides blinders that close off the affective elements in the ordinary.

Levin also notes that in-service, experienced teachers who are relatively secure in their classroom and able to maintain control are much more effective in utilizing AEP training than either pre-service teachers or those who tend to avoid defining behavioral boundaries—findings about humanistic teacher education I was to encounter wherever I went.

## MAYFIELD, OHIO: OJEMANN'S CAUSAL THEORY IN PRACTICE

### A Learning Disability Class
They begin with the rules, because the small class of ten makes its own, may revise them at each meeting, but will review them as a reminder: raise your hand before you talk; don't interrupt; use your eyes to look straight at people, your ears to listen to people, your mouths to talk and smile; don't tilt your chair; and when someone does well, clap your hands to praise.

The class is for children who have trouble getting along, who want to improve. IQs range from 50 to 81; ages from nine to 13. On the wall are charts with "smileface" stickers and, here and there, "sadface" ones. Talk in the circle is about what happened *today*. The teacher goes around the circle asking, "How has (so-and-so) been getting along with you?" If the news is good, everybody claps; a happy face goes up on the wall. When today is good, sad faces get removed.

Michael doesn't deserve a happy face—he started a fight on the playground—and he knows it: "I shouldn't have gotten mad."

"What could you have done?" asks the teacher, encouraging him to correct himself.

"I could have walked away, not gotten mad."

Michael has earned a sad face for today. There is no clapping, but nevertheless the teacher praises him for his honesty and for correcting himself.

"Who's a nice person in this room? Why do you think so?"

"Does it make you feel good to do something nice? What have you done today nice?"

Everybody tells, one by one, and then they clap, clap for themselves, for their being good, for being nice. The teacher leads, fast, slow, mixed rhythms—clap, clap; clap-clap-clap—while they follow, attentive, intent. They are moving and the movement clearly feels good.

### Underlying Theories: Ojemann and Others
Self-correction, goal setting, open-ended stories to facilitate practice in decisionmaking, the circle, room council meetings (similar to Glasser's concept of classroom meetings or Palomares' Magic Circle), and group management techniques that pull isolates into fuller participation—all these are important in the Mayfield elementary schools. (Glasser and Palomares are discussed below; the

Library
I.U.P.
Indiana, Pa.

370.1 Si58h
c.1

Magic Circle is presented in Appendix B.) Teachers are encouraged to use the leaders whom the children themselves identify, to put a "star" to work at some task with a child who doesn't participate, and to keep track of social changes through the use of sociograms. In one school, fifth graders tutor second graders with whom the teachers have matched them for personality and confer carefully with their tutee's teacher to determine what skills should be taught.

For some years, the Mayfield district was a member of the Educational Research Council in Cleveland where Ralph Ojemann (1970) is still developing the work that made him a forerunner in humanistic education many years ago under the rubric of preventive mental health. (See Chapter One) Teachers still attend workshops during the school year and in the summer. The "causal approach" underlies much educational practice in the district.

Ojemann believes that knowledge of the forces that operate in the world is essentially a knowledge of the forces that operate in human behavior in both individual and group interaction. Using the causal approach means attending to future consequences of acts, as well as to how behavior develops as a result of past actions. The training of teachers (and they of their students) focuses on the availability of alternatives under specified conditions—knowledge that a variety of choices is possible—and the need of the individual to be aware of the probable consequences, both immediate and remote, of his choices. "Discrimination"—that is to say, the evaluation of behavior—is considered important and practiced as "considered judgment," not "arbitrary, noncausal judgment." The issue is not *what* people do but *why* they do it. Behavior is caused and, once the causes are understood, future results may be influenced. Project *GOOD* (*G*uiding *O*ne's *O*wn *D*evelopment), aimed at increasing self-knowledge and responsibility, is a logical recent outgrowth of the earlier focus on knowledge of the causes of behavior of other individuals and groups.

Ojemann has made one of the few attempts in the field at a serious evaluation of the effects of humanistic education. Although the effects of training on academic achievement have not been studied, some evidence backs his claim for its utility as a means of preventive mental health in the grade schools and as a means for the education of disabled children.[11]

## PALO ALTO, CALIFORNIA: A GLASSER SCHOOL

"Ventura School," reads the brochure, "is a Palo Alto Unified School District public school. There are approximately 300 students from ages three-and-one-half through twelve years old (prekindergarten through sixth grade). The school population is highly integrated, with a minority population of about 45 percent. There are many students from highly enriched backgrounds. There are also like numbers of children from non-English-speaking families, families who must be on welfare, or families who represent low educational levels." Parent-teacher relationships are good at Ventura. According to a survey taken at the beginning of the year, the two groups agree closely on the proper goals for the school: motivation toward learning, reading comprehension, thinking skills, and self-concept. The school is devoted to the promotion and maintenance of a climate of mutual trust among all its community, including the students.

Members of the staff at Ventura describe it as a "Glasser school" and stress concern about cognitive goals of thinking and decisionmaking skills. But that emphasis alone would not explain the comfort with which children wandered into the teachers' lounge nor the welcome they received. It would not explain the lack of negative, disparaging comments about the students when they were absent. Nor would it have reduced the school's vandalism and truancy rates from the highest in the district to the lowest. In this environment, the child's relationships to his self, to his peers, and to adults are as central as his relationship to materials and ideas. Underlying these relationships, according to Glasser, is the development of a successful, positive identity derived from the belief that one is loved and a worthwhile, competent person.

Every person needs success in at least one important part of his life. "Nothing succeeds like success" is taken seriously at Ventura. The school climate is designed to identify and embrace the positive qualities, skills, and intellectual and social abilities of the students. The school generates and nourishes success in an environment of sharing, participation, and trust. Involved teachers help the child to focus on his own behavior and its implications. This climate enables the student to make a value judgment about the contribution that *he* is making to his own failure and, once the judgment is made, to commit himself to change.

### General Meetings, Class Meetings, and Conferences

Among the specific conditions providing this generalized emotional support are shared goal setting and evaluation of progress, peer contact and responsibility through the tutorial program, and class meetings. At a general meeting at the beginning of the school year, parents and teachers define school goals. Throughout the year, goal setting for individual students and the evaluation of their progress are mutual processes done in individual conferences on an average of twice a week. In these meetings, reaching toward new competencies is encouraged. Accomplishments rather than weaknesses or inadequacies are emphasized in assessing completed work. Grade cards are not used. Progress reports to parents are just that: reports on progress, not on omissions or failures. Although organized schoolwide, the peer tutorial program is highly individualized. It is designed to help both tutor and tutee learn caring, responsible behavior that also increases the sense of self-esteem and helps to develop cognitive skills.

The class meetings are a variety of support structure which, under different names and emphasizing different types of learning (e.g., the Magic Circle, home groups), I encountered across the nation. Glasser delineates three kinds of class meetings: (1) social problem-solving meetings; (2) open-ended meetings about intellectually important subjects; and (3) educational diagnostic meetings that assess how well the concepts of the curriculum have been understood. In these small groups at Ventura, the nonjudgmental setting provides life space for risk without fear of failure.

The staff at Ventura believes with Glasser that students must become involved with teachers who themselves have "success identities," can fulfill their own needs, and are responsible people. Indeed, the educational environment at Ventura and the complex learning that occurs there could not be maintained unless the teachers and community volunteers who assist in the school had these attributes. Ventura School is noteworthy because the affective component of education has been deliberately and responsibly structured into the school's program.

## FALL RIVER, MASSACHUSETTS: MUTUAL SUPPORT

### Fifth Grade Class: The Trust Walk

It was early but the big, dark room was already filled by the time we arrived. In the back a boy who looked heavier and older than the others was building a model on a board spanning two of the flip-top desks. When the teacher suggested the "trust walk," he and two other boys went on with what they were doing. The walkers went around them or under the board in dyads, one the guide, the other with eyes tight shut, as they explored the room together. In five minutes the teacher stopped them and suggested that the "blind" partner tell his guide how he had felt. "How did your guide make you feel?" he asked. "Comfortable? Safe? Worried about being led into things? Now switch roles and guide the other way you *would have liked* to have been guided."

When it was over, he asked them to take out their journals and write how they felt with their eyes closed and being led around, whether they'd choose the same person as a partner again, where they would like to walk, and how they would guide. "Write down what you found in the room," he said, "when you lost this important sense." The experience was valuable by itself, but it was consciousness, the analysis, that would give meaning to the feelings.

### Secondary School: A Nonacademic History Class

"Know thyself" is on the blackboard. The teacher, a young man, has passed out a ditto labeled "Framework." It says:

1. American history is not a collection of facts—it is a collection of group ideas and values.
2. To be a good citizen, a person must be aware of his surroundings, his ideas, and his values.
3. To be a good person, an individual must be aware of the feelings and values of others.

4. To do this, he must communicate his values and ideas to the group so the feelings and values of one belong to all.

The class—mostly young women—talks about the framework, communication, and values that are neither right nor wrong but only differ from person to person.

"Where does the minority value system fit in a majority system like the United States?" the teacher asks. Someone in bright orange pants begins to talk about competition as a majority American value and the teacher writes the word on the board followed by the phrase, "most Americans." The student repeats the words over and over again as she talks. When she finishes, he says, "But what about *you*? How do *you* feel about competition?

He draws a line, a continuum, across the chalkboard and labels the ends:

| Avoid any situation where there's a chance to win or lose | ———————————— | Will trample anyone for the chance to win, and use any means |

Then he says, "Now write down some things you'd like to win at."

Soon they are volunteering for the board, marking their initials on the continuum at the place each thinks she belongs on a specific issue. The discussion is lively about where the initials are put.

"What happens to those of you who feel different from the rest?" Now the issue of minority values is coming to life. They begin to see the point.

Another continuum is drawn below, and some put initials where they think one parent (or both) belongs on an issue. Some intergenerational differences are similarly examined. They have also used continua to look at other value conflicts. Later in the class they talk about the concept of freedom. The poles are laid out as "All decisions to be made for me" and "Complete freedom."

This class is full of drama and movement. The students are indulgent, good-natured. They come, they participate, and they enjoy.

### Practical Underpinnings: A Teacher Support Group

The enthusiastic Fall River teachers, elementary and secondary, are part of a project run by William Gastell, who has received training at the Center for Humanistic Education at the University of Massachusetts. He has found a compatible intellectual base for his practical work, work deriving from a highly successful drug program using humanistic education techniques. A "support group" meets once a week to share experiences in the classroom, to "process" for themselves and to help each other process whatever happened to them since they last met.

On the evening they let me join them on circled chairs, they began by reviewing the procedures—the ground rules—for my sake. No roles were to be worn to the meeting. Each came not as a "father," a "teacher," an "older person," a "beginning professional," an "administrator," but as himself. Concerns were with the here and now, the present needs of self and each other. Almost biblically, "Let thyself be known as you want it to be known" was intoned.

Members of the group, obviously accustomed to beginning this way, put forth comfortable pseudopods of private experience from the interval of separation—their feelings, their worries and pleasures, their inner responses to the external happenings in their professional lives. Acceptance, encouragement, support for a new attempt, a new way—the group members knew each other and were relaxed, willing to be supportive.

When they occurred, the tensions—I was told later—were traditional ones between elementary and secondary teachers, each group feeling its needs distinctive. At the beginning of the year the walls had been ten stories high. Now the barriers maintained a decent level, but alternatives, not criticism, found their way over and back. Here, as everywhere when I visited support groups, people spoke of the invisible, unpresentable contrast between their former patterns of behavior and understanding and the development they saw in themselves individually and later as a group. Progress was uneven—some individuals moved more slowly than others—but the ever-present consciousness of self, the reminding presence of those who also struggled to change, kept it alive for all.

## NEWTON, MASSACHUSETTS: A
## DEVELOPMENT PROGRAM

Ralph Mosher's work in humanistic education continues at Boston University through teacher training and student curricular programs in the Boston area. It began about five years ago with a "program to promote individual and human development" which he and Normal Sprinthall—together with a team of doctoral students at Harvard, teachers, and, later, high school students—developed for Newton High School. The authors of this program were aware that school personnel have their unconscious psychological agendas. At the same time they were convinced (as is the American Psychological Association, which is developing its own curriculum for psychological education) that formal education has done little to date to *intentionally* foster self-knowledge.

Designed for high school juniors and seniors, the program was twofold: (1) *cognitive* in its presentation of the data and generalizations derived from the discipline; and (2) *affective* or *personalized* in its concern that the students derive personal meaning from what they learned. Objectives for the affective component were drawn heavily from Krathwohl, Bloom, and Masia (1964) and ordered developmentally along a continuum from less complex to more complex processes. Children in primary school, for example, can identify their own and others' feelings, but cannot organize them with cognitive elements into a coherent personal philosophy—a more sophisticated task developmentally.

Built around the personal history of the student (Who was I as a child? Who am I now? Who am I becoming?), cognitive material examined early childhood, adolescence, and adulthood through literature including autobiography, film, and case studies that exemplified theoretical principles. Intelligence and personality testing were also included. This "core" course was taken by each student, who then also enrolled (after shopping around) in one "laboratory" activity to be studied in depth for two-thirds to three-quarters of the total course time. Laboratory experiences, which often used community resources and association with role models, ranged from film making or improvisational dance and drama through intensive group experience (such as self-analytic or sensitivity groups) to training to do individual counseling or teaching. Intended to allow the participant to slip from insider to outsider and back again, the laboratories involved him unselfconsciously, experientially, at the same time that he had a chance to apply what he had learned cognitively.

Like the other curricula we studied, the original course centered around communication with the larger world of experience, inner and outer, and had as its overriding goal increasing the capacity to attend and to perceive more acutely, to create and express ideas and forms of other kinds, and to interpret into personal meanings the emotional-laden experiences of life.

## NEW YORK CITY: RATIONAL-EMOTIVE THERAPY AT THE LIVING SCHOOL

Rational-Emotive Therapy is an approach to humanistic education conceptualized by Albert Ellis and practiced at The Living School in New York City. At the first meeting in the classroom the students and teacher ask, "What shall we do with our day?" The schedule is discussed, reworked by everyone, then posted on the board. Once it is agreed upon, each child is free to work on whatever he chooses, whenever he wants to, and in whatever order, until noon.

Rational-Emotive Therapy can be needed at any time and time set aside. If an emotional or intellectual crisis or upset occurs, a large four-pointed star is put on the blackboard. At each corner a letter is placed: S, T, A, R. *S* is for Situation, *T* is for Thought, *A* for Affect, *R* for Reaction. The children know the lessons implicit in the STAR model: nobody and nothing is perfect; inappropriate thoughts may cause troublesome feelings and unwanted reactions; we all have negative and positive parts; doing bad things does not make us bad persons.

On the board in the back of the room green paper hearts, pinned up, make a broken circle: *heart shape* for feelings, *green* for change and growth, a *head* for thoughts and a *name* on each symbol for individuality. A broken circle ... nothing is perfect.

William Knaus is Albert Ellis' cohort and colleague. As he described the school and his teacher-training work through Queens College, a familiar pattern emerged; openness to experience; for the self, personal growth; pattern practice to get rid of rejection fears (role play the rejector, role play the one who was rejected). "Touchy Joe," "Green Grasshopper"—the children learn through the help of the teacher that they do not have to accept the names they are called by others. The teacher can ask the class what else they know about Billy, help him to build a positive generalization about himself through the "Self-Concept Wheel," help him to remember that he is other things, as well as his negative traits. Without help, rejection can become a label—a generalization to "They don't like me."

A written curriculum has been published, *The Rational-Emotive Education Manual* (1974, available from the Institute for Rational Living, 45 E. 65th Street, New York, N.Y.). The school itself is now almost tuition-free, supported by the Ellis Foundation, and has a waiting list. They are all "normal" children, for Rational—Emotive Therapy is for the healthy. What they seek, says Knaus, is a reduction of the "upsetability dimension" so that learning and growing may go on unimpeded.

## HARTFORD, CONNECTICUT: AN ALTERNATIVE PUBLIC HIGH SCHOOL

Shanti—the Peace that Passeth all Understanding—is the name that students and staff gave Mulcahy-Sinner when the school became committed to educational structures and processes different from traditional forms. It has 86 students from 11 districts who meet in small groups of 12 to 15 led by anyone within the school, including the custodian, with the interest and competence to accomplish specific tasks. The two hour weekly meetings of the home groups are not instructional. Based on the concept of home room which Dewey invented at the turn of the century, they serve as points of reference, sources of peer support, and the principal means to identify student educational needs.

Funded by the districts whose children attend and with its school board made up evenly of community members and students, the school grants admission to anyone who applies, although there is a strong multiracial-multiethnic commitment. Shanti is the only comprehensive alternative secondary program in the area (although there are learning centers for curriculum development or failing youth). A lottery decides admittance if more students apply than can be taken.

Governance is by task force and the "community," with voluntary groups addressed to problems of (1) budget, (2) curriculum, (3) the internal environment of the school, and (4) communication among the school community. Aside from setting salaries, students make the budget and are required to stick to it. Maintenance of the physical facilities is also a student responsibility. Curriculum requirements are more or less traditional in content, but they may be met in a variety of ways, including apprenticeships of one kind or another within the larger community. Students are seen as capable of selecting their own programs with help in the identification of individual educational needs from their home groups. Parents are invited to participate and many do, as accountability is felt to be the mutual responsibility of school and parents. Students are coresponsible with staff for information sharing and parent reportings, as well as program planning and evaluation. Governance is a mutual process. For example, if a student fails to attend his class, the home group may decide to "disenroll" him, but the decision then goes to the school community for agreement and support.

Although I have not included the study of alternative public school programs in this report, Shanti is an example of how humanistic education may be carried out within, and by means of, social structure that intentionally connects emotional, social, and cognitive learning. Students are expected to be responsible not only for their own learning but also for the learning environment and the progress of others who share it with them. As a means of fostering development, emphasis is placed upon increased self-knowledge, the nurturing of genuine peer-peer and peer-adult interpersonal relationships, the availability of functioning adult models, and the expectation of shared decisionmaking.

## SANTA MONICA, CALIFORNIA: THE SYNANON SCHOOLS

It is a cliché that living and learning cannot be separated, but in Synanon it is most conspicuously true. A secular religion and an ethical system, the twenty-four hour communal life of this organization can no longer be considered solely an educational court-of-last-resort for drug addicts, alcoholics, and others the society presumes to be socially noneducable. Adults without these serious problems or character disorders who are committed to its "lifestyle" of absolute honesty, personal and group responsibility, cooperation, cleanliness, and the work ethic have also joined the community and become part of its learning environment. Synanon *is* a learning environment, one which derives substantial effect through affect, through its intensive group interaction called "The Game" and the strong emotional support of members of the community.

The Synanon Game is the central mechanism and modus operandi of Synanon. It encourages total freedom of speech and a complete expression of the range of emotions experienced by human beings. It is an intensive verbal interaction in which participants give each other honest, no-holds-barred feedback and discuss issues of common interest. The Game is an outlet for the full range of emotions experienced by human beings—the unfettered expression of the most intimate and innermost thoughts, feelings, fears, ambitions, obsessions, convictions, hatreds, prejudices, joys, and hopes. The Game is Synanon's most important educational tool, communication device, self-correction mechanism, and self-government activity. All residents play The Game at least once a week as a condition of residence there; children play The Game beginning around age four or five.

No life is unexamined at Synanon. There is an assumption that others in the community are as capable, if not more so, of recognizing the meaning of the individual's actions as is the person himself. Self-concept, upon which the capacity to learn and function adequately is built, is based upon absolute honesty. "Mutual self-education"—a guiding principle—implies the responsibility of the individual for his own learning and for his assistance to others. Teachers are expected to be learners and learners to be teachers. The range of experience is by no means confined to intellectual domains.

Who are the teachers? They are parents, adults, and peers—an "enhanced" family built into the formal structure of the Synanon schools. At the head of these schools is the director of education, Rod Mullen, who lives at the Tomales Bay Facility. Together with the "elders" of the community and staff members, he approves the curriculum. As in other aspects of the communal life, The Game provides feedback from students and acts as a change mechanism. During The Game the children got a discontinued weaving and textile class restored, for example, by persuading adults to help them find a community volunteer to teach it.

### Education at Synanon

Independence training begins very early. At six months the child goes to school. He is left to his own unrestricted explorations in a protected environment, an exploration that includes foods and ways of feeding himself. School rooms are open and uncluttered. The aesthetic sense is not neglected—color, plants, and handiwork are everywhere. The calmness of a serene environment is considered more important than a great deal of stimulation. Through donations and the skills of community members, the infant school for "New Life" is well equipped.

When teachers and materials are available, the seventy-six "Youngsters" and "Oldsters" in the infant-through-eighth grades of the Santa Monica school learn the subjects of the usual elementary curriculum, but in somewhat unusual ways. The learner is expected to inquire on his own, to take the initiative in learning what he wants to know. He may be helped by those in the school who are his peers and he is expected to help those less knowledgeable, younger members of the school. Content, methodology, and even the physical environment of his school will change frequently, in line with Synanon's belief that the community and, specifically, the schools should improve each year as defined by their own goals. Change as a means to growth is an important value. The schools must be able to renew themselves.

For the students between thirteen and eighteen the Interface program, Synanon's high school, attempts to facilitate the transition from youth to adulthood in ways that enhance the development of maturity and responsibility. To avoid the isolation from important adult activities that often characterizes this transition, work education is built into the more traditional curriculum. There are no separate vocational classes and no vocational faculty. Full time work alternates with intensive academic class sessions, field trips, and time off activities within or outside of the Synanon community.

Students learn from the workers themselves in the many departments that comprise the Synanon system, departments that range from animal husbandry through health and legal services to Synanon Industries and the Waste Water Control Plant. They work with the adult workers wherever skills can be taught them and responsibilities delegated. Here, as in the rest of the communal life, The Game provides a mechanism for free emotional expression by the members and engenders a trust that is carried over into the controlled transactions of life outside The Game.

## LOS ANGELES, CALIFORNIA: THE TUTORIAL
## COMMUNITY SCHOOLS

Emotional education as originally practiced by Synanon would have little chance of acceptance by the mainstream of the American public. But could Synanon values, in a different, but operationally related, form survive in a public school setting which is not a total environment? Gerald Newmark, Synanon Life Styler, has explored this question through the Ford-funded Tutorial Community Project (TCP) he directed from 1967 to 1974 in three Los Angeles public schools. Based on the ideal of an educational community in which parents, students, and school staff work together cooperatively, the program for the elementary public schools, like Synanon's, had to teach new methods of accurate communication to build trust.

Task-oriented encounter groups were initiated. Shared planning and decisionmaking were an integral part of the development of the school community. Cross-age and peer tutoring became a fundamental structural change, not simply an attractive effort by a few volunteers. The results of the tutoring effect were astonishing. Children whose feet had dragged to school came even when they did not feel well and took the task of helping another's growth more seriously than their own. They took their own learning to heart when it affected the learning of their own students. The project film shows young heads bent close to each other, young voices encouraging and explaining, as well as staff members confronting each other over educational issues. While feelings of progress fluctuated from day to day, tutor and tutee in delivering classroom and receiving classroom gradually changed their expectations and developed new methodologies and skills.

Clearly, such schools are teaching much more than conventional subject matter. At the least, they are teaching the enactment of values of cooperation, community, shared decisionmaking, and responsibility. Newmark believes that his project has developed a model for the development of tutorial community schools. As skills are developed, each teacher and each school may become re- sources for other teachers and schools. Eventually these, too, must become capable of self-renewal and self-correction, rather than relying upon the assis- tance of outside consultants.[12]

Can the TCP model be replicated? Parts of it, certainly. As a totality, only with great commitment. The social forces of twenty-four hour environment are not easily generated under other conditions. Unlike the introduction of smaller, discrete innovations, the holistic attempt at change requires enduring commitment by the school community. Without such a commitment, some of the pieces of the whole are not likely to survive nor is its determining character. Considerable evidence backs the notion that massive change may be more en- during than are piecemeal changes. Such commitment once achieved may insure its continuance. Replication should be tried. The tutorial communtiy school model offers an extraordinary opportunity for the implementation and trans- mission of important social and ethical values.

## TRENDS AND PROSPECTS

Our guided tour through classrooms displaying, teachers practiticing, and stu- dents learning humanistic education has been hurried and varied. Are such seemingly diverse enterprises truly part of a unitary phenomenon? They are. For all their separatenesses and disparities, they share basic goals and values of education: the self-as-curriculum; the integration and synthesis of affective and cognitive learning; a developmental framework; the seeking of mental health, autonomy, and the ability to empathize with others, to connect with the here and now, to be self-actualizing, open, alert, and expressive.

The report of the President's Panel on Youth (1973) recommended struc- tural changes in schools that seem to me remarkably congruent with the aims of humanistic education. Pointing up the fallacy of believing that schools should exist only for the self-development of cognitive skills and knowledge, panel members condemned the schools as "inappropriate settings for nearly all re- sponsibilities that affect others." The changes suggested included (1) the op- portunity for adolescents to specialize (possibly half a day) within the com- prehensive school, and (2) the reduction of overall size of the school or devel- opment of mechanisms by which internal small units might be combined on occasion—a suggestion consonant with the widespread, effective use of the small group already found throughout the nation.

Even more interesting, the panel suggested that the secondary school act as an agent using the outer environment to teach age-integrated—i.e., cross-age— public service and work skills. Work should not be an end in itself, but should provide the experiences of working cooperatively with others and of deriving satisfaction from a job well done. Academic (grades and test scores) and economic (income and occupation) success are not sufficient indexes for measuring the impact of educational institutions on the lives of those within them. More research, the panel concluded, is needed on noncognitive measures of personal development and social well-being. Clearly, "personal development and social well-being" are seen by this eminent group as legitimate goals of education. These recommendations make it obvious that the model of social and self-actualization described here as the aim of humanistic education is very much within the realm of mainstream educational thinking today. It represents a most desirable linkage of self, as the panel wrote, with "common purpose and a community of experience."

Interest in career education is growing. In the past, work education was practiced as job training for working class youth and as narrow vocationalism that retarded the development of the person, however much it provided access to manual labor skills. Revitalized today, work-as-curriculum is still likely to be aimed at certain segments of the society. It need not be so. In the Synanon Interface program, the Philadelphia secondary curriculum for human concerns, the California social action field programs for adolescents at Newport Beach High School or for undergraduates at Johnston College, and the community service component provided by such teacher-training programs as Confluent Education at the University of California at Santa Barbara or the new Humanistic Applications Center at the University of Massachusetts, "work" has been a means of learning valuable noncognitive skills that may be put to the service of social, as well as personal values. Many such programs exist, including internships and informal apprenticeships, and they are growing in number.

*Chapter 3*

# The Humanistic Education
# of Teachers

## INTRODUCTION

Teacher training goes on everywhere in the United States. Very little of it is humanistic education. I saw, read, and talked to participants about only a portion of that humanistic training that does exist, but I have tried to sketch representative examples of differing and useful models. Under a wide variety of labels these programs are ideologically similar.

## FAIRLEIGH-DICKINSON UNIVERSITY: THE CENTER FOR HUMAN DEVELOPMENT

The concept behind the Center for Human Development at Fairleigh-Dickinson University in Rutherford, New Jersey, began with Daniel Prescott (1957) at the Institute for Child Study of the University of Maryland, who became interested in the systematic observation of children using idiographic (descriptive, individual) methods. His student, and the founder of the Fairleigh-Dickinson center, Julia Gordon, became the first doctoral graduate in this field. She returned to her home in New Jersey and developed an in-service college credit program for personnel in the helping professions. Three years ago David Hobson succeeded her as director of the Center for Human Development.

Although technically part of the College of Education and offering a Master's Degree program for teachers, counselors, and correctional officers, the center does not offer a state certification program. In 1973 its full time professional staff supervised courses in the "Direct Study of Human Beings" in 12 out of 21 New Jersey counties. The typical group is made up of a minimum of 12 students through its two year, four semester program.

*37*

### The Study Groups

The emergence of the study groups was apparently truly grass roots, based on the self-perceived needs of members of the helping professions. Once formed, each chooses its own leader, who may already have had a training relationship with the Fairleigh-Dickinson center and who enrolls in the two year course on Consultant Development. Leaders keep a group study log in which they record their experiences, visit each other's groups, and meet with center personnel every two or three weeks for feedback. Four times during each semester the center faculty and the leaders of all the state groups meet to read to each other from their records.

Using group process techniques, the study groups' purpose is the development of awareness of others' feelings and responses and awareness of the self. Observational experience is central to the program, although integrative courses in psychological, sociological, and philosophical processes are taught concomitantly and an integrative essay is written instead of comprehensive master's examinations. Each participant is expected to select a person to study, someone whose "life space he can climb into," and to develop a sophisticated case study of that person. Although the group is referred to as a child study group, adults are equally acceptable as subjects if they are not class members. In fact, participants may choose to study themselves. Members contract for the work they choose on a four point form:

1. Who? (Will the subject be oneself? Another? Will there be sufficient access to observe?)
2. What? (Where do you want to go? What do you want to know?)
3. How? (How are you going to go about the study? What resources will you use?)
4. How will you know when you've gotten there? (What specific goals will you set for youself for the study? What criteria will you use to determine whether you've achieved them?)

### The Benefits of Close Observation

Careful objective observation is emphasized as a means of collecting scientific data. The goal is to record what is seen and not what is inferred, for example, "He is frowning," rather than "He is unhappy." An attempt is made to minimize observer effects through such teaching techniques as "echoing"—repeating the last part of the subject's sentence. By doing so, comments representing the stance of the observer do not reflect or distort the direction of the subject's thinking. Thus, idiographic methods provide a rich fund of anecdotal materials upon which an accurate and structured understanding of the person may be built.

It is unclear whether such reports are translated into generalizations about the specific individual studied (or comparable groups of individuals) based on theoretical paradigms of development and the process of learning. Little in the study group sessions I attended suggest this, but the utility of this research method for the helping professions seems obvious. The reports and the subsequent discussion showed that the participants had not only learned new reporting skills but had learned to *attend* in a special way, to listen and to see the person as he was to be heard and seen, as he was presenting himself, and not as he was mediated through the expections of those observing.

Why should such communication skills, based on objectivity and personal distancing, be an important asset to emotional education? First, because accurate knowledge of (as nearly as possible) objective reality becomes the baseline from which beliefs about—and, hence, affective reactions to—the universe and smaller matters are derived. Indeed, there are those who believe that affect is largely determined by cognition. (See, for instance, Kohlberg, LaCross, Ricks, 1972; Knaus, 1974; and Langer, in press.) Second, because analytic empathy (that is, role taking that is based on observation processed cognitively) has been shown to be much more accurate (according to the reports of those whose role is being taken) than is a global empathy whose processes are rooted in emotional and sympathetic identification (Flavell, 1968).

## GEORGE WASHINGTON UNIVERSITY: DIAGNOSTIC-PRESCRIPTIVE TEACHER PROGRAM

Robert Prouty, the coordinator of the Diagnostic-Prescriptive Teacher Program at George Washington University in Washington, D.C., insisted that he had no commitment to humanistic education, that he used the technology strictly "because it works." Formally, Prouty is a professor of Special Education—the education of children with learning or emotional disabilities. However, his intent was, and remains, to change the nature of schooling and, especially, the assumption that permits educators and parents to blame children for failures to learn. Students and teachers need the same things: skills to achieve the goals they value and psychosocial supports during the process of identifying, practicing, and maintaining these skills. Prouty's answer to these needs was to change the social system of the school and to create a new educational role— the diagnostic-prescriptive teacher, or DPT.

### The Role of the Diagnostic-Prescriptive Teacher

The name was deliberately chosen for its clinical sound. It gives the aura of medical, rather than psychological, authority to the delicate task of instructing, encouraging, and supporting the work of regular classroom teachers and avoids the familiar roles of peer or superior in the school hierarchy. The diagnostic-prescriptive teacher role model is a consultant, a source of curriculum (activities as well as materials), an insider in political balance who is perpetually an outsider whose status and utility exist only when she is removed from identification with either teachers or the power structure. Her room—the Activities Room—is an oasis, a place students choose to go to as an exciting treat, rather than as a humiliating assignment for treatment of disability.

How is this reversal of expectations achieved? First, children with learning or emotional disabilities are not isolated in classes that automatically identify them as liabilities to themselves and their peers. They are integrated into regular classes. Second, when their behavior prevents them or other children from learning, and the teacher believes herself unable to cope, she may "refer" the child out of the room. However, the child goes neither to the school counselor nor to the principal or his assistants, and he does not go alone, stigmatized or glamorized by the special attention given. Before any changes are made, his behavior is observed as often as seven times at different times of the day within his own classroom. When the child finally is assigned to the Activities Room, he goes with four or five others—volunteers who look forward to the games, the diversions, the opportunities that the imaginatively equipped room offers for new kinds of learning. Among these volunteers no more than two may be other "special" children. Among them may also be the most popular boy or girl in the class. Everyone wants to go.

During the time that the child spends in the room (usually from five to ten sessions), the teacher experiments with a wide variety of teaching techniques to determine what will involve him and sustain his interest. She keeps a careful log of the material resources used, the group and individual procedures they explore together each day, and the child's responses. Before the child returns to the classroom with his fellows, she has assembled the information needed, not to diagnose the pathology of the child's failings but to make explicit the pattern of behavior found and techniques that elicited specific changes.

The classroom teacher receives the diagnosis and the prescription—a written review of the child's needs and an account of strategies successful in involving him and in changing his view of himself. The regular teacher also received information and assistance to implement the child's future program and to integrate these new materials and methods into the already established processes of the classroom. The child is returned to the mainstream under improved conditions. The DPT continues to provide demonstrations and support for the teacher. The case, although subject to reopening at any time, is closed when both adults agree that assistance is no longer needed.

The Activities Room and the work with the DPT can be considered a species of short term play therapy that assumes that, within a relatively short time, some of the conditions that support the child's learning behavior in a more conventional environment can be determined and activated.

### Theoretical Underpinnings

Perceptual psychology underlies much of the substantive part of George Washington's Special Education training program, as do some of the standard, more conventional works in humanistic education—including values clarification—that are required reading. Learning how to find out is more important than learning lists of facts. The emphasis is less on the acquisition of a repertoire of methods and materials than the development of a point of view emphasizing personal meaning. The master's degree program is entirely in-service (two years of teaching experience are required for entry). The opportunity to use that orientation in practice in local district classrooms begins early, with supervised field work during the first semester of the program. By the second semester, the trainee has his own classroom.

Teacher training emphasizes understanding and accepting the self and building relations with others. Group processes and modified "encounter" are used as tools of psychological education. At the university, teachers in preparation as DPTs are evaluated using self-reports and the scores they receive in academic classes. In their field work, the criterion for teacher performance is the performance of the children.

### The DPT Program in Operation: Fairfax County, Virginia

Fairfax County in Virginia, with 156,000 children and an average family income of more than $17,000 annually, has adopted the DPT program. I observed the diagnostic-prescriptive teacher in the North Springfield School with her two trainees from the George Washington University program. Her bright, cheerful Activities Room provided a warm, encouraging setting in which children played the Developing Understanding of Self and Others (DUSO) game enthusiastically.[13] The wall posters say: "Don't interrupt. Tell how you feel about things. Be positive. Talk with each other. Be with it. . . ." The rhythmic song loudly sung by all is "Caring and Sharing." There is awareness, excitement, warmth, caring, and good feeling.

Robert Prouty made no bones about the fact that the program is intended to change teachers, not just those in Special Education but all of them, and all administrators, too, so that their positive feelings can also be used as supports for the children. If the teachers I watched were representative, both this training and the performance of other DPTs must be extraordinary. They were already thoroughly professional, purposeful, relaxed, and responsive, committed to the goals of the work and convinced of its efficacy and appropriateness for all elementary children.

Fairfax County has approved four DPT positions; Maryland has some two dozen full time teachers. The concept is spreading. South Carolina has a training program under Marlene O'Bryant at the Citadel in Charleston. The universities of North Carolina and Massachusetts are establishing programs. Douglas Prillaman at William and Mary College was the co-developer with Robert Prouty of the DPT program, and trainees have been coming to both William and Mary and George Washington University from other states.

Can the DPT concept and training be widely disseminated? There is little money available these days for structural changes that require new personnel. Perhaps teachers already in service could be retrained within their districts and on the job to become DPTs to others within their own schools. Under conditions of high peer trust, this may be feasible.

## THE UNIVERSITY OF FLORIDA: THE CHILDHOOD EDUCATION PROGRAM AND ARTHUR COMBS

Many people have suggested that the social purposes of the community must also be those of the teachers or they will not be carried out. Fewer have suggested means of attending directly to the purposes of teachers in training by organizing such education around the person, rather than around a specific body of content to be learned. Arthur Combs and his colleagues (1974) believe such a program must be an adaptive "open" system organized beforehand only about the general desired direction of growth. The assumption made in "closed" systems that mastery of many bits of desired competencies will lead to general competence is seen as false. On the contrary, the most deeply needed knowledge is broad: the nature of the self, how the self develops, and how it may be changed. The goal of teacher training is to facilitate the "adequate personality"—the growth of personality and intelligence—to minister to a process already underway.

### The Perceptual Theory

For the body of theory behind these assumptions, Combs has drawn on the "Third Force" humanistic, non-Freudian, nonbehavioral psychology which appeared in the late 1940s. This model perceives man neither as driven by his lower sexual and death instincts nor as controlled by external forces not subject to his will. Humans are most accurately seen as healthy, whole, free, and developmental. Persons are unique events in the process of being and becoming. The individual's view of himself, his self-concept, is learned not from introspection but from the responses of others to his actions.

The self-concept is of central importance and affects every aspect of life. Behavior is a direct function of the field of perception of the individual and results from interaction between how he views himself and the situation. Therefore, behavior is only a symptom that may be read backwards to understand the personal meanings attached to it. When those meanings are changed, then behavior will also change, but not before. The task of the teacher-training faculty, therefore, becomes helping students see that the understanding of personal meanings, which they and others assign to events, is more important than the facts themselves.

The future behavior of teachers as professionals is based on how the individual sees himself as self and himself in relation to administrators, students, subject matter, and the profession of teaching. Combs (1974) describes what he believes to be the perceptual organization of the good teacher. He must

1. be well informed about his subject matter;
2. have "accurate perceptions" and beliefs about people and broad identification with them (the capacity for empathy);
3. have a positive perception of his self, "leading to accuracy";
4. have accurate perceptions about the purpose and process of learning;
5. have personal perceptions about appropriate methods to carry out his purposes.

In addition, the good teacher must be *personally* open and aware that authority in the classroom is earned, not simply assigned automatically to the *role* of teacher.

### The Proposed Program

What are the characteristics of a teacher-training program that would facilitate the development of such perceptual organization? Success depends upon the selection of participants who to a large degree already have adequate "perceptual qualities." The atmosphere must support the search for personal meaning and the facilitation of self-esteem. Freedom from comparison and competition is essential to permit the widest possible personal experimentation. The structure of such a program would include close guidance counseling and relationships with faculty counselors who are also instructors in subject matter. This structure would not be intended as therapy for serious psychological disabilities but only to "assist the individual to make more effective use of himself in face-to-face relationships."

Clinical professors, themselves experienced teachers, would supervise the work of student teachers in the field. Learning specific methods would be far less important than beliefs about what was actually happening. Greater responsibility would be laid upon the student teacher in training, who must be involved in the planning and decisionmaking of the program. Discussion groups would serve as a means of involvement—first, as decisionmaking groups in which problems are examined and answers sought, and, second, as learning groups in which ideas and individual experiences are explored for the sake of uncovering their meanings for the participants.

An optimal teacher-training program would provide a curriculum laboratory to test and try techniques and materials, lectures, discussions, and reading. The management of such knowledge would be organized in ways quite different from the conventional teacher-training program. Participants would undergo simultaneous rather than sequential experiences. These would occur at any time within a two year period, largely at the option of the students. Students would be expected to seek information when they need it. The information provided would not only have to be made available more than once during that time period, it would have to manifest demonstrable relevance to the lives of the learners.

### The Program in Practice

When this hypothetical, ideal program was finally undertaken at the University of Florida, three broad categories of essential experiences were identified for the junior and senior years. First, *involvement with children* through field experiences and with the community through participation in various aspects of its life. Second, *exposure to ideas* through a substantive panel of faculty members. Third, *discovery of personal meaning* through attendance in discussion seminars. By the fall of 1973 this New Elementary Program was no longer experimental. It had graduated some 200 elementary teachers and had changed its name to the Childhood Education Program (CEP).

**Access to Practice Opportunity.** Student practice teaching in the Childhood Education Program is not confined to the traditional short period of classroom involvement toward the end of the pre-service professional training. The amount of time spent and responsibility assumed is continuous and graduated throughout the program. In the beginning, students work on a one-to-one basis with a single child while they visit the laboratory school and observe children at various developmental levels. Later, they become "teacher aides" in an elementary classroom, then "assistant," and then "associate" teachers. At least four quarters of partial responsibility prepare for the opportunity to practice the full role of teacher during the last half quarter of the program. The decision about when the student should attempt more involvement is made by discussion among students, seminar participants, and the public school and college personnel with whom he has worked.

Field experience is intended to provide other benefits besides role practice opportunity. It includes the experience of different approaches to teaching (including team teaching, modular teaching, the open classroom) with pupils of differing age levels and maturity from different socioeconomic and cultural backgrounds. Participation in the broader community remains an ideal.

**Access to Ideas.** Weekly sessions may provide knowledge required of all students, be established at the request of students, or simply be made available without requirement by faculty members of the substantive panel. What any one student takes may be required of all, selected from a range of alternatives, or proposed by the student and approved by the instructor as "negotiated activities." Contracts spell out what is proposed and how and when it is to be done.

Each term begins with orientation meetings in various areas of inquiry, such as language arts and math, which provide knowledge in the field and procedures and requirements for completing the work. Optional small group meetings for demonstrations, discussions, and lectures are held thereafter. Faculty members work with students on independent studies, although cooperation in learning activities is encouraged. Usually, a student would attend the math orientation sessions and afterward sign up for small group meetings on various topics of his choice, participate in the laboratories, and do the associated readings, although he may also choose independent study if appropriate meetings are not available.

The small group discussions may be faculty or student initiated or led. In content they may range from required learning activities to the intellectual interests of individual students in any area, say, from feminist movement to the American Indian.

**Access to Personal Meaning.** An important aspect of humanistic education centers is the emotional home provided by "circles," small groups, or seminars designed to facilitate the integrative development of students. In CEP, 30 students and one faculty member form such a community which meets informally twice a week in groups of 15. Students are assigned to them as vacancies occur through graduation. Such contact is mutually enhancing through the sharing of information and the building of familiarity and trust. It may take the form of games (such as values clarification), communication laboratories, social gatherings, or field experience discussions in dyads or triads. These seminars are neither for intellectual nor experiential exploration solely, nor for the investigation of inner life alone, but rather for the personal integration of these in professional behavior.

Because the seminar leader remains constant throughout the training program as personal counselor, academic advisor, record keeper, and coordinator of evaluation, he is able to provide feedback to the student that is both accurate and nonthreatening.

**Organization and Evaluation.** In CEP, responsibilities roughly equated with a conventional college course load may be shared by several faculty members. The 10 to 12 professors, who, together with the 120 students and a program director, make up a team act as the four seminar leaders and as substantive panel members in each of the following areas: art, curriculum, language arts, mathematics, reading, science, social foundations, multiethnic studies, music, health, physical education, and children's literature. Careful liaison with the field schools is crucial, but these professors do not supervise the student in the field. That is left to the classroom teacher, although the seminar leaders are concerned with the meaning of the experience to the student teacher. Each seminar sends one delegate to biweekly program meetings that are an important governance structure. There, students and faculty—all those who will be affected —share in making decisions for the future of the overall program.

Careful record keeping is indispensable because student progress is made along a broken front. Student evaluation is by the students themselves, substantive panel members, teachers in the schools, and the seminar leaders who act as evaluation coordinators and are responsible for summarizing the student's work for inclusion in his placement credentials. Students whose contracted work is felt to be inadequate may be asked to supplement it or to redo it in some agreed upon way. Substantive panel members are formally evaluated once a year; and seminar leaders and the entire program, three times a year, although the latter two may be informally evaluated in open discussion at any seminar. The last procedure is especially valuable because the feedback is immediate and thus the instructor may explain his actions or change them if he is convinced of their inappropriateness.

While Combs believes that the behavioral objectives, performance-based criteria approach to accountability has value for the learning of precisely defined skills or the production of clearly defined simple behavior, he sees it as much less useful for the assessment of complex, problem-solving skills that involve affect as much as cognition. He does believe that the characteristics of the effective teacher, described earlier in terms of perceptual organization, can be assessed and he has made some attempt to do so.

Similarities between the Florida program and Barbara Biber's at the Bank Street College are strong. Independently arrived at, the convergences of these and other programs lend significance to their synchronous appearance across the nation. Margaret Mead may have been right when she suggested that not invention but the dissemination of what is already known is the crucial issue in the world today.

## THE UNIVERSITY OF MASSACHUSETTS: THE CENTER FOR HUMANISTIC EDUCATION AND GERALD WEINSTEIN

Gerald Weinstein described to me the program of the Center for Humanistic Education that he directs and that started with Ford Foundation support in 1970. About 300 teachers have been formally trained in various school districts; 19 doctoral students in humanistic education have graduated; many lives have been changed. There were some 500 professionals influenced by the center's work who were at that moment actively involved in classrooms. Thousands more had been trained within Youth Tutoring Youth, a National Commission on Resources for Youth project in New York City. A new professional group—school counselors—was beginning to extend their traditional role to include the teaching of self-education through group counseling. (See *The Personnel and Guidance Journal, 51,* May 1973).

The center began its work and the training of teachers by limiting itself to one narrow track of humanistic education, focusing on feeling, emotion, the person inside himself and in relation to others. Self-actualization was the goal.

Personal growth through planned experiences based largely on Gestalt techniques was seen as the way. Human potential was not, broadly speaking, *human*
potential at all, but the actualization of the lone seeker. In the beginning, those
who came to work at the center came to work on themselves, to experience
themselves. Larger, more lasting, meanings were not sought.

This beginning has persisted in the public eye long after its reality has passed,
for the program has changed. It is more humanistic—more balanced in its cognitive and affective elements and in its content and the experiences provided. It
has also redistributed its emphasis from self-knowledge of the person as private
and unique to include that self as a professional, and that self as a member of
organizations and other groups, as a part of systems. The approach is now on
three levels: personal, professional, and organizational.

### Self-Science

Self-science as Weinstein's approach to the psychological aspects of humanistic education is called, uses the self as content, much as biology uses
living organisms and sociology uses groups as content. Dealing with the experiences of the inner person, it is not designed as a healing or therapeutic
process (although that may at times occur), but as one that is at once preventive and developmental. Like a scientist, the individual and not an outsider
is responsible for his own explorations inward to consciousness or outward to
reflexive observation of his own behavior. Like a scientist, the learner may begin deductively with a generalization that he holds about himself and tests
through systematic observation. Or, more commonly, he may begin inductively
by gathering data in which he can gradually discern generalizable patterns that
he can transfer to other situations.

The Trumpet March (so named because of the shape in which it is usually
presented) is the ingenious scheme through which the latter is done.

The Trumpet
#### INDIVIDUAL CONCERNS
(Identity, Connectedness, Power)

| | |
|---|---|
| Step One: | Experience confrontations |
| Step Two: | Inventory responses |
| Step Three: | Recognize patterns |
| Step Four: | Own patterns |
| Step Five: | Consider consequences |
| Step Six: | Allow alternatives |
| Step Seven: | Make evaluations |
| Step Eight: | CHOOSE |

(See Appendix B for details about the Trumpet March, including a diagram and a
detailed presentation of the steps.)

An interesting parallel could be made between this scheme and Dewey's scheme for the accumulation and testing of observable data, the building of testable hypotheses, replication, verification, and the development of theories and, eventually, laws.

But, although self-science may be behavioral science, it is not as it is usually taught with emphasis on learning an accumulated body of hypotheses, theories, and laws about individual thinking, feeling, perceiving, behaving. Self-science begins with the person most of interest to the learner—himself—who then connects his personal knowledge of an individual to the public knowledge available about many individuals, the science of psychology.[14]

Weinstein at the University of Massachusetts, and Borton and Newberg in the Philadelphia schools, with their special emphasis on individual learning directed to the person, were among the first to believe that the self is subject matter content important enough to deserve its own time slot in the school day. Theoretically, Weinstein's self-science might appropriately move from education about the self of one learner to education about the selves of the species—to valid generalization about *human* behavior. In practice, however, the patterns discerned have been extended only to generalizations about the learner's own life. The balance in the self-science program between consciousness and behavior is as tilted as in conventional psychology courses, but in the opposite direction.

The importance of the self-science curriculum has little to do with its potentiality as a behavioral science or as an extension of traditional scientific thinking. It rests with its capacity as theory and methodology to facilitate learning. Self-knowledge and self-respect are preconditions of humane development and the capacity to learn democratic values. Self-study helps the person to cope with "blockages," with inner matters that get in the way of useful, generous, inclusive behavior.

### Learning and Teacher Education

How should teachers be educated? Ideally, Gerald Weinstein believes in all three of the ways that Alfred Alschuler, who works closely with him, has suggested as a typology for education procedures: *congruent, confluent,* and *contextual* approaches. The *congruent* approach is through the intensive study of self-science and its focus on personal knowledge about one's own self. *Confluence* occurs through adapting the traditional—that is, cognitive—subject matter content taught in the schools to include affective or feeling components. Weinstein strongly feels the need for good professional curricula in the schools but recognizes the conflict between that need and the important experience teachers gain when they develop their own materials. But this potential conflict is probably minimal. Depending on their needs, teachers tend to adapt even prepared packages they think are very good. It is the clear definition of those needs and objectives that is indispensable. *Contextual* training involves organizational development work to improve the entire climate of the school, including the relationship between teachers and students, and to cope with the system within which humanistic education occurs.

The teacher education programs I perceived were largely devoted to the congruent procedures of self-education. Nowhere was context—the school environment—attended to as a major means of learning.

## Current Developments

The work at the University of Massachusetts has changed greatly, not only during the three years of the Ford funding, but since that ended in 1973. Then, the need for evaluation of outcomes was expressed, but those in the program were "unclear on what to measure"—a typical problem when primary objectives are affective. Now, appropriate goals for their work in humanistic education are seen as increments of self-knowledge along a developmental continuum.

Weinstein and Alschuler have begun to examine self-knowledge as a developmental process. The outcome of their work will be of scientific as well as educational interest. Following Piaget's theory of cognition, they hypothesize not only that there is an invariant structural sequence by which individuals learn to characterize themselves, but that education may facilitate movement through the stages of that sequence. Those largely cognitive stages are then seen as operational outcomes whose attainment may be measured.

Another change has taken place. The value framework, which began with the highest goal of life as the development of human potential and self-actualization, has been modified from a self-centered focus to a socially centered focus. We "must help people become all that they can become," but appropriate procedures for accomplishing cognitive, affective, and behavioral subgoals may differ for different ages, different social classes, and different institutional settings. An outgrowht of this new emphasis on social actualization and social responsibility is the addition of a "Humanistic Application Cluster" within the School of Education which offers course work and practice toward master's and doctoral degrees. Governance of the cluster is shared broadly. Its approaches to change range from the individual to the system and are applied onsite within a wide variety of educational settings: schools, mental hospitals and prisons, detention centers, halfway houses, community mental health centers, drug education units. The draft list of general professional competencies required is revealing:

1. the ability to present (in writing, orally, or pictorially) a clear statement of what is meant by becoming "more fully human";
2. competence in "promoting full humanness"
3. competence in practical field work in two or more settings;
4. *"demonstrated commitment to combating the causes and effects of racism, sexism, and other forms of systematic dehumanization"* (emphasis added);
5. skills in "demystifying" the educational methods used—that is, teaching them to "non-professionals."

## THE UNIVERSITY OF CALIFORNIA, SANTA BARBARA: THE CONFLUENT EDUCATION PROGRAM AND GEORGE BROWN

George Brown in Santa Barbara invented what he calls "confluent education" after his first systematic attempt, in 1967, to train teachers and develop curricula in a balanced way. (1971, 1975) Brown, director of the Confluent Education Program at UCSB, sees the concept simply as an appropriate way to refer to the two most important components of human personality—feeling and thinking—and how education concerns itself with both. Nothing intrinsic in his expressed theory of confluent education posits the values derived from the traditions of the humanities, from the mental health education movement, or from "Third Force" psychology.[15]

However, in practice the matter is different. Brown in his programs and operations accepts and implements such values and their links to personal and social competence. In Chapter One, I suggested that the concept of humanistic education includes education for personal integration to which explicit values are attached and in which none of the streams of personality—affect, cognition, will, psychomotor functions—is undervalued. In his practice, George Brown seems to me to agree and to draw heavily upon theories of Gestalt and Psychosynthesis psychology.

### Affect and Learning Process

Earlier I described three principal ways affect directly shapes the learning process: (1) through such preconditions for learning as self-esteem and motivation; (2) though the intrinsic emotion-arousing qualities of curriculum materials and experience; and (3) through the personal, private, and, perhaps, immediate concerns of the learner himself. All three areas appear in the program at Santa Barbara. First, practice draws on the empirical and theoretical work of John Shiflett who sees three sequential aspects of each learning task, in cyclical and spiral repetition, eliciting affective responses from learners: the *orientation* or preparation for the task, *engagement* or its performance, and *accomplishment* or its completion and the beginning of preparation for another cycle. Such responses may not be self-conscious, yet they nonetheless deeply affect the motivation of the learner.

While some forms of so-called affective education deal only with intrapsychic awareness of interpersonal knowledge, Brown sees the second of these affective manifestations—the impersonal or extrapersonal dimension of subject matter substance—as an important part of confluent education. The task of the teacher is to utilize the opportunities for emotional experience within the classroom climate to enable the student to connect those experiences to what he brings from his prior, rich engagements. Delicacy may be required, and a light touch, for with affect as with other kinds of content, readiness is all. The teacher's function is not only to guide the way but also to detour the learner around the passage that leads to premature knowledge.

The third way that affect shapes the learning process—through the personal concerns of the learner—is dealt with in many ways, including the small group that demonstrates caring and support without the threatening implications of therapy. Confluent education is for the healthy, not the ill; for the facilitation of development and not for remediation. The in-house teacher education program, with its emphasis on professional growth, makes this distinction clear. Implicit, however, is the belief that personal growth undergirds professional growth.

### The Teacher Education Program and
### Gestalt Psychology

The students enrolled in master's and doctoral programs already have spent at least two years in the classroom. They are working with other teachers still in the classroom and, in keeping with the new, extended meaning of education, with other communtiy groups. Some have come through encounter and sensitivity training and the Gestalt way to personal growth. All have come for professional growth and the core expansion of self-awareness that accompanies it in this program.

Courses are given in "Gestalt (theory and practice), encounter group leadership, the creative process, dynamics of planned change, philosophical dimensions of confluent education, human relations in education, instructional strategies and curriculum design in confluent education." Some techniques are taken eclectically from other theories, but both Gestalt and Psychosynthesis are especially useful to confluent educators because they are synthesizing in nature, reclaiming human wholeness from fragmenting analysis.[16]

**Gestalt Psychology.**  Gestalt psychology began in Germany almost two generations ago as a discovery about the nature of visual perception: seeing is inherently ordered as a dynamic configuration (*Gestalt*) of figure and background which alters according to attention, interests, and other factors. From this beginning grew the concept of the "organism-as-a-whole" and knowledge that the recognition or reorganization of wholeness out of parts may occur as sudden insight—the "aha!" experience. The central thesis of Gestalt psychology is that phenomena that are unitary wholes must have that wholeness respected and can be broken into bits analytically only at the cost of annihilating what in fact was, and is no longer, there. The integration of the organism that is the person and how that irreducible unity can be served by education are the foci of Brown's explorations and of all confluent education.

Two aspects of Gestalt thinking are especially prominent in Brown's work— the "here and now" as a way to increase personal awareness; and the emphasis on self-responsibility, on claiming those actions, thoughts, feelings that are

one's own. Affect is not denied, ignored, repressed. Through passionate investment, emotion aids learning as it can, in other ways, obstruct or distort it. The
distinction is clearly maintained between furthering awareness and therapeutic
exploration. However, the well of creativity is invited to flow through fantasy,
the invention of symbols, and imagination actively exploring both inner and
outer worlds. The belief of Freudians that negative emotions must be recognized
and coped with before more positive ones can be put to service is taken seriously
and so is the Greek ideal of moderation—nothing in excess. The polarities of
reason and emotion, both fully recognized, are reconciled within the unity of
the person. As Michael Scriven (1973: 103) has written:

> Reason is . . . never enough. It is always the slave of the passions, the in-
> strument of man's prerational needs. That, in sum, is what it is for. We
> must not exaggerate its utility, but neither can we afford to discard it, or
> to suppose that it cannot influence its masters, the passions.

## DRICE: Development and Research in Confluent Education

DRICE was the  acronym given a collection of curriculum development and
teacher-training projects of the Confluent Education Program at UCSB initially
funded by the Ford Foundation. DRICE's successor, CEDARC (the Confluent
Education Development and Research Center) is now independent of the Graduate School of Education. DRICE was established as a center to design and carry
out projects in curriculum development at all levels of education and, when
feasible, to carry out research on these activities. The many efforts of DRICE
participants to carry out this mandate have been reported in a noteworthy series
of occasional papers and monographs.[17] The original DRICE grant ran from
1970 through 1973 and was extended for one year through 1974.

There were three major thrusts of DRICE activity: first, three in-service
projects that provided training and practice in the development of curriculum;
second, the teacher-training and field school testing project; and, finally, the
research about the effects of humanistic education on teaching quality and classroom environment.

**The DRICE In-Service Program in Curriculum Development**. Of the in-
service programs under the original DRICE grant from Ford I will discuss three
sequentially: the Elementary Social Studies Project, the Community College
Project, and the Elementary Reading Project.

*Curriculum Development: The Elementary Social Studies Project.*  All of the
40 participants—almost equal numbers of men and women, older and younger,
teachers of upper and lower grades—came to this project in California's Goleta
Union School District with some prior experience with humanistic education.
They came with a sense of urgency, knowing that they had only one school year

to accomplish the tasks that were set. They wanted immediate help, lesson plans for the classroom.

The directors of the project—Gloria Castillo and Liles Grizzard—took as a major goal for the year the development of social studies curricula by each teacher, a goal that easily fits into the existing concept of in-service teacher-training programs. A principal function of the group itself was to help the teachers to define behavioral and affective objectives and then to decide what activities and materials were needed to attain them in the classroom. Another function was evaluative: to give feedback about the units or lessons presented as they were developed. Gloria Castillo has since written a book, *Left-Handed Teaching* (1974), that gives teachers practical help with humanistic methodology.

Aware of the need for greater self-understanding, the directors during the first three months showed Gestalt films and encouraged role playing and "readiness activities" from Psychosynthesis that allowed the participants to become aware of their subselves. However, these were kept secondary to the curriculum development focus. Both directors reported growth of the group as a group: increasing interdependence and decreasing reliance on the leaders; decrease of internal tensions caused by age, teaching level, or personality differences; and development of a rhythm that carried them through the specific substance of lessons and classroom reality to work on interpersonal relationships and subsequently on personal growth. By the end of the year, the social studies group had developed identity, autonomy, and belief in its own leadership capacity—including its capacity to raise funds to continue its own training in the fall.

These happy results were not without external complications, however. At the same time that faith in the growth of their own professionalism was reinforced, many felt inadequate to cope with the educational needs of peers and parents and the administrative needs of principals trying to accommodate other teachers who were threatened by innovation. Other internal complications were the teachers' own desires to stress narrowly *affective* rather than broadly *humanistic* education and their resistances to writing about (and thereby clarifying, consolidating, and routinizing) the activities they were developing.

In my experience, this is a common problem. It is perhaps a necessary reaction to the insight that problem solving and other thinking skills are drastically overemphasized in the conventional curriculum. It can be dealt with by emphasizing materials in which cognitive and behavioral elements are clearly related to affect and by using the training group for brainstorming to provide suggestions to strengthen substantive weakness in the curriculum. To formalize and record curricula, Castillo suggests exploring such alternative ways as sound tape, video tape, and film.

**Curriculum Development: The Community College Project.** Born of dissatisfaction with current approaches to the teaching of English language and literature, this two-and-a-half year project went through sequential emphases on personal growth and on the application of what had been learned to classroom practice, moving from the intrapersonal to the interpersonal and then the impersonal, and, finally, to the integration of the three domains. A confluent theory of English teaching based on Psychosynthesis was developed by Tom Yeomans, the director. It and the "book" of curriculum pieces (published in mimeo by DRICE), written, tested, and revised by participants, make up a useful package for promulgating their work.

*Curriculum Development and Teacher Training: The Elementary Reading Project.* Directed by Sara Miller, the elementary reading project was a cooperative three year effort between the UCSB and the Esalen Institute in San Francisco. Like the other DRICE teacher education programs, this was structured around intensive weekend workshops and monthly evening meetings. At the workshops, methods and techniques were tried or experienced by the participants as they were presented. The followup evening seminars provided opportunity for reflection on, and analysis of, the experience and the chance to practice what was learned within a sheltered laboratory environment. Participants were asked to keep extensive personal and professional logs, which included notes on research, reading, meetings, and an ideal model against which they measured themselves, their appreciations, resentments, and future plans. These were read by the director to provide immediate reinforcement. At the end of the year each presented a project that reflected the knowledge gained. The presentation of methods and ideas was concentrated in the first two years. The individual year end projects were coordinated for the sake of pursuing serious curricular development during the third year of the project.

What happened as the teachers learned to manipulate the techniques drawn from psychological theory and practice, from philosophy, from the arts? A few examples will suffice. Ordinary teaching became transformed by the addition of feeling. Simple, large print vocabulary cards spelled out "mad," "sad," and "glad" for the children to identify and display not only their knowledge of the word but their own—and owned up to—feelings. Reading became an expansion of awareness—from reading bodies, feelings, objects, symbols, to letters and finally sentences. They "read" with their bodies by listening with stethoscopes; they read each other's bodies formed into letters.

The child was taught to "center" himself within himself, to collect himself-his feelings and his mind—within his body to quiet himself in preparation for cognitive learning. Through adaptations of *aikido*—a nonviolent Japanese martial art—he learned to "blend" with his environment to avoid conflict and foster harmony. Through "receptive" meditation, he learned to listen to inner messages, to intuition that can complete the slow grope toward knowledge in an instant.

By the close of the project, a confluent curriculum outline had been developed based on current theory and research in reading. Interactive in nature, recognizing the importance of self- and other-acceptance and the rejection of stereotypes, it utilizes a vocabulary of human experiences, rather than one limited by class and culture. Four major units, each with cognitive, interpersonal, and affective themes, comprise the program, which is sequential and cumulative. For each unit, focus is on specific exercises related to body, feelings, and intelligence. For Unit One, for instance, *body* is centered around the general notion of *awareness* (the students learn to read their bodies, and more). *Feelings* is devoted to *recognition* (the students learn to "mirror" another's expressions and actions, to "read" about feelings by listening to stories). *Intelligence* centers around *relaxation* (the student learns to recognize his tense or relaxed body, to relax his mind from concern for the past or the future to being in the present "here and now"). The final unit treats *thinking* and problem solving under *intelligence; controlling* under *body* (leading to the control of pictures and words); and *accepting* (self, differences, and their expression through writing) under *feelings*.

Carefully done in outline, the curriculum/training program has been completed since the end of the formal project. The conception differs in structure, sequence, and scope from other curricula that, however useful, are solely assemblages of activities. Nowhere, to the best of my knowledge, is such an integrated program in reading available commercially. The children are part of it; they enjoy it. Does it teach? It couldn't fail to do so. Does it teach reading? This is the question that should be put to the test, widely and soon.

**DRICE Field School Testing.** The purposes of this effort, coordinated by Aaron Hillman, were twofold: to enable small groups of interested teachers to meet to study humanistic theory and practice with credit through the Extention School of the University of California at Santa Barbara, and to enable schools in the field to test already developed curriculum materials and to use confluent educational practices with current materials. During the course of one year (1972-1973), some 25 study groups across the nation and in several locations in Canada and Mexico were formed. These are ongoing and the number continues to enlarge. Locally developed, like the study groups under the Fairleigh-Dickinson program, they represented grassroots interest tied to and emotionally and professionally supported by DRICE through the group's local coordinator and consultation services.

Identification of field testing schools, based on contact with staff members already trained in humanistic education, was more difficult. At the end of the school year of 1973, only five were reported; one was in Mexico City, another in Vancouver, British Columbia. Elaborate administrative requirements may be a deterrent. So may the time, energy, and opportunity required for adequate communication about both the objectives and means of confluent education.

Although sanguine that his voluminous and sustained correspondence from institutions and individuals and unrealized field contacts still imply future teacher training possibilities within the public schools, Hillman believes that roadblocks to dissemination and the feedback needed for elaboration and revision of activities and materials do exist. These include the lack of more adequate curricula in fields outside of English and Social Studies and a systematic definition of humanistic education and its general goals, behavioral objectives and measurement instruments. At present, in what looks like a promising attempt, Edwin Bridges at UCSB is working with Hillman on the identification of the latter two through the analysis of action patterns and their prospects in the classroom.

Like Arthur Combs and others, Hillman believes that over time the progress represented by study groups and field test schools may disappear if it is not supported from an outside central source. The course of school changing goes slowly, against the powerful forces of conventional wisdom and the social pressures generated by it. However hard working and committed to humanistic education, teachers alone cannot restructure the schools.

**DRICE Research: The Problem of Evaluation.** Two sets of findings from DRICE studies have direct relevance to humanistic classrooms and curriculum development. The studies are limited in purpose, sensible in design and method, and modest in their claims.

John Shiflett and George Brown presented interesting findings in a monograph entitled *Confluent Education: Attitudinal and Behavioral Consequences of Confluent Teacher Training* (1972). Ingenious scales were adapted and devised to measure the consequences of the Gestalt awareness training that was part of a fifth year elementary teacher-training program at the Confluent Education Project in Santa Barbara. The authors concluded that:

> . . . the confluently trained, compared to the non-confluently trained, exhibited significantly greater classroom informality, and possessed a significantly higher sense of existential mastery by the conclusion of training. . . . Confluent training was seen to lead to an increased orientation to "the Now," which, in turn, contributed to greater classroom informality. [pp. xi–xii]

Similar findings are reported by Mark Phillips and Bettye Elmore in their monograph *Follow-up Report on DRICE Participants, 1974.* Their goal was to determine "whether confluent education, as operationalized in the DRICE project, made any contribution to improving teaching quality, classroom environment, and student behavior. . . ." (1972: 1) Their conclusions, qualified by the limits of their methods (which measured solely subjective perceptions of teachers and students) and by the small size of their sample (26 out of 43

DRICE teacher participants responded to the mail questionnaire), are sufficiently provocative to be cited at length:

1. The DRICE project, as perceived by both the participating teachers and
   their students, appears to have had considerable impact on their personalities and behavior. The greatest impact reported by the DRICE
   participants appears to be in what is usually considered personality
   changes in themselves and in their students. This is partially substan-
   tiated by student responses as well. The teachers perceived themselves
   as having increased their self-awareness, awareness of others, self-
   esteem, and affective expression. They also perceive the students as
   being more self-aware, open in displaying emotions, and more responsible. Additionally, many students perceive themselves as having gained
   both increased self-confidence and self-awareness. . . .
2. It is also possible to tentatively conclude that the project did have considerable impact on the classroom environments of participating teachers. Changes were noted by the teachers in their teaching styles and in
   the curriculum used, with the emphasis being upon more student-
   centeredness, openness, flexibility, and with an overt emphasis on
   affect. These perceptions are reinforced by those of the students who
   perceive the confluent teachers as warmer, more open, closer to students, and more caring. In general, the teachers and students perceive
   the confluent classrooms as ones in which feelings are expressed more
   openly and closer relationships among students and between teachers
   and students exist. . . .
3. The DRICE project appears to have been highly successful in meeting
   teachers' needs for interpersonal contact (connectedness, a sense of
   community). Given the limited opportunity for teachers to share values, feelings, ideas, and even skills within the typical institutional
   structure of most public schools, it is possible that this is a widespread
   teacher need that is generally not being met. . . .
   Similarly, student responses also emphasized how beneficial they felt
   the close interpersonal contact was to their functioning both in and out
   of the class. It is possible that the need for affiliation between students,
   through sharing of problems, feelings, and values is also one which is
   rarely met in our schools and which, through being met by confluent
   teachers, both facilitates student personal development and generally
   improves the classroom environment. (1974: 33–35)

To those of us schooled in the pristine rigors of behavioral methodology,
faint cautioning echoes are heard: the Hawthorne effect, the halo effect, con-
taminated samples, improper design, and the rest of the litany by which purists
determine the importance of findings. Nevertheless, we are beginning—very
slowly—through such studies as the above to have some notions about what
humanistic education does, to whom, and how, and what can be done to improve the process.

## RELIGIOUS SCHOOLS:
## DIVERSE DENOMINATIONS

Religious education has not escaped the crisis in the classroom. Attendance has been diminishing, and students have been increasingly restless and resentful. The confluent approach, which links emotion to substance and private to public knowledge, may reverse the tide. These four examples typify humanistic education in religious contexts: The Hebrew Union College; the Roman Catholics; the American Baptist Convention in Valley Forge, Pennyslvania; and the Unitarian-Universalists headquartered in Boston.

### The Hebrew Union College in Los
### Angeles, California

The Hebrew Union College in Los Angeles has a teacher-training course in confluent techniques for its religious school teachers meeting once weekly. Aaron Hillman instructed the seminar I took part in. There are some 800 Reform Jewish congregations in the United States. Hebrew Union College in Los Angeles, under Rabbi William Cutter, is one of three Reform schools of education in the country focusing on graduate training. Only four years old, it is the only one involved in confluent education. During that time, about 200 religious teachers have had some confluent training. Recently, 12 were chosen to have leadership training and will continue to meet monthly with HUC staff. A summer curriculum is planned, with confluent education workshops for professionals already in positions of responsibility. Camp leaders and local teachers not enrolled in the teacher-training programs are also offered confluent education training year round.

**The Roman Catholics.**  At a Toronto meeting of their Religious Education Association, Roman Catholics centered their discussions about the issue of values and their meaning to the individual. While the integrating principle of spiritual life remains Jesus and Catholic Christianity, with God as a superordinate organizing force, the individual is seen as liberated to work through his own personal values. No national curriculum has evolved from this concern for education of the self, but religious teacher training now attempts to incorporate some psychological approaches. Father Nichola Spagnolo and other Stagmatine Fathers use Transactional Analysis in teacher training at the Espousal Center in Waltham, Massachusetts. Others include such psychological and philosophical orientations and methodologies as Transcendental Meditation. Nor is ideological conflict felt by those Catholics who use the curriculum materials developed by the Unitarian-Universalists.

**The American Baptist Convention.**  These Baptists call their approach to humanistic education "experiential." In their manual on *Team Building in Church*

*Groups,* for example, they suggest a sophisticated variety of exercises and activities derived from group dynamics and National Training Laboratories training procedures. Bible education is seen as a group process through which the individual explores himself as he explores his relationship to the authority of the Holy Word. Role playing is important.

**The Unitarian-Universalists.** The Unitarian-Universalists refer to their educational approach as process-oriented and "life-enhancing." They have developed multimedia kits based on "discovery" processes and a view of life compatible with much humanistic psychology, including the work of Gordon Allport and the developmental theories of Erik Erikson.

A field staff conducts workshops to train religious teachers. Techniques from Transactional Analysis, Gestalt, and group dynamics are used to focus on the avoidance of self-deception and the increasing of knowledge about one's own desires and needs and those of others. Role playing and the simulation of life situations are commonly used as a means to self-examination and introspection.

Training programs also accompany the curriculum. Directed at students from the third grade through junior high, these kits center around themes that represent the beliefs and values of the Universalist-Unitarian Association. "Decision-making," "Freedom and Responsibility," and "Person-to-Person" (problems of communication) are typical themes designed to increase inner knowledge and generalizable knowledge of the outer world. Inquiries about the availability of these materials should be directed to Unitarian-Universalist Headquarters, 25 Beacon Street, Boston, Massachusetts 02108.

This humanistic approach to education is often seen as nonsectarian and representative of values that transcend differences of dogma. The Catholics, for example, are willing to use UUA materials, just as both groups use some of the value clarification techniques popularized by Sidney Simon.

## NONPROFIT AND OTHERWISE: FOUNDATIONS, ENTREPRENEURS, AND OTHER DISSEMINATORS

A major source of dissemination of information about humanistic theory and practice appears to come from an influential handful of individuals and organizations that are highly mobile or have established networks of consultants throughout the nation. By no means all of these are external to university programs, but many are, or they effectively detach themselves to gain increased access to their clientele. The work of William Glasser (1969; 1965) has been described in connection with Ventura School in Palo Alto, California. Thomas Gordon's programs (1975; 1970), like the rage for vitiated Transactional Analysis ("I'm OK—You're OK") in the classrooms of both teachers and students (see the discussion below of Self-Enhancing Education), have now reached national scope.

It is unclear whether the success of the specific programs discussed here and others of their ilk results from the learn-it-and-apply-it-now simplicity of the methodology or from some important substance. In their common forms, it appears likely that many will sputter and die rapidly once launched, drowned as much in the large and complex seas of human personality as in the ever-recurring tides of innovation. Nevertheless, the impressive investment of time and money by school districts and individuals in these programs suggests strongly that they are filling a widely felt gap in available educational resources. I will discuss two examples of these programs: the Human Development Program and Self-Enhancing Education.

### The Human Development Program:
### Bessell-Palomares-Ball

Far more sophisticated and influential than most programs is the work of Harold Bessell, Uvaldo Palomares, and Geraldine Ball at the Human Development Training Institute in La Mesa, California. Based on the theory of Karen Horney that the essential human drives are to achieve mastery and to gain approval, the "standard" program also incorporates insights from other psychoanalytically oriented therapists such as Harry Stack Sullivan, whose notion of universalization provided a concept for the process by which persons might realize that being unique or different from others did not necessarily mean being inferior to them.

The Human Development Program (HDP) is designed for teachers and students in environments as different as Beverly Hills and Watts. In-service teacher training is district supported both financially and through the participation of the principal or superintendent. The program was known to almost everyone to whom I talked—more so than the work of the centers at either Santa Barbara or the University of Massachusetts. The institute itself claims to have trained over 30,000 professionals and paraprofessionals in the past several years through its theoretical, experiential, and demonstration model workshops and institutes.

**The HDP Curriculum.** Out of the human needs for mastery and approval, Bessell, Palomares, and Ball developed a preventive curriculum framework around the constructs of awareness, self-confidence, and social interaction. Awareness is defined as recognizing one's own needs, motives, and experiences, and being receptive to the outer world and in contact with the inner. Self-confidence or mastery refers both to belief in oneself as a capable human being and to the harmonious behavioral integration of knowledge and skills. Such integration, in practice, means to use one's capabilities for the enhanced happiness of oneself and others. According to the Human Development Program, awareness and mastery are both the products of reactions to, and by, other people. A positive self-concept is largely the creation of others. The social interaction dimension of the curriculum is intended to increase understanding about the causes and effects of behavior in interpersonal relationships.

**The Magic Circle.** "The Magic Circle," says the brochure, "is a communication system which incorporates group dynamic techniques in a structured learning environment." Used by teachers for children of all ages, the curriculum of sequentially developed objectives was first based on the assumption that whole class teaching was inefficient and, before the junior high level, was better done in dyads and triads. Within the shelter of its sequential framework, daily small group activities directly related to program goals are carried out. "Acting out" is not allowed. Although the atmosphere is carefully casual, relaxed, and accepting (but not necessarily condoning), the structure, rules, and expectations of the learning process are clearly visible. Emphasis is on communication skills—both process and content—and the format is rigid. Everyone is involved and each person gets a turn at being listened to, if he wishes to talk.

As the teacher withdraws—but not beyond the range of control—each person is encouraged to develop leadership skills and to practice them responsibly within the circle. Such skills include learning to give honest positive recognition and feedback, to look directly at the speaker, to listen closely ("active listening"), and to respond courteously without interruption. The teachers and children are also taught to watch for signals that others wish to speak and to ask open-ended questions that allow the individual to express himself in his own way. Paraphrasing is an importan technique for helping speakers organize their ideas and complete them. Feelings, and the reactions of the participants to each other, are important and are not labeled good or bad through moral pronouncements by the teachers. The sessions are often so engrossing that the allotted 20 to 30 minutes are filled and run over, with the teacher standing by in amazement at the length of attention span even very young students have when they become truly involved.

While the Magic Circle fosters other kinds of skills in the mastery component of the program (similar to Glasser's Classroom Meetings), much of the interaction that goes on is highly dependent upon verbal, cognitive facility. Indeed, the knowledge acquired in the circle is summarized or "reviewed" cognitively at increments during the session—to clarify cognitive ideas that have been generated by an affective experience, to control aggression, and to reward those who have participated. Reviewing leads to practice in the observation of similarities and differences and acceptance of both. Like other programs described earlier, at the end HDP also uses verbal labeling to define and close the experience that has taken place within each session. (See Appendix B for examples of awareness, mastery, and social interaction activities within the Magic Circle.)

### Self-Enhancing Education, Inc.

Self-Enhancing Education (SEE), Inc., originated in 1959 by Norma Randolph and William Howe and based in Santa Clara, California, is a combination of curriculum and counselling in which a self-discipline plan is developed by teachers co-planning with students. "Self-discipline" means commitment to behavior that has been agreed upon as appropriate for specific activities or situations—stable, consensual limits, for example, rather than school rules. Inherent in the development and practice of such a plan is growth in self-control over learning and self-concept.

This highly eclectic program has human development as its long range goal. Two conditions of such development (nurturance and the freedom and opportunity to become) are clearly spelled out for participants. Nurturance is seen as both physical (food, shelter, safety, etc.) and social (stimulation, structure, and recognition from other human beings). Short range goals are intended to effect "intimacy in life opportunities" which appear in 12 areas: sexual, emotional, intellectual, aesthetic, creative, recreational, work, crisis, conflict, commitment, spiritual, and communication—the last the source of all types of true intimacy.

**The Use of Transactional Analysis.** SEE draws heavily on Transactional Analysis (TA), especially its description of how persons seek social nurturance and the recognition of their existence. The aim is to be "stroked" or to gain legitimacy for stroking oneself. This is done by making oneself available to stroke or be stroked through structuring time into any of several basic patterns: *withdrawing* from relating and transacting with others to relating and transacting with oneself; developing *rituals* which are stereotypic, repetitive, and often traditional ways of behaving toward self or others; filling in time with others with trivia through *pastimes;* and playing *games* designed to maintain existential life postures decided upon in early childhood.

There are four basic *posture types:* (1) rejection of self and acceptance of others ("I'm not OK—You're OK"); (2) rejection of self and others ("I'm not OK—You're not OK"); (3) acceptance of self and rejection of others ("I'm OK and you're not OK"); and (4) acceptance of self and others ("I'm OK and so are you.") *Intimacy* is the culminating and most valued way to structure time in the quest for the opportunity to give and receive social nurture. Its achievement depends upon the capacity to present oneself as real, rather than as expediently modified, to communicate directly with others, and to trust their capacity to receive messages honestly and with acceptance.

The SEE program is designed to build the capacity for intimacy through the practice of communication skills and processes within a group. "Reflective listening" and "congruent (that is, maintaining the authenticity of the self) forthright confrontation," followed by clear evidence of the willingness to discuss ("Can we talk about it?") are built into the structure of the program. The form that this has taken in practice in the field varies from one social context to the next. Work in the schools has focused less on TA as a system and more on the building of self-concept and self-esteem by a variety of methods centering around personal and social awareness. These are intended to help children feel stronger and more adequate about academic competency, feel more adequate physically, feel that they are unique resources of their own feelings in the interaction with significant adults, and feel accepted as worthy individuals by their peers.

**Teacher-Student Authority Relations.** Although the classroom self-discipline or "management" plan is developed by the teacher with the students ("What behavior will you need to be responsible for . . . for what activity?"), the authority of the traditional role is less relinquished than rendered inconspicuous. It remains ready but out of sight, able to take over when needed. Teachers use their legitimate authority in three ways: (1) as role models conveying listening and responding skills; (2) through direct influence on behavior, attitudes, and values—for example, through "admonishment and commands" while respecting feelings; and (3) as the "how to" provider of information and facilitation in identification of problems, approaches to solutions, and assessment. A number of structural arrangements assists in the balancing of teacher-student authority relations: group problem solving and the provision of "escape hatches" (places set apart for legitimate retreat from the class situation); "islands" for separate work as opposed to one "continent"; and a room set aside for the plastic arts and/or socially accepted ways of working out anxiety or unhappiness (including, perhaps, a rocking chair). Cards posted by the children (for example, "I'm getting myself back in") serve as a defense for whatever activity they are engaging in and so remove the teacher from the role of policeman. The "self-freedom" sign legalizes a period of independent activity at the end of the class period or a free moment for hobby sharing.

Like other programs in humanistic education, SEE utilizes direct practice and observer feedback as basic educational tools. Perhaps because of its entrepreneurial organization, SEE appears to be the most conservative of the programs examined—highly cautious, adaptive, and aware of the political and educational importance of community involvement.

## THE END OF THE JOURNEY

Our brief journey through the humanistic education of teachers has taken us criss-cross across the geography of our land: from Massachusetts to California, from New Jersey to Florida. Several models or styles of teacher education have been presented. All contain useful elements; all differ in content, structure, and process, although they also have many commonalities.

Among the significant elements that all these examples share and that bind them together as models for humanistic education are a belief in the importance of awareness and the development of self- and other-knowledge and respect; an emphasis on using group processes to facilitate learning; an environment that promotes informality and familiarity (in its meaning as a cognate to family); an emphasis on interaction between information gained and its practical application; and a focus on developing the powers of observation, communication, decisionmaking, and expression.

The Affective Education Development Program in the School District of Philadelphia with its process training (described in Chapter Two); the Center for Human Development at Fairleigh-Dickinson University in New Jersey with its study groups and close observation; the Diagnostic-Prescriptive Teacher Program at George Washington University based on perceptual psychology; the Childhood Education Program at the University of Florida developed by Arthur Combs emphasizing access to practice opportunity, ideas, personal meaning, and organization and evaluation; the Center for Humanistic Education at the University of Massachusetts organized by Gerald Weinstein with his self-science; and George Brown's Confluent Education Program at the University of California, Santa Barbara, with its teacher education program and DRICE projects —all these share in the traditions that have emerged to produce humanistic education. Too, they illustrate some of the range of its diversity.

By way of conclusion and summary, I would like explicitly to identify some of the methodologies inherent in humanistic education that have been implicit or only partially specified in the foregoing descriptions of practice, teacher training, curriculum development, and research. Finally, I shall briefly set down some suggestions about the tasks ahead.

### Methodologies Integral to Humanistic Education

First, social technology derived from the behavioral sciences has produced a valuable invention and powerful format for self-directed change: *the small group experience.* In one form or another—usually a circle of some kind—this useful structure has become ubiquitous as support, experience, reference, community, and mirror.

Second, another change made in curriculum—*simulation exercises and educational games*—has permitted a shift in teacher-student authority relationships and provided an in-house base for the active experiencing of planned, shared, emotional, and intellectual content. These games have often provided a legitimized mode of temporarily stepping outside self-consciousness and rationality— license for *being* during an intense and thought-free involvement similar to that of certain forms of aesthetic or athletic experience. Return passage is vouchsafed through the analysis that unites the experience with its meaning.

Third, *language as a major symbol system* in description, report, creation, and analysis has been used to expand the conceptual ability of the learner and to consolidate and integrate affective explorations through free associations, story telling, games, poetry, dance, drama and ritual, imagination, fantasy, dreaming. All serve to combine feeling and intellectual experience.

The fourth methodology is the curriculum of *the planned environment— contextual learning*—either within the school or without. Questioning, observing, responding, manipulating objects, students encounter the community beyond the school walls as they also do in play, in the search for answers and holistic experience, and, increasingly, in cooperative work or community service. They are put to action, to the active exploration of reality at all stages of human life, set out to learn from those who know, who are themselves primary sources. This curriculum is built of human resources, drawn upon *in situ* and not artificially transported to the schools, in ways that engage the learner and increase his knowledge of himself, his relationship to the social life of his time, and the meaning of that relationship.

Fifth, the *use of the body for the physical embodiment of abstract concepts* through movement, dance, drama, and role play builds psychomotor, feeling, and thinking competence. Drawing on knowledge of early developmental stages when thought and feeling were embodied in action, this methodology serves to integrate them at a higher level. People know more than they can put into words. The body provides another sensitive modality of expression. In a society where sensuality has been conventionally repressed, the natural state of physical awareness may have to be taught. Role play and dramatization, when properly used, are simple yet exceedingly powerful tools to achieve this.[18]

Role playing is effective when it is not the taking of roles as abstractions of tasks, norms, and expectations in the sociological sense. It enlarges the aptitude for empathy only when the player is able to take on the dilemma and circumstances of another *whole* person—one who is in three dimensional, living color and not a stereotype. Forced into two dimensions by a narrow script, players almost invariably find their own way out of the fraud, either by remaining themselves and responding as such or by spontaneously contributing responses and traits to the rounded development of the pallid figure who neither breathes nor acts except within the boundaries of rigid social role definitions. For many, the capacity for empathy does not automatically unfold in the course of biosocial maturation; it is the product of environmental interaction. Often it needs to be taught, so the fact that others have their own, often differing, perceptions and feelings is brought to consciousness, and practice is facilitated in the identification of these perceptions and feelings.

Sixth and last (and related to the previous item), the *expression of the creative unconscious through the arts* is a powerful and little used means of self-development. The arts provide opportunities for knowing and for description that neither logic nor science can present. Art is expression and response. Clinicians have testified that unconscious creative processes are integrative. Art, both as content to which the student responds and a process which he does, provides an unobtrusive yet powerful means for the development of self within the curriculum.

### Some Suggestions About the Tasks Ahead

Most conspicuous as I visited across the nation was the lack of knowledge about common goals and common practices. Communication is poor.[19] The existing journals are narrow and devoid of theory or intellectual vigor. National meetings of "humanistic" educators are exclusive more from ignorance than intent. Distortion and misrepresentation abound between workers in the field and those who view it from afar view it with suspicion. Isolation may breed innovation and useful variation. But it may also discourage workers who do not have public reinforcement for their work and who believe themselves to be the few apart from the many. Humanistic education is past its infancy and is now a widespread phenomenon which, like any organism, can be expected to mature within an enabling environment.

A clearinghouse is needed to provide facts about available and appropriate curriculum materials, training opportunities, consultant resources, and mentors and apprenticeships. Descriptions of exemplary programs, persons, and places—that is, learning environments—should be available for examination as models. An intellectually respectable journal that does not sacrifice practicality or applicability is needed, as are informal newsletters for rapid exchanges of information.

Research is also needed, and of all sorts: multimodel, longitudinal, short-term, clinical, descriptive, experimentally controlled, subjective (data of consciousness), objective (data of behavior). Research methodology should be chosen for its appropriateness for the problem, not for its academic stylishness. Emphasis should be on the importance of the question and its clear conceptualization, not on the manipulation of data. Problems should be chosen not only for their applicability to the solution of significant educational questions but also for their compatibility with the values of humanistic education. For example, an immediate problem is that of affective measurement, the compilation of available instruments and analysis of their reliability and validity. Even more basic is the need to delineate the kinds of problems that exist for which means of measurement are needed.

**The Further Extension of Humanistic Education.** Unlike teachers in British schools whose financing is national, American teachers often avoid innovation as threatening. In local schools supported by local money the task that should be educational may easily become political overnight. "Humanistic" is the catch word of the year.

There is little way of knowing whether the centers in Santa Barbara and at the University of Massachusetts more or less passively coincided with forces already at work or themselves were powerful instigators, but it is clear that the timing of their work was right. In remarkable synchronicity, they and many others rose to protest the neglect of the person. Today concern for the one is being enlarged by concern for the many, and self-actualization accompanied in part by social actualization.

Will humanistic education continue its astonishing growth? At least three sets of power relationships affect the answer to that question: the relationship of the teachers to academic and other research and development personnel, to the district administrators, and to the community in which they work. These external forces (and others, including the economy) will affect whatever happens next.

Humanistic education may concern itself with any justifiable subject matter in which is imbedded knowledge of the whole self in relation to itself, to the other, and to the eternal environments of space and time, inner and outer mysteries.[20] Its methodologies, however, represent a set of values derived from a model of human nature and an ideal of human life, which make them especially appropriate processes for learning content that requires personal development as well as intellectual assimilation.

This substance includes social issues of global importance. Drug education, widely taught through humanistic means, is certainly one of these. Intercultural or intergroup education (the management of conflict and real difference) and peace studies are much more neglected areas. So is reading (although, as noted above, an excellent start has been made.) So are career or work education (seen as education for social responsibility) and law-related studies that attempt to shape politicolegal socialization through experiences with the process of law within both classroom and community. Many educational thinkers have suggested we need to learn to cope with constant change, to learn to value the temporary and the transitional. George Brown suggests that change be taught as a living opportunity, a challenge in which "idiosyncracy, divergence and the strange" have value.

The behavioral science curricula now emerging take the person as subject matter, but by no means always include the study of consciousness with the study of behavior, or the study of the learner's self with the study of the many. In this area, the exploratory work of Barbara Ellis Long (1974) for younger learners and of Alfred Alschuler and Gerald Weinstein in self-knowledge development shows considerable promise. In psychology, cognition rules the day, but understanding of self and others is dependent upon integration. Symbol systems generate personal as well as abstract meanings, feeling as well as thinking. To understand them, we need more than one set of answers. Neither perception nor cognition alone can explain William Blake's fourfold vision. Intuition and imagination remain vague and relatively unexplored lands—*terrae incognitae*— on the slowly appearing map of human personality. Much more needs to be known about the effects of environment—of context—and how to alter that environment to make it a more effective means of education.[21]

Humanistic education is at once theory, practice, and yeasty possibility. If that possibility is to be fulfilled, it will be because vision and enterprise will combine to apply these underused means and humane goals to such other areas of human learning as those described above and not solely to those formerly labeled "affective." I have suggested where I think humanistic education is today and the future to which its present course is bent, not irresistibly or irreversibly, but propelled by human will and human choice. The future lies beyond theory and beyond practice. The basic question is: What are the implications of what is taught for the lives of individuals and groups?

# Appendixes

There are three appendixes. Appendix A lists the major educators consulted about their work in humanistic education at this time.

Appendix B presents a wide variety of examples of different kinds of humanistic curricula, including those that focus on cognitive content and processes, those that focus on emotional content and processes, those that emphasize psychomotor or physical processes, and some that combine two or more of these foci. The curriculum "slices" are from all levels: elementary, secondary, college, and some adaptable across levels.

Appendix C is "A Pathfinder Guide to Humanistic Education" prepared by Mary Anne Gray. It systematically presents the major readings, references, periodicals and other material about humanistic education and should provide the interested reader with an excellent method of acquainting himself with the field or with extending the scope of his knowledge about it.

Mary Anne Gray has also prepared "A Comprehensive Annotated Bibliography of Humanistic Education" which forms the second part of this volume. This 200 page annotated bibliography is systematically organized and represents one of the most useful available guides to the history, theory, and practice of humanistic education.

# Appendixes

# Principal Contacts in Exemplary Programs

Terry Borton
59 Westview Street
Philadelphia, Pa. 19103

George I. Brown
Department of Education
University of California
Santa Barbara, Ca. 93106

William Cutter
Hebrew Union College
Jewish Institute of Religion
3077 University Mall
Los Angeles, Ca. 90007

William Gastall
Fall River Middle School
Melrose Street
Fall River, Mass. 02723

David Hobson, Director
Center for Human Development
Fairleigh Dickinson University
Rutherford, N.J. 07070

Hugo J. Hollerorth
Director of Curriculum Development

Unitarian-Universalist Association
Department of Education and
    Social Concern
25 Beacon Street
Boston, Mass. 02108

William Howe
Self-Enhancing Education, Inc.
1957 Pruneridge Avenue
Santa Clara, Ca. 95050

Evelyn M. Huber, Leader Development,
    or Milton Owens, Curriculum Ser-
    vices
Board of Educational Ministries
American Baptist Churches
Valley Forge, Pa. 19481

Human Development Training Institute
7574 University Avenue
La Mesa, Ca. 92041

Human Development Training Institute
4455 Twain Avenue
Suite H
San Diego, Ca. 92120

William Knaus
Institute for Advanced Study in
   Rational Psychotherapy
45 East 65th Street
New York, N.Y. 10021

Ralph Mosher
School of Education
Boston University
765 Commonwealth Avenue
Boston, Mass. 02215

John Moore
Director of Curriculum
Mayfield City School District
784 S.O.M. Center Road, Mayfield
Cleveland, Ohio 44143

Gene Mulcahy, Director
Shanti School
480 Asylum Street
Hartford, Conn. 06103

Norman Newberg, Director
Affective Education Program
Board of Education, Room 323
Parkway at 21st Street
Philadelphia, Pa. 19103

Gerald Newmark
Synanon
1910 Ocean Front Walk
Santa Monica, Ca. 90405

Robert Prouty
School of Education
George Washington University
Washington, D.C. 20006

Willima Purkey
Arthur Combs
College of Education
University of Florida
Gainesville, Fla. 32601

Gerald Schmidt
Ventura School
3990 Ventura Court
Palo Alto, Ca. 94306

Sidney Simon
School of Education
University of Massachusetts
Amherst, Massachusetts 01002

Norman Walker
Superintendent of Schools
Louisville Public Schools
506 West Hill Street
Louisville, Ky. 40208

Gerald Weinstein
Center for Humanistic Applications
University of Massachusetts
Amherst, Massachusetts 01002

**USEFUL INFORMANTS**

David Aspy
Flora Nell Roebuck
National Consortium for Humanizing
   Education
College of Education
Northeast Louisiana University
P.O. Box 4048

Monroe, Louisiana 71201
Teacher Training Programs in Humanizing the Classroom

Victor Atkins
16 Granville Road
Cambridge, Mass. 02138

Charles J. McCann, President
Evergreen State University
Olympia, Wash. 98505

Eli Bower
Educational Psychology
Tolman Hall
University of California
Berkeley, Ca. 94720

Donald Cochrane
School of Education
State University
Northridge, Ca. 91324
Moral Education

John Ekstedt, Executive Director
Department of the Attorney General
Parliament Buildings
Victoria, B.C., Canada
Specialized Programs

Martin Engel
National Institute of Education
U.S. Department of HEW
Code 600
Washington, D.C. 20202

Joseph W. Griggs
U.S. Department of HEW
National Institute of Mental Health
Room 12C
26 Parklawn Building
Rockville, Md. 20852

William Hitt
Battelle Center for Improved Education
505 King Avenue
Columbus, Ohio 43201

Howard Kirschenbaum, Director
National Humanistic Education Center

Springfield Road
Upper Jay, N.Y. 10025

Lois Knowles
Education Network
Association for Humanistic Psy-
chology
325 Ninth Street
San Francisco, Ca. 94103

Lawrence Kohlberg
Human Development
Harvard University
Cambridge, Mass. 02138

Lisa Kuhmerker
Department of Curriculum and
Teaching
Hunter College of the City University
Box 937
695 Park Avenue
New York, N.Y. 10021
Values Education

Barbara Ellis Long
17 Granite Court
San Carlos, CA 94070

Thomas Long
Educational Psychology
College of Education
University of Illinois
Urbana, Ill. 61801

Clark Moustakas
The Merrill-Palmer Institute
71 East Ferry Avenue
Detroit, Mich. 48202

Paul Nash
School of Education
Boston University
765 Commonwealth Avenue
Boston, Mass. 02215

Sheldon R. Roen
Human Sciences, Inc.
2852 Broadway
Morningside Heights
New York, N.Y. 10025

William Russell
Education Programs
National Endowment for the Humanities
Washington, D.C. 20506

Robert Samples
Box 129
Tiburon, CA 94920
*Essentia*

Harold Skorpen, Director
Program in Human Development
SUNY 1400 Washington Ave.
Albany, N.Y. 12206

Wid Slick
Foundation for Educational Skills
3520 Cedar Springs
Dallas, Texas 75219

Keven Van Camp
Confluent Education Project
Box 219
Minnedosa, Manitoba, Canada

Norma Watson, Administration Assistant
Mid-Continental Regional Educational Laboratory
104 East Independence Avenue
Kansas City, Mo. 64106
Inner-city Teacher Training

## USEFUL INFORMANTS: AT THE COLLEGE LEVEL

William Leer
Mills College
Oakland, Ca. 94613

Layne Longfellow
Prescott College
Prescott, Arizona 86301

Charles J. McCann
President
Evergreen State College
Olympia, Wash. 98505

Eugene Oulette, Chancellor
University of Redlands
Redlands, Ca. 92373

Fred Rosenzveig
Humanities Department

Dawson College
350 Selby Street
Montreal 215, Quebec, Canada

Nevitt Sanford
The Wright Institute
2728 Durant Avenue
Berkeley, Ca. 94704

Raymond Wilkie
College of Education
University of Kentucky
Lexington, Ky. 40506

Roger A. Wingett
Jamestown Community College
SUNY
Jamestown, N.Y. 14701

## OVERSEAS

Hiroshi Kamura
Associate Director
Japan Center for International
   Exchange
7A Hermano Akasaka Building
4-3, Akasaka 8-chrome
Minato-ku, Tokyo, Japan

Hans-Martin Muller-Wolf
UNESCO National Commission
5 Koln

Cacilienstrasse 40-42
Germany

Lawrence Stenhouse, Director
Centre for Applied Research in
   Education
University of East Anglia
University Village
Norwich, NOR 88c
England

## CURRICULUM PROJECTS AND MATERIALS

APA Clearinghouse on Precollegiate
   Psychology and Behavioral Sciences
American Psychological Association
1200 Seventeenth Street, N.W.
Washington, D.C. 20036

Robert W.C. Brown
539 East 87th Street
New York, N.Y. 10028
Religious Education

Jerry Coombs
Faculty of Education
University of British Columbia
Vancouver 8, British Columbia,
   Canada
MERV (Moral Education and Research
   into Values)

Robert W. Fox
*Inside/out*
National Instructional Television
   Center
Box A

Bloomington, Indiana 47401

Ellen Greenberger
Department of Social Ecology
University of California
Irvine, CA 92664
The development of psychosocial
   attitudes and values

Anita Simon, Director
Humanizing Learning Program
Research for Better Schools, Inc.
Suite 1700
1700 Market Street
Philadelphia, Pa. 19103

William Ward
Coordinator of Field Relations and
   Dissemination
Improving Teaching Competencies
   Program
Northwest Regional Educational
   Laboratory
Lindsay Building

710 S.W. Second Avenue
Portland, Oregon 97204

Violet C. Weiss
Senior Teacher for Staff Development
Brevard Teaching Center

905 Pineda Street
Cocoa, Fla. 32922

Harold Wells
9497 Ridgecrest Drive
La Mesa, Ca. 92041
"A Becoming Curriculum"

✳ *Appendix B*

# Slices of Curriculum

These activities attempt to provide work in the following areas, sometimes with a clear emphasis but always in combination.

1. *Cognitive content and processes*
   knowledge of self and others, including values and beliefs; analysis, differentiation, imagining, comparison, etc.

2. *Emotional content and processes*
   the experience of feeling response

3. *Psychomotor or physical processes*
   skill mastery of the physical and social world including communication

   Examples are drawn from the following levels:

I. *Elementary*
   A. The Magic Circle
   B. The Sky Lab: A Guided Fantasy
   C. Walnuts: A Game

II. *Secondary*
   A. Values in Mathematics
   B. The Greek Philosophers and Philosophies
   C. Essentia

III. *Adaptable for all levels*
   A. Processing

*77*

    B. Brainstorming
    C. Role playing
    D. Physicalization
    E. Improvisation

IV. *The Trumpet March: Diagram and Details*

Other examples are given in the body of the report. In practice, all the exercises are adaptable for all levels. The above classification is based on the specific example given and not the general methodology.

## ELEMENTARY

### The Magic Circle
This label is associated with the work of Harold Bessell and Uvaldo Palomares and the *Human Development Program*. However, as an intimate, familiar structure within which meetings for a variety of purposes can take place, the small circle is found everywhere that confluent or humanistic education is practiced. More formally put, the circle may be considered any communication system incorporating group dynamics techniques within a structured learning situation.

In the Human Development Program Magic Circle, session topics include, in sequence, the three elements of *awareness, mastery,* and *social interaction.* Where focus is on specific areas of human endeavor, other kinds of attitudinal work are included, such as those related to parent, bilingual, drug, or career education. What follows are syllabi of topics related to *awareness* (self-perception in elementary career education), *mastery,* and *social interaction* in the kindergarten.

### Awareness in Career Education

### Interests and Proficiencies:

**Something I Like About You.**  By participating in this session each child is given an opportunity to give and receive validation, which helps him to recognize his personal attributes.

Be sure each child is chosen to hear a positive statement from one other child.

In the summary, ask the children how it feels to tell someone what you like about them. Also ask them how it feels to hear someone tell you something that they like about you.

**Something I Like About Myself.**  This activity is an extension of "Something I Like About You." Today the children will "own" a positive quality in themselves, thereby increasing their awareness of the positive aspects of their own personalities. Strong feelings of self-worth and awareness of one's attributes and capabilities are basic to career choice and effectiveness.

If time permits, allow the children more "rounds" so that they may name several things they like about themselves. However, do not sacrifice discussion.

Summarize by asking the children how they feel. Discuss how 'funny' it feels to talk openly about one's strong points, but how good it is for us to realize how many fine qualities each of us possesses.

**If I Could Do Anything I Wanted It Would Be . . . . .** Our human ability to dream and fantasize has led us to some of our most brilliant accomplishments. Today the children should be encouraged to become more aware of what they enjoy doing by imagining that there are no obstacles and that what they do would be their choice.

In the summary, ask the children what things keep us from doing what we want to do. Help them to recognize that limitations are not always exterior, but some are those we "put on ourselves."

**Someone Disappointed Me.** Through this activity the children are given an opportunity to examine and accept limitations in other people and to gain awareness of their own feelings.

In the discussion, urge the children to concentrate more on describing their feelings surrounding the event than on describing the person or the occurrence itself.

Summarize by discussing the idea that "nobody's perfect" with the children. It is inevitable that people will sometimes disappoint one another. Discuss also how they have a right to their feelings of disappointment.

*I Disappointed Someone.* By examining yesterday how someone else disappointed them, the children are possibly now more ready to "own" how they disappointed someone else.

In the discussion, concentrate on the feelings of the people who were disappointed and on the feelings of the child telling the story. Also, ask each child who participates to tell about a time when they made that person (or someone else) feel good. Even though the topic for the session relates to something negative, it should be our purpose to make each session a positive experience for the child.

Summarize by asking the children what they learned from the session. Review the points discussed as the end of yesterday's session.

*I Disappointed Myself.* The most serious kind of disappointment is when we have disappointed ourselves. Awareness on the part of the children in this area may be extremely varied. Some may not be painfully oversensitive to their own limitations.

In either case, treat the topic as matter-of-factly as all the others.

After each child who wishes to participate tells how he disappointed himself, ask him to tell about a time when he accomplished something that he felt very good about.

By way of summary, ask the children what they learned from the session.

***How I Feel When I Do My Favorite Things.***   This topic again focuses the children's attention on their personal interests and proficiencies and continues to develop their awareness of how they feel.

In the discussion, allow the children to tell all about their favorite activities and then ask them how they feel when they are doing them.

In the summary, ask the children why they think it is good to discuss the things that they enjoy doing.

**The World of Work:**

*Something I Worked Hard At.*
*When I Work Hard On Something I Feel. . . . . .*
*Something I Did (or Made) That I'm Proud Of.*
*People Who I Need.*
*Someone Who  Needs Me.*
*Jobs People Have That Help Me.*
*I Did It All By Myself.*
*I Got It Done.*
*Jobs I Like.*
*Jobs I Don't Like.*

**Change:**

*Something I Used To Do That I Don't Do Anymore.*
*I Changed My Mind About What I Wanted To Be When I Grew Up.*
*My Friend Moved Away.*
*When My Family Moved.*
*We Got Some New Neighbors.*

**Economic Aspects of Work:**

*A Time When I Was the Boss.*
*A Time Someone Else Was the Boss.*
*How I Spend My Money.*
*A Way I Earned Some Money and What I Did With It.*
*A Time I Traded With Somebody.*
*How I Could Save My Money for Something.*
*A Time When I Was Broke.*

**Other People**:

*I Was Alone and I Liked It.*
*I Was Alone and I Didn't Like It.*
*Things I Like To Do In Groups.*

### Mastery in Performance Skills
"I can use things."
Clear demonstration is very important during this week.

### Tasks for kindergarten children:

| | |
|---|---|
| I can open and shut a drawer. | (Without banging it or spilling the contents.) |
| I can cut a paper in two. | (Use small papers. Later the child may use the paper to cut some more or for making pictures.) |
| I can draw on the chalkboard and then use the eraser. | (Have the children each draw a geometric shape.) |
| I can fold a cloth. | (Each child folds a square cloth, no larger than two feet by two feet, with at least two folds.) |
| I can fit things in a box. | (Have several items that can be fitted into a box in various ways. The child fits them in, but the task is not completed until he has placed on the lid and it fits down on the box securely.) |

### Social Interaction
"I can show what I did that someone liked."
Today we begin to look at our own behavior and consider how it affects other people. Having acknowledged last week through discussion that *other* people's behavior causes feelings in *them,* the children are ready to deal with this more responsible concept.

In simple terms, discuss these ideas briefly with the children and then enact something you did that made someone feel good, possibly with the assistance of one of the children to play the part of the person in your story while you portray yourself. Allow a brief guessing period about what it was that you did and then tell what you did and how the person responded so that you knew that he liked your action. Tell how it made you feel. Then ask for volunteers to do likewise.

As each child completes his turn, ask another child to reflect back to him what he observed and heard. Be sure to give them credit for paying attention and listening.

By way of summary ask the children, "Can you cause other people to feel good?"

### The Sky Lab Trip: A Brief, Guided Fantasy for
### Children ("What do you dream about?")
### Fall River, Mass.

"Get comfortable," says the teacher, and 19 small bodies flop to the floor, curl up, close their eyes, and reach inward in anticipation. "You are now entering the Sky Lab. The doors are shut and latched and you have fastened yourself in place. In a minute you will be blasting off."

Nineteen voices are added to hers as the countdown begins.

"The ship is off! Shall we stop on the way?" Loud agreement—the bodies are restless.

"All right. We have landed at our first location now. You can get out, but don't forget you have your space suit on and you need your equipment."

There is lots of movement around the room, stiff legs, crouched bodies, pantomine of lively flesh trapped within survival bounds.

Back to the Sky Lab for another blast-off. "Now we have landed at Mars. When you get out, you can have anything you want. Mars has a magic spot. If you're willing to look for it, you can have anything you want." The search is made; each reaches inside himself and finds the hidden dream.

Back on earth, the teacher asks softly, "What did you carry away?" According to his own nature, each shares this information (or does not), joyful or anxious, bragging, or a little sad, a little inadequate, feeling the choice was not the one really wanted, but knowing the trip will be offered again.

. . . . . . . . . . . . . . .

**Note**: Sometimes this exercise is done by asking the children to choose others to join them. The search for what they want on Mars is then made together, the pair or group to return with something all of them want together.

### Walnuts: A Game (Eli Bower)

Children are blindfolded after they have had the opportunity to examine a numbered walnut given to each small group. The walnuts are mixed up in a bag and spilled on the floor. Ostensibly, the object is to recover the proper walnut within a given time period.

(Or, each child may be given his own walnut to examine.)

Usually the group whose members sit close to each other and share data will win.

. . . . . . . . . . . . . . .

The purpose of games is to experience the relationship between affect and cognition within a structured microcosm. An event is devised which requires physical and emotional participation—something is *done* that stimulates a variety of feelings. The experience is then examined intellectually and identified. ("What happened? What did you feel?") Emotion seeks *discharge* while cognition seeks *connection.* Understanding of emotion is dependent upon its correct labeling (anger, joy, etc.) Thus, the two processes are inseparable.

## SECONDARY

### Values In Mathematics (Harmin, Kirschenbaun, Simon, 1973)

**Problem:** Bill bought a three speed bike for $35. Three years later, he sold it for $15. While he owned the bike, he spent $9 on repairs. How much did it cost Bill to use his bike each year? What percent of the purchase price did he lose when he sold it?

**Values Levels:**

1. Under what conditions would you tell a buyer what was wrong with something you were trying to sell him? What if he didn't ask?
2. Would you lower the price to someone who was poor?
3. If you didn't sell your old playthings, what else might you do with them?

**Project:** Have the students keep a record of how they spend their money. They work out problems and values questions based on that record. For example: What percentage of your expenditures goes toward purchases that last only a short time, like a soda or a movie ticket? What percentage goes toward purchases that last a long time, like a baseball or a record? What fraction of your income required work? Would you want your life's work to be any more enjoyable than this work?

**Project:** Have the students keep a time diary—a chart that shows how they spend all their time, each day. Then work out problems and values questions based on their own statistics. Here are some examples, with values questions in parentheses.

1. What percentage of your waking hours is spent with others? What percentage is spent alone? (Do you like this balance? Is it right for you? For everyone? Why do some people always need people around them? In what ways do you spend time differently from others your age?)
2. Using the total time you slept last week as an average, how many hours per year do you sleep? What is the ratio of your sleeping time to the time you spend in nonschool activities? (Do you get enough sleep to satisfy you? What activities might you eliminate if you wanted more time to sleep? What

is the best time of day for you to do difficult things? How does not getting enough sleep affect your behavior?)

3. On the average, how much free time a day do you have? What percentage of this time is spent watching TV? (How do you handle conflicts with other members of your family over what to watch? The last time your television wasn't working, what did you do with your free time?)

### The Greek Philosophers and Philosophies
### (Aaron Hillman)

These exercises were taken from a lengthy course outline that was published as a DRICE paper. This one and others, such as *Sociology of Human Relations,* published as Quarter Course Outline no. 8 by DRICE, are interesting attempts to integrate subject matter with structure and processes suggested by Gestalt theory.

#### Assimilation and Integration.

*Part I:* Protagoras believed that opinions are tested by the practicality they exhibit. Those that work are acceptable. Those that fail are unacceptable. How do you understand what is acceptable? What is unacceptable?

*Part II:* Socrates was of the opinion that the function of questioning is not destructive but constructive. If that is so, then prepare five questions that you want me to answer. They must be short answer questions and they must also be questions that you yourself would not hesitate to answer. They can be on any subject.

*Part III:* Plato devised three classes of knowledge. One of those classes was called *Ethics,* or the *Rules of Good Conduct.* Let your mind wander and, on your own, draw up ten rules of good conduct for yourself. One restriction: The rules must be specific. No generalizations allowed.

### Essentia: An Environmental Cluster (Environmental
### Studies, Evergreen State College)

This cluster of short exercises is typical of those that are appearing in ecology, outdoor, or environmental studies of various kinds that are concerned with the human factor as part of the physical world. In this case, they are packaged on cards with striking photographs and graphics.

#### Psych-Out.

The Action:

With someone who chooses to cooper-

More:

See if the whole class can make a

ate, try to reach as many conclusions as you can about their personalities from their lifestyles and mannerisms.

people profile check list that works on others. Invite someone from the community in for the class to psychout. Do not role play this. Use a 20 questions approach or . . .

### Stupidaction.

The Action:
Make a list of the stupidest things that happen to you in school and a list of the stupidest things you do in school.

Set up a plan to change both. Carry out your plan.

More:
Repeat, using the community, the state, the nation. What makes something stupid? What makes it smart? Does it really matter whether or not you do stupid things? Who cares? Why should they? Why should you care?

### Expectations.

The Action:
Figure out what kinds of things people expect you to do without asking your permission.

Figure out things you expect other people to do without asking their permission.

More:
Determine which expectations are fair and which are unfair. Create "Don't lay that on me" lists that are kept in the room and written on freely. Do people have a right to expect anything of you? Do you have a right to expect anything of others?

## ADAPTABLE FOR ALL LEVELS

### Processing
*Processing* is the subsequent analysis of experience. It may be done privately (through ditto sheets with questions to which responses can be made in writing, through the opportunity to write in individual journals, etc.) or publicly, among the members of the group before it disbands after each session. It may be as simple as asking each student to complete three open-ended statements, such as "Because of this lesson, I feel . . . , I learned . . . , as a result, I'm going to . . . ," or asking students to respond to questions about the session by moving or holding up colors to parts of the room which represent their response choices. A more thorough and complicated procedure is reprinted here.

1. Review and summary of experience.
2. Identification of *feelings* that were experienced.

3. Identification of *preferences* that were expressed.
4. Identification of *similarities and differences* in behavior, thoughts, and feelings.
5. Identification of *choices* that were made and *how* they were decided.
6. Identification of the roles that each member took in the experience, e.g., active participant, decisionmaker, funmaker, facilitator for others.
7. Identification of *changes in behavior* and the *conditions* under which it changed.
8. Identification of some alternative behaviors that could have been used.
9. Identification of "unfinished business," if there is any.
10. Dealing immediately with any "unfinished business."

### Brainstorming

This method of problem solving consists of the wild generation of as many ideas as possible, without regard for quality or the opinion of others in the group. Combinations, modifications, additions—all are encouraged. Evaluation is forbidden because it dampens the willingness to be extreme.

### Setting Up A Role Play Session

1. Warmup: Exercises to prepare class for activities in role playing.
   a. These activities should involve as many students as possible.
   b. The students should have a number of choices to pick from. For example: emotional and unemotional responses to questions, e.g., "It is 5:30 A.M. and your alarm clock has just gone off. Show us what you do," or "Walk down the street and look at yourself in the mirrors as you go by."
   c. Warmup activities may be verbal or nonverbal, e.g., Who am I? Improvisations, etc.
2. Preparation: Directions.
   a. Give as many as possible. Make them clear.
   b. Establish a setting, e.g., "This area is the doorway. You enter here and leave there."
   c. Sometimes it is a good idea to have the students run through a short fantasy to visualize the setting.
   d. Ask the class to help with the physical aspects of the setting by moving chairs and creating a stage.
3. Techniques.
   a. *The interview.* Ask students who are assigned roles certain questions about themselves: "How do you feel now? What are you going to do about your situation? How old are you? Do you like him? What kind of person are you?"
   b. *Side coaching.* This helps the students in the audience and the students in the role play to focus their attention on the action or the solution to

the problem. This is an important role for the teacher. The teacher should walk around the players and stand in back of them or beside them. The teacher must encourage the students to take a course of action, e.g., "What are your plans? Show us . . . Remember you are angry. Don't let him get off so easily! How is he making you feel? Are you tense? etc."

   c. *The Freeze.* Stop the action and get suggestions from the audience. "What do you think he should do now?" Interview the participant further: "How do you feel now? Are you making progress?" Be ready to change the course of action if necessary.

   d. *Doubling.* The teacher may act as the double or he may use a student double. The double copies the posture and facial expressions of the player. This gives the player feedback about his interpretation of the role. Doubling gives more students a chance to get in touch with each role. The double should stand or sit as close to the player as possible. The teacher can prepare the student double by telling him to feel what the player feels: "He's tense, nervous, happy."

   e. *Alter ego.* Alter ego is an extension of the double. The alter ego stands or sits in back of the player. He does not have to copy posture or facial expressions. The alter ego speaks the innermost thoughts of the character. The student playing the role may decide to be polite. He's really being put down by another character. In his mind, he's calling this character names or thinking things that aren't so polite. (Coach: "What isn't he saying? What does he really want to say?" etc.) The alter ego picks up these thoughts and speaks them for the player. When he speaks these thoughts, *he speaks as the player.* The alter ego and the player *become one.* The alter ego makes the thoughts of the player explicit. This gives depth to the role play and dimension to the role.

4. Closure.

Make the students focus on a solution or the ending. Sometimes it is necessary to set a time on the solution, e.g., "You have two minutes to reach a solution."

5. Followup and Evaluation.

Always allow time for discussion of the role play. Ask the students about their roles. Get feedback from the audience. Ask the students in the audience what they would have done. A role play can be followed with discussion, written assignments, and readings.

## Physical Embodiment

*Physicalization* is the term used by Viola Spolin (1963) to describe nonverbal (as opposed to intellectual or psychological) processes used to present material to students. The concept has been extended to include the active learning by students through concrete and objective experiencing by their own bodies. The physical is the known. In psychomotor activity, action is simultaneously thinking and feeling. There is no space for conscious awareness of either of these processes. The actor creates reality—"the whole organism is alerted"—as the freedom of physical expression opens the door for insight. Using the body as a building unit, e.g., to build types of shelters, is one kind of physical embodiment. Another is the use of the body, other than the voice, to create noise (clacks, whistles, slaps, taps, etc.) and rhythms alone or in orchestration with others. Mime or improvisations for groups or individuals are also used with such topics as:

Scenes
        beach (with water skier)                movie theater
        barnyard                                playground
        school room                             market
        bus                                     race track

Objects or Situations
        can or an electric canopener
        book (with someone turning the pages)
        washing machine
        swimming in a cold lake
        riding a burro down into the Grand Canyon

**Improvisation**

**The Ice Cube**
1. You are an ice cube. Stand very rigidly, the way you think an ice cube would be.
2. The sun has come out. You are melting slowly, from the top of your head. Soon you will be a puddle on the floor.
    Or, you are an ice cube that accidently falls into a hot pan. You begin to melt from the bottom up.

Both improvisation and physicalization are designed to enlarge the imagination and the capacity for empathy. An extension fo them leads to practice in self-metaphor building and nonverbal communication of other kinds. The former might be done by asking, "If you were a book (pie, car, animal, etc.), how would you be? What would be your form, color, size, taste, function, other attibutes?" The latter might take the form of identification exercise or improvisation.

## THE TRUMPET MARCH: DIAGRAM AND DETAILS

Part of the self-education process taught at the Center for Humanistic Education of the University of Massachusetts, the ingenious Trumpet March teaches the student to generalize from the data he has gathered about himself and others. Weinstein and Fantini (1970: 164–165) note that:

> The trumpet depicts the process of personal integration as having three phases in each of which a different function assumes the most important role—awareness of concerns, abstract thought, and conscious action (the flowing lines at the head of the chart).

They diagram the trumpet below:

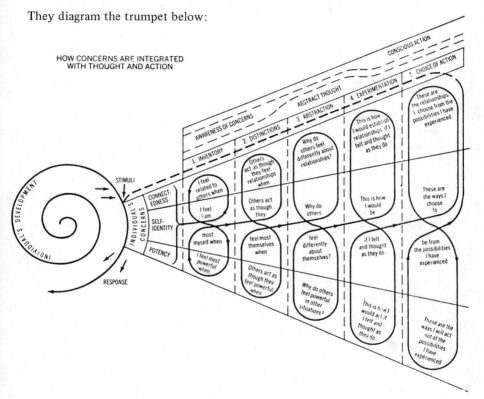

A typical Trumpet March might go through the following procedures:

## 1. Step One: Experience Confrontations
I interact with a situation that generates data; and

## Step Two: Inventory Responses
How did I respond? What was unique? What common?

*Questions* for steps one and two (inventorying thoughts, feelings, and behaviors that occurred) might include:

   a. What did you just do? Describe your behavior.

   b. What were you aware of?

   c. At what points did you feel comfortable or uncomfortable?

   d. At point X, how did you think or feel?

   e. Where in your body did you feel something?

   f. What sentences did you say to yourself? Were these *should, can't,* or *won't* sentences?

   g. How was your response similar or different from other people's responses?

   h. If you felt like doing something else, what hindered you or permitted you to do it?

   i. Were you affected by the responses of others? How did their behavior affect your behavior?

   j. What were the things that stopped you from getting involved?

   k. Were there things you felt like avoiding? What were they?

   l. What sentences did you say to yourself?

   m. Were you more concerned with yourself or with the other persons(s)? How did you show your concern?

   n. Were you concerned with how you were appearing to other people? Did this affect your behavior?

2. **Step Three: Recognize Patterns**

   What is typical of me?

   *Questions:*

      a. Did you do anything that surprised you?

      b. Did you do anything different from what you usually do?

      c. How do you usually respond in similar situations? Can you think of a similar situation where you've responded the same?

      d. How often have you thought, felt, or acted like this? In what circumstances?

      e. Where were you on a continuum (from one extreme possibility of response to the other) in this exercise? Where are you usually?

      f. What particular part of your response was most like you?

      g. What particular part of your response was least like you?

      h. Look at your feelings inventory and try to find a pattern in your responses.

      i. Where, when, and with whom, do you typically act this way?

3. **Step Four: Own Patterns**

   What function does this pattern serve for me?

   *Questions:*

      a. How does it serve you?

      b. How does your pattern make you feel good?

    c. What does it protect you from?

    d. What kinds of freedom does it give you?

    e. What kinds of structures do you function with best?

    f. What part of your pattern annoys you?

    g. What does it enable you to do that you enjoy doing?

    h. What does it get for you?

    i. What needs does it satisfy?

    j. What does it give you?

    k. What does it enable you to do that you want to do?

4. **Step Five: Consider Consequences**

   What does happen or could happen in my life because of this pattern?

   *Questions:*

    a. What price do you have to pay?

    b. How much does it cost you?

    c. Are you missing out on anything? If so, what?

    d. What precautions would you give somebody to take before using your pattern?

    e. What pleasure and what pain do you get?

5. **Step Six: Allow Alternatives**

   Will I allow myself any additional patterns of response?

   *Questions:*

    a. What are the first steps you could take to change?

    b. What are the options you have?

    c. Using each alternative, go through the trumpet again.

6. **Step Seven: Choose**

# A Pathfinder Guide to Humanistic Education

A Pathfinder Guide to Humanistic Education
by Mary Anne Gray

An introduction to humanistic education appears in The Encyclopedia of Education, Lee C. Deighton, ed. New York: Crowell-Collier Educational Corp., 1971, under the title of "Behavioral Sciences, Teaching of" by Sheldon R. Roen, pp. 446–449.

BOOKS dealing with humanistic education are listed in the subject card catalog. Look for the subjects:

| | |
|---|---|
| "education, humanistic" | (highly relevant) |
| "education, confluent" | (highly relevant) |
| "educational psychology" | (relevant) |
| "guidance and counseling" | (more general) |

Frequently mentioned books include:

Borton, Terry. *Reach, Touch, and Teach.* New York: McGraw Hill, 1970.

Bower, Eli M. and Hollister, William G. (Eds.) *Behavioral Science Frontiers in Education.* New York: Wiley, 1967.

Brown, George I. *Human Teaching for Human Learning: An Introduction to Confluent Education.* New York: Viking Press, 1971.

Brown, George I., ed. with Yeomans, Thomas, and Grizzard, Liles. *The Live Classroom: Innovations Through Confluent Education and Gestalt.* New York: Viking Press, 1975.

Greer, Mary, and Rubenstein, Bonnie. *Will the Real Teacher Please Stand Up? A Primer in Humanistic Education.* New York: Macmillan, 1969.

Heath, Douglas H. *Humanizing Schools.* New York: Hayden Book Company, Inc., 1971.

Jones R. J. *Fantasy and Feeling in Education.* New York: New York University Press, 1968.

Krathwohl, D. R.; Bloom, B.; and Masia, B. *Taxonomy of Educational Objectives. Handbook II. Affective Domain.* New York: David McKay, 1964.

Lederman, Janet. *Anger and the Rocking Chair. Gestalt Awareness With Children.* New York: Viking Press, 1960.

Lyon, Harold C. *Learning to Feel—Feeling to Learn.* Columbus, Ohio. Charles Merrill, 1971.

Patterson, C. H. *Humanistic Education.* Englewood Cliffs, New Jersey, Prentice-Hall, Inc., 1973.

Raths, Louis E., Harmin, M. and Simon, S. *Values and Teaching: Working With Values in the Classroom.* Columbus, Ohio: Merrill, 1966.

Read, Donald A., and Simon, Sidney B., eds. *Humanistic Education Sourcebook.* Englewood Cliffs, New Jersey: Prentice-Hall, Inc., 1975.

Weinstein, Gerald, and Fantini, Mario D., eds. *Toward Humanistic Education: A Curriculum of Affect.* New York: Praeger Publishers, 1970.

Other books including material on humanistic education are shelved under call numbers:

LB 1027
LB 1051
LB 1067

ENCYCLOPEDIAS that contain information on humanistic education are:

*The Encyclopedia of Education.* Lee C. Deighton, ed. New York: Crowell-Collier Educational Corp., 1971. "Affective Learning," by David W. Ecker, pp. 113-120.

*Encyclopedia of Educational Research.* Robert L. Ebel, ed. Fourth edition. New York: Macmillan Co., 1969.

Bower, Eli M. "Mental Health," pp. 811–828.
Gordon, Ira J. "Social and Emotional Development," pp. 1221–1230.
Ojemann, Ralph. "Behavior Problems," pp. 98–105.
Schmuck, Richard A. "Group Processes," pp. 551–559.

*International Encyclopedia of the Social Sciences.* David L. Sills, ed. New York: Macmillan Co., 1968, "Moral Development," Lawrence Kohlberg, pp. 483–494.

BIBLIOGRAPHIES that contain material on humanistic education include:

Alschuler, Alfred S. *Developing Achievement Motivation in Adolescents: Education for Human Growth.* Englewood Cliffs, New Jersey: Educational Technology Publications, 1973. Bibliography on pp. 267-306.

Burgess, Bonita. *A Bibliography.* ED 049118* Philadelphia: Philadelphia School District, 50 pp.

Canfield, John, and Phillips, Mark. Humanisticography. *Media and Methods,* 8 (1), 41-56, September 1971.

*Curriculum Projects and Materials in  Elementary School Behavioral Sciences.* ED 067358 Washington, D.C.: American Psychological Association Clearinghouse in Precollege Psychology, 1972.

Kuhmerker, Lisa. *A Bibliography on Moral Development and the Learning of Values in Schools and Other Social Settings,* ED 054014 New York: Center for Children's Ethical Education, 1971, 45 pp.

Roen, Sheldon R. *References to Teaching Children About Human Behavior: Pre-High School,* ED 066411 1970, 29 pp.

*Teaching of Psychology in the Secondary School: Research Studies 1964–1971: Teaching of the Behavioral Sciences in the Elementary School. Selected Bibliographies.* ED 052074 Washington, D.C.: American Psychological Association Clearinghouse in Precollege Psychology, 1971.

Thomas, Walter L. *A Comprehensive Bibliography on the Value Concept,* ED 024064 Washington, D.C.: Office of Education, June 1967, 45 pp.

JOURNAL ARTICLES and other literature on humanistic education are indexed primarily in the guides listed. The quote subject headings are those in use since 1965 unless other dates are given.

*Current Index to Journals in Education* (Began in 1968)

| | |
|---|---|
| "affective behavior" | "humanistic education" |
| "affective objectives" | "interpersonal relations" |
| "behavioral sciences" | "mental health" |
| "educational psychology" | "self . . ." |
| "human relations" | "values" |

*These numbers refer to documents which are listed in the journal *Research in Education* as ERIC publications.

*Education Index*

"curriculum . . ."         "interpersonal relations"
"education . . ."          "mental hygiene"
"emotional . . ."          "psychology . . ."
"health education"         "self . . ."
"human relations"

*Psychological Abstracts*

Section on Educational Psychology

Other indexes, listed here, should be used for an exhaustive search. Only a limited return can be expected for the time spent. Directions are generally given in front of each issue.

*ABS Guide to Recent Publications in the Social and Behavioral Sciences.*

*Mental Health Book Review Index. An Annual Bibliography of Books and Book Reviews in the Behavioral Sciences.*

*Public Affairs Information Service. Bulletin.*

*Social Science and Humanities Index.*

JOURNALS that often contain relevant articles are:

*AHP Newsletter* and *Journal of Humanistic Psychology* published by Association for Humanistic Psychology, 325 Ninth Street, San Francisco, California, 94103

*Edvance* published by Combined Motivation Education Systems, 6300 River Road, Rosemont, Illinois, 60018.

*People Watching: Curriculum and Techniques for Teaching the Behavioral Sciences in the Classroom.* Behavioral Publications, 2852 Broadway, New York, New York, 10025.

*New Directions in Teaching.* Department of Education, Bowling Green State University, Bowling Green, Ohio, 43402.

*Periodically* (a newsletter for high school teachers of psychology) is available free from American Psychological Association Clearinghouse on Precollege Psychology, 1200 Seventeenth Street, N.W., Washington, D.C. 20036.

REVIEWS and YEARBOOKS containing material on humanistic education are:

Association for Supervision and Curriculum Development. *Perceiving, Behaving, Becoming.* Yearbook 1962. Washington, D.C.

Association for Supervision and Curriculum Development. *Humanizing Education: The Person in the Process.* Yearbook 1967. Washington, D.C.

Association for Supervision and Curriculum Development. *To Nurture Humaneness: Committment for the '70's.* Yearbook 1970. Washington, D.C.

Carr, Williams G., ed. *Values and the Curriculum.* ED 042731 A Report of the Fourth International Curriculum Conference School for the '70's Auxiliary Series. Washington, D. C. 1970, 144 pp.

National Society for the Study of Education. *Mental Health in Modern Education.* Fifty-Fourth Yearbook, Part II.

National Society for the Study of Education. *The Curriculum: Retrospect and Prospect.* Seventieth Yearbook. Part I. Mark R. Shedd, Norman A. Newberg, Richard H. Delone, "Yesterday's Curriculum/Today's World: Time to Re-invent the Wheel."

REPORTS and other types of literature containing material on humanistic education are indexed in this guide:

*Research in Education.* See particularly the following subject headings:

| | |
|---|---|
| "affective behavior" | "humanistic education" |
| "affective objectives" | "interpersonal relations" |
| "behavioral sciences" | "mental health" |
| "educational psychology" | "self . . ." |
| "human relations" | "values" |

Important JOURNAL ARTICLES that discuss the theory of humanistic education include:

Bower, E. M. "Mental Health in Education." *Review of Educational Research, 38:* 447-59, December 1968.

Brown, George. "I Have Things To Tell; Confluent Education." *Elementary English, 50:* 515-520, April 1973.

Combs, Arthur W. "Can Education Be Relevant?" *Colorado Journal of Educational Research, 9* (3), 2-8. Spring, 1970.

Dinkmeyer, Don. "Developing Understanding of Self and Others: Central to the Educational Process." *People Watching, 1* (1), 12-16. 1971.

Kohlberg, Lawrence. "Moral Education in the Schools: A Developmental View." *School Review, 74,* 1-20, Spring 1966.

Maslow, A. H. "Some Educational Implications of the Humanistic Psychologies." *Harvard Educational Review, 38,* 685–696, Fall 1968.

Weinstein, Gerald. "The Trumpet: A Guide to Humanistic Psychological Curriculum." *Theory Into Practice, 10,* 196–203, June 1971.


CURRICULUM MATERIALS that have been developed in the area of humanistic education include:

Dinkmeyer, Don. *Developing Understanding of Self and Others* (DUSO). American Guidance Service, Inc., Dept. EL-4, Publisher's Building, Circle Pines, Minnesota 55014.

Limbacker, W. *Dimensions of Personality.* Pfaum, George A., 38 West Fifth Street, Dayton, Ohio 45402.

Ojemann, Ralph. *Education for Human Behavior and Learning to Decide.* Educational Research Council of America, Rockefeller Building, Cleveland, Ohio 44113.

Palomares, Uvaldo, and Bessell, Harold. *Methods in Human Development.* Human Development Training Institute, 4455 Twain Avenue, San Diego, California.


RESEARCH findings that support curriculum projects in humanistic education include:

Cowen, Emory, et al. "A Preventive Mental Health Program in the School Setting: Description and Evaluation. *Journal of Psychology, 56,* 307–356, October 1963.

Griggs, Joe W., and Bonney, Merle E. "Relationship Between 'Casual' Orientation and Acceptance of Others, 'Self-Idea Self,' Congruency, and Mental Health Changes for Fourth and Fifth Grade Children." *Journal of Educational Research, 63* (10), 471–477, July 1970.

Koval, Calista B., and Hales, Lloyd W. "The Effects of the DUSO Guidance Program on the Self-Concepts of Primary School Children" *Child Study Journal, 2* (2), 57–61, 1972.

Kuhlman, Charles ED 070250 and Wiley, William. ED 070251 "The 'Inside/Out' Evaluation"; The First Five Year Programs, Part I, Part II, Bloomington, Ind.: National Instructional Television Center, July, 1972, 67 pp., 216 pp.

Long Barbara Ellis. "To Teach About Human Behavior." *Educational Leadership, 27,* 683–686, April 1970.

Ojemann, R. J., et al. "The Effect of a 'Casual' Teacher Training Program and

Certain Curricular Changes on Grade School Children." *Journal of Experimental Education, 34,* (24), 95–114, December 1955.

Slobetz, Frank, and Lund, Alice. "Some Effects of a Personal Development Program at the Fifth Grade Level." *Jouranl of Educational Research, 49,* 373–378, January 1956.

Several periodicals have carried CURRICULUM LESSONS in humanistic education.
"Interaction Briefs," Today's Education *58,* nos. 6, 7, 9; and *59,* nos. 1, 2, 4, 6. September 1969 to September 1970.

Long, Barbara Ellis. A series of nine lessons in *Grade Teacher* on the subject of teaching about human behavior, vol. 89, nos. 1–9, during 1971–1972.

Zeitz, F. F., "Lessons in Awareness." *Instructor,* August 1972 to June 1973, vol. 82.

TEACHER EDUCATION is a very important part of humanistic education. Several articles on this subject include:

Avilla, Donald L., et al. "The Florida Experimental Program in Elementary Education." *Improving College and University Teaching, 20* (2), 148–149, Spring 1972.

Brown, George I. "The Confluence of Affective and Cognitive Learning: Requirements for Teaching." Paper prepared for the National Symposium: Critical Issues in Teacher In-Service Education. Chicago, October, 1975.

Combs, Arthur W. "Some Basic Concepts for Teacher Education." *The Journal of Teacher Education, 23* (3), 286–290, Fall 1972.

Iannone, R. V., and Carline, J. L. "Humanistic Approach to Teacher Educaton." *Journal of Teacher Education, 22,* 429–433, Winter 1971.

Johnson, Mel. *Model Program for Teacher In-Service Emphasizing the Affective Dimension* ED 034747 Washington, D.C.: Elk Grove Training and Development Center, Office of Education, 1969.

Jones, Donald W. *Human Relations in Teacher Education.* ED 055965 Chicago: North Central Association of Colleges and Secondary Schools, August 1970, 113 pp.

Khanna, J. L. *A Humanistic Approach to In-Service Education for Teachers.* ED 045573 Washington, D.C.: Bureau of Elementary and Secondary Education, 1970, 226 pp.

Long, Barbara Ellis. *Implications of a Teacher Training Program Developed for a Curriculum in Psychology Elementary Level.* ED 066373 Washington, D.C.: American Psychological Association, July 1971, 26 pp.

PERIODICALS have devoted whole issues to the subject of confluent education.

*American Annals of the Deaf, 117* (5), October 1972.

American School Health Association Committee on Mental Health in the Classroom.

"Mental Health in the Classroom." *Journal of School Health 38,* May 1968.

*Eduational Opportunity Forum, 1* (4), Fall 1969.

Teaching Psychology and the Behavioral Sciences in the School. *Journal of School Psychology, 5,* Spring 1967.

A Regeneration of the Humanities. *Theory Into Practice, 10* (3), June 1971.

*Personnel and Guidance Journal 51* (9), May 1973.

# Notes

1. So-called "human relations" education, whether in organizational management; teacher effectiveness training; ethnic, domestic intercultural or multicultural training; urban studies; or international-intercultural education—wherever primary focus is on the self and interpersonal processes—has been excluded here for the sake of drawing necessary practical boundaries, however arbitrary.

2. "Affective education" in its extreme forms illustrates perfectly the disastrous consequences of an antitheoretical and exclusivist orientation. Affective *education* is a construct without empirical referents, for neither mind nor heart are educable without the other. As Piaget wrote, "affectivity is nothing without intelligence. Intelligence furnishes affect with its means and clarifies its ends." The label "affective," where accurate, only points out which aspects of behavior have significant feeling components. Much of so-called affective education is really cognitive, no more the education of the emotions than of other areas, but with the self and people as content—people at hand and singly and people in general. As such, like most other types of education, it is linguistically, as well as emotionally or experientially, mediated. Richard Jones was right when he said that the affective education movement showed "signs of aborting itself by way of inviting its own polarization and possible destiny as a cult instead of a cause."

3. Parts of this section were published previously in E. L. Simpson, "Can the Humanities Provide a Humanistic Education?" *California Humanities Association Bulletin,* Winter 1974.

4. During the early part of the twentieth century *behaviorism* emerged as an influential philosophic and psychological theory. Rejecting the data of consciousness, of awareness, of self-perception, early behaviorists (and some of their contemporary descendants) insisted on using data derived solely from direct observation of overt phenomena and contended that all human behavior was determined by forces outside the individual. The issue today, however, is

no longer simply behaviorism versus humanism. Neither is entirely what it used to be. Some humanists, rejecting empirical science as a means of problem solving, have also abandoned the view that intellect and reason are the means by which humans shape their destinies. Some behaviorists have reneged on what has come to be called conventional behaviorism and on reliance on direct observation, denial of consciousness, and rejection of self-report.

*Radical behaviorism,* an evolutionary outgrowth from that earlier thinking, is typically represented by the work of B. F. Skinner. While Skinner's theoretical rationale acknowledges that private events occur in inner life, his empirical inquiries do not treat self-reports as authentic scientific data. In practice, therefore, his stimulus-response-stimulus model is only a toddler's step from Watson's early work. Skinner denies that responses covert within the individual are autonomous or spontaneous and suggests that they are, rather, the result of prior public learning. However, to understand the causes of human behavior—whether internal *or* external—he asserts that not only must preceding events (*stimulus control*) be carefully observed, but so must the events that follow particular actions (*outcome control*).

The most recent development in behaviorism, called *social* or *behavioral humanism,* displays considerable deviation from Watson's *conventional* model. Behavior is not conceptualized in operant response terms, that is, as stimulus-behavior-response. Trait, motive, and drive explanations of behavior are also disregarded. This theory does not assert that internal events and processes are irrelevant to behavior, but rather that they are a dynamic sequence of complex processes that involve attentional, retentional, reproductive, and motivational factors. Skinner's external stimulus and reinforcement paradigm is replaced by a three part model of *stimulus control, internal symbolic control,* and *outcome control.* Covert internal symbolic responses mediate the behavior of the individual. Like the perceptionists, social learning theorists believe that the significance or meaning of particular situations to the person affects behavior powerfully. Thus, internal sensory and symbolic processes determine to a large degree whether behavior will be learned while outcomes (contingencies of reinforcement) determine whether the learned behavior will then be utilized. Behavior is determined primarily by the immediate environment, including *both* the external and the internal. Hence, the individual is best described and understood by examining actions in a particular situation.

*Behavioral humanism* represents an interesting co-optation and reduction of some of the goals of confluent thinking. (One recent author [Thoresen, 1973], for example, "translated" certain phrases into response terms, e.g., "experience tranquility and calmness in everyday life" became "decrease the frequency of stress and tension responses within the body.") Its proponents claim to develop methods that help people to act in more humane ways and will help the individual to learn skills to direct and control his own life in ways that can increase its personal meaning and satisfaction. But *social* behaviorism is a technology *only.* It is concerned with processes and means, rather than with the goals for which these are utilized. It *may* be put to the service of such humane ends as "translated" above, but it need not be. Frequently, these techniques are harnessed to the immediate, the trivial, and the compensatory—to remediation rather than to development, to therapy rather than to prophylaxis. Without alteration they may serve selfish, not to say sinister, ends.

5. The approach to value clarification of the psychologist Milton Rokeach is less widely known. (1968; 1973) Rokeach has explored a wide range of value questions and devised a ranking measure of instrumental values (means) and terminal values (goals) that has been used to provide feedback to students, teachers, and many others about their personal value stances. His research suggests that individuals who become aware through the task of ranking of discrepancies between their values, or between the ranking of their values and their actions, will modify their behavior to eliminate the discomfort such discrepancies cause. Newport Harbor High School in California is currently using Rokeach's approach as part of a schoolwide teacher and administrator training effort.

6. For example,". . . students who have been exposed to this approach have become less apathetic, less flighty, less conforming as well as less overdissenting. They are more zestful and energetic, more critical in their thinking, and are more likely to follow through on decisions. In the case of under-achievers, values clarification has led to better success in school." (Simon, Howe, and Kirschenbaum, 1972: 20–21)

7. R. Ekstein and R. Motto (1969) provide examples of contemporary uses of psychoanalytic insights in education and also describe the European origins of psychoanalysis in education.

8. However, their unity, in all forms, does not necessarily lead to humane outcomes. In Milan, Italy, a 600 member humanist movement, the Centro Coscienze, operates nursery school through adulthood educational programs based on Renaissance ideals of reason and aesthetic experience. The schools emphasize the use of language, a high level of adult-child interaction, and the absence of raw materials for imaginative play. The *experience* of feeling is deeply imbedded in the curriculum, while the *analysis* of feeling, which is so much a part of American humanistic education, is not. Analysis is directed at objects and experience just as, from simple enjoyment to more complex discrimination, emotion is learned as a response to art, music, dance, and drama rather than to other people. The *direction* that feeling receives in the educational process surely affects its utilization in maturity. May not such an education, in extreme form, leave the individual responsive to artistic experience and indifferent to human beings?

9. Loevinger has published (1966, 1970) an empirically derived scoring methodology for the assignment of stages. Weinstein and Alschuler at the University of Massachusetts have begun investigating the developmental aspects of *self-awareness,* and Weinstein has incorporated Loevinger's schema in his thinking. However, no systematic attempt has been made to develop curricula that could facilitate movement through these stages of ego development. (Cf. Kohlberg's curriculum work in the schools and with delinquents to facilitate the development of moral judgment.)

10. The final stage of training is devoted to implementing humanistic education as proposed by Newberg and Levin, "The Classroom as a Laboratory for Living: A Humanistic Model for Redefining Education," in *The Psychology of*

*Open Teaching and Learning: A Teacher's Guide,* edited by Silberman, Yanoff, Allender (Boston: Little, Brown and Co., September 1975).

11. See also Joe Griggs, "Relationships Between 'Causal' Orientation and Acceptance of Others, 'Self-Ideal Self' Congruency and Mental Health Changes from 4th and 5th Grade Children," *The Journal of Educational Research, 63* (10), 471–477, July–August 1970.

12. A brochure, *About TCP,* describing the main goals and results of the project, is available from the Ford Foundation. A black and white film, *Tomorrow We'll See What Happens,* showing graphically the interactions among students, teachers, parents, and administrators as they go about the basic TCP processes of tutoring, feedback, parent involvement, and shared planning and decision-making is available from Phoenix Films, 470 Park Avenue South, New York, N.Y. 10016. Newmark himself is preparing for publication a manual about how to organize a school based on tutorial community principles. He may be reached at the Educational Communications Corporation, 1910 Ocean Front, Santa Monica, California 90406.

13. DUSO is an important humanistic education program that ranks in usefulness and student appeal with the Affective Education Program's primary *Sharing Book* and the confluent reading curriculum which Sarah Miller has described to me but I have not seen. While the lessons are often delivered didactically, the multimedia message bearers (storybooks, posters, song cassettes, puppets, role-playing cards, and props for the puppets) draw in and involve the children. The puppets are an extremely effective psychomotor outlet for sending and responding to threatening communications that would not be given or accepted between persons. DUSO can do many forbidden or risky things and express many frightening, or otherwise intimate, thoughts.

The DUSO program has also been used effectively by Clark Moustakas and Cereta Perry during their work in the Detroit inner city schools. Unfortunately, teachers at these schools were on strike when I might have visited them. However, while this variant of humanistic education is not described in this report, it has been reported at some length in their book, *Learning To Be Free* (1973).

14. The science of psychology is increasingly popular in the secondary schools and is filtering down to the middle schools and below. The American Psychological Association now has a secondary school curriculum development project on human behavior directed by John Bare at Carleton College. Barbara Ellis Long, now in California, has done nationwide teacher training and curriculum activities for middle school and elementary children. (See the APA *Clearinghouse for Precollegiate Psychology.*)

15. Brown and his associates have defined "confluent education" as "a process in which intellectual and emotional growth is integrated in an educational setting: it is human teaching for human learning." (CEDARC Bulletin.) So defined, confluent education clearly falls within (although it is not co-terminous with) what I call "humanistic education." Unless I am referring directly to Brown's theories and work or that of his colleagues and students, I shall continue to use the more inclusive term "humanistic education."

16. Psychosynthesis is a psychological theory developed by Italian psychologist Roberto Assagioli that is used to conceptualize the integrated person.

Psychosynthesis is seen as an ideal inner state, an alignment between mind and feelings affected by external events. Within the person are "elements"—mind, body, feelings, and subpersonalities—that must be brought together for psychological organization. Within, the person may become a detached observer, "disidentifying" with his separate aspects as he recognizes and claims his integrated self. Part of this integration is building a sensibility linking inner to outer world, connecting personal experience and knowledge to interpersonal and public knowledge.

This theory has been influential in the development of George Brown's theory of confluent education and in practical efforts at curriculum development carried out at Santa Barbara and the Esalen Institute.

17. Publications and descriptions of current activities are now available from DRICE's immediate successor, CEDARC, the Confluent Education Development and Research Center, P.O. Box 30128, Santa Barbara, California 93105. CEDARC publishes *The Confluent Education Journal* and sponsors workshops in Gestalt awareness training, group dynamics, values clarification, Psychosynthesis, interpersonal relations, and body awareness and movement. The list of workshops is interesting in its inclusiveness, including group psychological techniques, individual psychological approaches, the values clarification approach linked to the humanities, and an approach blending the physical and psychological.

18. See, for elaboration, Barker and Gump (1964), Gump (1969), and Insel and Moos (1974).

19. But improving. See Brown (1975) and Read and Simon (1975).

20. Mario Fantini (1974) has suggested that humanistic education (which he calls "the humanism movement") should turn itself to more meaningful and humane pursuits than sensitivity and sexuality training. It has, as I hope this report shows. (Drug education is the most obvious example; others are discussed within the report.) If indeed that stereotype ever existed, it may now be beaten, like any dead horse, only for the pleasure of it. I found the remediation he suggests—social concern—already part of the planning of most humanistic educators and beginning to be widely implemented.

21. Kohlberg (no date: 49–51) has suggested that the approaches of humanistic psychologists and educators to personal growth or development are incompatible with those of the cognitive developmentalists. I do not agree. The contrasts he presents are not entirely real. For example, he believes education labeled *affective* to be opposed to the *cognitive* reorganization of experience. But I hope I have made clear in this report that nowhere in the serious work being done in this area are emotional processes separated from intellectual ones. Over and over again we have seen commitment to the view that emotional experience is not assimilated until it is analyzed (and, usually, labeled). This misunderstanding seems to take form in two ways—on the one hand, the belief of the cognitive developmentalists that affective education does not include cognitive elements, and, on the other, the belief that values or ethical systems are largely the product of rationality coping with dissonance. The latter notion sometimes appears under the flimsy umbrella of an interactionist theory that, in practice, ignores active elements other than cognition.

The orientations of the humanistic educators (as the term is used here) and the cognitive developmentalists do not seem to me so far apart. Authentic (as opposed to pseudo) humanistic education does accept spontaneous emotional experience and expression *under certain conditions* as goods or aims in themselves, whether oceanic or "peak" experiences or smaller, less tumultuous ones. But so did Dewey (1934) in *Art as Experience*. It is possible to believe in the worth of consummatory, nonrational, even Dionysian, experience and also believe that the test of present experience is its worth for fruitful and creative living in subsequent experiences. Like cognitive developmental education, authentic humanistic education attempts to link present experience to the future, as well as to the past, through integration.

It seems to me that there are two principal barriers to the reconciliation of cognitive developmental and humanistic educational views as they exist today. First, developmentalists do not see that at the highest stage of the hierarchy of moral reasoning, their methodology and emphasis on cognition becomes irrelevant because process becomes content (in fact, another of the inescapable "bags of virtue"), and, second, the unwillingness of humanistic educators to own up, to make their values explicit, to accept that the methodologies and the processes of their approach (however different, or sometimes not so different, from the cognitive developmentists) are employed for the sake of fostering values and principles that are not far separated from those universally applicable ones described as the "ultimate highest stage or end of development" in the cognitivists' moral hierarchy: justice, equality, reciprocity, and authenticity. Although these are not necessarily delineated by humanistic educators in such high-falutin' terms, they are indeed a consequence of openness to experience, trust, and interpersonal and self-awareness, among other factors.

# References

Allport, G. *Pattern and Growth in Personality*. New York: Holt, Rinehart, and Winston, 1961.

Alschuler, A. "Psychological Education." *Journal of Humanistic Psychology,* Spring, 1969.

Alschuler, A. *Developing Achievement Motivation in Adolescents: Education for Human Growth*. Englewood Cliffs, New Jersey: Educational Technology Publications, 1973.

American Psychological Association Clearing House on Precollegiate Psychology and Behavioral Science, 1200 Seventeenth Street, N.W. Washington, D.C. 20036

Atkins, V., and Solomon, L. "A Conversation About Affective Learning: A Frontier Between Education and Psychotherapy." In *A Study of Education,* edited by P. Nash. New York: Wiley, forthcoming.

Back, K. *Beyond Words: The Story of Sensitivity Training and the Encounter Movement*. New York: Russell Sage Foundation, 1971.

Barker, R., and Gump, P. *Big School, Small School*. Stanford: Stanford University Press, 1964.

Biber, B. "Integration of Mental Health Principles in the School Setting. In G. Caplan (ed.). *Prevention of Mental Disorders in Children*. New York: Basic Books, 1961, p. 326.

Brown, G. I., ed. *The Live Classroom: Innovations Through Confluent Education and Gestalt*. New York: Viking, 1975.

——. *Human Teaching for Human Learning: An Introduction to Confluent Education*. New York: Viking, 1971.

Bullis, H. E. "How the Human Relations Class Works." *Understanding the Child, 10,* 5–10, 1941.

Castillo, G. *Left-Handed Teaching*. New York: Praeger, 1974.

Combs, A., ed. *Perceiving, Behaving, Becoming.* 1962 Yearbook of the

Association for Supervision and Curriculum Development. Washington, D.C.

Combs, A.; Blume, R.; Newman, A.; and Wass, H. *The Professional Education of Teachers.* 2nd ed. Boston: Allyn and Bacon, 1974.

Cremin, L. *The Transformation of the School.* New York: Knopf, 1961.

Dewey, J. *Art as Experience.* New York: Putnam, 1934.

Dewey, J. *Democracy and Education.* New York: Macmillan, 1916.

Ekstein, R., and Motto, R. *From Learning for Love to Love of Learning.* New York: Brunner/Mazel, 1969.

Erikson, E. *Childhood and Society.* New York: W. W. Norton, 1955.

Fantini, M. "Humanizing the Humanism Movement". *Phi Delta Kappan,* February 1974, 400–402.

Flavell, J. *The Development of Role-Taking and Communication Skills in Children.* New York: John Wiley, 1968.

Freud, A. *Introduction to Psychoanalysis: Lectures for Child Analysts and Teachers.* 1922–1935 New York: International University Press, 1974.

Glasser, W. *Schools Without Failure.* New York: Harper and Row, 1969.

Glasser, W. *Reality Therapy.* New York: Harper and Row, 1965.

Gordon, T. *Teacher Effectiveness Program.* New York: Wyden, 1975.

Gordon, T. *Parent Effectiveness Program.* New York: Wyden, 1970.

Gump, P. "Intra-Setting Analysis: The Third Grade Classroom as a Special But Instructive Case." In *Naturalistic Viewpoints in Psychological Research,* edited by J. P. Willems and H. L. Rausch, pp. 200–220. New York: Holt, Rinehart, and Winston, 1969.

Harmin, M.; Kirschenbaum, H.; and Simon, S. *Clarifying Values Through Subject Matter.* Minneapolis: Winston Press, 1973.

Insel, R. M., and Moos, R. H. "Psychological Environments: Expanding the Scope of Human Ecology." *American Psychologist, 29,* 179–187, 1974.

Jahoda, M. *Current Concepts of Positive Mental Health.* New York: Harper and Row, 1958.

James, W. *Talks to Teachers on Psychology.* New York: Norton, 1958.

Knaus, W. J. *Rational-Emotive Education: A Manual for Elementary School Teachers.* New York: Institute for Rational Living, 1974.

Kohlberg, L. "The Concepts of Developmental Psychology as the Central Guide to Education: Examples from Cognitive, Moral, and Psychological Education." *Proceedings of the Conference on Psychology and the Process of Schooling in the Next Decade: Alternative Conceptions.* Leadership Training Institute/ Special Education. Washington, D.C.: Bureau for Educational Personnel Development, United States Office of Education, no date.

Kohlberg, L.; LaCrosse, R.; and Ricks, D. "The Predictability of Adult Mental Health from Childhood Behavior." In *Manual of Child Psychopathology,* edited by B. Wolman. New York: McGraw-Hill, 1972, 1217–1286.

Krathwohl, D. R.; Bloom, B.; and Masia, B. *Taxonomy of Educational Objectives. Handbook II: Affective Domain.* New York: David McKay, 1964.

Langer, J., and Kuhn, D. "Relations Between Logical and Moral Development." In *Recent Research in Moral Development,* edited by L. Kohlberg and E. Turiel. New York: Holt, Rinehart, and Winston, in press.

Levin, M. "Teacher Preparation for Affective Education." Paper presented at the American Educational Research Association, April 1972.

Loevinger, J. and Wessler, R. *Measuring Ego Development,* Vols. 1 & 2. San Francisco: Jossey-Bass, 1970.

——. "The Meaning and Measurement of Ego Development." *American Psychologist, 21,* 195–206, 1966.

Long, Barbara Ellis. *The Journey to Myself: A Curriculum in Psychology for Middle Schools.* Austin, Texas: Steck-Vaughn, 1974.

Maslow, A. *Toward a Psychology of Being.* 2nd ed. Princeton, New Jersey: Van Nostrand, 1968.

Mead, E. J., Jr. "Confronting a Society in Confrontation." In *Facts and Feelings in the Classroom,* edited by L. J. Rubin, pp. 61–80. New York: Walker, 1973.

Moos, R. "Conceptualizations of Human Environments." *American Psychologist, 28,* 652–665, 1973.

Moustakas, C., and Perry, C. *Learning to be Free.* Englewood Cliffs, N.J.: Prentice-Hall, 1973.

Ojemann, R. *A Brief Summary of Statistically Significant Findings of Some of the Research Studies Involving* the *"Causal" Approach to Preventive Mental Health in the Classroom.* Cleveland: Educational Research Council of America, 1970.

Perry, R. B. "A Definition of the Humanities." In *The Meaning of the Humanities,* edited by T. M. Greene. Princeton, New Jersey: Princeton University Press, 1966.

*Personnel and Guidance Journal, 51,* May 1973. Whole issue on Psychological Education.

Phillips, M., and Elmore, B. *Follow-up Report on DRICE Participants, 1974.* DRICE Monograph no. 6. Santa Barbara, California, June 1974.

Prescott, D. *The Child in the Educative Process.* New York: McGraw-Hill, 1957.

Raths, Louis E., et al. *Values and Teaching: Working With Values in the Classroom.* Columbus, Ohio: Merrill, 1969.

Read, Donald A., and Simon, Sidney B., eds. *Humanistic Education Sourcebook.* Englewood Cliffs, New Jersey: Prentice-Hall, 1975.

Roen, S. "Behavioral Studies as a Curriculum Subject." *Teachers College Record. 68,* 541–550, 1967.

Rokeach, M. *The Nature of Human Values.* New York: The Free Press, 1973.

——. *Beliefs, Attitudes, and Values.* San Francisco: Jossey-Bass, 1968.

Rubin, L. J., ed. *Facts and Feelings in the Classroom.* New York: Walker, 1973.

Scriven, M. "Revolution Within Reason." in *Facts and Feelings in the Classroom,* edited by L. J. Rubin, pp. 85–106. New York: Walker, 1973.

Shiflett, J., and Brown, G. *Confluent Education: Attitudinal and Behavioral Consequences of Confluent Teacher Training.* University Center, Michigan: 1972.

Shoben, E. J. "Guidance: Remedial Function or Social Reconstruction?" In *Guidance: An Examination,* edited by R. L. Mosher, R. D. Carle, and C. D. Kehas. New York: Harcourt, Brace, and World, 1965.

Silberman, C. *Crisis in the Classroom.* New York: Random House, 1970.

Simon, S. B.; Howe, L.; and Kirschenbaum, H. *Values Clarification.* New York: Hart Publishing Company, 1972.

Simpson, E. L. "A Holistic Approach to Moral Development and Behavior." In *Moral Development and Behavior,* edited by T. Likona. New York: Holt, Rinehart, and Winston, 1976.

——. "Can the Humanities Provide a Humanistic Education?" *California Humanities Association Bulletin,* Winter 1971.

——. *Democracy's Stepchildren: A Study of Need and Belief.* San Francisco, Jossey-Bass, 1971.

Smith, M. B. "On Self-Actualization: A Transambivalent Examination of a Focal Theme in Maslow's Psychology." *Journal of Humanistic Psychology, 13,* 17–33, 1973.

——. "Mental Health Reconsidered: A Special Case of the Problem of Values in Psychology." *American Psychologist, 16,* 299–306, 1961.

Taba, H., and Elkins, D. *With Focus on Human Relations.* Washington, D.C.: American Council on Education, 1950.

Thoresen, C. "Behavioral Humanism." In *National Society for the Study of Education Yearbook, 72,* pp. 385–421, 1973.

Weinstein, G., and Fantini, M. D., eds. *Toward Humanistic Education: A Curriculum of Affect.* New York: Praeger, 1970.

White, R. W. "Motivation Reconsidered: The Concept of Competence." *Psychological Reviews, 66,* 297–333, 1959.

Spolin, V. *Improvisation for the Theater.* Evanston, Ill.: Northwestern University Press, 1963.

# A Comprehensive Annotated Bibliography of Humanistic Education

Mary Anne Gray
*Research Assistant and
Principal Bibliographer*

# Bibliography Format

The following classification may seem as arbitrary to the reader as it has at times to the classifiers: many items could appropriately be cross-referenced. We have tried to be as obvious as possible without cross-referencing. Seek and ye shall find, but not all which might be expected here. There are two notable omissions: 1) general, popular, easily-available books which point out deficits in the school's capacity to educate humane human beings, and 2) books, articles, and reports which we have not either read ourselves or found professionally summarized.

## A. SUBJECT CATEGORIES

1. *Rationale and Rhetoric: Justification and Call for Action*

2. *Broad, Underlying Theory*

3. *Theory and Practice*

4. *Reports of Research*

  a. *Effects of Curriculum on Students*

  b. *Teacher-Training Programs*

  c. *Surveys of Student and Teacher Attitudes*

  d. *Relevant Psychological Research into Attitudes and Beliefs*

5. *Descriptions of Classroom Activities*

6. *Descriptions of Programs and Curricula*

7. *Instructional Technology, Programmed Learning, and Media*

8. *Teacher Training*

9. *Evaluation and Measurement*

10. *General*

11. *Bibliographies*

## B. CLASSIFICATIONS WITHIN CATEGORIES

Each category is divided into the following sub-categories:

I. *Books*

II. *Magazines and Journals*

III. *Chapters in Books and Reports; Articles in Encyclopedias*

IV. *Whole Issues*

V. *Reports*

## HUMANISTIC EDUCATION SEARCH STRATEGY

This strategy has been included here to avoid further duplication of effort. These are the materials which have been checked. Future bibliographers should confine themselves to other sources or new ones.

### Reference Books

*Library Journal (Reference, Psychology,* and *Education* from January, 1960 to September 1973).

*Reference Quarterly* (Volume I through Volume X).

*Wilson Library Bulletin* (From 1960 to November, 1973).

Winchell's *Guide To Reference Books (Education* under *Social Sciences)* and the three supplements.

*Reference Services Review* (Volumes One and Two).

*Choice* (Under *Education* and *Psychology,* 1964-1972).

*American Reference Books Annual* (Volumes 1970, 1971, and 1972).

*Reference and Subscription Book Reviews* (Formerly *Subscription Books Bulletin Reviews)* (1962-1972).

**Educational Indexes**

*Education Index* (July 1961–September, 1973).

*Research in Education* (Volumes 1960–1973) affective behavior, affective objectives, affective techniques, annotated bibliographies, behavioral sciences, bibliographies, educational psychology, educational philosophy, emotional . . . , human development, human relations, human relations programs, human relations units, humanistic education, humanization, intergroup relations, interpersonal relationships, self-actualization, self-concept, self-esteem, self-evaluation, values, mental health . . .

*Current Index to Journals In Education* (Volumes 1969 to September, 1973) affective behavior, affective objectives, annotated bibliographies, behavioral science, bibliographies, educational philosophy, educational psychology, emotional . . . , human development, human relations, human relations programs, human relations units, humanization, humanistic education, mental health . . . intergroup education, interpersonal relations, self-actualization, self-concept, self-esteem, self-evaluation, values.

*Psychological Abstracts* (1960–September, 1973) Educational psychology.

**Encyclopedias**

*The Encyclopedia of Education.* Lee C. Deighton (Ed.) New York: Crowell-Collier Educational Corp., 1971. "Affective Learning," by David W. Ecker, pp. 113–120 and "Behavioral Sciences, Teaching of," by Sheldon R. Roen, pp. 446–449.

*Encyclopedia of Educational Research.* Robert L. Ebel (Ed.) New York: Macmillan Company, 1969. "Mental Health," "Behavior Problems," "Group Processes," and "Social and Emotional Development."

*International Encyclopedia of the Social Sciences.* David L. Sills (Ed.) New York: Macmillan Company, 1968. Lawrence Kohlberg, "Moral Development," pp. 483–494.

**Associations**

*Encyclopedia of Associations.* Fisk, Margaret, 6th Edition. Vol. I National Associations. Detroit, Michigan: Gale Research Company, 1970: Educational and Cultural Organizations.

*Education Directory Part IV.* U.S. Office of Education. *Part IV Educational Associations,* Washington D.C., 1971–1972. Childhood education and welfare, education-general, elementary education, guidance and placement, health education, higher education, mental hygiene, orthopsychiatry, psychology, research, secondary education, teacher education.

**Miscellaneous**

Burke and Burke, *Documentation in Education,* New York: Teacher's College Press, 1967.

Mannheim, Theodore; Dardarian, Gloria L.; Satterthwait, Diane A. *Sources in Educational Research,* Detroit, Michigan: Wayne State University Press, 1969. Descriptor: Social Studies Education *NEA Journal* (now called *Today's Education*) (May issues in 1963-1973).

*Bibliographic Index* (1960-1973) Descriptors: education, human relations, mental health.

*Books in Print*

education, education-philosophy, education-U.S., education-elementary, education-higher, education-humanistic, education-preschool, education-secondary, education of children, educational innovations, personnel service in education, educational psychology, emotional problems of children, emotions, interpersonal relations, mental health, moral education, self, self-actualization

*Personnel service in education*
1966-1968
1969
1970
1971

*A World Bibliography of Bibliographies* Besterman, Theodore Geneve: Societas Bibliographica, 1966-1967, Descriptor: education.

*PAIS Bulletin* (1960-1973) Descriptors: *behavioral sciences, child guidance and psychology, education.*

**Not Included**

*Social Science and Humanities Index*

*Cumulative Book Index*

*Alternatives in Print*

*Alternatives Index*

*Mental Health Book Review Index*

*ABS Guide*

# Bibliography

## 1. RATIONALE AND RHETORIC: JUSTIFICATION AND CALL FOR ACTION

### II. Magazines and Journals

Abruscato, Joseph. "Integrative Education." *Education,* 89:353-358, April-May 1969.

   Provocative presentation of the need for an educational curriculum that would, at the very minimum, help students become aware of the nature of his fellow man. The author describes our society as an instantaneous electric age which places all men in constant contact with others. Therefore, a major aim of education should be to provide students with an opportunity for developing empathy toward others. Most important in carrying out such a program is a teacher who is not only loving and patient, but also firm so his students will not become overly dependent on him.

EJ 095 545

Alpren, Morton. "Curriculum Significance of the Affective Domain." *Theory Into Practice,* 12:46-53, February 1974.

   The author predicts that the affective movement in education will subside because the proponents of the movement have failed to develop curricula and other materials for potential practitioners outside the movement.

Alschuler, Alfred and Ivey, Allen. "The Human Side of Competency-Based Education." *Educational Technology,* 12:53-5, Nov. 1972.

   Addresses the problem of the lack of attention paid to psychological and vocational curricula in schools. Discusses what is important to learn, ethical issues in psychological education plus intentionality, a metagoal of psychological education.

Alschuler, Alfred. "Psychological Education and Growth Communities." *Educational Opportunity Forum,* 1:172–183, Fall 1969.

Identifies problems and possibilities that are present when introducing psychological education into the schools. Extrinsic problems include the following: more classrooms will be needed, who is to teach the courses, what are basic values, to whose advantage is this innovation, and most educators are not serious enough in their concern for the whole student. Intrinsic problems include the fact that at present there are no definitive descriptions of eupsychic states and processes, and little research exists on the following important question: does psychological education have significantly greater long-term impact than other forms of therapy and education? If so, what makes it more effective? Finally, the author discusses the impact of this type of education upon communities.

Anonymous. "Watergate Emphasizes Need to Teach Ways of Choosing Values." *Pennsylvania School Journal,* September 1973, pp. 20–22.

The article opens by noting that recent socio-political events have stimulated a rebirth of values education. Several examples of specific school efforts to incorporate the process of values clarification with students, teachers, and parents are noted. In conclusion a brief narration is offered describing how values clarification can be adapted for use in subject matter teaching.

Baker, Harold S. "It All Begins With the Individual." *Education Canada,* 11:4–12, June 1971.

In education one should be closely involved with the main needs of the individual. In this article the author groups these needs into five categories: 1) existential—referring to such things as personal identity, recognition, security, and esteem; 2) vocational; 3) leisure and recreational; 4) intellectual; and 5) evaluative, particularly with reference to social moral, and spiritual concerns. Each category is discussed in its education context.

Banikotes, Paul G. "A Preventative Approach to Mental Health in Schools." *Counselling and Values,* 17:112–17, Winter 1973.

The school appears to be an ideal place for applying a preventative approach to mental health. The emerging role of the school counselor-consultant offers some hope for systemwide impact. Coordination with community mental health services would further strengthen the consultant's role in the school.

Beatty, W. H. "Emotions and Learning." *Educational Leadership,* 22:517-19, April 1965.

Emotions support and determine the strength of commitment which we have to our values. Need is for further studies in the area. Last studies were done in 1933 by American Council of Education.

Beatty, Warren H. "Emotions: The Missing Link in Education." *Theory Into Practice,* 8:86-92, April 1969.

This paper explores how a person organizes his self-concept. There are four areas around which perceptions of self and adequacy are clustered: worth, coping, expressing, and autonomy. The author explores how feelings and emotions relate to this self-concept theory. Finally, he challenges teachers to utilize their knowledge of self-concept theory to make classrooms humane environments in which children can develop an adequate self-concept.

Behling, Herman E., Jr. "What Do We Value in Teacher Education?" *The Informer,* 1:3; February/March 1973.

The article discusses the need for educators to become more aware of themselves and the values that guide and influence their lives and activities. The author sadly notes the present lack of emphasis schools and colleges place on values clarification and the valuing process. The article concludes with a description of research findings by Carl Rogers in the area of positive teacher behavior changes after exposure to a program of values clarification.

Belensky, Robert. "Guidance and the Teaching of High School Psychology." *Community Mental Health Journal,* 2:41-46, Spring 1966.

Suggests that counselors would be more effective if they facilitated change through field work, exposure to psychological literature, plus supervised self-scrutiny in a specially designed psychology course.

Bidwell, Corrine. "The Teacher as a Listener-An Approach to Mental Health." *Journal of School Health,* 37:373-383, October 1967.

For a teacher to assume the responsibility of teaching the whole child, the teacher should get to know each child individually. To accomplish this, the author suggests that classroom time be set aside at least once a month for personal conferences between teacher and child in which the child is encouraged to talk about himself and express his own interests and problems. At these sessions the teacher should be a nonjudgmental, nonauthoritarian listener. The author feels that such sessions are an important step in attempting to promote positive mental health in both the students and teachers.

Bishop, Inez E. and Alice B. Donovan. "Teaching Problem-Solving as a Component of Mental Health." *Journal of School Health,* 39:411-413, June 1969.

The problem-solving method, in which the process of inquiry and discovery is deemed more important than the amount of material covered, is important to mental health because it allows for maximum student involvement. Summaries of studies indicate that there exists a direct correlation between this student-involved method of study and the more effective development of perceptions, emotions, and interpersonal relationships of students.

Blake, Robert W. "I See You, I Hear You, You're OK—Humanizing the English Classroom." *English Journal,* 63:41-6, May 1974.

In these times when the terms "humanistic" and "humanism" are bandied about, Blake examines the following questions: (1) What is humanism? (2) What is humanistic teaching? and (3) What is it to be human? If we teach humanistically what humanism is all about, we might come up with human beings.

Blosser, P. E. "Principles of Gestalt Psychology and Their Application to Teaching Junior High School Science." *Science Education,* 57:43-53, January 1973.

Posits that science teachers should provide opportunities for students to change. States 19 guidelines for the teaching of science. Discusses Gestalt Psychology and how it relates to science teaching.

Borton, Terry. "What's Left When School's Forgotten?" *Saturday Review,* April 19, 1970. pp. 69-71, 79+.

The crux of this article is that there is a great interest in process education today because of the knowledge explosion, the development of the computer, and the desire to be relevant to the concerns of kids. The author cites the danger that to teach about processes is not to be assured that students use these processes in their lives. As the author states, "In a process education, the student himself is clearly the most important content, and his own consciousness the most important teacher."

Botkin, R. "Can We Teach Values." *Education Record,* 49:189-96, Spring 1968.

Discusses the role of the teacher in teaching human values in light of the teacher's two responsibilities: 1) as a conveyor of information and as an authority in a discipline, 2) as a nurturer of a climate of devotion rather than fanaticism. Failure to teach values imperils the human spirit.

10871

Bowen, Andrew J. "Carl Roger's View on Education." *American Journal of Occupational Therapy,* 28:220-1, April 1974.

Presents a humanistic, person-centered approach to education based on C. Roger's idea of education as the facilitation of learning and the development of people as learners. The relationship between facilitator and learner is discussed and related to the qualities of genuineness, empathetic understanding and nonpossessive warmth.

Bower, Eli M. "K.I.S.S. and Kids: A Mandate for Prevention. *American Journal of Orthopsychiatry,* 42:556-565, July 1972.

    Characterizes KISS, "key integrative social systems" as 1) health services, 2) families, 3) peer-play arrangements, 4) schools. Describes a need to integrate these systems to prevent mental health problems at a later date. This institution would be called the Child Growth Center.

Bower, E. M. "Mental Health and Education: A Play in Three Acts." *Educational Leadership,* 21:8-10+, October 1963.

    Gives reasons why delinquency needs to be prevented before it happens. Collaboration between mental health and education will be one of investigating together the nature of cognitive and affective experiences so that learning processes will be more effective in both these areas.

Bower, Eli M. "Mental Health in the Schools," *NEA Journal,* 53:64, September 1963.

    Describes opportunities provided by HEW's 1963 Appropriation Act. Some suggested programs: behavioral science training, home-school cooperation, mental health consultation, screening methods in early childhood, etc.

Bower, Eli M. "On Teaching Human Behavior to Humans." *Journal of School Psychology,* 5:237-240, Spring 1967.

    Through the technique of a fictitious interview with a visitor from another planet, the author brings to light the need for elementary schools to incorporate the study of human behavior in the school curriculum. Understanding the basic concepts and modes of thinking in a field of knowledge and being able to use such concepts and modes of thinking freely is to master a subject matter. To study the theory of behavior would provide a crossbridge for students between the formal subjects and the realities of life.

Brameld, T. "Education as Self-fulfilling Prophecy." *Phi Delta Kappan,* 54:8-11, September 1972.

    Education can become a device to reconfirm our human limitations, or it can become a way to build for something, "a city of man" that still awaits our future. Self-fulfilling prophecy is reducible to cultural expectations, can become personal expectations. Some critique of Silberman and Ilich.

Brody, H. S. "Humanism in Education." *Journal of Aesthetic Education,* 7:67-77, April 1973.

    Discusses the new humanistic approach to education as a way of making an effort toward individuality and authenticity in a technological society. Author believes that a more promising route lies in exploring the cultural heritage of the sciences, the humanities, and the fine arts.

Broudy, Harry S. "Science and Human Values." *Science Teacher,* 36:23-28, March 1969.

The goal of science in general education is the exploration of value, including its scientific components. Interdisciplinary exploration of value needs to be undertaken deliberately and systematically. The future depends on citizens being able to carry on interdisciplinary thinking or the exploration of value.

Brown, George L. "A Plague and Some Medication." *Improving College and University Teaching,* 18:92-96, Spring 1970.

Another article by the author to stress the importance of feelings in achieving maturity and personal growth. Author states that a prerequisite for maturity is an ability to experience feelings and to stay with feelings both pleasant and painful. Once a person makes contact with his feelings, genuine growth occurs, for at that moment he is experiencing reality. This condition of experiencing reality the author refers to as awareness, which involves the cognitive or intellectual process as well as feeling. Author feels society should allow within its schools and colleges for the existence of feelings and desires because these have a strong effect on cognitive learning.

Brown, George L. "Confluent Education: Exploring the Affective Domain." *College Board Review,* 4-10. Summer 1971.

Author defines term, "confluent education," and presents case that schools are best place to present this form of education. Confluent education would bring relevance into the classroom and would result in personal growth for the individual. Aspects of what and how the learner feels can be integrated with what schools believe he should know. To accomplish this goal, there is a need for training teachers, for "developing materials, lessons, and teaching units in the various subject areas, and for implementing these approaches for use by the educational establishment as a whole."

Brown, Glen J., and Rentschler, James E. "Humanizing the Schools." *Contemporary Education,* 45:90-5, Winter 1974.

Focuses on the changes in schools which are necessary to bring about more humane environments. Lists the 12 statements used by J. Lloyd Trump to describe a humane school and then discusses the three divisions of people who are of concern to the school administrator who aspires to increase the humaneness of the school—parents, students, and teachers.

Bruce, P. "Alternative to Alienation." *Educational Leadership,* 23:301+. January 1966.

States that since Dewey, education has been existing in a state of alienation with no sense of purpose. Identifies three forces in educational psychology and calls for education to identify itself with humanistic psychology and rethink its objectives and practices in light of humanistic principles.

EJ 092 489
Buchholz, Ester S. "The Proper Study for Children: Children and Their Feelings." *Psychology in the Schools,* Vol. 11:10-15, January 1974.

This article examines the need for and feasibility of including children's feelings as school work, sets forth some expectations that arise from such work, and describes ongoing work with children at a public elementary school and the problems encountered.

Budzik, Jerome M. "The Realities of Developing Humanistic Public Schools." *Education Digest,* 37:22-4, April 1972.

Divides schools into two categories: humanistic and custodial-type. Discusses the affecting forces on teachers and administrators. Calls for more humanistic styles of administrative control, inservice programs for teachers, and alternative programs and methods for dealing with deviant students.

Buhler, Charlotte. "Humanistic Psychology as an Educational Program." *American Psychologist,* 24:736-742, August 1969.

Educators should utilize a student's interest in himself and his life in starting out with studies of human life. These could serve as starting points for studying more specific aspects of psychology.

Buscaglia, Leo F. "Listen to the Children." *Academic Therapy,* 7:443-6, Summer 1972.

This is a call for a return to a more humanistic kind of education which would include wisdom, joy, love, and courage.

Churchman, C. West. "Humanizing Education." *Center Magazine,* 1:90-93, November 1968.

Author presents two viewpoints on goals of educational system: economic versus individual development. The economic-benefit goal is formulated by the systems-science approach which looks at education as a system with recognizable inputs and outputs. The opponents of this approach recognize education as a means to help students learn about themselves and the world around them. Suggested policy changes for educational systems are to drop required courses, provide real-life problems for students to study, and drop the distinction between teachers and students. To develop every person's natural inclination to inquire should be the primary purpose of education.

Cimini, Peter D. "Humanizing as a Teaching Strategy." *School Health Review,* 2:15-21, Jan./Feb. 1974.

The logical place in the schools for the scientific development of inner transactions should be in the health program. Topics should be approached from an informational and a humanizing base. We must develop affecting techniques along with the information. Four examples of humanizing areas are elucidated: value clarification exercises, self-concept exercises, communication exercises, and decision-making exercises. Evaluation should also be part of this approach.

Cleverdon, S. A. "To Thine Own Self: Building a Personal Curriculum." *Teacher,* 90:18+, February 1973.

Author feels that each individual teacher can get at the common learning of young people: reading, writing, math, science, social studies. Teacher planned projects should excite the children's interest and be something they can deal with on their own level. Should provide opportunities for activity and actual use of concrete materials, have goals, and provide opportunity for extension in a variety of directions.

Coleman, James S. "Introduction: In Defense of Games." *American Behavioral Scientist,* 10: pp. 3-4, October 1966.

The author sees games as a caricature of social life. Games represent a magnification of some aspects of social interaction. The sociologist, as well as the young child, can gain insight into the functioning of social life through the construction and use of games. This, then, is the fascination of the sociologist with social simulation games.

Combs, A. W. "Human Side of Learning." *National Elementary Principal,* 52:38-42, January 1973.

Posits that the behavioral objectives are useful devices for dealing with simplest aspects of education, but not for intelligent behavior requiring a creative approach to a problem. Trouble with education is lack of humanity. Student must discover meaning of new information. Teachers must be aware of other person's point of view. Must make systematic search to weed out things that destroy effective learning. Need to recognize how we influence self-concept.

Combs, Arthur W. "The Human Side of Learning." *National Elementary Principal,* 52:38-42, January 1973.

The author suggests that behavioral objectives and accountability in education deal with only a small aspect of the educational problem while the problems of self-concept, human attitudes, feelings, beliefs, meanings, and intelligence are going unexplored. This article illustrates how schools are dehumanizing and suggests how education can be humanized.

Combs, Arthur W. "New Concepts of Human Potentials: New Challenge For Teachers." *Childhood Education,* 47:349-355, April 1971.

This paper first takes a look at factors that influence how well children can live in and make use of the world and then calls on teachers to find ways of challenging instead of threatening children, utilizing new concepts of human potential.

Combs, Arthur W. "Helping Young People Discover Commitment." *Educational Leadership,* 22:164-9, December 1964.

Young people need commitment, involvement in some course of action, need to discover this themselves. Need to eliminate barriers to commitment.

Comes through relationships with significant people. Teachers have responsibility to be significant, build confidence in youth.

Combs, Arthur W. "New Concepts of Human Potentials: New Challenges for Teachers." *Childhood Education,* 47:349-55: April 1971.
Discusses limitations and possibilities of living in an expanded world. Physiology, lack of opportunity, human needs, self-concept, challenge and threat, are limitations placed on ghetto child. Teachers have benefit of science's answers and directions, but must operate on faith and belief that what they do is important. Stupidity and maladjustment are not "the will of God" but the lack of will of man. Teachers must act upon new understandings for the child, the parents, our institutions.

EJ 080 994
Cooper, Saul; Seckler, Donald. "Behavioral Science in Primary Education: A Rationale." *People Watching,* 2:37-39, Spring 1973.
Discussed are the issues and activities involved in creating a curriculum aimed at helping children understand the nature of feelings, human growth and development, and the process of learning.

Corazzini, John G. "Psychological Education: Three Perspectives." *Counseling and Values,* 17:126-131, Winter 1973.
A new approach to education is needed. Psychological education seems to be one alternative. It challenges and attacks the educational process as we know it because it educates the whole man in all that he is. Whether it is affective, cognitive-developmental, or problem-solving, psychological education seems to be true education for growth.

Cornebise, J. M. "Self: A Concern For The Teacher." *High School Journal,* 46:189-94. February 1963.
Discusses Hopkins' need-experience approach in finding out children's needs and meeting them in the classroom on an individual basis. A friendly informal classroom, an empathetic teacher, and freedom for children are needed. Teacher's role is facilitating growth and acting as a resource person.

Cottingham, Harold F. "Psychological education, the guidance function, and the school counselor." *School Counselor,* 20:340-45, May 1973.
Examines the implications of two current, significant trends in guidance: (a) disenchantment with limited role and restricted impact of counselors and (b) demands for humanized and individualized educational systems. These elicit implications regarding deliberate psychological education, reexamination of guidance functions, and the changing responsibilities of school counselors. It is noted that counselor focus on personal growth requires a shift from remedial emphasis to growth functions. Broader cognitive experiential

learning opportunities encourage consideration of counselor involvement in extra-school settings.

Darling, D. W. "Why a Taxonomy of Affective Learning?" *Educational Leadership,* 22:473-522. April 1965.

Gives rationale for taxonomy of affective learning. Interests, attitudes, values are apparent when a child accepts, prefers and makes a commitment to a value. This is a long-term objective for a teacher. A taxonomy can clarify a school's responsibility for promoting learning in the affective realm needed for this changing society.

Daubner, Edith Schell. "Making Moral Education Possible." *Elementary School Journal,* 70:61-73, November 1969.

Advocates use of John Stuart Mill's ethical theory to settle moral disputes in the classroom. Teachers should familiarize themselves with the principles of ethical theory to make it a reality in the classroom.

DeArmond, Murray and Parker, Austin T. "Becoming Human: An Educational Process." *Journal of Higher Education,* 39:506-511, December 1968.

Author feels that universities must integrate development of intellect with development of affective abilities. Discusses 5 areas of concern in young adults and 3 ways in which universities can meet these concerns.

Dickens, Mary Ellen. "Values, Schools, and Human Development." *The Clearing House,* 48:473-477, April 1974.

There is great confusion about values in American schools. Shaver defines values as "standards or principles of worth" and outlines three categories of values. Values are not separate from knowledge. Schools must encourage students to question values. Progress in personal human development depends on the ability to understand one's own values. Through reflection about the values we hold, we can integrate our knowledge of the disciplines and relate ourselves to our experiences.

Dinkmeyer, D. "Teacher As Counselor: Therapeutic Approaches to Understanding Self and Others." *Childhood Education,* 46:314-17, March 1970.

Describes how the teacher can counsel children with emotional problems in school. Basic function is to facilitate human effectiveness. Teacher must serve as model. Guidance and curriculum are highly interrelated. Teachers must begin to understand the significance of misbehavior. DUSO program (Developing Understanding of Self and Others) is currently available in developing a planned classroom guidance period. Discusses C group in education.

Dirlam, Karen S., and Buchanan, Roland L., Jr. "Human Relations: These Approaches Can Succeed." *Educational Leadership,* 32:22-26, October 1974.

There must be two thrusts in human relations programs: (a) an inter-personal component, by which students and educators become better aware of self; and (b) intergroup relations to develop an improved understanding and appreciation of human differences. This article explores these two thrusts and their integration.

Dodge, Marjorie T. "Should Values Be Taught in  the Classroom?" *Journal of American Indian Education,* 11:15-17, January 1972.

Calls for the values of self respect and respect for others to be taught in the classroom to Indian children.

Dreischmeier, W. B. "Teaching for a Change in Attitude: Values Clarification." *Agricultural Education Magazine,* 47:129-30.

Presents the ideas of Raths, Harmin, and Simon to teachers of agriculture and challenges them to work on value clarification with their students.

Drews, Elizabeth Monroe. "Beyond Curriculum." *Journal of Humanistic Psychology,* 8:97-112, Fall 1968.

Author lists series of assumptions about the psychology of self. The role of the teacher, format changes in methodology and content, ways of learning basic to self-actualization, and ways to expose students more to the world outside the classroom are discussed. All assumptions are documented by noted psychologists. Among the assumptions discussed are unconditional trust and valuation of the student, individualization, group discussions, self-affirmation and commitment, and world as setting and curriculum. Education should help young people become self-actualizing and prepare them to live in today's society.

Dyer, Prudence. "Love in Curriculum." *Theory Into Practice,* 8:10-107: April 1969.

Love can be taught in the classroom. Love or respect of self, love or ro-mance between a man and a women, love or concern for family, love or regard for fellow man, love or devotion for country, and man's love or commitment to an ideal and reverence for God can all be included in the curriculum. Literature, films, music, and works of arts are listed for each type of love mentioned. These serve as exemplars. Love is a highly relevant concern of today's youth. Teachers must be exemplars. Teachers must love their children if they wish to teach children to love.

Edman, M. L. "Can Children Achieve Humaneness?" *Educational Horizons,* 51:107-10, Spring 1973.

A teacher dealing with education of children in a world of change, con-fusion and unprecedented opportunities needs a humane approach. Schools must set up proper situations and climate, know and appreciate their model "teachers," and must be able to identify with and cooperate with human beings no matter what their race, culture, economic or social status may be.

Eickhorn, Donald H. "The School As Center for Human Development." *Educational Leadership,* 29:24-7, October 1971.

The philsophic commitment to develop schools which "promote the dignity and worth of the individual" must be a top priority goal of American education.

Eisner, Elliot W. "The Humane School Is the Human Relations Curriculum." *Educational Leadership,* 32:7-9, October 1974.

Outlines a 3-dimensional approach to the creation of a humane school. (1) We need to conceptualize the features that define such an environment. (2) There must be support from parents who send their children to the school. (3) We must deal with the problems of evaluating the school, the teaching, and the quality of life and learning that exists there.

Elliott, Lloyd H. "Teaching for Life Adjustment, Sixth-Grade Level." *Elementary School Journal,* 51:152-154, November 1950.

A first-hand account by a school principal of his sixth-grade teacher, Mrs. Davis. Mrs. Davis brought into the classroom a sincere concern for every child. She offered guidance and became personally acquainted with each child's family. The success of her boys and girls in some measure could always be attributed to her genuine feelings and sympathetic interest in her students. The author concludes that perhaps such a quality of sincere concern for fellowmen is the first essential for life adjustment.

EJ 095 103
Elberty, William T., Jr. "Problems Associated With Humanistic Teaching." *Journal of College Science Teaching,* 3:193–196, February 1971.

The author discusses some of the human, psychological, and educational problems that he has encountered in introducing humanistic teaching to his college classes as an alternative to conventional education.

English, Horace B. "Education of the Emotions." *Journal of Humanistic Psychology,* 1:101-109, 1961.

Thought-provoking article on need for training and development of one's emotions to lead a fuller, freer life. Author states that "for a full life people need to emote freely, spontaneously." And to be able to emote both freely and appropriately, there must be training. Freedom lies in participation with equals. We are free only when we share in the lives of others. And this sharing is always deeply emotional.

Esler, William K., and Armstrong, J. "Humanistic Curriculum. Is it for Everyone?" *Clearing House,* 48:189-190, November 1973.

"Schools have only a limited ability to shape society. Rather, they must operate within the society as it exists. Children of all ages come to school with a variety of personalities and needs. A truly humanistic school, open and unstructured, would no more be right for all children than is the more traditonally structured one. This condition implies that the children who require order in their daily activities should be able to find this structure in the school, and children who are best served by an openly humanistic setting should be able to operate in their best setting. It would seem that the most humane of schools would be one that provides a mixture of humanistic unstructuredness and traditional structure. This would enable each child to find learning activites that best bring forth his own unique style of human growth."

EJ 093618   H62567
Fantini, Mario D. "Alternative Schools and Humanistic Education." *Social Education,* 38:243-47, March 1974.

Two important trends in public education of the 1970's are identified as humanistic education and a wide choice of educational options. An analysis of the interrelationships between these trends emphasizes the need for educational alternatives in order to humanize education.

Fisher, E. "Open Letter to the President." *School Counselor,* 20:137-8, November 1972.

Describes a personal experience with humanistic education as a justification for $1800 worth of federal monies spent. Skills learned included achievement motivation, value clarification, the creative process and reinforcement of personal strengths. Author spread materials around and spoke at other places to share information.

Fleres, Carol, and Benmaman, Virgina. "Designing a Human Relations Curriculum." *Educational Leadership,* 32:31-34, October 1974.

Authors discuss key concepts essential to any program for improving the quality of interpersonal relationships in the classroom and suggested activities to bring about such improvement.

Garner, John. "Psychology in Schools: A Consideration." *Education and Social Science,* 1:105-109, October 1969.

Author presents an overview of the case for the introduction of psychology into the British schools. In a society of increasing complexity, teachers feel the need to prepare the young at a personal, as well as at a vocational level. The question arises whether only one theory of learning or motivation should be endorsed and taught, or whether many views of psychology should be presented. "What is being suggested, then, is that the psychology taught in schools would have as its aim that of showing that there are many varied views of the person, and that there are some grounds for discriminating between them." Educators and psychologists together must prepare a curriculum that would help students "to become more sophisticated and discriminating in their search for an understanding of themselves and their predicament."

Gearing, Frederick O. "Toward a Mankind Curriculum; From Kindergarten through Twelfth Grade." *Today's Education,* 59:28-30, March 1970.

Author deems it advisable that social studies classes for all grade levels deal with the nature of man. "A mankind curriculum persistently asks: What is human about all humans? How do people, wherever they are, uniquely express that common humanity?" Such a curriculum would view "the lives of many men, remote in time and place and close at hand. Men are thus seen in the full sweep of the total human career." The main purpose of such a course would be to help the student gain a deeper understanding of himself and of his own human nature, thereby enabling him to better relate to a heterogeneous nation and world.

Gersir, Robert L. "Help Them Learn About Themselves." *Teacher,* 90:27-8, September 1972.

Author contends that teachers need to teach for the present rather than for the future. Teachers should relate to their students as human beings, put humaneness first in schools, and emphasize the non-intellectual areas of human development.

Glasser, William. "Reaching the Unmotivated Science Teacher." *Science Teacher,* 38:18-22, March 1971.

In an article addressed to science educators, Glasser suggests that educators must help students develop a positive self-identity. He must get the students involved, teach relevant material and get them to think. Contains many practical ideas which will help reach the unmotivated.

Goldman, Leo. "Psychological Education: Where Do We Go From Here?" *School Counselor,* 21:22-26, September 1973.

Describes the failure of recent guidance programs in schools and warns of failure in the current trend toward involvement in psychological education in the schools, unless certain precautions are taken. Selection and training procedures for counselors should be reexamined. Alternative plans for delivery of some services may be necessary. Ideas for implementation must be exchanged.

Gonzalez, M. "Humanistic Learning." *Science Teacher,* 39:25, February 1972.

Lists 20 beliefs that, if followed, will create a humanistic learning and foster its lifelong survival. These 20 beliefs must be felt and experienced as well as perceived.

Goodlad, J. I. "Humanistic Curriculum." *Music Educators Journal,* 53:91-5, March 1967.

States a need for development of education for the value of the individual, not for some future college entrance exam. States several lessons which have been learned about education in recent years to turn curricula toward a more humanistic approach. Author feels that if answers to future problems do not lie in education, there are no answers.

Gordon, J. W. "Values in the Classroom." *National Elementary Principal,* 42:30-4, November 1962.

Describes forces that affect the expression and development of values in the classroom, an illustrative list of values children should hold, and the behavior of the adult in the classroom that allows these values to prevail. It is inescapable that one must make choices in values. Values humans need include 1) openness to experience, 2) flexibility, 3) objectivity, 4) complexity, 5) perfection, 6) spontaneity, 7) rationality, 8) integrity, 9) autonomy, 10) responsibility, 11) charity. Teachers must have these values: 1) regard the child as equal, 2) respect the child's integrity, 3) be real, 4) make the present good.

Gray, Charles E. "Values Inquiry and the Social Studies." *Education,* 92:130-7, November–December 1972.

The paper takes the position that if value inquiry in the social studies is to become something more than a mere "fad," it will have to be grounded upon a sound rationale from which appropriate curricular designs and teaching strategies can be developed.

Hafemann, John. "Teaching and the Valuing Process." *Wisconsin Education Association,* 100:5, May 1968.

This article, an editorial comment, supports the need for schools and educators to teach a process of valuing modeled after the work of Raths, Harmin, and Simon. The author feels this is a major way for teachers to combine the affective domain with the cognitive to help students develop their maximum potential. Finally the article states that students who have learned a process for determining their own values can become more effective law-abiding citizens of a democratic society.

Hamm, R. L. and Arvolt. "Existential View of Affective Learning." *Contemporary Education,* 44:76-9, November 1972.

Existentialism is a revolt against traditional philosophy. It implies individual choice and freedom with responsibility. For schools it suggests the open classroom with alternatives; choices and individuality for teachers as well as children. A choice calls for judgment which leads to value and value leads to life.

Happ, Joyce W. "VC for Sixth Graders." *School Health Review,* 5:34-35, January/February 1974.

Speaks of her observance of the growth of interest in values clarification and her doctoral research work in several 6th grade health classes.

Hargrove, W. R. "Learning in the Affective Domain." *Peabody Journal of Education,* 47:144-6, November 1969.

Hargrove finds five affective goals which he feels we must not neglect in schools: 1) quiet contemplation, 2) relationship to nature, 3) valuing the good and beautiful, 4) respect for self and others, 5) development of values and behaviors necessary for sustaining democracy. He goes on to outline several specific ways to begin to implement these goals.

Harrison, Jr., A. and Scruin, E. G. "Educational Controversy: A Gloomy Prediction." *Contemporary Education,* 44:115-17, November 1972.

Gloomy prediction is that the humanistic educators and the materialist reform movers will be in conflict within the schools. American culture is not a favorable environment for humanistic education. That numbers of young people are disenchanted with materialism is a favorable factor, but unlikely to turn society around. Predicts education will move into free market arena and will be similar to industrial corporations.

Hartley, W. H. "Love and Laughter in the Social Studies." *Social Education,* 30:71-3, February 1966.

This is the text of the President of the National Council for the Social Studies address at the Council meeting. Discusses how humanizing qualities of teachers, i.e. "love" make the classroom come alive. Casts doubt upon some new innovations in education. Attention to high standards as well as love is important in good teaching.

Heath, D. H. "What Education For a More Violent World?" *American Association University of Women Journal,* 63:160-165, May 1970.

Makes proposals for educational change to prepare youth for a world of tomorrow. 1) Expand the awareness of our students about their own predisposition to violence. 2) Provide more systematic programs to develop more allocentric students. 3) Help students learn how to form and test more integrative ways to deal with conflicts. 4) Test in a wide range of frustrating and conflicting situations to develop a stable identity and autonomy in the potential leaders.

Heath, D. H. "Student Alienation and the School." *The School Review,* 78:515-528, August 1970.

Discusses reasons for increasing student alienation in the schools. Includes reasons for characterological changes such as estrangement from self, others, and traditions. Societal causes include overlarge schools and too much TV watching. Apathy, loneliness and meaninglessness challenge us to develop an educational environment that will help each youth to develop more integratively and more humanely.

Henderson, T. "Review of the Literature on Affective Education." *Contemporary Education,* 44:92-9, November 1972.

Reviews literature and authors on affective education. Among those referred to are John Holt, Jonathan Kozol, William Glasser, Charles Silberman, George B. Leonard, Frank Gole. Makes a case for training teachers in affective domain by quoting research from various leaders in fields such as Rogers, C. *Freedom to Learn.* New methods must be found to enable prospective teachers to recognize and to express their feelings.

Henson, K. T. "Teach Students Not Subjects." *School and Community,* 59:26, May 1973.

Discusses teacher's role in teaching students. Activities of each lesson must be structured and have variety of activity as well as content.

Hirschlein, Beulah M., Jones, John G. "Education of Affect: A Social Imperative." *College Student Survey,* Vol. 4:68-71, Winter 1970.

The article on the education of affect discusses the various deterrents to the development of affective learning experiences. It is now imperative educational institutions find strategies for dealing constructively with the attitudes, emotions, and feeings of individuals.

Hoffman, D. "Teaching Self-Understanding for Productive Living." *National Association of Secondary School Principals Bulletin,* 57:74-9, February 1973.

Attempts to show that it is possible to help young people modify their actions in the area of risk-taking behavior through stressing the consequences of motivation. Suggest questions teachers should be encouraging students to ask are "Who Am I?," "What Influences Me?," and "How Can I Control the Influences Upon Me?"

Hogenson, Dennis L. and Jean M. Nixon. "Why Not Psychology?" *Minnesota Journal of Education,* 48:25, November 1967.

Authors suggest courses in psychology be made available to elementary and junior high school students. The study of psychology would help students understand themselves better and would aid them in formulating their direction in life more intelligently. In elementary school, a psychology course could deal with learning, the defense mechanisms, and emotions. At the junior high school level, a course in psychology could deal with conditioning, psychological aspects of sex, parent-child relationships, and peer-group dynamics.

Howe, L. W. "Educating to Make a Difference." *Phi Delta Kappan,* 52:547-9, May 1971.

There are four natural growth stages in the process of self-definition: fantasizing, gaming, encountering, and actualizing. Each of these processes are explored and teachers are challenged to provide the opportunities, climate and encouragement which children and adolescents need to explore themselves and their relationship to the world.

Hubbard, G. "Our Most Precious Possession." *Instructor,* 83:12, April 1973.

Author believes education has disregarded those qualities that enable each individual to achieve and appreciate his potential for curiosity, emotional expressiveness, delight in personal achievement, and sense of belonging. Creative writing, arts and crafts, drama, dance, music and aesthetics deserve special attention at school.

Jensen, M. "Humanistic Education: An Overview of Supporting Data." *High School Journal,* 56:341-9. May 1973.

Defines humanistic education as a value commitment toward certain educational goals. Humanists seek to provide opportunity to come to grips with sense of identity, attend to "whole" child, be concerned with content which is relevant to student's own needs and interests, seek to foster a sense of personal effectiveness, and provide education for tomorrow. Traditional classrooms fail to meet humanistic goals. Piaget and others give convincing evidence for humanistic education. Society is cognizant of need for change and there is advanced technology to help, but institutions are difficult to change.

Jones, Loren S., Jones, Virginia. "Creating Opportunities for Individual Growth." *National Association of Secondary School Principals Bulletin,* 56:38-42, February 1972.

By raising pertinent questions about the process of humanization, the writers highlight several characteristics which principals can weigh in their pursuit of humanizing education.

Jones, R. M. "Role of Self-Knowledge in the Educative Process." *Harvard Educational Review.* 33:200-9, No. 2. Spring 1962.

This article looks at the psychological aspects of the classroom as normal rather than pathological. The author considers emotional interactions, usually ignored by teacher and student, in relation to the learning situation. Jones feels that awareness of psychological processes can lead to enhancement of learning. He underlines how important it is for the student to be free to draw on his personal resources in creative thought.

Jourard, Sidney, Combs, Arthur. "Conversation: Two Humanists." *Media and Methods,* 8:4:24-9, December 1971.

Rather than changing the education system to make it more humanistic, the authors advocate altering teachers' philosophies.

Katz, Richard. "A Solo-Survival Experience as Education for Personal Growth." *Educational Opportunity Forum* 1:38-53, Fall 1969.

Describes how a solo survival experience which is part of the Outward

Bound Program can lead to personal growth. Details aspects of one experience and author's reaction to it. Discusses key aspects: the solo and survival aspects, the path toward personal growth, characteristics of participants and underlying structure of the experience. Finally, transformation of the solo experience could make significant contributions to educational institutions.

Kelley, E. C. "Place of Affective Learning." *Educational Leadership,* 22:455-7, April 1965.

How a person feels is more important than what he knows. Education must learn how to plan for affective learning. Curriculum committees should ask a new set of questions about the individual and his reaction to school. Student should feel more positive about himself at the end of class than the beginning.

Klein, Thomas D. "Personal Growth in the Classroom: Dartmouth, Dixon, and Humanistic Psychology." *English Journal,* 59:235-243, February 1970.

The author concentrates his remarks on the teacher-student relationship, especially as it embodies the social, generational, racial, and political gaps that threaten to break down communication in the classroom. Continuing to teach subject matter with its typical disregard of the student's deepest concerns is educational suicide. It is the teacher and his relationship with the child (or adult) that is far more important today than any technique, method, curriculum, or technological innovation. That principle is what this article is about. The approaches the author discusses are based on John Dixon's paper, "Growth Through English," which was presented at the Dartmouth Seminar of 1966.

Kraft, Arthur. "Time Out." *Journal of School Psychology,* 8:291-295, Summer 1970.

Recommends that school psychologist conduct 1/2 hour discussions with entire classes with teacher present. In these sessions trust and acceptance of feelings and ideas are developed.

Kruger, Cynthia C. "The Social Sciences and the Humanistic Curriculum." *Social Studies,* 65:257-258, November 1974.

This article examines how the social sciences should provide the foundation upon which educators can modify old curricula to achieve a humanistic curriculum. Emphasis is placed upon the fact that social science disciplines have a common denominator of man which is readily adaptable to humanistic education.

Kurtz, Paul. "Why Moral Education?" *Humanist,* 32:5+. November-December 1972.

In delineating a program of moral education for the schools, the question must be asked whether a framework of moral education can be provided that is constructive and responsible and that does not simply impose a set of authoritarian values, yet gives a child some guidance.

Landsman, T. "Role of the Self-Concept in Learning Situations." *High School Journal*, 45:289-95, April 1962.

Centers around the effect of the self-concept upon learning, and how the learning experience rebounds upon the self-concept. Discusses the significance of "peak" experiences in the development of a "beautiful" person.

Liles, Jessee. "A Dilemma of Teaching Values to Young Children." *Contemporary Education*, 45:296-8, Summer 1974.

"How should one go about teaching values like honesty and responsibility? The solution to this dilemma must satisfy two criteria. First, the solution must permit teachers to utilize those nonrational affective domain strategies such as conditioning and modeling which are effective with young pupils. Second, the use of whatever non-rational technique is selected must not damage the subsequent ability of the pupil to achieve rational understanding of and assent to the value system he acquired as a youngster." Several affective domain strategies are given which satisfy these criteria.

Lippel, E. "Feelings are Important." *Childhood Education*, 42:212-15, December 1965.

A teacher at the University of Florida lab school, the author expresses her views on feelings in the classroom. A child's feelings must be considered, trusted and respected. Teachers should nurture feelings and accept negative feelings. Many times feelings are communicated nonverbally and teachers thus must be alert. Finally, teachers must be authentic adults with clearly visible feelings.

Long Barbara Ellis. "Where Do You Learn To Be People Now—In Schools?" *American Journal of Orthopsychiatry*, 39:291-93, March 1969.

Calls for a program of mental health education to be developed in the schools. Describes a program the author developed at the Webster College Experimental School and posits the argument that children can learn behavioral science.

McBride, A. "Values are Back in the Picture." *America*, 128:359-361, April 1973.

Father McBride notes that values are occupying a prominent position in education today. He cites the work of Sidney B. Simon who has popularized the values clarification movement. The author notes, however, that values clarification "games" do not answer such questions as, "Is it true or false, good or bad?" He feels that judgment and decision are central to value education and must follow value clarification. The article concludes with a discussion of values in Catholic religious and school education.

Mackey, James A. "Moral Insight in the Classroom." *Elementary School Journal,* 73:233-8, February 1973.

Describes a frame of reference which teachers will find useful in clarifying values and in value education.

Maslow, A. H. "Peak Experiences in Education and Art." *Theory Into Practice,* 10:149-53, June 1971.

Relates some of his peak experiences in life. Explores triggers for peak experiences. Says effective education in music, art, dancing, and rhythm can help one come closer to learning his identity, his values, and his alternatives than the so-called "core curriculum."

Matson, Hollis N. "Values: How and From Where?" *School Health Review,* 5:36-38, Jan./Feb. 1974.

Hollis gives a definition of value and then speaks about the sources of "Traditional values": survival, Greek rationalism, hedonism, and Judeo-Christian.

Michalak, Daniel A. "The Clarification of Values." *Improving College and University Teaching,* 18:100-01, Spring 1970.

Calls for a structure for clarifying values that can be used in man's quest for solving problems of science or society. There is a need to look more closely at the role of values and their clarification as one significant way of many for improving human relations and understanding. Knowledge without values is senseless. Understanding based on value clarification is priceless.

Miller, G. A. "Psychology as a Means of Promoting Human Welfare." *American Psychologist,* 24:1063–1075, November 1969.

Psychology has not provided the intellectual leadership needed in the search for new and better personal and social arrangements. Careful diagnosis and astute planning based on what we already know can often resolve problems which seem insurmountable. There is a need for psychological technologists who can apply our science to the personal and social problems of the general public. Competence motivation uses psychology to give people skills that will satisfy their urge to feel more effective.

Mixer, A. S. and Milson, J. L. "Teaching and the Self." *Clearing House,* 49: 346-50. February 1973.

Need of the child to be met with approval by the teacher are discussed. Learning that takes place within a child depends upon his self esteem. Teachers must recognize and develop the uniqueness of the students.

Moore, H. K. "The Advent of Psychology as a Unit in Junior High School Science." *Science Education,* 16:199-200, February 1932.

An early recommendation for the teaching of psychology in the junior high school. The need for psychology in the classroom results from the growing demand for character material based upon that phase of science which deals with motives and habits.

Muessig, R. H. "To Humanize Schooling." *Educational Leadership,* 30:34-60, October 1972.

Recommends some specific suggestions for humanizing education: 1) change curriculum to center on personal concerns, 2) emphasize commitment to global purpose, 3) encourage more variety, 4) plan student scheduled days and student-faculty lunches, 5) make available individualized funds for teachers, 6) create preschool retreats for teachers and students, 7) provide education for happiness and recreation, 8) keep school buildings open nights and Saturdays for credit and non-credit opportunities for community, 9) allow teachers to do what they are best at, 10) substitute letter grades with a conference and written comment, 11) follow-up procedures for teachers to keep in touch with former students, and 12) make a comprehensive study of rules and requirements.

Nyquist, E. G. "Making Education More Humanistic." *New York State Education,* 58:21-2, October 1970.

Humanistic education is the new goal of education. Education is humanistic when it emphasizes mankind, human values and making a life. In a technological and material oriented society, we must stress the importance of man, his values, his relationships to others and his ability to control his own destiny.

O'Banion, Terry. "Humanizing Education in the Community College." *Journal of Higher Education,* 42:657-668, November 1971.

Author calls upon community colleges to change their educational objectives from preparing students to fit industry to preparing them to encounter the extent and the excitement of what it means to be a human being. If the educational process is to be humanized, then a concern for human development must become a central focus of education. Several guidelines suggested by the author are: the student must become the subject matter; educational trappings, such as grades and testing programs, should be removed; and the difference between teacher and student should become less discernible. Education is a meeting between persons, so a better term for teacher would be human development facilitator.

Ohlsen, M. M. "Focus on Issues: Affective Education." *Contemporary Education,* 44:194, January 1973.

Discusses the November 1972 issue which discussed affective education. Gives pro and con arguments for making teachers responsible for it in the classroom.

Ojemann, Ralph H. "Education For Change." *Educational Forum,* 34:447-56, May 1970.

Educational institutions must educate their students to be prepared to face and cope with the many changes that are daily occurring in their world. With the benefit of such an education, they will be able to influence the course of these changes.

Ojemann, Ralph H. "Humanizing the School." *National Elementary Principal,* 50:62, 65, April 1971.

Discussions of "humanness" and "humaneness" often emphasize such human traits as compassion, sympathy, empathy, rationality, listening, individuality, and so forth. These take on meaning when one recognizes the basic tasks human life presents and the problems encountered in working them out. Each individual has a life to build. Being human means recognizing what those tasks are and developing strategies that stimulate the individual to realize his potential and others to realize theirs.

Ojemann, Ralph H. "Self-Guidance and The Use of Prepared Lists of Objectives." *Elementary School Journal,* 73:269-278, February 1973.

Suggests that the school considers the familiar lists of objectives in education as tools or means toward the development of the pupil's "socialized" self-guidance.

Ojemann, Ralph H. "Some New Perspectives in Child Development." *Theory Into Practice,* 8:192-7, June 1969.

In this article Ojemann calls upon the schools to provide opportunities for young people to examine critically their ways of living and to develop a conception of a plan and purpose for their life.

Ojemann, Ralph H. "Who Selects the Objectives For Learning—And Why?" *Elementary School Journal,* 5:262-273, February 1971.

Four questions need to be asked in selecting decisionmakers in the area of learning objectives: 1) To what extent has the individual or the group clarified for themselves the life goals or life purposes of the learners? 2) To what extent are they aware of the potentials of the learner? 3) To what extent are they aware of the role of scholarly research and analysis in providing knowledge about the long-term consequences for the learner of alternative objectives? 4) To what extent are they emotionally free and motivated to use the findings of such scholarly analysis of the task?

Palomares, Uvaldo H. "Nuestros Sentimentos Son Iguales, La Diferencia Es En La Experiencia." *Personnel and Guidance Journal,* 50:137-144, October 1971.

The author concludes that counselors may be the prime cause of miscommunication and prejudicial evaluation in relations with persons from divergent racial and ethnic groups. Counselors must recognize and value the ethnicity of other persons if they are to foster an open, trusting, and productive counseling relationship with them.

Paschal, B. J. "Values as Basic in Education." *School and Society,* No. 2302. pp. 77–8, chapter 96. February 1968.

Paschal calls for a new emphasis on the distinction between education and indoctrination. A child must have the opportunity to question what he prizes, what he should prize, and what the alternatives are in a permissive secure atmosphere in which he is free from having to cling to his values lest he be caught defenseless in the middle of a crisis.

Patterson, F. "How Can Men Become Human?" *Teachers College Record,* See *Record,* 67:25-9, January 1966.

Describes problems of technology, sociology, and urban living in an uncertain present and future. Describes how education must plan for future and meet those needs now. Needs are 1) concept of self as individual living healthy and free, 2) concept of individual as group member, 3) continual reeducation of perception, 4) communication with a minimum of distortion, 5) flexible approach to problem solving and making responsible individual choice.

Peck, Robert F. "Why Should We Teach Elementary School Children About the Principles of Human Behavior?" *Journal of School Psychology,* 5:235-236, Spring 1967.

The author contends that it would be very beneficial to society to include a study of the principles of human behavior in the elementary school curriculum. Attitudes and habits in adults are extremely hard to change, but in the child they are easy to modify. Therefore, teaching children to understand the causes of behavior will improve that child's ability to get along with ohers. Behavioral science instruction in the classroom will provide an intellectual basis for rational judgment about people and rational self-control. Consequently, it will serve to increase the vocational efficiency and stability of the adult population.

Primack, R. "Accountability For The Humanists." *Phi Delta Kappan,* 52:620-1, June 1971.

Develops guidelines whereby humanists can be accountable: 1) must develop techniques to the point where those who profess humanism will function better, 2) must develop clearly defined philosophy to verify assumptions, 3) should be able to specify clear-cut patterns of behavior, 4) must act on principle that one cannot effectively segment one's life, 5) must use intelligence, scholarship and research, 6) must be cautious it does not become rigid ideology, 7) must not abandon all reasonable levels of assured competence, 8) requires a wider sense of community, 9) must learn how better to open channels of expression, 10) must be sensitive to great issues of the day.

Rice, G. "Exploring Feelings." *Instructor,* 82:39, March 1973.
  Makes suggestions for classroom teachers about how they can make their students become more aware of their feelings via various activities.

Roen, Sheldon. "Behavioral Studies as a Curriculum Subject." *Teachers College Record,* 68:541–550, April 1967.
  Explains why behavioral studies should be taught in the elementary school, and gives a summary of specimen lessons.

Roen, Sheldon. "The Behavioral Sciences in the Primary Grades." *American Psychologist,* 20:430–32, June 1965.
  An experience has been presented which argues that the behavioral sciences have become an important field of knowledge possessing interesting, useful learning for children and society. Should be taught as an elementary school subject.
  Author states that "the temper of the times makes it extremely likely that the behavioral sciences be taught in the lower grades." Children are naturally inquisitive about themselves, their social institutions, and their cultural environment. Including the behavioral sciences in the school curriculum can be justified because such a curriculum possesses an intrinsic interest for children and is useful to them and to society at large. To implement this program, the author suggests that universities should offer special graduate programs for teaching the behavior sciences in the lower grades.

Roen, Sheldon R. "Teaching The Behavioral Sciences in the Elementary Grades." *Journal of School Psychology,* 5:205–216, Spring 1967.
  Author advocates teaching of behavioral sciences in public schools. "To teach growing children about their development in the context of their environment would seem, in itself, to be a legitimate educational endeavor." Author briefly sketches historical development of contemporary education from Rousseau, John Dewey, Montessori, and Conant. Similarly, historical developments of behavioral science in education are traced from William James to the University of Iowa studies where research-minded psychologists first manifested an interest in teaching the behavioral sciences in the public schools. The author proposes that universities offer today special programs to qualified students who wish to pursue a career in teaching the behavioral sciences in the schools.

Roen Sheldon R. "Teaching the Behavioral Sciences to Children." *Bulletin of the Institute for Child Study Journal,* 29:21–31, Spring 1967.

Roseman. "School and Self-Realization." *Educational Theory,* 14:286-292, October 1964.

"Education for self-realization requires the awakening of the intelligence and the fostering of an integrated life." The school may contribute to growth by providing learning experiences which challenge the imagination.

Rubin, L. "Curriculum, Affect, and Humanism." *Educational Leadership,* 32: 10-13, October 1974.

Author begins with a clarification of the terms "affective" and "humanistic." He then delineates humanistic and affective differences and describes the virtues of affective and humanistic education. Finally he discusses the implications for the structuring of education in schools.

Ruth, L. "Way Things Shouldn't Be." *English Journal,* 62:817-9, May 1973.

States people are dehumanized by bureaucracy, regimentation, technology, and become "robopaths." Suggests antidote in group approaches to human interaction.

Samler, Joseph. "Basic Approaches to Mental Health: An Introduction." *Personnel and Guidance Journal,* 37:26–31, September 1958.

This article is an introduction to the contents, six mental health programs, which are described in succeeding issues. A rationale is offered for the presentation of articles dealing with preventative mental health.

Samples, R. "Science, A Human Enterprise." *Science Teacher,* 39:26-90, 1972.

Discusses "free inquiry" in science, growth of attitude that science is a human activity as is art or athletics. This is consistent with realization of capacities, potential, and aspiration in the context of exploration in science. Humanistic education adds self-realization to content and process in science education.

Sanford, Nevitt. "Education for Individual Development." *American Journal of Orthopsychiatry,* 38:858-868, October 1968.

"Education ought to be concerned with the development of personality characteristics such as flexibility, creativity, openness to experience. In this sense, the goals of education parallel those of psychiatry. This paper offers a theory of personality that enables speculation about how such development takes place, and analyzes the experience of a student whose intellectual work in college contributes to his development."

Saputs, Helen N. and Gill, Nancy L. "How Should Human Relations Be Taught?" *American Vocational Journal,* 47:38-39, April 1972.

Authors stress need for human relations course for vocational students to prepare them to get along with others on the job. The course should be structured around the students themselves. Examples of case problems are presented.

Schrag, F. "Learning What One Feels and Enlarging The Range of One's Feelings." *Educational Theory,* 22:382-94, Fall 1972.

Discovering what one feels and learning to feel are two tasks which ought to play a prominent part in an education of the emotions. The author justifies his view of these experiences as essentially educative rather than therapeutic.

Schulte, J. K. "Self-Centered Social Studies; Children Share Feelings." *Teacher,* 90:71-2, October 1972.

Teacher and class discussed their feelings together and developed rapport. Some feelings discussed were fear, anger, self-consciousness, jealousy, and joy. Class felt it helped them to understand selves.

Scriven, Michael. "Student Values as Educational Objectives." *Social Science Education Consortium,* Publication 124, March 1966.

In this paper author briefly states views of present research in the field. Four problems author discusses are: 1) Can one justify trying to change student values at all? 2) Can one justify one particular set of values for one's students? 3) Can one demonstrate the occurrence of changes in student values due to the educational factor? 4) Can one measure student values in any important sense? Author contends that moral behavior should be taught in the schools. It can be taught by role-changing games, audio-visual material, and by direct field experience supplemented by discussions and interviews.

Sieferth, Berniece. "Religion and Morality." *Educational Horizons,* 3:99–108, Spring 1969.

Posits that although the schools are secular, they must teach morality. The fact that today's youth not only question the established society but reject it is evidence that there has been a failure to teach morality. There is need for a formulation of a code of moral and ethical behavior and for the preservation of the code from one generation to another for the sake of society.

Shattuck, J. Bruce. "Value Clarification from Science Teaching." *Science and Children,* 8:16–18, April 1971.

Discusses results of the revision in science education which took place after the launching of Sputnik I: children were doing more science and more experiments were being done in the classroom. Author contends that teachers need to make subject matter relevant and should attempt to illuminate a student's value structure. Places scientific questions into three categories: fact level, concept or generalization level, and values level. Calls for utilization of value-clarifying questions to help students rely upon their own abilities to consider questions.

Simon, S. B. "Pushing for Passion." *Nation's Schools,* 89:49-52, February, 1972.

Illustrates ways in which schools need to recognize strong emotions and to help children accept them as part of our humanity. Discusses socialization roles of men and women and the school's part in this.

Skaggs, E. B. "Psychological Studies in Grades and High School." *School and Society,* 46:598-599, October 1937.

An early plea by author for need to include psychology, or the study of human nature, into the school curricula. He cites lack of textbooks and lack of skilled teachers as obstacles standing in the way of including psychology in the grades and high schools. However, author feels these obstacles can easily be overcome once there is a demand for them by educational directors.

Smith, Robert R. "Personal and Social Values." *Educational Leadership,* 21: 483–486, May 1964.

Education has centered too narrowly on the formal academic curriculum, achievement standards, school management, provisions of facilities and the like. It has failed to devote needed attention to the storm clouds gathering in the personal-social value dimensions of young people's lives. Education needs to hold and extend the major gains we have made in shaking down the curriculum with new knowledge and innovation in techniques.

Sprinthall, N. A. "Humanism: New Bag of Virtues for Guidance." *Personnel and Guidance Journal,* 50:349-56, January 1972.

Discusses need for guidance programs in graduate schools to develop an adequate basis in theory: guidance in need of guidance. There is a growing consensus that concepts of humanistic education and human relations skills are the goals and objectives for guidance. A developmental framework of human values needs to be defined. Gives a current example from a program in psychological education (Mosher & Sprinthall, 1970). Guidance could take leadership in preparing teachers for personal growth.

Stanford, Barbara Dodds. "Needed: Human Relations Training." *School and Community,* 57:6-7, December 1970.

Author briefly states need for human relations training program for children as well as teachers. Children need help in developing healthy attitudes toward themselves and others. Teacher trainees need help in learning to handle and overcome harmful attitudes, such as race and class prejudice. Educators and psychologists should begin studies to determine the most efficient means of teaching human relations.

Stanford, Gene. "Sensitivity Education and the Curriculum." *Educational Leadership,* 28:245-249, December 1970.

Author stresses need for learning in the affective domain through the careful integration of sensitivity education with the existing curriculum. The affective and cognitive domains are inseparably interrelated. To support this view, several recent experiments testifying to the success of combining sensitivity education with subject matter are discussed. They are the pilot project to explore ways to adapt approaches in the affective domain to the school curriculum, the Human Relations Education Project of Western New

York and the author's experimental English classes in St. Louis during the school year 1969–1970.

Sterling, M. McMurrin. "What Tasks for the Schools?" *Saturday Review,* 50: 41, January 14, 1967.

Points up the need for development of aims and purposes in national education. Need for a full commitment of our intellectual, moral and spiritual resources to preserve the distinctive personal quality of life of a free people.

Stewart, C. E. "Human Interaction: A Source of Affective Learnings." *Educational Leadership,* 22:487-91, April 1965.

Studies show disadvantaged children have negative attitudes toward school. Teacher leadership is essential in changing attitudes. School-wide approaches are promising. Disadvantaged need technical competence and values required to direct it. School and community must participate.

Taft, Jessie. "The Relation of the School to the Mental Health of the Average Child." *Mental Hygiene,* 7:673-687, October 1923.

Author points out how important a child's emotional adjustment to school, teacher and classmates is for that child's ability to learn. Unfortunately, there were at the time this paper was written two obstacles to the development of an attitude in the teacher that would promote mental health in the child. These were lack of knowledge and experience in the principles of mental hygiene and conflict between teaching for subject content and teaching the child as a whole person whereby he could most successfully develop in the school environment. Therefore, schools and teachers should be helped to see that their vital responsibility to education includes the child's mental growth and adjustment.

Tageson, Carroll W. "Humanistic Education." *Counselling and Values,* Vol. 17: 95–96, Winter 1973.

When administrators and teachers alike mutually search out ways to make their schools more person-centered, schooling then becomes the humane experience it ought to be. All the available resources can be brought to bear in the service of the student's self-actualization, the development of his unique potential. This is an essential part of humanistic education.

Thal, H. M., and Holcombe, M. "Value clarification." *American Vocational Journal,* 48:25-29, December 1973.

Thal and Holcombe advocate the use of values clarification as an important component of any vocational educational program. The authors note that students are faced with many areas of conflict and confusion. They feel that values clarification helps students recognize and define their own values and to see values in relation to others. The more relaxed atmosphere of a vocational classroom provides a natural setting for the inclusion of values clarification along with the other elements of the regular vocational education program. The authors note that one positive result from such an approach is the spark of motivation provided to previously apathetic students. Several examples of classroom strategies are given for the interested reader.

Van Gorder, Edwin and Kermerer, Frank R. "Values and Decision-Making: Helping Students Achieve Self-Actualization." *Independent School Bulletin,* 32:26-31, October 1972.

Describes method by which schools can help students realize their own self-actualization through graduated processes of decision making.

Weiser, Margaret G. "Teaching and the New Morality." *Childhood Education,* 46:234-238, February 1970.

The author describes the new morality as the duty of the teacher to treat each student as an individual with feelings. "Teaching is a matter of human interactions, of inter-personal communication of subjective as well as objective relationships. One teacher can open the hearts and minds of children, can instill a feeling of true worth and human dignity. Acceptance of the thesis that the fundamental basis of teaching is a relationship between two persons would result in overwhelming changes in our classrooms and schools."

West, Earle H. "The Affective Domain." *Journal of Negro Education,* 38:91-93, Spring 1969.

Given the pressing problems of race and poverty, the author states that "it is evident that we need the explicit setting of goals in the affective domain and the explicit development of ways to achieve them. Objectives in the affective domain should be concerned with the study of feelings, emotions, commitments, and appreciations. An adequate conception of the role of public education must include efforts to change attitudes especially those attitudes related to critical social problems."

Winthrop, Henry. "Can We Educate for a Sense of Value?" *Journal of Humanistic Psychology,* 1:35-47, 1961.

Author's plea is to bring human values into the curriculum. One approach would be to develop programs of integrated education not restricted only to the synthesis of information and skills about understanding and problem-solving, but which also take the development of consciousness of value in all its ramifications as a major objective. Author states problem that the intellectual emphasis in education has provided no techniques for imparting a sense of felt value and there has been little interest in examining values conceptually. Author feels these trends must be reversed, and that educational leaders must now rise to the challenge of educating the citizen to the fullest meaning of a sense of value.

Yamamoto, Kaoru. "Humanization of College Teaching." *Teachers College Record,* 73:585-594, May 1972.

Author regards teaching as a serious human enterprise, and as such meriting a concentrated study of its own. Various disciplines are primarily concerned with their own explorations and not with the teaching of those disciplines. Education should become a discipline of disciplines which studies logical and psychological structures and their interrelationships. Teachers should pride themselves on wisdom, vision, and compassion rather than information, rigor and detachment.

### III. Chapters in Books and Reports; Articles in Encyclopedias

Atkins, Victor and Solomon, Leonard. "A Conversation About Affective Learning: A Frontier Between Education and Psychotherapy." To appear as a chapter in *A Study of Education* edited by Paul Nash. Wiley Publications.

The participants in this dialogue first address themselves to the central focus of affective education and three different identifiable emphasis: Feelings Growing out of Curriculum, Feelings in the Service of the Learning Climate, and Feelings Become Curriculum. Next they examine how these three emphases influence teaching strategies. A crucial question which they address is "Are the teachers equipped to deal with treating feelings as a separate part of the curriculum?" The authors point out some techniques that teachers can adopt from psychotherapeutic theory and practice. They would like to see teachers able to take account of the affective dimension of the life in the children with whom they work. This article is important for the questions it raises as well as for its discussion of the realm of affective education.

### IV. Whole Issues

Bybee, R. W. and Welch, I. D. "Third Force: Humanistic Psychology and Science Education." *Science Teacher.* 39:18-22, November 1972.

Teaching science humanistically 1) starts with the teacher examining his own attitudes, beliefs, values, 2) means creating conditions that emphasize maximum development, 3) deals openly with attitudes and values, 4) requires the teacher to understand that concepts of self are important, 5) gives emphasis to personal meaning, 6) gives emphasis to the ends of science as well as the means. New emphasis in science education is on the processes and products of science as they affect the individual and society.

### V. Reports

ED 022829

Appell, Clara and Appell, Morey. *More Tender Hearts.* 1965.

Personal sensitivity and self-understanding are attributes which are very important for those who would teach the disadvantaged. "Sensitivity training" is recommended for self-discovery and self-actualization. Through such training the teacher can foster a climate in which a disadvantaged child can feel "valued, wanted, and worthy." Sensitivity training in teacher education classes may use such approaches as circle seating for discussions, minimal use of structured lectures and assigned readings, and inclusion of films, resource persons, and role playing in the course. An understanding of the nature of prejudice is important for development of accepting attitudes. Creative expression may also be used in sensitivity training.

ED 059935

Byrne, T. C. *The Role of the Social Studies in Public Education.* Ontario Institute for Studies in Education, Toronto.

This paper was prepared for a social studies curriculum conference in Alberta in June, 1967. It provides a point of view on curriculum building which could be useful in establishing a national service in this field. The basic assumption is that the social studies should in some measure change the behavior of the students. Since values held by an individual or group are powerful determinants of behavior, the social studies teacher must be concerned with values and value systems. The curriculum should be designed around student needs and interests to generate relevancy, rather than reflect the dictates of the discipline. Knowledge is essential but if outcomes are not so much what a student knows but how he behaves in certain situations, content becomes not the end but the means. Students who have been exposed to several years of social studies should exemplify the following behaviors: 1) examine social issues critically, 2) question assumptions, 3) be suspicious of actions that limit the rights of others, 4) identify and reject prejudice, and 5) determine reliability of information sources. When the social studies program accomplishes some of these purposes, it has justified its role. The success of such curriculum design resides with the teacher who is broadly educated within the social sciences.

ED 042731

Carr, William G., (ED.) *Values and the Curriculum.* A Report of the Fourth International Curriculum Conference. School for the 70's Auxiliary Series. June 1970.

This report is a synopsis of the conference, texts of papers delivered at the conference, and lists of participants. There are three headings for the papers: 1) "Behaving and Believing," 2) "Values and the Curriculum," and 3) "The Choices Before Us." The papers outline values implicit in the editorial systems of England, Canada, and the United States, the process by which an individual acquires values, and ways of modifying the curriculum to include implicit and explicit education in values.

ED 050464

Curtis, Thomas E. *What Is a Humanizing Curriculum?* Paper presented at American Association of School Administrator Annual Convention, Atlantic City, New Jersey. 1971.

This short paper discusses education which centers on the student. Four types of curricula are discussed. One type emphasizes humanities instruction while the other three see man as a social creature, a unique individual, and an introspective analyst.

ED 051064

National Association of Elementary School Principles. *The Elementary School: Humanizing? Dehumanizing?* Washington, D.C. 1971.

This report contains forty-one articles from 1969–70, issues of the *National Elementary Principal* devoted to the theme that the school as an institution must operate on and reflect human values.

ED 065388

Fraenkel, Jack R. *Values: Do We or Don't We Teach Them?* 1971.

"The key issue here is not whether values should be taught, but rather, the justification of certain values over others to be taught and the decision on how to teach them."

ED 002009

Heaton, Margaret M. *Feelings Are Facts.* National Conference on Christians and Jews. 1951.

Concern about feelings has always been important to the teacher. There are four main tasks for the teacher who wishes to promote better human relations in the classroom: diagnosing or understanding children's feelings, bringing feelings into the open, rearranging school and classroom situations, and direct teaching about feelings. Many examples of teaching techniques are given.

ED 024630

Johnson, John L. and Seagull, Arthur A. *Form and Function in the Affective Training of Teachers.* 1968.

All too often education professors fail to use the techniques they advocate: team teaching, programmed texts, and group process. Consultations with specially trained teachers of disturbed children revealed that teachers found it difficult to make explicit demands on colleagues or children, were unaware of their value as models, feared to generalize from past experience, saw no relationship between rules governing the behavior of normal children and that of disturbed children, and were fearful of negative criticism. It is vitally necessary that the form of teacher education be amended to follow its function. Teacher education must encourage creativity and experimentation and provide a model for flexible, dynamic, innovative action so that mistakes may be viewed as opportunities for growth and development.

ED 035072

Kelley, Earl C. *Humanizing The Education of Children: A Philosophical Statement.* Elementary, Kindergarten, and Nursery School Education. 1969.

This booklet contains short articles on humanizing the education of children to help elementary teachers focus on their main purpose in education —helping children to fully recognize their humanity.

ED 051053

Shaver, James P. *The Teacher in a Multivalue Society.* 1970.

"Given the general recognition that what we do is influenced as much or more by our value commitments as by our factual knowledge, it is ironic that social studies, the area of the curriculum supposedly focused on citizenship education, has paid so little attention to values.

## 2. BROAD, UNDERLYING THEORY

### I. Books

Allport, Gordon W. *Becoming; Basic Considerations for a Psychology of Personality.* New Haven: Yale University Press, 1955.

"Personality is far too complex a thing to be trussed up in a conceptual straight jacket. Starting with this conviction, the essay argues for conceptual open-mindedness and for a reasoned eclecticism. It also attempts to lay certain groundwork that is needed before an adequate psychology of personality can develop." Some topics discussed: the necessity of self concept; chance, opportunistic, and oriented becoming; motivation and tension; schemata of value; and structure of personality.

Bantock, G. H. *Education and Values: Essays in the Theory of Education.* London: Faber & Faber, 1965.

"These essays are intended as reminders that judgments about value are essential to the educator. The aim of education must be to help towards a satisfactory life experience at the level of consciousness implicit in the individual child." Some titles of the essays are: "What is Wrong With English Education?" "Freedom in Education," "Education and Society," and "Education, Social Justice and the Sociologists." Of interest to educators who wish to do some philosophical reading about educational values.

Bettleheim, B. *Love Is Not Enough: The Treatment of Emotionally Disturbed Children.* New York: Macmillan Co., 1950.

In this book Dr. Bettleheim reports on the day-to-day life at an institution for the treatment of emotionally disturbed children. By presenting the material in this way, he shows how the everyday activities of children can be used in a purposeful way, how they can be made carriers of personal relations and of the experience of mastering tasks that were previously avoided in which the child usually experienced defeat. He also gives a composite picture of how the emotional problems of children may be handled. Love is not enough to rear a child in today's world. Many additional things are needed to raise children successfully in our complex present day environment. Anyone who is concerned about the development of children who can successfully cope with our world will find this book filled with insights and ideas.

Bugental, James F. T. *Challenges of Humanistic Psychology.* New York: McGraw-Hill, 1967.

A collection of thirty-four articles on humanistic psychology, which illustrate humanistic studies of human experience, and explore the growthful encounters of psychotherapy and basic encounter groups and the immense storehouse of the humanities, including literature, philosophy, religion, the arts, and all man's varied efforts to understand and improve his own experience. The book is divided into six sections. These are: 1) The Nature and Task of Humanistic Psychology, 2) The Human Experience, 3) Research Areas and Methods, 4) Some Research Products, 5) The Growthful Encounter, and 6) Reunion of Psychology and the Humanities. Of general interest to psychologists, students, teachers, and the general public.

Buhler, Charlotte and Massarik, Fred (Eds.). *The Course of Human Life; A Study of Goals in the Humanistic Perspective.* New York: Springer Publishing, 1968.

"The book is focused on the interplay of the principal codeterminants of goal setting. Concern with the person's goal setting as a procedure contributing to his eventual fulfillment or failure represents the book's humanistic orientation." Twenty-four papers are presented. Four papers of interest are: 1) C. Buhler and A. Horner, "The Role of Education in the Goal-Setting Process." 2) R. Friedman and M. Wallace, "Vocational Choice and Life Goals." 3) W. McWhinney, "Role of the Small Group in Goal Development." 4) F. Massarik, "Goal Setting as Codetermined by Institutional and Class Factors."

Caplan, Gerald (Ed.). *Presention of Mental Disorders in Children: Initial Explorations.* New York: Basic Books, 1961.

A technical book of readings in child psychiatry, this book is concerned with the understanding of mental disorders in children. However, in the field of school mental health, three articles by Biber, Bower, and Ojemann are included.

Glass, John F., and Stande, John R., eds., *Humanistic Society: Today's Challenge to Sociology.* California: Goodyear Publishing Co., 1972.

The authors have an expressed interest in furthering a humanistic approach to the study of man and society through this collection of articles. "Part I . . . is concerned with humanistic views on the nature of man by psychologists and sociologists. Part II deals with the role of science and values in studying human behavior and the moral commitments of scientists and scholars. Part III introduces a variety of different approaches to humanistic sociology. And Part IV discusses some issues in the application of the social sciences to personal and social change, including the classic debate between Carl Rogers and B. F. Skinner on the control of human behavior."

Hamachek, Don E. (Ed.) *The Self in Growth, Teaching, and Learning; Selected Readings.* Englewood Cliffs: Prentice-Hall, 1965.

"This book represents an effort to bring together a collection of readings which focus specifically on the self as it is influenced by growth, teaching, learning, and perception. Also included are selections which reflect both the theoretical and philosophical undercurrents beneath its growth as a psychological frame of reference. The readings represent a wide variety of sources and emphases." Some papers dealing with education are: 1) J. Staines, "The Self-Picture as a Factor in the Classroom." 2) H. Davidson and G. Lang, "Children's Perceptions of their Teacher's Feelings Toward Them Related to Self-Perception, School Achievements, and Behavior." 3) C. Rogers, "Personal Thoughts on Teaching and Learning." 4) B. Borislow, "Self-Evaluation and Academic Achievement." This book is a useful tool in courses concerned with the training of teachers, counselors, and psychologists.

Jourard, Sidney M. *Disclosing Man to Himself.* New York: Van Nostrand Reinhold, 1968.

"A psychology which strives to enlarge man's grasp of his situation and his freedom is the direction taken by this thoughtful study. It treats the human being as an end to be fostered, not as a source of error in experiments or as a barrier to institutional control over human conduct. New dimensions for psychological research and new ways of performing as a psychotherapist are suggested. Psychology is pointed toward the service of all persons, rather than the control of the many by a few. Well-executed line drawings, clear summaries, and valuable charts, tables, and bibliographies supplement the discussion."

Jourard, Sidney M. *The Transparent Self.* New York: Van Nostrand, 1971.

"Shall I permit my fellow men to know me as I truly am, or shall I seek instead to remain an enigma, and be seen as someone I am not? Throughout history, Sidney M. Jourard maintains, man has chosen the road of concealment rather than 'openness,' a route that all too often results in sickness, misunderstanding, and alienation from self. In this enlarged and revised edition of *The Transparent Self,* Professor Jourard explores the implications of a new premise: man can attain health and fullest personal development only insofar as he gains courage to be himself with others and only when he finds goals that have meaning for him, goals which include the reshaping of society so that it is fit for all to live and grow in."

Matson, Floyd W. and Montagu, Ashley (Eds.) *The Human Dialogue: Perspectives on Communication.* New York: Free Press, 1967.

An anthology of forty-nine articles on a wide variety of current perspectives on communication in the major disciplines concerned with the subject. The articles are presented under the following topics: communication as science, communication as dialogue, person-to-person psychological approaches, democratic dialogue, modern persuasion—the rhetorics of mass society, symbolic interaction, culture as communication, and the philosophy of communication. Scholarly approach to the subject of communication in many disciplines.

Otto, H. and Mann, John. *Ways of Growth.* New York: Grossman, 1968.

This book is a collection of nineteen articles written by people who are part of the human potential movement. All seek to help the reader expand his own personal dimensions. There are several types of articles: personal expressions of an individual viewpoint, accounts of new methods requiring professional background and specialized training before they can be successfully applied, and approaches that the layman can directly apply to his own life for self study and development. Valuable for someone who wishes to know what is happening in the human potential movement.

Purkey, William Watson. *Self Concept and School Achievement.* New Jersey: Prentice-Hall, Inc., 1970.

There is a growing emphasis in education today on the student's subjective and personal evaluation of himself. First Dr. Purkey gives the reader an overview of theories about the self, its history and some important characteristics of the self. Next he explores the relationship between the self concept and academic achievement. After explaining how the self begins, how it develops in social interaction, and what happens to it under the impact of school, he suggests ways for the teacher to become a significant force in building positive and realistic self concepts in students. Particularly valuable for teachers who are trying to make what we know about the self concept become an important part of what goes on in schools.

Read, Donald A., and Simon, Sidney B., eds. *Humanistic Education Sourcebook.* New Jersey, Prentice-Hall, 1975.

What is humanistic education all about? In this timely and well-rounded collection of articles Simon and Read "touch on every aspect of the humanistic emphasis in student-teacher relationships." "The Interpersonal Relationship in the Facilitation of Learning" by Carl Rogers opens the book and is followed by a section on "Bringing Together Ideas and Feelings in Learning" by such contributors as Alfred Alschuler and Arthur W. Combs.

Arthur Jersild begins a series of articles on "The Teacher As Psychologist" and leads to a section entitled "Sensitivity Education: Problems and Promises." Also included are articles on human relations training and teaching with feeling. Finally there is a chapter on current techniques of humanistic education. Anyone who wishes to become better acquainted with humanistic education must have this book.

Rogers, Carl. *Freedom to Learn.* Ohio: Charles E. Merrill Publishing Co., 1969.

For Dr. Rogers there are several elements involved in experiential learning: it must have a quality of personal involvement, it must be self initiated, it must be pervasive, it must be evaluated by the student.

The purpose of this book is to help all who are involved in education find how learning can take place. In the first two sections of the book he gives teachers specific ways to experiment with their classes. In the third section he provides some of the conceptual basis for such experimentation. The fourth part develops the personal and philsophical bases for the whole approach. Finally, he offers the reader a program for bringing about self-directed change in an educational system, and the beginnings of the implementation of such a program. Excellent reading for anyone working toward making schools more humanizing.

## II. Magazines and Journals

Bruce, D. "Three Forces in Psychology and Their Ethical and Educational Implications: Third Force: Humanistic Psychology." *Educational Forum,* 30:282-5, March 1966.

Discusses diverse views of human nature as neutral, evil or good and the important ethical and educational implications of these views. States man is a highly educable creature and his development can be influenced by environmental conditions.

Chaney, R. and Passmore, J. L. "Affective Education: Implications for Group Process." *Contemporary Education,* 42:213-16. April 1971.

Evaluates the present crisis in education, lists qualities of the affective teacher and consequent implications for teacher training. From his analysis of objectives in teaching and learning, he builds a model for implementing affective education in the schools.

Combs, A. W. "Perceptual Views of the Adequate Personality." *Association for Supervision and Curriculum Development,* 50-64, 1962.

Four characteristics seem to underlie the behavior of a truly adequate person: 1) positive view of self, 2) identification with others, 3) openness to experience and acceptance, 4) a rich and available perceptual field. One learns a positive self concept from having been treated as though he is liked, wanted and accepted. Warmth and humanity come easily to people with a feeling of oneness with their fellows. The more secure the individual's self, the less he will feel threatened by events. To be an adequate person one must have a field of perceptions rich and extensive enough to provide understanding of the events in which he is enmeshed and available when he needs them. To produce adequate persons requires not that we do something entirely new and different, but that we all do more efficiently and effectively what some of us now do only sometimes and haphazardly.

Craig, Robert. "Lawrence Kohlberg and Moral Development: Some Reflections." *Educational Theory,* 24:121-9, Spring 1974.

In this paper the author presents L. Kohlberg's cognitive developmental theory, shows the implications of his theory for education, and analyzes his views philosophically.

Kohlberg, Lawrence. "A Developmental Approach to School Psychology." *School Psychology Digest,* 1:3-7, Summer 1972.

Discusses how school psychologists can assist schools in contributing to the development of all children rather than dealing only with those who are labeled as problems. Instead of a mental health and treatment model, a community mental health approach is recommended with stress placed on moral and psychological education within the classroom group. It is suggested that while moral education may have a negative connotation to school psychologists, they could be of great assistance to teachers who must and do act as moral educators. Brief examples are given of the cognitive developmental approach to moral development applied to classroom settings.

Kohlberg, Lawrence. "The Development of Children's Orientations Toward A Moral Order. I. Sequence in the Development of Moral Thought." *Vita Humana,* 6:11-33, 1963.

"The paper presents an overview of the author's findings with regard to a sequence of moral development. It is based on empirical data obtained mainly from boys aged 10, 13, and 16 in lengthy free interviews around hypothetical moral dilemmas."

Kohlberg, Lawrence. "Moral Development and the New Social Studies," *Social Education,* 37:369-375, May 1973.

First, he discusses ways in which the new social studies have worked out assumptions developed in Dewey. The new social studies, however, has neglected two central assumptions of the Deweyite canon: the psychological assumption of cognitive and moral stages and the philosophic recognition of ethical principles as defining the aims of social education. Kohlberg feels that these two themes have been elaborated in his work on moral stages. Finally he outlines how one can use the moral stages to further develop the new social studies programs.

*Learning,* 1:19, December 1972. "An Exchange of Opinion."

This article is a dialogue between Kohlberg and Simon as they explain their different ideas on morals and values education.

Rogers, Carl. "Characteristics of a Helping Relationship." *Personal Guidance Journal,* 37:6-16, September 1958.

A helping relationship might be defined as one in which one of the participants intends that there should come about, in one or both parties, more appreciation of, more expression of, more functional use of the latent inner resources of the individual. Includes a wide range of one to one relationships such as mother-child, physician-patient, teacher-pupil. It also includes some individual group relationships.

Rubin, Eli Z. "A Psycho-Educational Model for School Mental Health Planning." *Journal of School Health,* 40:489-493, November 1970.

"If school workers are to be effective in mental health planning, they must be able to recognize high-risk subjects early and introduce meaningful programs. School environmental conditions, teacher attitudes and the specific demands of learning bear a significant relationship to the production of maladjusted behavior. It follows from this that the interruption of this behavior and its alteration toward more effective functioning can fall within the province of the school and its methodology."

Samples, Robert. "The Intuitive Mode: Completing the Educational Process." *Media and Methods,* 11:24-27, May/June 1975.

Until recently we have overemphasized the rational aspects of learning to the exclusion of the intuitive. While we have defined a cognitive/affective functioning of the human mind, the meaning of these terms has shifted from process to product. To clear up confusion about these terms and begin again to think about process and not product we should perhaps replace these terms with the more accurate one of "rational/intuitive"—a distinction which is based upon research into the two hemispheres of the brain. In order to initiate a learning sequence that encourages the use of both cerebral hemispheres, we should seek to invest our teaching with ambiguity. By doing so we will create more synergic educational settings.

Samples, Robert E. "Value Prejudice: Toward a Personal Awareness." *Media and Methods,* 11:14-15, September 1974.

According to Samples, values are closely allied to prejudices. Both Sidney Simon and Lawrence Kohlberg have contributed much toward a renewal of the subject but have also brought a new element to values education: the affective/cognitive controversy. Samples focuses our attention on the intrinsic side of values and identifies three core personalities: authoritarian, dependency, and intrinsic. These three core personality postures indicate the places where people go in search of the value prejudices that guide their lives. Samples has developed an introspective, intrinsic approach to value prejudices which he calls "incounter" and gives several examples of techniques to help individuals engage in "incounter."

Smith, M. Brewster. "Mental Health Reconsidered: A Special Case of the Problem of Values in Psychology." *American Psychologist,* 16:299-306, May 1961.

Author attempts to conceptually clarify term "mental health." He treats term as a rubric or chapter heading under which fall a variety of evaluative concerns. He tries to show that such a view of the term may help to clear the ground for both practical and theoretical purposes."

Williams, Frank E. "Models for Encouraging Creativity in the Classroom by Integrating Cognitive-Affective Behaviors." *Educational Technology,* 12: 7-13, December 1969.

Develops and diagrams a three dimensional chart for the convergence of the affective and cognitive levels of learning.

Vander Velde, Philip B., and Kim, Hyung-Chan. "A Critique of Arthur Combs' Third Force Psychology. The Perceptual Field." *Western Carolina University Journal of Education,* 4:18-25, Fall, 1972.

Critically analyzes humanistic psychology in relation to new programs and ideas in teacher education. Personal analyses and observations are reported. It is concluded that Third Force Psychology is not an alternative to behavioristic and/or Freudian psychology. Its validity as a scientific undertaking is questioned because of the emotionally unclear terminologies.

### III. Chapters in Books and Reports; Articles in Encyclopedias

Allport, G. "The Mature Personality." *Pattern and Growth in Personality,* Chapter 12. New York: Holt, Rinehart and Winston, 1961. pp. 275-301.

In a volume which covers many aspects of personality including development, structure, assessment, and knowledge, Allport has written a succinct chapter on what is meant by a mature personality. He finds that there are six characteristics: an extended sense of self; an ability to relate warmly to others; possession of a fundamental emotional security and self-acceptance; a perceiving, thinking, and acting nature in accordance with outer reality; capability of self-objectivification, insight and humor; and living in harmony with a unifying philosophy of life. He would have us encourage the development of these potentialities in all six directions from childhood to the end of life. The whole book and particularly this chapter are important reading for those formulating theories of teaching and learning.

Bower, Eli M. "Three Rivers of Significance to Education" in Eli M. Bower and William G. Hollister (Eds.) *Behavioral Science Frontiers in Education.* New York: John Wiley & Sons, Inc. 1967. pp. 3-46.

In a penetrating essay, Bower describes in detail three rivers of significance to education: 1) Knowledge, qualities and quantity; 2) Public health concepts and methods: applications to human development; and 3) Competence in the use of symbols. The combined force of these three rivers is pointed squarely at the processes of education. We must create an educational system which will help develop effective ego-development of children.

Bower, Eli M. "The Confluence of the Three Rivers—Ego Processes," in Eli M. Bower and William G. Hollister (Eds.) *Behavioral Science Frontiers in Education.* New York: John Wiley & Sons, Inc., 1967, pp. 47-72.

The confluence of the three rivers of significance to education lies in the ego-processes. The ego processes have several functions. They act as mediators of knowledge, perform a binding function, test reality, and program specific ego-processes into educational experiences. They also have several dimensions: the differentiation-diffusion dimension, fidelity-distortion dimension, pacing-overloading dimension, expansion-constriction dimension, and the integration-fragmentation dimension.

Bower, Eli M. "Primary Prevention of Mental and Emotional Disorders: A Frame of Reference." *The Protection and Promotion of Mental Health in Schools* Lambert, N.M. (ed.). Bethesda, Maryland: National Institute of Mental Health, Revised 1965, pp. 1-9.

Author develops his conceptual framework for primary prevention of mental and emotional disorders and maintains that schools are one example of primary institutions for preventive action. Children may be helped in their emotional problems by managing and mediating their crises within the structure and role of the educational institution. Those in the field of school psychology must find the profession's identity and uniqueness in this institution's efforts to serve the health and educational needs of its children.

Kohlberg, Lawrence. "Moral Development." *International Encyclopedia of the Social Sciences.* New York: Crowell Collier and Macmillan, Inc., Vol. X. 1968. pp. 483-494.

Kohlberg writes an article which covers the following factors in moral development: internalization versus situational factors, some specific moral determinants, culture and cultural agents, major questions, stages of moral development, factors in development, and neurotic behavior. Extensive bibliography is appended.

Kohlberg, Lawrence. "Development of Moral Character and Moral Ideology." *Review of Child Development Research,* Hoffman, M. L. and Hoffman, L. W. (Eds.). Volume I, New York: Russell Sage Foundation, 1964, pp. 383-431.

In this chapter Kohlberg gives his views on the development of moral character. He considers the extent to which moral behavior is determined by moral character, the major interpretations of the nature of moral character, stages of moral development, guilt formation, the role of morality in children's personality functioning, and some implications of the foregoing for moral education.

McClelland, David C. "Values for Progress." *Education and the Development of Nations,* Burns, Hobert W. (Ed.). Syracuse: Syracuse University, 1963, pp. 60-78.

    Author explains one key factor of economic growth as people who value or want the "right things." It has become widely recognized that peoples' wants, desires, motives or values differ on the average from country to country or culture to culture and these differences are related to rate of economic growth. This paper examines human motivation and national achievement goals to promote economic growth and development.

Maslow, A. H. "Some Basic Propositions of a Growth and Self-Actualization Psychology." *Association for Supervision and Curriculum Development Yearbook,* 1962. 34-49.

    Gives basic propositions of "holistic-dynamic" psychology. States that we are in the middle of a change in the conception of man's capacities, potentialities and goals. The "new" psychology has arisen as a reaction against the limitations of behaviorism and associationism (Freudian psychoanalysis).

**V. Reports.**

ED 043577

Overly, Norman V. (Ed.) "The Unstudied Curriculum: Its Impact on Children." *Association for Curriculum and Supervision.* Washington, D.C., 1970.

    Booklet contains six papers which focus on the affective part of the curriculum—alterations in attitudes, motives, values and other psychological states related to the experience a child has in the classroom. Of particular interest are the following two articles: "The Impact of School Philosophy and Practice on Child Development" by Barbara Biber and Patricia Minuchin, and "The Moral Atmosphere of The School" by Lawrence Kohlberg.

Powers, John F. "The Implications of A. H. Maslow's Humanistic Ethics for Philosophy of Education." *Dissertation Abstracts International.* Vol. 33 (5-A), 2244. November 1972.

    Essentially this study shows that Maslow's ethics are a viable goal for American education.

ED 056934

Roberts, Thomas. *Beginning a Humanistic Normal Science: Developing Thoughts on Developmental Psychology and Moral Development.* North Illinois University, DeKalb College of Education, 1971.

    There are four purposes of this paper: 1) to give an example of how to begin to reformulate current intellectual interests in a humanistic scheme by using developmental psychology, 2) to contribute to a train of thought which emphasizes self development, 3) to construct a holistic framework for understanding man by closely interweaving the separate views of life, and 4) to humanistically ask what sort of cultures result in what sorts of children, and what sorts of society these children form when they mature.

Scriven, Michael. "Value Claims in the Social Sciences," *Social Science Education Consortium, Publication 123,* March 1966.

"The aim of this paper is to provide a sound understanding of the nature of value judgments and other claims about values, and to attack a number of common fallacies about the relationship of value judgments to factual and scientific claims. In particular, reasons will be given for the views that value judgments are inescapably involved in all the sciences, that in the social sciences moral value judgments are sometimes involved."

ED 069733

Wight, Albert R. *Affective Goals of Education.* Interstate Educational Resource Service Center. Salt Lake City, Utah, November 1971.

Describes affective domain in education with particular reference to goals and objectives.

ED 069734

Wight, Albert R. *Toward a Definition of Affect in Education.* Interstate Educational Resource Service Center. Salt Lake City, Utah. May 1972.

Develops a model for the expansion of educational objectives beyond the usual narrow focus on low-level cognitive abilities and the transmission of facts.

## 3. THEORY AND PRACTICE

### I. Books

Allensmith, W. and Goethals, G. W. *The Role of Schools in Mental Health.* New York: Basic Books, Inc., 1962.

This book is the seventh of a series of monographs to be published by the Joint Commission on Mental Illness and Health as part of a national mental health survey culminating in *Action for Mental Health,* the final report containing findings and recommendations for a national mental health program. This book was aimed at professionals as well as citizens without special training and attempts to answer the question of what schools should do about mental health. It includes a field study of selected school systems and colleges for potential trouble spots with a view toward preventative action. Another major part of the book report is a survey made of the bulk of the literature on the topic published after World War II. Their aim is to describe the range of practices being tried, to call attention to some paths that may merit exploration, and to spell out implications for health and education. A large bibliography and copies of questionnaires and statistical tables used are appended.

Alschuler, Alfred S., Tabor, Diane, and McIntyre, James. *Teaching Achievement Motivation Theory and Practice in Psychological Education.* Middletown, Connecticut. Education Ventures, Inc. 1971.

This book is an outgrowth of the Achievement Motivation Development Project at Harvard University Graduate School of Education. Achievement motivation is an area of psychological education in which each individual is encouraged to find his own unique way of satisfying his concern for excellence. Basically the book gives instructions for a teacher run workshop in which individuals can work through the process of arousing and internalizing achievement motivation. Many games and specific procedures are detailed along with ways to explore related questions. In addition, the book delineates ways for teachers to make their classroom a more motivating place and gives examples to illustrate ways to implement achievement motivation training in schools.

Andreas, Burton G. *Psychological Science and the Education Enterprise.* New York: John Wiley & Sons, 1968.

This provocative book focuses the attention of teachers on applying psychological principles of behavior to enrich and revitalize the educational enterprise. After asserting his belief in individualized instruction and the acquisition of learning and thinking processes as two goals of education, he discusses the relevance of psychology and analyzes the educational system. Next he focuses on motivation and goal attainment, sensory reception and response activation, and accomplishing associations automatically. Finally he outlines ways to fight against forgetting and promote potent process. This book should stimulate teachers to re-evaluate what they are doing in the classroom.

Association for Supervision and Curriculum Development. *Life Skills in School and Society.* Association for Supervision and Curriculum Development Year-Book, Washington, D.C. 1969.

An anthology of papers concerned with the development of human skills in the school curriculum. Four of the authors, within the framework of their very different approaches, hit hard at the matter of interpersonal relationships. "We get along together less well than we might, and the school must begin to pay as much attention to feelings as it has to facts." These papers are: Meade, "The Changing Society and its Schools;" Bettelheim, "Autonomy and Inner Freedom: Skills of Emotional Management;" MacKinnon, "The Courage To Be: Realizing Creative Potential;" and Seeley, "Some Skills of Being for Those in Service in Education" Of general interest to administrators and curriculum planners.

Aspy, David N. *Toward a Technology for Humanizing Education.* Champaign, Illinois: Research Press, 1972.

The author summarizes his extensive work over the last decade about enabling schools to humanize the educational process. The author describes the concepts, procedures, and techniques he has used to maximize learning in the classroom. In this context, he produces the results of the empirical research and the research tools which he utilizes both to explore his theories and to train his teachers and students. Written for educators, administrators and teachers. A handy sourcebook for new and more effective approaches to classroom teaching.

Bay, Angelo V. and Pine, Gerald J. *Expanding the Self: Personal Growth for Teachers.* Dubuque, Iowa: Wm. C. Brown Co., 1971.

Since teaching is a personal expression of the self, a healthy positive view of self—an expanded self—results in self-actualizing teaching. It is in response to and in relationships with a person that the student's personal growth occurs. Therapeutic experiences—human, vocational, religious, recreational—enable the teacher to become a person who can generate healthy personal growth and development in students. This book elucidates how the teacher can expand himself through therapeutic experiences in the four areas mentioned above, and it draws implications for teaching and learning. As the teacher moves toward becoming a psychologically whole person, he will be better able to create conditions in schools whereby students also can grow and become more fully functioning persons.

Beck, C. M., Crittenden, B. S., and Sullivan, E. V. (Eds.) *Moral Education; Interdisciplinary Approaches.* Toronto: University of Toronto Press, 1971.

This book is based on a 1968 conference on Moral Education under the sponsorship of The Ontario Institute for Studies in Education. Of particular interest to the subject of moral education in the public schools were the following three papers. 1) Kohlberg, "Stages of Moral Development as a Basis for Moral Education." Paper states that the development of moral reasoning is central to political and social studies education. The unit of effectiveness of education, in so far as it has social value, is the group rather than the individual. 2) Loubser, "The Contributions of Schools to Moral Development: A Working Paper in the Theory of Action." The author maintains that various aspects of the structure of schools are not conducive to moral development, but rather inhibit or retard it because schools are organized in ways that minimize participation and involvement, relying rather on regimentation as a means of education. 3) Oliver and Bane. "Moral Education: Is Reasoning Enough?" Authors are skeptical about using social studies curriculum for teaching moral education. Case materials were used for basis of class discussons, but clinical institutions hold that students see conversations more as a forum for combat or persuasion rather than as a context for the clarification of personal value premises upon which public policy issues are grounded. The book as a whole offers an excellent scholarly presentation on the topic of moral education. The introduction of the book by Beck and Sullivan offers a background overview of the topic in addition to summaries of the papers. Discussions on the topic by the contributors of the conference papers conclude the book.

Benne, K. D. and Muntyan, Bozidar (Eds.) *Human Relations in Curriculum Change.* New York: The Dryden Press, 1951.
   Although this book was written over twenty year ago, its research on human relations and group process in change is valuable today. There are several unique features about the book. The principles and concepts involved represent a fusion of resources from several social sciences and they involve the collaboration of social scientists and social practitioners, including educators, in their formulation and testing. The approach of the book is that of a *participant* rather than an observer of change and is based on a *democratic* value system. The book is divided into two main parts: conceptual tools for analyzing change situations and groups, and group methods in curriculum change. Filled with many accounts of techniques and principles in action, this book is especially pertinent to all who are involved in directing groups.

Boocock, Sarane S. and Schild, E. O. (Eds.) *Simulation Games in Learning.* Beverly Hills: Sage Publications, 1968.
   "This is a book about an educational innovation: games with simulated environments, or simulation games. These games have two major uses: one, as research tools for the study of the process simulated; and two, as teaching devices. It is with the latter function that the book is concerned. The book is a progress report on recent thinkings and findings in this area." Some chapters of interest are: 1) E. O. Schild, "Interaction in Games"; 2) S. S. Boocock, "An Experimental Study of the Learning Effects of Two Games With Simulated Environments"; 3) M. Imbar, "Individual and Group Effects on Enjoyment and Learning in a Game Simulating a Community Disaster." Of interest to teachers and behavioral scientists.

Borton, Terry, *Reach, Touch, and Teach.* New York: McGraw-Hill, 1970.
   This autobiographical account of how and why Borton began to work on a curriculum aimed at students' fundamental concerns is an excellent introduction to the field of humanistic education. He sees as a goal for affective education the ability to educate a person "in his own humanity, in his power to change his life by changing the processes he used to form himself." The author outlines many possible ways to teach process education and comments on various projects for humanistic education.

Bower, Eli M. and Hollister, William G. (Eds.) *Behavioral Science Frontiers in Education.* New York: John Wiley and Sons, 1967.

This book is a collection of articles about the relationship of the behavioral sciences to education. It is divided into two parts: 1) in Part One each author seeks not only to stretch conceptual horizons but also to herald a parade of new program possibilities, new ways to reintegrate and reinvigorate the "old marriage" of education and the behavioral sciences; and 2) in Part Two our attention is focused on the utilization and application of research and experience which will integrate "themes" worthy of public performance. The articles are written by leaders in the field and contain extensive documentation of ideas and bibliographies. This book is essential for anyone wishing to study humanistic education in depth.

Bower, Eli M. (Ed.) *Orthopsychiatry and Education.* Detroit: Wayne State University Press, 1971.

A collection of thirty papers originally appearing in the *American Journal of Orthopsychiatry* on the subject of schools and mental health. Papers presented fall under one of the following eight topics: 1) Education/General Theoretical Perspectives, 2) Education and the Preschool Child, 3) Curriculum Innovations, 4) Readings as a Significant School Skill, 5) Children with Learning and Emotional Problems, 6) Children with Retarded Intellectual Development, 7) Children of the Inner City, and 8) Higher Education. The editor introduces each of these eight areas as they appear in the book and briefly describes the contents of the articles appearing in each section. Excellent anthology of articles written by experts in the field. Recommended for administrators, educators, and teachers concerned with mental health in the schools.

Brown, George I. *Human Teaching For Human Learning.* New York: The Viking Press, 1971.

This book is derived from a report to the Ford Foundation on the Ford-Esalen Project in Affective Education. It focuses on confluent education or the integration of the affective and the cognitive domains of education. Many affective techniques, some of which are derived from Gestalt therapy, are described and given classroom applications. There are several detailed outlines of affective techniques used in high school and first grade as well as suggestions for ways in which to begin to innovate in schools. There is also a comprehensive bibliography.

Brown, George Isaac. *The Live Classroom.* New York: Viking Press, 1975.

"In the live classroom, the learning involves living. . . . The live classroom could be considered one or two steps beyond the open classroom [in that] confluent education requires an open teacher for the open classroom. This book is directed toward bringing more life and better learning into classrooms through confluence learning." This collection of articles shows how principles of Gestalt therapy can be applied to teaching and learning. The four main sections are as follows: (1) Gestalt: theory with practice; (2) the theory of confluent education; (3) the practice of confluent education; and (4) examples of lessons, units, and course outlines in confluent education. "Confluent education provides substance for both the open classroom and the alternative-school structure. It could be thought of as new meat for those new bones."

Carkhuff, Robert R. *Helping and Human Relations.* Vol. I, "Selection and Training." New York: Holt, Rinehart & Winston, Inc., 1969.

"This volume builds upon the empirical and experiential basis of evidence for effective helping and makes translations to both selection and training." Part One looks at the present state of affairs in the helping profession, emphasizing particularly the potential sources of effectiveness of both lay and professional helpers. Part Two gives a model for the development of psychological health and psychopathology and examines factors that influence the success of the treatment program. Part Three focuses on the development of procedures for selecting effective helpers while Part Four attends to the development of effective training procedures. Finally, Part Five presents a summary and overview and develops a model for a formula for effective selection and training. This volume should prove valuable not only to traditional helpers such as nurses, counselors, educators, psychiatrists, ministers, and lawyers, etc., but also to lay people concerned with effective helping.

Carkhuff, Robert R. *Helping and Human Relations.* Vol. II, "Practice and Research," New York: Holt, Rinehart & Winston, Inc., 1969.

This volume which is based on a great body of existing literature, concerns itself with practice and research. Part One introduces the literature on the present state of affairs in the treatment processes, including the results of the ongoing search for sources of efficacy in helping. Part Two elaborates effective modes of treatment, including operationalizations of the goals of the exploratory and emergent directionality phases of treatment as well as of the intermittent crises of therapy and life. The emphasis of Part Three is on some of the issues and problems involved in making systematic and enlightened inquiries into effective modes of training and treatment. The summary and overview contained in Part Four is devoted to some of the larger issues of life that are not easily summarized and operationalized in a primer for human relations. This volume contains much practical, useful help for the teacher.

Clarizio, Harvey F. (Ed.) *Mental Health and the Educative Process: Selected Readings.* Chicago: Rand McNally, 1969.

"This collection of readings addresses itself to the school's role in mental health. Basic to the theme of this collection is the notion that the teacher is the mainstay of the school mental health program." The editor includes fifty-five articles written within the last decade. Chapter headings include:

Mental Health and the Schools, Social and Emotional Aspects of Educational Adjustment, Group Aspects of Classroom Functioning, Mental Health of Teachers, and Intervention Procedures in the Schools. An excellent sourcebook of readings for those interested in current developments in the school mental health field.

Combs, A. W. (Ed.) *Perceiving, Behaving, Becoming.* Association for Supervision and Curriculum Development Yearbook, 1962. Washington, D.C.

This yearbook took as its task to explore the implications for education inherent in four definitions of the fully functioning or self-actualizing person. Four authors, Earl C. Kelley, Carl R. Rogers, Abraham H. Maslow, and Arthur W. Combs have written position papers outlining what they mean by a fully-functioning or self-actualized person. These papers were used as a focal point in working out implications for education in such areas as: motivation and growth of self; positive view of self; creativity and openness to experience; the feeling of identification; the adequate person is well-informed; convictions, beliefs, and values, dignity, integrity and autonomy; and the process of becoming.

D'Evelyn, Katherine E. *Developing Mentally Healthy Children.* American Association of Elementary, Kindergarten, Nursery Educators. NEA Center, Washington, D.C. 20036, 1970.

In response to the challenge to remediate the 80 percent of mental health problems of children caused by training or experience and difficulties in adjustment, the author has written this volume which outlines for the teachers of the young areas of involvement where they can be participants in providing a corrective emotional experience for at least a segment of these children.

After outlining the "musts for mental health and ego development," she proceeds to discuss the child as a class member, the expectations of teachers, interaction and involvement with others, development of self-discipline, importance of achievement, and the school as a positive force. This book is extremely valuable for teachers seeking to develop a curriculum which fosters mental health.

D'Evelyn, Katherine. *Meeting Children's Emotional Needs: A Guide for Teachers.* Englewood Cliffs, New Jersey: Prentice Hall, 1957.

The author has written this book to give teachers constructive assistance in meeting the emotional needs of children in the classroom. The first part discusses how the school can meet those needs. In the second section, she presents specific cases of disturbed children and suggests ways of dealing with their problems. Cooperation between school and home is stressed in the final part. This book emphasizes the interrelationship between good mental health and in so doing underscores the importance of emotional well-being in the educative process. A very practical book for teachers.

Dinkmeyer, Don C. *Child Development: The Emerging Self.* New Jersey: Prentice Hall, Inc., 1965.

*Child Development* provides a comprehensive survey of the child development area and implications for practical work with children in school or home, and presents many influential viewpoints in research, child study techniques, and theories in the field of child development.

The chapters focus on principles of development, learning, social development, emotional development, development of self-concept and intelligence and mental processes, motivation, personality, academic growth, and family life. Each chapter presents some significant research and ends with a brief discussion of the implications of the material for teachers and parents. In addition, there are long lists of background readings for each area. This well researched and documented book should be of special value in child development courses.

Dinkmeyer, Don and Dreikurs, Rudolf. *Encouraging Children to Learn: The Encouragement Process.* Englewood Cliffs: Prentice-Hall, 1963.

A basic reader about personality development in children and the use of encouragement to facilitate development in academic areas as well as in the personal-social areas. Chapter headings include: The Principles of Encouragement, Encouragement Techniques Adapted to Developmental Levels, and Encouragement in the Classroom Group. Of interest to teachers who want to gain deeper insight into the philosophy and techniques of the encouragement process in the classroom.

Dreikurs, Rudolph. *Psychology in the Classroom.* New York: Harper and Row, 1957.

Dreikurs believes that if teachers become familiar with psychological and group approaches, they can exert strong and effective influences on the child, for both the prevention and the correction of maladjustment. This book offers teachers training in psychological methods specifically applicable to the classroom. "Part I. presents the theoretical premises for the application of the psychological approach in the classroom. A specific concept of man underlies any educational philosophy. (His) is based on the philosophy of democracy, with its implied principle of human equality and on the socio-teleological approach of the psychology of Alfred Adler. In this frame of reference, man is recognized as a social being, his actions as purposive and directed toward a goal, his personality as a unique and indivisible entity. We are teleo-analytically oriented, concerned with the goals of the child's behavior and the means of changing goals when necessary." Part II consists of a discussion of selected reports on actual classroom situations in which children with problems were involved. Excellent for teachers who wish to find a clear-cut, sound method for helping children in the classroom.

Duggins, James. *Teaching Reading for Human Values in High School.* Ohio: Charles E. Merrill, 1972.

One of a series in humanistic education by Charles E. Merrill Co., this book is concerned with teaching human values in a high school reading program. Emphasizing a Rogerian outlook, it contains contributions by Nila Banton Smith, Mario Fantini, Louise Rosenblatt, Richard S. Alm and others. The book would probably interest the generalist rather than the reading scholar. Of particular interest is a chapter in bibliotherapy at the high school level.

Ecker, David W. "Affective Learning." *Encyclopedia of Education.* Vol. 1 pp. 113-120. Lee C. Deighton (Ed.) New York: Macmillan, 1971.

Presents a broad overview of the subject of affective learning. Covers the following topics: development of affective characteristics, taxonomy of educational objectives, cognitive theories of instruction, guided observation, psychological methods, and methods in the arts. Excellent overview of the current status of the subject. Includes an extensive bibliography.

Fairfield, Roy P. (Ed.) *Humanistic Frontiers in American Education.* Englewood Cliffs, New Jersey: Prentice-Hall, 1971.

A diverse range of views on what the frontiers of American education should be in humanistic ideologies in the classroom. Twenty-eight papers are presented. Each paper presents the view of the respective author. Among the papers presented are: 1) M. Fantini, "Relevance-Humanistic Education;" 2) R. Darcy, "Economic Education, Human Values, and the Quality of Life;" 3) O. Krash, "Several Humanisms and John Dewey;" 4) A. Lerner, "Black Studies: The Universities in Moral Crisis;" 5) A. Maslow, "Education, Art, and Peak Experiences;" 6) J. Jerome, "Toward an Ideal College;" 7) R. Fairfield, "A Teacher as Radical Humanist." A book of general interest to teachers and educators.

Glanz, Edward C. and Hayes, Robert W. *Groups in Guidance,* Second Edition. Boston: Allyn & Baron, Inc., 1967.

Although this book is probably of most benefit to a school counsellor, anyone who works with groups will find it valuable. After an introduction to the use of groups in guidance, Glanz and Hayes discuss the nature and formation of groups. Specific characteristics and group processes are elucidated and many suggestions for group techniques and activities are offered. Of particular interest to teachers are the following chapters: "Words and Meanings in Groups," "Problem Solving in Groups," "People and Tasks in Groups," "Student Activities," and "Articulation and Orientation." An excellent book for any one who wants to discover more about how to work with groups effectively.

Ginott, Haim. *Teacher and Child.* New York: Macmillan Co., 1972.

In this book Ginott offers tools and skills to deal with emotional problems in the classroom. Numerous anecdotes and classroom scenes are recounted to help teachers focus on congruent communication or words that fit feelings. This practical book helps teachers find positive ways to respond to children so that their self-worth and self-respect is not only unharmed but even increased.

Glasser, William. *Schools Without Failure.* New York: Harper & Row, 1969.

In this book, Glasser applies his theories of reality therapy to contemporary education. Believing that our present educational system is the main cause of school failure, Glasser outlines starting points for new directions in education based on increased involvement, relevance, and thinking. Glasser gives many specific ideas for changing the schools including daily group counseling sessions and a suggested grading system. Ideas are applicable to all educational levels.

Goodykoontz, Bess (Ed.) *Basic Human Values for Childhood Education.* Report of a Colloquy, October 16-18, 1972, at Childhood Education Center, Washington, D.C. Association for Childhood Education International, 1962.

"After identifying some of the pressures on children in American society today and pooling their knowledge of the effects, members of the Colloquy discussed possible outcomes if today's trends continue, and analyzed some of the basic human values which educators should bear in mind as they work with children. Following the Colloquy report, is a summary of the basic human values and some implications for action in the schools for young children." Among the topics under discussion were today's pressures on children, self-discipline, the effect of cultural deprivation, developmental opportunities for young children, the physical development of children, and early learning. Of some interest to teachers and educators.

Gordon, William J. J. *Synectics: The Development of Creative Capacity.* New York: Harper, 1961.

Synectics theory means the integration of diverse individuals into a problem-making, problem-solving group, using the preconscious psychological mechanism in man's creative activity. "This book is an interim report on the research of the Cambridge Synectics Group. It describes the evolution of the Synectics theory of creative process, the hypotheses underlying the theory, and the actual implementation of the theory in specific cases. Excerpts from tape recorded problem-solving sessions are included."

Gorman, Alfred H. *Teachers and Learners: The Interactive Process.* Boston, Allyn & Bacon, Inc., 1969.

As the author says, "this is a book for teachers who wish to improve that area of teaching that lies within the sphere of interactive behavior in the classroom." Written to be used in preservice and inservice teacher education programs, the author first presents a short overview of the past, present, and future of teaching and learning. He then discusses the theory underlying his approach to teaching, his concept of the nature of groups, ultimate goals in teaching, and specific objectives of his approach. The major part of the book concentrates on interaction exercises and reaction and evaluation instruments. This book is a must for anyone who works with groups, especially teachers.

Greenberg, Herbert M. *Teaching With Feeling; Compassion and Self Awareness in the Classroom Today.* New York: Macmillan, 1969.

The theme of this book is that within the teacher's emotional life are the forces that most powerfully affect the teaching process. Greenberg discusses learning and behavior problems of children, struggles of teachers learning to live with themselves and others, parental concerns, and responsibilities of those who direct and supervise the training and development of teachers. Always he relates these to the feelings of teachers. This provocative book will help teachers learn ways to deal with their feelings that will not be harmful to themselves, to children, and to parents.

Greer, Mary and Rubinstein, Bonnie. *Will The Real Teacher Please Stand Up?* California: Goodyear Publishing Co. Inc., 1972.

Calling their book "A Primer in Humanistic Education," the editors of this volume have creatively drawn together a collection of materials about affective education. This book is a stimulating introduction to such topics as students, teachers, groups, feelings, and ideas. Interspersed between the major articles are a wide variety of techniques to stimulate creative and affective thinking, feeling, and teaching in the classroom.

Gustafson, James M. and others. *Moral Education: Five Lectures,* Cambridge, Massachusetts: Harvard University Press, 1970.

Five renowned educators here examine problems of school and society as they relate to moral education. James Gustafson expresses the concern for responsibility for the acquiring of virtue by children. R. S. Peters looks at principles of morality and their effect on human activities. Laurence Kohlberg's outstanding essay explicates Plato's view of education for justice by using a Charlie Brown framework. Young radicalism and the intense moral crisis of the post war era receive the attention of Kenneth Kenniston. Finally, Bruno Bettleheim contributes "Moral Education." This timely collection is richly relevant for educators in all settings as they explore the goals of moral autonomy and accountability.

Hawley, Robert C. *Human Values in the Classroom.* Amherst, Mass.: Education Research Associates, 1973.

In this book "Hawley sets forth a basic approach to teaching and learning based on human needs and human values. Proceeding from the position that teaching human values is, in fact, equipping students with survival skills, Dr. Hawley delineates a sequence of teaching concerns which form a basis upon which to build classroom climate in which human beings can thrive and grow. Also included are many specific suggestions—teaching techniques and classroom procedures—which help to promote personal and social growth."

Heath, Douglas H. *Humanizing Schools.* New York: Hayden Book Company, Inc., 1971.

Based on his experience with predominately white suburban youth, the author discusses at length the growing alienation of youth and the changing times we live in. He then posits the goal of healthy maladjustment as a way of educating our youth for the future. He compellingly calls for humanistic schools and offers many avenues for schools to explore in their effort to provide a rich, affectively oriented curriculum which will be meaningful for students in their present and future growth.

Henderson, George and Bibens, Robert F. *Teachers Should Care: Social Persectives of Teaching.* New York: Harper and Row, 1970.

Henderson and Bibens meant this book to be a foundation upon which can be built a repertoire of useful knowledge and teaching techniques. The book deals with all aspects of teaching: the teachers, the students, parents, and the classroom situation. Of particular interest is its focus on such problems as the white teacher-black student problem, prejudices, and human relations in the classroom. Because it realistically and wisely discusses so many of the problems in classrooms today and attempts to formulate answers which are within the capability of the teacher, this book should be read by anyone who is preparing to enter teaching today.

Hih, William D. *Education as a Human Enterprise.* Worthington, Ohio: Charles A. Jones Publishing Co., 1973.

Intended as a textbook for beginning students in education, this book seeks to present a humanistic approach to education. It is the author's contention that the human model of education must be united with the technological model to find an educational model that will be relevant to all needs of the student. After outlining the principles of a humanistic educational philosophy, the author addresses himself to these questions: "What are the characteristics of people who have achieved their potentialities?" "What should the objectives of education be?" "What type of instructional process should be carried out to achieve those objectives?" "How should the school system be managed?" and, "What should be done to effect constructive educational change?"

Hunter, Elizabeth. *Encounter in the Classroom: New Ways of Teaching.* New York: Holt, Rinehart & Winston, Inc., 1972.

Hunter believes that meaningful change in education must involve a change in the process of teaching rather than merely structural or content change. In an age when students are clamoring for relevance, she offers this book of practical suggestions to provide involvement in the classroom. Intended for use in professional education courses and, with suitable modifications, in classrooms with children, this book gives techniques to facilitate personal and interpersonal effectiveness group behavior, teaching-learning behavior, classroom communication, and adult relationships within schools. This extremely readable, practical book provides much thought-provoking information for people seeking to restore meaningful relationships within the teaching-learning process.

Ivey, Allen E. *Microcounseling Innovations in Interviewing Training.* Illinois: Charles C. Thomas Publisher, 1971.

Microtraining attempts first to identify specific counselor behaviors and then to systematically train the counselor-candidate in these behaviors. It utilizes a "shaping" process involving immediate and concrete feedback. Ivey sets forth a definition of microcounseling and puts it into perspective. He discusses attending behavior, the component skills of microcounseling, and how to use it as a teaching tool. Finally, he describes the use of the technique in other settings, research implications, and microtraining as an open system. This book is helpful for anyone wishing to become more skillful in therapeutic relationships.

Johnson, David W. *Reaching Out: Interpersonal Effectiveness and Self-Actualization.* Englewood Cliffs, New Jersey: Prentice-Hall, 1972.

An excellent presentation on learning new interpersonal skills. Chapter headings reveal the scope of this work: self-disclosure, development and maintenance of trust, verbal expressions of feelings, non-verbal expression of feelings, acceptance of self and others, and constructive confrontation. Recommended for anyone interested in improving his interpersonal relations with others.

Jones, Richard M. *Fantasy and Feeling in Education.* New York: New York University Press, 1968.

Jones gives a perceptive critique of *Man: A Course of Study* developed by Jerome Bruner and the curriculum theory on which it was built. He focuses on the failure of the program to recognize the potential that the materials contain for fostering the emotional growth of children. To buttress his argument he draws heavily on the work of Erik Erikson and illustrates his criticisms with many examples taken from his own classroom observations. Finally, he makes specific recommendations for new approaches to affective education.

Joyce, Bruce R. *Strategies for Elementary Social Science Education.* Chicago:

Science Research Association, 1965.

Although this book is primarily designed to present materials and strategies for planning a social science curriculum in the elementary school, the author focuses attention on three goals which should direct such a curriculum. These are: Humanistic Education—social studies should help a child comprehend his experience and find meaning in life; Citizenship Education—each child must be prepared to participate in the dynamic life of his society; and Intellectual Education—each child needs to acquire analytic ideas and problem-solving tools. "The simple thesis of this book is that instruction in elementary social studies should be centered on the child's examination of his social world, that he should be helped to examine social topics in such a way that he progressively learns to apply—not merely memorize—the intellectual tools of the social sciences." An excellent guidebook and sourcebook for teachers in the elementary grades.

Kaplan, Louis. *Education and Mental Health.* 2nd ed. New York: Harper & Row, 1971.

"The basic theme of this book is that schools must educate for mental health so that as youngsters acquire knowledge they find an authentic human role for themselves. Part 1 describes the problems of adjustment in society, shows how these problems affect the schools, and outlines some of the efforts that have been made to prevent and treat maladjustments. Part 2 deals with biological and environmental influences on the development of mental health. Part 3 describes psychological factors in human development, including the forces that shape behavior and the symptoms of maladjustment. Part 4 makes practical application of these principles to the school setting. Part 5 is concerned with the human aspects of school administration and organization." The many references to research and the extensive bibliographies at the end of each part make this a valuable book for college courses in mental health or integrated courses dealing with the influences of the school on the growth and development of children.

King, Edith. W. *Educating Young Children . . . Sociological Interpretations.* Dubuque, Iowa: William C. Brown Co., Publishers, 1973.

This is a valuable book for teachers of pre-school and primary age children who are looking for theory and for practical ways to develop positive concepts of self and others. King focuses on the classroom as a social arena where children are stigmatized and often mistreated, and as a possible setting in which to educate the child to function in a world society. The numerous concrete implications for classroom practice and sources of classroom materials make it an excellent reference tool for teachers.

Kowitz, Gerald T. and Kowitz, Norma G. *Guidance in the Elementary Classroom.* New York: McGraw-Hill, 1959.

"This book was written to aid teachers who are interested in the philosophy of guidance and its practical relationships to mental hygiene, to child development, to teaching, and to learning. Throughout the book an attempt has been made to keep the daily classroom operation in mind. Two goals of the book are 1) to increase sensitivity in the teacher to the relationship of the child's personality to his behavior in the classroom and his structured activities, both academic and nonacademic, and 2) to discuss specific techniques for the teacher's use in helping children to meet and to solve their problems." Some chapter headings are: The Goals of Guidance, The Roles of Guidance and Teaching in Learning, Mental Hygiene, Collecting and Using Pupil Information, Understanding the Child's Behavior, and Providing Guidance Through Classroom Activities. Good presentation of the subject for both teachers and prospective teachers of the elementary grades.

Krathwohl, D. R., Bloom, B. and Masia, B. *Taxonomy of Educational Objectives. Handbook II: Affective Domain.* New York: David McKay, 1964.

The purpose of this book is to hold the affective domain's terms well enough in place to facilitate research and thinking on these problems. The authors found it difficult to structure the affective domain and profess to be less than satisfied with the results. "In Part I, Chapters 1 and 2 give the background of the project and indicate how and why it came to be. Chapter 3 describes the basis of classification (internalization) and the nature of the classification structure, and relates internalization to terms common to the field. Chapter 4 analyzes the relation of the affective to the cognitive domain. Chapter 5 describes how the affective-domain structure can be used to classify both objectives and test items, and it permits the reader to test himself on how well he can use the Taxonomy. Chapter 6 relates the affective domain to the contemporary views of curriculum, evaluation, and educational research and suggests some points for further exploration. Part II contains a complete and detailed description of the categories and subcategories of the affective domain and gives illustrative objectives and test items for each category." The appendices contain condensed versions of both the cognitive and affective domain. This book is a basic reference tool for anyone doing research in the affective domain.

Krumboltz, John D. and Krumboltz, Helen Brandhorst. *Changing Children's Behavior.* Englewood Cliffs, New Jersey: Prentice-Hall, 1972.

This book is designed for parents, teachers, camp counselors, social workers and all others interested in helping children learn more effective ways of behaving. Many principles of human behavior are described, and each principle is liberally illustrated with concrete examples based on actual happenings. The thirteen principles covered are 1) positive reinforcement, 2) modeling principle, 3) cueing principle, 4) discrimination, 5) substitution, 6) intermittent reinforcement, 7) satiation principle, 8) extinction principle, 9) incompatible alternative principle, 10) negative reinforcement, 11) avoidance, 12) fear reduction, and 13) successive approximation principle. Chapter headings are: strengthening existing behavior, developing new behavior, maintaining new behavior, stopping inappropriate behavior, modifying emotional responses, and changing your behavior. Book is aimed at the understanding of behavior problems of young children.

Lacey, Richard A. *Seeing With Feeling. Film in the Classroom.* Philadelphia: W. B. Saunders Co., 1972.

Lacey calls upon teachers to resist their tendency toward forced evaluation of a film. Instead he proposes the technique of the image sound-skim to focus the attention of the student upon the specifics of the film experience from which he can develop his own meaning of the film. He then offers many specific devices to help teachers and students express their feelings about the film. This book is an excellent introduction for teachers seeking to use film as parts of a curriculum of affect.

Lambert, Nadine M. *The Protection and Promotion of Mental Health in Schools.* Bethesda, Maryland: National Institute of Mental Health, Revised 1965. (Mental Health Monograph 5).

"The Annual Conference of the California Association of School Psychologists and Psychometrists, meeting in Los Angeles in March 1962, addressed itself to the role of education, from the twin standpoints of preventing learning and behavior disorders in young people and of building strengths through learning. The papers presented at the conference are published in this volume. They represent an effort to illustrate the essential role of the schools in the development of personality and the potential of educational institutions to assist in preventing learning and behavior problems in children." The contributors include Bower, Caplan, Ouggam, Hollister, Klein, Lambert, Sanford, and Schreiber. Excellent reading for educators in the study of the conceptual basis for prevention of mental and emotional disorders in children, and what role the school could play in this program.

Lane, Howard and Beauchamp, Mary. *Human Relations in Teaching: The Dynamics of Helping Children Grow.* New York: Prentice-Hall, 1955.

Fine easy-reading presentation on children as human beings and individuals with feelings and emotions, and the teacher's role in helping that child develop as a whole child. Chapter headings include On Becoming Human, Human Beings are Social, How Human Beings Learn, The Meaning of Social Health, Group Life is to Enhance Individual Dignity, Roles of Group Membership, and Using Group Discussion and Role Playing. Recommended for all elementary teachers who want a better understanding of what a child's world is all about. All facets of life are explored in this book.

Lederman, Janet. *Anger and the Rocking Chair: Gestalt Awareness with Children.* New York: Viking Press, 1969.

In a moving, poetic manner, Janet Lederman describes her work in the classroom with children who have been negatively affected by the educational system. Using principles of Gestalt Therapy, she attempts to increase an awareness of reality for her students, helping them to "get-in-touch" with the resources and strengths of the real self and to develop feelings of personal responsibility.

Lyon, Harold C. *Learning to Feel—Feeling to Learn.* Ohio: Charles Merrill, 1971.

This book is a good introduction for people who know little about the area of affective education. First the author presents a rationale for humanistic education and then he outlines briefly pioneering efforts in this field. He describes a wealth of humanistic education techniques for teachers to use although no attempt is made to coordinate them into one approach.

Mann, John. *Learning to be: The Education of Human Potential.* New York: The Free Press, Macmillan, 1972.

The purpose of this book is to describe a comprehensive alternative which draws from both traditional and progressive approaches and reaches toward an educational experience in which the goal is to teach the student how to understand, direct, and develop himself. The book is divided into three main parts: Part I spells out processes for educating human potential; Part II enumerates strategies for changing behavior; Part III is a scenario of what a day might be like at a school which attempted to build an Internal Curriculum. Several appendices focusing among other subjects on the study of behavioral strategies and the component strategies derived from behavior change methods nicely round out this stimulating book for teachers. Similar to *Human Teaching for Human Learning* by Brown, this book should provide much food for thought for educators.

Manning, Duane. *Toward a Humanistic Curriculum.* New York: Harper & Row, 1971.

The author presents a dynamic look at what humanizing education can mean in today's schools. For example, problem solving should be keyed to and directed at the real social problems that exist. He sees the school as an instrument of leadership in social change. A humanistic school will nurture and enlarge a healthy form of self-control and self-rule. The school can be used as a laboratory for social education. The social studies program should provide opportunities to help children experience social education in a realistic and guided setting. The entire thrust of this book is one of moving toward a more authentic and humane environment. Provides good reading on the subject for administrators and teachers.

Miles, Matthew and Charters, Jr., W. W. *Learning in Social Settings.* Boston, Massachusetts: Allyn and Bacon, 1970.

This is a revision of an earlier book entitled *Readings in the Social Psychology of Education* that attempted to bring together a wide range of empirical work by social psychologists involved in the study of educational settings. Both books are sponsored by the Society for the Psychological Study of Social Issues. The book is intended for use in a variety of educaton courses at the graduate and undergraduate level and by researchers who explore special problems of educational environments. Contents include collection of articles under the following titles: Educational Environments, Inside the Classroom, The Race Problem, Aspirations and the School, Educational Procedures, Education as Personal Change, College Consequences, The People Who Educate, and Changing the Schools. Includes an index of persons and subjects. Valuable as a reference work in the area of education.

Miles, Matthew B. *Learning to Work in Groups: A Program Guide for Educational Leaders.* New York: Teachers College, Columbia University, 1959.

"This book is written in the belief that teaching school personnel more about the skills of working together is a high-priority need. This book is an attempt to bring together what is now known about the practical problems of helping people learn better group behavior, and to apply this knowledge to the special and important case of American public education." The values and uses of role playing are discussed on pages 191–194. The book should be of interest to principals, teachers, and counselors.

Moustakas, Clark. *The Authentic Teacher: Sensitivity and Awareness in the Classroom.* Massachusetts: Howard A. Doyle Publishing Co., 1966.

In a book which describes and analyzes many classroom experiences of a variety of teachers, the author discusses how the teacher can be a more authentic, unique person in the classroom, "facilitate actualization of potentialities in himself and in children," and how creative capacities can be fostered by sensitive encounters and interactions in the classroom. After a discussion of authenticity or its opposite betrayal, and ways to create the authentic relationship, Moustakas discusses emotional education from kindergarten through high school showing successes and failures and reasons for these outcomes.

Moustakas, Clark E. and Perry, Cereta. *Learning to be Free.* New Jersey: Prentice-Hall, Inc., 1973.

The authors of this book have drawn a beautiful picture of what happens when an educational institute (Merrill-Palmer) becomes involved in a working relationship with a school and a community (The Williams School in Detroit and the Williams School Neighborhood Committee). In the first chapter Moustakas outlines his philosophy of education: education which leads to self-awareness and freedom with the concomitant values of commitment, involvement, and active participation. The rest of the book is an account of the working out of this philosophy in the school. Perry describes some self-awareness techniques and then participants give their reactions in a very moving chapter. Also included are descriptions of the various programs used in the school: mathematics, play therapy, and the DUSO program among others. Following this there is a discussion of the teacher-training program, the involvement of the community in the program, and ways of integrating classroom teachers into the program. This book gives a well-balanced picture from many points of view of what happens when educators and communities become involved together in schools and the educative process.

*National Special Media Institutes.* "The Affective Domain: a Resource Book for Media Specialists." Washington, D.C.: Gryphon House, 1972.

"This book is intended primarily for the instructional technologist who is involved in designing, developing, or reviewing instructional systems. Seven facets of human feelings, or affect, are presented by authors who have been engaged in the basic research and instructional applications of that particular approach." Some of the chapters presented are 1) Barber, "Human Relations Training and the Innovation Consultant," 2) McDonald and Kielsmeier, "Social Learning Theory and the Design of Instructional Systems," 3) Edwards and Porter, "Attitude Measurement."

Nyberg, David. *Tough and Tender Learning.* Palo Alto, California: National Press Books, 1971.

Nyberg's main interest is in the relationship established prior to and during the learning process. He would have students and teachers develop a relationship based on empathy and self-understanding. He emphasizes personal development within the framework of the school situation. Offers provocative ideas to teachers or prospective teachers.

Otto, Herbert A. *Group Methods to Actualize Human Potential: A Handbook.* 2nd limited ed., Beverly Hills, California: Holistic Press, 1970.

"This is a handbook for persons who have a background in conducting groups or who are interested in working with groups. The methods described here are of interest to group facilitators or group leaders from such diverse fields as psychology, counseling, psychiatry, education, and social work. The methods are experimental or expressive and have been widely used in basic encounter groups, sensitivity training, and in group therapy. They are a part of the growing edge of the human potentialities movement. Two purposes have been dominant in the design of the methods in this handbook: 1) to furnish a general framework useful in expanding awareness and understanding and which can serve to actualize potential; 2) to create an interpersonal environment characterized by deep caring, love and personal authenticity where open communication, confrontation and the sharing of feelings is encouraged."

Osborn, Alex F. *Applied Imagination: Principles and Procedure of Creative Thinking.* New York: Charles Scribner's Sons, 1953.

The purpose of this book is to present principles and procedures of creative thinking. It also gives workable methods which utilize what is known about the creative imagination. Extremely detailed and precise, this book provides a wealth of material for anyone who is concerned with the development of creative thinking.

Parnes, Sidney J. and Harding, H. F. *A Source Book of Creative Thinking.* New York: Scribners, 1962.

This is a collection of twenty-nine articles and seventy-five research summaries on creative thinking. It is divided into five sections: 1) creative education in the space age, 2) the creative process-philosophy and psychology of creativity, 3) creative imagination research into its identification and development, 4) operational procedures for creative problem-solving, and 5) case studies of educational programs for the deliberate development of creative problem-solving ability.

Patterson, C. H. *Humanistic Education.* New Jersey: Prentice-Hall, Inc., 1973.

Intended as a textbook for teacher education, this book deals primarily with two aspects of humanistic education: teaching subject matter in a more human way and educating the affective aspects of the student. This book gives a historical introduction to affective education, outlines goals for education of this nature, and then describes how to foster human teachers, teaching, and learning. Although pedantic, the author does build a framework for affective education and concludes with an excellant chapter on the humanistic education of humanistic teachers.

Prescott, Daniel Alfred. *Emotion and the Educative Process.* Washington, D.C.: American Council on Education, 1938.

An early exploratory study on the part played in education by all affective experiences. Feelings, emotions, and all attitudes with emotional components are factors which affect one's interpretation of life and consequently one's behavior. While the word "emotion" is given in the title because it occurred in the original request for a grant, the terms, "affective experience" or "affective factors" are substituted throughout the book because they describe more broadly the three aspects of experience that are studied. Some chapters of interest are: The Influence of Affective Factors Upon Learning, Affect and Education, Aspects of Education Needing Study.

Raths, Louis E. *Teaching for Learning.* Columbus Ohio: Merrill, 1969.

"In this volume the emphasis has been placed upon teaching which will help to meet the needs of the individual in our ever-changing dehumanized society. Accordingly, a set of teaching functions is presented which considers the student's emotional needs, the use of thinking processes, the diagnosis of learning difficulties, the clarification of human values, development of group power and morale, status within the group, and the relations between school and community."

Raths, Louis E. (and others). *Values and Teaching: Working with Values in the Classroom.* Ohio: Merrill, 1966.

Offers new insights into teaching values. After outlining a values theory, the authors describe in detail a value clarifying process and specific instructional strategies that have been designed to implement their values theory. Raths, et al, are more concerned with how students actually behave rather than how they say they behave, and the process a student uses to acquire a value rather than any particular value a student uses at a particular time or place. A synopsis of research that supports the value-clarifying process concludes the book.

Romey, William D. *Risk—Trust—Love. Learning in a Humane Environment.* Ohio: Charles E. Merrill Publishing Co., 1972.

Based on the assumptions that a student has much to contribute to his own learning and that the learning environment is rich in proportion to the number of alternatives for learning that it allows and the freedom of individual students to be doing different things at the same time, this book is a provocative inquiry into what is going on in schools today and the possibilities for introducing risk, trust, and love in a humane environment as a means of growth for the student. There are five basic sections. Chapter I is largely an autobiographical account of the influences important in the author's own learning. Chapter II gives some of his impressions based on a number of recent visits to elementary and secondary schools and identifies positive and negative factors. This chapter also describes some more ideal school situations that give hope for providing better alternatives in the future. Chapter III is a series of essays examining the various aspects of the teacher's role as a facilitator of learning. Chapter IV contains essays concerning the problems of creating open, student-center schools. Finally in Chapter V he describes his ideas for ideal school situations. These ideas draw together a number of things he has actually seen working and describes models that he is presently involved in implementing. This book has much to offer the beginning teacher as well as the veteran. Anyone who is concerned with making schools more humane would certainly find many stimulating ideas in this book.

Rubin, Louis J. *Facts and Feelings in the Classroom.* New York: Walker and Company, 1973.

This book is a somewhat disjointed collection of articles and author-editor comment designed to aid in the reforming of schools toward a more humanistic curriculum. The author comments on articles presented in the volume by Bloom, Eisner, Jones, Maslow, and others and then proceeds to outline changes which he feels can be initiated at once to provide a starting point for reform.

Rucker, W. Ray, Arnspiger, V. Clyde, and Broadbeck, Arthur J. *Human Values In Education.* Iowa: Kendall/Hunt Publishing Co., 1969.

This book takes the eight basic values set forth by Lasswell and applies them to eudcation. Contending that the teacher is directly involved in the valuing process in education, the authors address the following areas: (1) discovery of valuing in education, (2) the release of learning potential, (3) giving form to value thinking, and (4) contextual reconstruction of education. There are a multitude of ideas to help the reader apply the valuing process in education.

Schmuck, Richard A. and Schmuck, Patricia A. *Group Processes in the Classroom.* Iowa: William C. Brown, Co., 1971

This book appears as part of a series in education titled Issues and Innovation in Education. Designed for teachers who are involved in pre-service and inservice education, this book focuses on the "mediational model" of group processes. "The mediational model views the effects of a teacher's behavior as being mediated by classroom group processes and not as occurring in two-person units." Awareness of these mediating group processes will enable the teacher to effectively use them to aid the learning process. The book contains a discussion of basic concepts, group processes, leadership, attraction, norms, communication, cohesiveness, developmental stages, and organizational characteristics. The many instructional strategies included and the discussion itself should prove useful to anyone involved in work with groups.

Schmuck, Richard A., and Schmuck, Patricia A. *A Humanistic Psychology of Education.* Palo Alto, California: National Press, 1974.

In this book the authors focus on "what humanized schooling means, what humanized schools look and feel like, and, most important, how such schools can be created." Although it will probably most often be used in educational psychology courses, it can be read with benefit by individual educators, parents, students, and citizens interested in humanizing schools.

Seidman, Jerome M., (Ed.) *Educating for Mental Health: A Book of Readings.* New York: Crowell, 1963.

"Understanding the problems of children and helping them solve their problems more effectively" are the two major themes of this collection of fifty-six articles on mental health and education. "Part One deals with the socialization process and with concepts that broaden our understanding of mental health, teaching-learning processes, and human development. Part Two seeks to demonstrate the extent to which everyday classroom practices can aid the teacher in stimulating thinking and the learning of wholesome attitudes and behavior. Part Three aims to show how the efforts of parents and teachers can be made more effective when joined with school and community programs."

Shaftel, Fannie R. and Shaftel, George. *Role-playing for Social Values: Decision-making in the Social Studies.* New Jersey: Prentice-Hall, Inc., 1967.

One of the major concerns in education today is the inculcation of values. Fannie and George Shaftel have written an excellent book for teachers on the theory and method of utilizing role-playing or "reality practice" in the teaching of this important area. In the first part they discuss the theory and the necessity for "reality practice" in value education. They also present the process of role-playing, how to guide it, role theory, ways of leading into it, and other uses of role-playing. Part II contains materials for role-playing, stories which teach such concepts as individual integrity, group responsibility, self-acceptance, and managing one's feelings. These stories simulate problem situations a child is likely to meet and end with a dilemma to be solved by the class. Usually to solve the dilemma "the child must choose between a social value and a personal interest; between loyalty to the group and honesty, between winning dishonestly and losing honorably; between concern for a friend and protection of self; between fairness to another child and fear of ostracism."

Simon, Sidney B., and Kirschenbaum, Howard. *Readings in Values Clarification.* Minneapolis: Winston Press, 1973.

Values clarification is one approach to teaching a process of valuing. In the first section of the book Harmin, Simon, and Kirschenbaum among others present an overview of the values-clarification approach. Other perspectives are discussed as well. The next sections treat values clarification and school subjects, values in religious education, and values in the family. The last deals with other applications of values clarification. An annotated bibliography is appended.

Simpson, Bert K. *Becoming Aware of Values.* San Diego, California. Pennant Press, 1973.

The ideas in this book are an outgrowth of the valuing process originated by Dr. Harold Lasswell of Yale University and its adaptation to the field of education by Dr. W. Ray Rucker. Simpson sees valuing in terms of eight basic needs which are common to all men. These basic needs or values are developed in three-dimensional process: (1) to develop within ourselves each one of these basic need areas, (2) to participate in the sharing and shaping of these eight basic areas in the lives of others, (3) and to recognize the ways in which others influence the shaping and sharing of values within ourselves. The book discusses valuing, the principles and processes of valuing, and then offers materials and strategies for teachers interested in implementing this approach. This is a helpful book for teachers seeking new approaches and strategies.

Spolin, Viola. *Improvisation for the Theater: A Handbook of Teaching and Directing Techniques.* Illinois: Northwestern University Press, 1963.

In an attempt to help a child develop spontaneity and opportunities for integrating his intellectual with his emotional self, Viola Spolin has developed a series of theater games. Basically the book is divided into three parts. The first is concerned with the theory and foundations for teaching and directing theater, the second with an outline of workshop exercises, and the third with special comments on children in the theater and directing the formal play for the community theater. The main emphasis is on helping students to communicate non-verbally, that is, to show, not to tell, to feel free to respond spontaneously to problems under certain circumstances, and to develop their sensory equipment. Particularly valuable for those who are planning strategies to implement affective education.

Strang, Ruth and Morris, Glyn. *Guidance in the Classroom.* New York: Macmillan, 1964.

Covers the main points of guidance: Methods and Techniques of Guidance, Essentials of Guidance, Guidance Personnel and Program, Positive Procedures, Perplexing Problems, Guidance During the Preschool and Elementary School Years, and Guidance in the Secondary Schools. Reaffirms the principle that good teaching and guidance are inseparable. Excellent book for teachers.

Stratemeyer, Florence B.; Forkner, Hamden L.; McKim, Margaret G.; Passow, A. Harry. *Developing a Curriculum for Modern Living.* 2nd ed. revised and enlarged. New York: Teachers College, 1957.

"This volume is an attempt to look at the curriculum as a whole and in terms of a particular set of beliefs. It is focused upon a particular curriculum design and the ways in which this design may be put into practice. The purpose is to spell out, first, general principles of curriculum development that recognize the importance of relating individual needs to those of society, and, second, suggestions as to the implications of this relationship for each of the basic curriculum issues discussed in the book." Of general interest to teachers and administrators.

Strom, Robert D. and Torrance, E. Paul. *Education for Affective Achievement.* Chicago: Rand McNally & Co., 1973.

This book is a collection of articles by many authors grouped around the following themes: family and community, changing the school, and curriculum and learning. Issues that are dealt with cover a wide variety of topics such as mind-altering drugs, alienation, ethnic education, and achievement motivation.

Taba, Hilda; Brady, Elizabeth Hall; Robinson, John T.; Vickerey, William E. *Diagnosing Human Relations Needs.* Washington, D.C.: American Council on Education, 1951.

This book describes "several devices helpful in diagnosing gaps in social learning of children and adolescents introduced by their cultural backgrounds, their social relationships and patterns of belonging, and their feelings and concerns about their relationships with their families and peers. The six methods used for obtaining descriptive evidence which can be incorporated into instruction while being used for diagnosis were diaries, parent interviews, participation schedules, sociometric procedures, open questions, and teacher logs."

Taba, Hilda and Elkins, Deborah. *With Focus on Human Relations: A Story of an Eighth Grade.* Washington, D.C.: American Council on Education, 1950.

An eighth-grade teacher's account of how she personally came to know all the students in her class. She diagnosed her students' needs through sociometric questions designed to reveal the structure of pupil society in the classroom, through interviews with the students, as well as interviews with the parents. With this new information about her students, the teacher was able to pattern her class according to the interests and concerns of the students. A good book to read for all teachers who have a genuine interest in getting to know their students.

Tanner, Laurel N. and Lindgren, Henry Clay. *Classroom Teaching and Learning: A Mental Health Approach.* New York: Holt, Rinehart & Winston, 1971.

"It is the purpose of this volume to present new knowledge and research evidence from education and the behavioral sciences as a conceptual framework for preventing learning and behavior disorders in children, and for building strengths through learning. The authors have taken an ecological view of the school environment, identifying both positive and negative influences on learning and mental health." Chapter 1 takes a long-needed look at mental health in relation to personal and social competency. Chapter 2 examines the research on the relationship between the teacher's personality and pupil behavior. In Chapter 3 we are confronted by the perennial conflict over the curriculum and its significance for the present and future well-being of the learner. The development of the child is discussed in Chapters 4, 5, and 6, while factors that underlie children's behavior are the concern of Chapters 7 and 8. The effects of socioeconomic deprivation and segregation on school progress are discussed in Chapter 9, while Chapter 10 explores the relationship between evaluation, mental health, and learning. Chapters 11 through 14 are concerned with the parents' and teachers' attitudes and behaviors as they relate to the childrens' progress in school. Recommended for teachers and educators interested in the field of mental health for the schools.

Waetjen, Walter and Leeper, Robert R. (Eds.) *Learning and Mental Health in the*

*School.* Washington, D.C. Association for Supervision and Curriculum Development, National Education Association, 1966.

The authors of this book view mental health as a process which results in the competent person. Potentialities for influencing mental health exist in all of the classroom learning activities. The teacher must accept pupils' thoughts and feelings and help the pupils challenge the generalizations and concepts inherent in the curriculum. The contributors to this volume discuss theory and practice which will help to produce the competent person, one adept at learning, sensitive to his environment, compassionate to his fellow man, and can manage stress.

Weinberg, Carl, (Ed.) *Humanistic Foundations of Education.* Englewood Cliffs, New Jersey: Prentice-Hall, 1972.

A foundation reader in humanistic education for prospective teachers. There are nine articles presented; half are written by the editor of this book. The editor introduces each chapter with comments about what the article has to say in light of humanistic values. Each article is also preceded by a photograph of the author. For each of his articles, the editor takes a slightly different approach to the humanistic task. With sociology, he is concerned with application of scientific knowledge to human needs. With literature, he approaches humanism from the perspective of coming to know oneself and to grow through this knowledge. In guidance, he takes the clinical view of humanism, which is a perspective emphasizing mental health and how it is produced. Of interest to students and teachers who want to see what some university professors have to say about humanistic education and its relevance to students today.

Weinstein, Gerald and Fantini, Mario D. *Toward Humanistic Education: A Curriculum of Affect.* New York: Praeger Publishers, 1970.

Written as a report to the Ford Foundation about the status of their funded program entitled Elementary School Teaching Project, directors Fantini and Weinstein present an account of their project which was designed to develop a fundamental approach to education and relevant curriculum materials to meet the needs primarily of the disadvantaged student. Particularly addresses the affective domain of learning, elucidates a model for developing a curriculum of affect, and explains many concrete ways to implement this model in the classroom. Valuable as a starting point for anyone interested in this area of education.

Wilson, John; Williams, Norman; Sugarman, Barry. *Introduction to Moral Education.* Harmondsworth: Penguin Books, 1967.

An attempt to define and discuss the topic of moral education. Part I of the book is entitled, "What is Moral Education?" It includes Morality and Freedom—Intentions and Reasons, and Dispositions and Feelings, as well as problems in moral education. Part II is presented in two parts: "What the

Psychologist Has to Say," and "What the Sociologist Has to Say." The book is a philosophical overview of moral education.

## II. Magazines and Journals

Alschuler, Alfred and Thompson, Roy. "How to Increase Achievement Motivation." *Educational Opportunity Forum,* 1:95–108, Fall 1969.

Explains nature of "motivation" and in particular, achievement motivation. Procedures that will increase achievement motivation and other motives as well include the following: increasing the motive syndrome, goal setting, self study, and emotional supports. Discusses applications of achievement motivation training, for teachers, community leaders of minority groups and other people who are working to alleviate pressing social problems.

Alschuler, Alfred S. "Developing Achievement Motivation in Adolescents." *Education for Human Growth.* New Jersey: Educational Technology Publications. 1973.

Alfred Alschuler has identified educational tactics and strategies that will effectively increase achievement and has generalized these conclusions to other aspects of mental health education. In part one he gives a historical overview of the nature and origins of psychological education and achievement motivation. Part two presents research studies on achievement motivation training and offers solutions to the problems of training in the classroom. Part three describes his methods of working with schools as systems. This book is valuable for its insights into classrooms and school systems, for the questions it raises, for the solution it offers, and the implications drawn for the future of psychological education. Contains an extensive bibliography.

Alschuler, Alfred S. "Humanistic Education." *Educational Technology,* 10: 58–61, May 1970.

Describes the goals of humanistic education, a sequence of learning to follow in structuring humanistic education courses, and a 4-phased strategy to follow in effectively introducing humanistic education in a school.

Alschuler, Alfred S. and Ivey, Allen E. "Internalization: The Outcome of Psychological Education." *Personnel and Guidance Journal,* 51:607–610, May, 1973.

This article defines internalization as occurring "when a skill, idea, value, or motive has been voluntarily incorporated into a person's repertoire to such an extent that the behavior has become the person's own." The authors present ways to measure internalization and the steps to internalization. By using these measures, psychological educators and practicing counselors can involve themselves in meaningful evaluation.

Alschuler, Alfred. "The Origins and Nature of Psychological Education." *Educational Opportunity Forum,* 1:1–16, Fall 1969.

First explains ideologies and origins of psychological education by reviewing the work of Kraepelin and Freud and other more recent developments in the treatment of mental illness. Four eupsychian goals of humanistic education are: develop a constructive dialogue with one's own fantasy life, engage in nonverbal exercises, develop and explore one's emotional responses to the world, and live intensely in the "here and now." Clarifies differences and similarities between these courses and existing academic and vocational courses.

*American Journal of Orthopsychiatry.* Digests of Papers, Forty-Sixth Annual Meeting, 1969. "School Mental Health." 39:268–305, March 1969.

Digests of symposium papers presented on school mental health. Some papers were relevant to humanistic education. 1) Kellam and Schiff, "Effects of Family Life on Children's Adaptation to First Grade." Concerned with study of differences in family life of adapting and maladapting first-grade children in Chicago. 2) Solnit, "The Emotional Setting of the Classroom." Concerned with that part of the psychological environment in the classroom established by teachers and their students. 3) Stone, Wilson, Spence & Gibson, "A Survey of Elementary School Children's Behavior Problems." A survey in Iowa to compare schools, classes, and grade levels by the number of student behavior problems. 4) Long, "Where Do You Learn to be People Now In Schools?" The development of a curriculum in the behavioral sciences at Webster College Experimental School with 4th, 5th, and 6th grade students.

1689

Bateman, Barbara. "Humanistic Goals and Behaviorist Technology." *School Psychology Digest,* 2:39, Winter 1973.

Discusses the desirability of combining the behavioristic and humanistic approaches in educational settings. It is suggested that a merger of the skills of the behaviorist with the caring of the humanist facilitates relationships among special services personnel, teachers, administrators, parents, and children in reaching desired goals. An illustration of how the humanistic and behaviorist orientation may be successfully combined is provided as the elements one might include in consultation with teachers and in other forms of inservice training.

Bower, Eli M. "Psychology in the Schools: Conceptions, Processes, and Territories." *Psychology in the Schools,* 1:3–11, January 1964.

Examines the relationship between psychology and education and considers the following four points: 1) present-day realities and assumptions in this collaboration, 2) implications for psychology of the evolution of the school as a primary agency, 3) models for programs in primary prevention, and 4) the normal epilogue of scientific inquiry and discussion-research gaps and needs.

Brown, B.; Long, B. E.; and Morse, W. C. "Mental Health in the Classroom." *Today's Education,* 61:48-54, September 1972.

Brown writes about "stress," how the teacher can deal with it, how mental health professionals help teachers and the role of the National Institute of Mental Health. Long writes about "A Climate for Learning" in which she proposes that education must help children make sense of their environment and form predictions of what will happen next. Morse writes about "The Crisis Teacher," a special resource teacher available in the school to provide crisis intervention service for a pupil when his coping process beings to fall apart.

Brown, George I. "Confluent Education: Exploring the Affective Domain." *College Board Review,* No. 80. pp. 5-10, Summer 1971.

Author stresses need for schools to introduce confluent education—the term for the integration or flowing together of the affective and cognitive elements in individual and group learning—into the school curriculum. The aspect of what and how the learner feels can be integrated with what schools believe he should know. To accomplish this, there would be needed an initial national expenditure of millions to train teachers and to develop materials, lessons, and teaching units in the various subject areas. The author feels that every society in this world needs emotional education. Helping other societies achieve this could be a great investment in world peace.

Brown, George I. "Human is as Confluent Does." *Theory Into Practice,* 10: 191-5, June 1971.

Gives a description of confluent education: the merging of the cognitive and affective domains by conscious teaching in an attempt to make the educational process and the student more humane. Also discusses how techniques of confluent education help a student to learn his personal existential responsibility. Calls for confluent teacher training programs and points of departure for teachers innovating in this area. Also outlines scope and sequence of programs in progress.

Brown, George I. "I Have Things to Tell; Confluent Education." *Elementary English,* 50:515-20, April 1973.

Defines confluent education as that which seeks to integrate, in teaching and learning, the realm of emotions, attitudes and values with that of thought and intellect. A goal is to teach students responsibility for their own behavior. Thought processes are continually affected by feelings. There are techniques which help people get in touch with their will to live. Advocates beginning to change by becoming aware of what goes on in the classroom.

Burnes, Alan J. "Laboratory Instruction in the Behavioral Sciences in the Elementary School: Models for Inquiry." *Journal of School Psychology,* 5: 217-224, Spring 1967.

"This paper has alternately considered conceptualization of laboratory experiences in behavioral science for elementary school children and has given some concrete illustrations of applications. With respect to the use of instruments or the setting of experimental conditions, this paper has set guidelines and shown preference for a particular approach which involves the use of simple materials, the building of laboratory devices by students themselves, and a proviso that the process of inquiry be student-determined."

Dizenhuz, Israel M., *et al.* "School Mental Health." *American Journal of Ortho-psychiatry,* 41:307–314, March 1971.

Presents digests of six papers presented at 48th annual meeting of American Orthopsychiatric Association in 1971. Covers liaison educator, in-service mental health training for teachers, ways of modifying aggressive behavior in elementary schools, and mental health consultation.

Ellis, Albert. "An Experiment in Emotional Education." *Educational Technology,* 11:61–64, July 1971.

Describes the principles of Rational Emotive Therapy and their application to a specific classroom situation.

Ellis, Albert. "Emotional Education in the Classroom: The Living School." *Journal of Clinical Child Psychology,* 1:19–22, Fall 1972.

Dr. Ellis describes the process of Rational-Emotive Therapy and its application to education.

Ellis, Albert. "Teaching Emotional Education in the Classroom." *School Health Review,* 1:10–13, November 1969.

An explanation is given of Rational Emotive Therapy and its possible application to the classroom environment.

Forcinelli, J., and Engeman, T. S. "Value Education in the Public School." *Thrust,* 4:13-16, October 1974.

The authors briefly discuss the issue of whether or not values education should be taught in schools. Two reasons are offered in support of a school values education program. Four value-oriented programs are reviewed: Values Clarification (Sidney B. Simon), The Cognitive-Developmental (Lawrence Kohlberg), Lifeline (Per McPhail), and Character Education (American Institute for Character Education, San Antonio, Texas). Finally, the authors evaluate each program according to a set of personal criteria.

Fraenkel, Jack. "Value Education in the Social Studies." *Phi Delta Kappan,* 50: 457–461, April 1969.

Contends that the systematic design of appropriate teaching strategies to bring about desired values is crucially important in social studies education. Discusses how to break down societal goals into expected student behaviors, appropriate teaching strategies, and a value-developing strategy.

Frick, Ralph. "Values: Games Are Not Enough." *Teacher,* 91:8-9, December 1973.

Although games are useful for teaching values, they are not sufficient for the following reasons: (1) games involve pretense, (2) the student is asked to make a decision rather than consider consequences, (3) value clarification frequently becomes value justification, and (4) games are necessarily a superficial treatment of the study of values. Instead we must be sure that a study of values is built around a study of alternatives and students must be helped to understand that decisions have consequences.

Hillman, Aaron, *DRICE Monograph No. 3.* "Concepts and Elements of Confluent Education." 46 pp. February 1973.

In this monograph Hillman sets forth the concepts and principles of the process basic to confluent education which developed out of the work of Frederick Perls in Gestalt psychology.

Ivey, Allen E. and Alschuler, Alfred S. "An Introduction to the Field." *Personnel and Guidance Journal,* 51:591–599, May 1973.

The authors advocate a new definition of the counselor role: that of the psychological educator who actively intervenes in the life of institutions and teaches healthy skills to others. There are four aspects of this new role: goals of psychological education, psychological education strategies, tactics of psychological education tactics, and demystifying the nature of helping. These four aspects are discussed in detail and a bibliography is appended.

Ivey, A. and Weinstein, G. "The Counselor as Specialist in Psychological Education." *Personnel and Guidance Journal,* 49:98-107, October 1970.

In this dialogue, the authors describe psychological education. Ivey speaks about training teachers to help children with intrapersonal and interpersonal negotiations. Weinstein discusses a new pattern of school organization called the "three-tiered model." He also describes skills which are involved in learning about oneself. Finally the authors draw implications for the guidance field.

Kohlberg, Lawrence. "A Cognitive-Developmental Approach to Moral Education." *Humanist,* 32:13-16, November–December 1972.

Developmental findings on moral stages, moral-philosophic conceptions of principles and the tenets of constitutional democracy cohere to define a philosophically and psychologically viable conception of moral education. Though outlined in 1909 by John Dewey, this conception has only recently gained the research support needed to make it truly convincing.

Kohlberg, Lawrence. "Moral and Religious Education and the Public Schools: A Developmental View." Theodore R. Sizer (Ed.), *Religion and Public Education.* Boston: Houghton Mifflin, 1967, pp. 164-183.

Author presents studies he has conducted on boys aged 9 to 23 in several countries to show that the goal of moral education is the stimulation of the natural development of the individual child's own moral judgment. His findings show that liberty and justice are culturally universal moral values. Basic morality develops naturally through a variety of intellectual and social stimulations in the home, the peer group, and the school. The school or classroom atmosphere has an extremely important influence on a child's moral conduct.

Kohlberg, Lawrence. "Moral Education in the Schools: A Developmental View." *School Review,* 74:1-30, Spring 1966.
"In this paper the author attempts to deal with some of the value issues involved in moral education and approaches these issues from the standpoint of research findings. A number of research facts offer some guide through the problems of moral education when these facts are considered from Dewey's general perspective as to the relationship between fact and value in education."

Laas, M. and Anderson, J. "Causal Approach to Behavior." *Instructor,* 76:25, November 1966.
Describes the causal approach to human relations as one in which the teacher attempts to identify and work on the causes of hostile or socially unacceptable behavior. Gives examples of experiences for children of causal behavior.

Levine, E. "Affective Education: Lessons in Ego Development." *Psychology in the Schools,* 10:147-50, April 1973.
Discusses trend toward humanized learning process in schools. Describes Magic Circle technique of daily 20-minute sessions, where groups of children, with the teacher acting as leader, discuss predetermined personal themes. Outline of Human Development Program given as example of affective curricula.

Lewy, Arich. "Affective Outcomes of Musical Education." *Journal of Research in Music Education,* 19:361-365, Fall 1971.
Applies affective taxonomy of Krathwohl, Bloom and Masia to goal formulation in music education.

Limbacher, Waler J. "Mental Health Training for Elementary School Pupils." George H. Moreau (Ed.) *Guidance Awareness in Elementary Education.* Washington, D.C. National Catholic Educational Association, 1967. pp. 82-109.
The author discusses the school's role in mental health, and states that concepts in mental health can be successfully taught in the 5th and 6th grades. An overview of a course taught to 5th grade students once a week is described. The course provides a systematic, direct, organized presentation of mental

health principles aimed at giving the child insights into the causes and purposes of his behavior and the means to directly affect his own mental health.

Llewellyn A. and Cahoon, D. "Teaching for Affective Learning." *Educational Leadership,* 22:469-72, April 1965.

Principles of affective learning include the following: 1) openness between teacher and student, 2) a stress on the uniqueness of the individual, 3) teacher and students must share feelings, thoughts and actions, 4) teacher must provide warmth, acceptance, and empathy, 5) learning has personal significance for learner. Students "reactions" to teacher in the affective area and problems of implementation are explored in a seminar.

Long, Barbara Ellis. "Pebbles in the Pool." *Grade Teacher,* 89:118-130, September 1971.

This is an introductory piece for a series of articles on human relations in the classroom. Children study their own behavior to develop greater self-knowledge and human awareness. The author names and explains her ideas about projective education.

Long, Nicholas. "Helping Children Cope With Feelings." *Childhood Education,* 45:367-372, March 1969.

Article explains how teachers at Hillcrest Children's Center, a therapeutic elementary school for emotionally disturbed children in Washington, D.C., learn to understand, relate to, and educate their students. Considerable time and effort are spent discussing and demonstrating the concepts of decoding behavior, labeling and accepting feelings, and redirecting behavior. Three case histories are presented as examples.

Lyon, Don and Lyon, Berthamay. "Human Relations Education—Who Needs It?" *American Secondary Education,* 1:15-17, June 1971.

Human relations education is described as cooperative team action in which students, teachers, and administrators work together to meet the needs of all people. Background reading is given and techniques resulting in feedback are described. Such techniques which are useful in helping people to interact more successfully are brainstorming, creative dramatics, laboratory settings, case studies, and action-research projects such as random interviews.

Lyon, Don O. and Lyon, Berthamay. "Human Relations Education—Who Needs It?" *Teacher Educator,* 7:2-6, Autumn 1971.

Human relations education is described as cooperative team action in which students, teachers, and administrators work together to meet the needs of all people. Background reading is given and techniques resulting in feedback are discussed. Techniques which can be used to help people interact more successfully are brainstorming, creative dramatics, laboratory settings, case studies, and action-research projects such as random interviewing.

McMullen, Ronald S. "The Achievement Motivation Workshop." *Personnel and Guidance Journal,* 51:642-645, May 1973.

Discusses the principles of achievement motivation and describes the six-step sequence of an achievement motivation course.

Maslow, A. H. "Humanistic Education vs. Professional Education." *New Directions in Teaching,* 2:6-8, Summer-Fall 1969.

Maslow's response to an article by a graduate student who participated in Maslow's seminar at Brandeis University on the topic, "Advanced Educational Psychology."

Maslow states that through the seminar he came to recognize the need for a sharper and more explicit distinction between professional training and humanistic education. In addition, Maslow became aware through the seminar of the students' hunger for contact, for intimacy, and for community.

Maslow concludes that if these basic humanistic jobs could be started in nursery school or kindergarten, then graduate education would be far more efficient than it now is.

Maslow, Abraham. H. "Some Educational Implications of the Humanistic Psychologies." *Harvard Educational Review,* 38:685-696, Fall 1968.

In this essay the relevance for education of much of Maslow's psychological theorizing is examined in detail. The author explores the reinforcing role of peak-experiences, and discusses the general educational imperative to be derived from his views of the process of self-actualization. The author explains the Third Force psychology, a belief in the reality of higher human needs, motives, and capacities, and its meaning for learning and education.

Mears, Michael. "Who's Sid Simon and What's All This About Values Clarification?" *Media and Methods,* 9:30-37, March 1973.

Presents ideas contained in two books: *Values and Teaching* by Louis Raths, Merrill Harman, and Sidney Simon, and *Values Clarification* by Sidney Simon, Leland Howe, and Howard Kirschenbaum. After an explanation of why teachers should teach values, the author presents many values clarification strategies.

Mogar, Robert E. "Toward a Psychological Theory of Education." *Journal of Humanistic Psychology,* 9:17-52, Spring 1969.

Mogar first attempts to formulate a psycho-social model based on the works of leading psychological and sociological theorists that will lead to alternative innovative educational systems relevant to all kinds of educational needs of children. He then goes on to discuss the dynamics of self-directed growth in the classroom.

Morgan, H. "Curriculum is the Self." *Music Educators Journal,* 47:27-32, December 1970.

Explores concrete ways music can be utilized to meet affective needs of children: feeling, emotion, friendship, love, and a sense of positive self-worth. Music can be used to facilitate real self-expression and relevation, genuine communication between teacher and student, and communication between home and school.

Morse, William C.; Finger, Craig; and Gilmore, George C. "Innovations in School Mental Health Programs." *Review of Educational Research,* 38:460-477, December 1968.
Discusses innovations under several headings: search for new guidelines, classroom teacher as mental health worker, realignment of mental health personnel, services focusing on pupils, and changing the school milieu.

Mosher, Ralph L., *et al.* "Psychological Education: A Means to Promote Personal Development During Adolescence." *Counseling Psychologist,* 2:3-82, Winter 1971.
Formulates a curriculum whose objectives are: achieving self-knowledge, enjoying one's capacities, and more effective relating to others.

Murphy, M. L. "Values and Health Problems." *Journal of School Health,* 43: 23-31, January 1973.
Defines eight categories of human values: affection, enlightenment, skill, power, respect, rectitude, wealth, and well-being. Describes how negative self-concept is a self-fulfilling prophecy in children. Discusses how values framework can be applied to curriculum areas to increase understanding, by implementation of relevant skills. Identification of high risk takers has correlation with drug abuse. Children need to learn to deal with cause and effect.

Myers, D. A. "Humanistic School, A Critical Analysis." *Educational Forum,* 37:53-8, November 1972.
Suggest five components for humanistic schools: conventional content with a mankind perspective, interpersonal relations, teachers, action and Geist. Integration of knowledge, a necessity, also helps with interpersonal relations. Teacher needs to be loving, self-actualizing, humane, authentic, autonomous, and well informed on pedagogy, psychology and instructional programs. Students must be able to utilize knowledge. Schools must provide a friendly, positive environment conducive to learning. Self understanding must be predominant. Curriculum will teach traditional disciplines as vehicles for arriving at an understanding of mankind. Society will be less efficient, more cooperative.

Nolte, A. E. "Acquiring Values: Mental Health." *Instructor,* 81:51-3, August 1971.
From a larger section entitled "Health Values For Your Children" dealing largely with physical fitness and nutrition as other areas which involve acquiring values. The section on mental health gives a list of desirable mental

health qualities for children to achieve and suggestions for teachers in the classroom.

Ojemann, Ralph. "Education in Human Behavior in Perspective." *People Watching,* 1:58–67, Spring 1972.

Examines problems of teaching behavioral sciences to children from preschool years through the secondary school. The objective of a "scope and sequence chart" is to help students develop a causal approach to behavior rather than an arbitrary, judgmental, stereotype approach.

Ojemann, Ralph H. "Incorporating Psychological Concepts in the School Curriculum." *Journal of School Psychology,* Section 9. pp. 5, 195–204. Spring 1967.

Delineates the difference between consideration of behavior as it appears in its outward form and consideration of behavior by its underlying dynamics called the causal approach. Describes some testing done with fourth, fifth and sixth graders which showed that dealing with causal behavior was effective in changing it. Two significant contributions of increased understanding and appreciation of the dynamics of behavior: it helps the child now and it provides a needed foundation for later development.

Ojemann, Ralph H. "Self-Guidance as an Educational Goal and the Selection of Objectives." *Elementary School Journal,* Vol. 72:247-57, February 1972.

Identifies four forms of self-guidance: a) impulsive decision, b) tradition-bound decisions, c) future-oriented decisions which neglect immediate consequences, d) choices made by immediate and future effects. Self-guidance will not directly determine direction of society but will produce individuals capable of influencing society. This has a direct impact on the role of the teacher in the classroom.

Patterson, F. K. "Values and Social Studies Curriculum." *National Catholic Education Association Bulletin,* 62:386-94, August 1965.

Describes five frontiers in social science which have direct bearing on curriculum: 1) nature and behavior of the individual, 2) understanding about social groups, 3) perception, 4) communication, and 5) problem-solving. Three principal ends which social studies should serve are generalization, idea of causality and the process of valuing.

Payne, Buryl. "Uncovering Destructive Self-Criticism: A Teaching Technique Based Upon General Semantics." *Educational Opportunity Forum,* 1:85–94, Fall 1969.

Principles developed by Alfred Korzybski can be effectively used to help students examine and modify their self-critical behavior. Describes background of Korzybski's formulations and teaching procedures that can be developed from these formulations.

Payne, Buryl. "Uncovering Destructive Self-Criticism: A Teaching Technique." *Rational Living,* 6:26-30, Winter 1971.

    This is an application of Korzybski's principles to help students examine and modify self-critical behavior.

Peck, Bernard and Prescott, Daniel A. "Basic Approaches to Mental Health: The Program at the Institute for Child Study, The University of Maryland." *Personnel and Guidance Journal,* 37:114-122, October 1958.

    Outlines in some detail a three-year program of child study by teachers who met in child study groups. This program developed out of work relating to the in-service training of teachers in human growth and development and is now being developed by the Institute for Child Study at the University of Maryland.

Rappaport, Julian and Sorensen, James. "Teaching Psychology to 'Disadvantaged' Youth: Enhancing the Relevance of Psychology Through Public Education." *Journal of School Psychology,* 92:120-126, Winter 1971.

    Describes psychology course taught in a summer "upward bound" program to "disadvantaged" students.

Roen, Sheldon R. "Relevance of Teaching Children About Behavior. *American Journal of Orthopsychiatry,* 40:307-308, March 1970.

    Behavioral science as a new elementary school subject would be a way to meet the current demand for relating education to social realities. Some teachers already try to weave the topic of the understanding of behavior into their classroom discussions of literature, history, geography, and current events. Preliminary findings of a survey to ascertain interests and activities in teaching children about behavior revealed that the fourth-grade is chosen most often for the program with lessons taught once or twice a week. The fifth and sixth grades were runners up. The materials used for these lessons were almost always designed locally.

Roen, Sheldon. "Behavioral Studies as a Curriculum Subject." *Teachers College Record,* 68:541-550, April 1967.

    This essay concentrates on behavioral studies as a curriculum subject from the perspective of teachers. Discusses prerequisites for curriculum innovation, potential benefits for students from their study of behavior, skills of social survival, curriculum integrations, behavioral science as a discipline, and the teaching program and special methods involved in creating lessons in this area.

Roen, Sheldon. "Teaching the Behavioral Sciences in Elementary Grades." *Journal of School Psychology,* 5:205-216, Spring 1967.

    Suggests that the behavioral sciences have become important fields of knowledge which possess intrinsic interest for children, and can be useful to them and society at large. It is easy to justify the behavioral sciences as being important enough to be included in the elementary school curriculum, especially when one considers the progress made by proponents of foreign languages and physical sciences.

Romig, D. and Cleland, C. C. "Educational Applications of Humanistic Psychology." *Journal of School Psychology,* 10:289-98, Spring 1972.

Reports on studies being done about Maslow's theory of human motivation. Presents a hypothetical school, with suggestions on using Maslow's theory. The school seeks to produce truly human beings. Discusses the systematic implementation of the research and theory current in humanistic psychology.

Samler, J. "School and Self-Understanding." *Harvard Educational Review,* 35:55-70, Winter 1965.

In this article Samler examines the possibility of mental health programs in the schools and various ways of obtaining self-understanding. Some of the subjects touched on are as follows: the school, cognition, and self-understanding, the control of behavior, the explicit support of values, on the examined life, maintaining self-records, and the interpretation of dreams.

*Saturday Review of Education.* "Inside Out! Confluent Education." 1:51, January 1973.

Discussion of confluent education first used by George I. Brown at UCSB to describe learning that involved the confluence or flowing together of thoughts and feelings. Describes the Ford-Esalen Confluent Reading Project's confluent reading curriculum for elementary school teachers. Children also learn about feelings.

ED 054018
*The 70's, Decade of Environmental Decision: Education and Action Guidelines. Environmental Information Source Guide and Bibliography.* 1970.

Three goals of environmental action are as follows: survival of man and improvement of life, relationship of environmental action with academic disciplines and informal education, and values of environmental education in relation to democracy. Paper focuses on strategies and curricula. Bibliography lists other bibliographies and national sources of free and inexpensive materials.

Shallcross, Doris J. "Creativity: Everybody's Business." *Personnel and Guidance Journal,* 51:623–626, May 1973.

Author provides an introduction to the literature and methodology of creativity. Discusses theory and techniques in using creativity to eliminate barriers and to increase ideation.

Shapiro, Edna and Biber, Barbara. "The Education of Young Children: A Developmental-Interaction Approach." *Teachers College Record,* Columbia University. 74:55-79, September 1972.

This article describes current educational trends in the area of preschool education which focus on either intellect or emotion. The authors develop a theory which integrates the two areas. Items discussed are general goals for the education of young children, developmental concepts, characteristics of ideal teachers and the utilization of the community.

Shattuck, J. B. "Using the Sciences for Value Clarification." *Science Education,* 54:9-11, January/March 1970.

The first part of the article is devoted to analyzing how science education has changed in the past 10–15 years. The author, unhappily, noted a major thrust to increase the stress on factual learning and content improvement. The author notes that rarely does the science curriculum attempt to improve in terms of people. Science education has become dehumanized. Instead of a conventional approach which emphasizes only factual and conceptual levels, Shattuck advocates the addition of a third level—a values or "you" level. This level would utilize values clarification in an attempt to lead students toward a greater awareness of thoughts and feelings. The author provides examples of how science questions and information can be presented at the factual, conceptual, and values levels.

Simon, Sidney B. "Promoting the Search for Values." *Educational Opportunity Forum,* 1:75-84, Fall 1969.

The author explains seven different value-clarifying strategies which he has used with high school and college students. These are methods for helping students to learn values without the teacher getting caught in the bind of moralizing, inculcating, or teaching values. Among the strategies for value-clarification discussed are weekly reaction sheets, weekly values cards, autobiographical questionnaires, time diaries, and confrontation questioning.

Simon, Sidney B. "Sid Simon on Values: 'No Moralizers or Manipulators Allowed.'" *Nation's Schools,* 92:39-42, December 1973.

Written as an interview of Simon by Joel Goodman, this article explains the theory and practice of values clarification education.

Simon, Sidney B. "Values Clarification vs. Indoctrination." *Social Education,* 35:902-905+, December 1971.

In place of indoctrination, the author posits a process approach to the area of dealing with values in schools which focuses on the process of valuing, not on the transmission of the right set of values. Illustrates this concept with five value-clarifying strategies and ways to use them.

Sliepcevich, Elena M. "School Health Education: Appraisal of a Conceptual

Approach to Curriculum Development." *Journal of School Health,* 36:145-153, April 1966.

"The theory underlying the conceptual approach to curriculum development in health education is that the identification of major concepts and supporting generalizations from a discipline facilitates the organization of its knowledge and forms a structure for developing meaningful relationships. It was hypothesized that such a curriculum would improve the efficiency and effectiveness of both the teaching and learning project." The curriculum demonstration project was conducted in 1964–65 in Alhambra, California; Evanston, Illinois; Great-Neck Garden City, New York; and Tacoma, Washington. This project is part of the School Health Education Study begun in September 1961 for the purpose of improving health instruction programs in schools. "Three key concepts serve as the unifying threads of the curriculum. These were: 1) Growing and Developing—The Dynamics of the Growing and Developing Individual, 2) Decision Making—Choices and Decisions the Individual Makes, 3) Interactions—Interactions Between the Individual and his Environment."

Sprinthall, N. A. "Curriculum for Secondary Schools: Counselors as Teachers for Psychological Growth." *School Counselor,* 20:361-19, May 1973.

Author describes a three-year attempt with different approaches to give psychological education to pupils using high school personnel, graduate students and faculty with students. Two levels of assessment were skills and psychological impact. Issues raised were explanation of positive effects of the program, relation of approach and adolescence, and the personnel to implement curriculum.

Stewart, William. "A Humanistic Study of the Visual Arts, the Commitment, Risk, and Potential." *Art Education,* 25:2-3, February 1972.

"The visual arts are seen as an effective way of bringing all the rich dimensions of the real world into the school for examination and experiencing. A humanistic study of the visual arts considers encounters with ideas and works of man as learning experiences that function as determinants of human behavior. The basic subject matter of this domain appeals to feeling, emotion, expressiveness, and the deeper meaning of life."

Tempelton, D. E. "The Arts: Sources for Affective Learning." *Educational Leadership,* 22:465-72, April 1965.

Art may be received as a discipline of self-expression. Child must perceive in his own experience universals, which free the spirit. To involve emotion and feeling and discovery through creation of art is what visual arts are about and why they're a valid source for affective learning.

Tolor, Alexander and Griffin, Ann M. "Group Therapy in a School Setting." *Psychology in the Schools,* 6:59–62, January 1969.

Outlines considerations associated with group therapy activities in a school setting. Discusses advantages, disadvantages, and considerations for enhancing the chances of success.

Weinstein, Gerald. "Trumpet: A Guide to Humanistic Psychological Curriculum." *Theory Into Practice,* 10:196–203, June 1971.

Details a strategy for selecting and sequencing affective activities that will lead to the expansion of an individual's response pattern.

Weinstein, Gerald. "Trumpet: A Guide to Humanistic Psychological Curriculum." *Theory Into Practice,* 13:335-42, December 1974.

The Trumpet is a strategy for selecting and sequencing affective activities that will lead to the expansion of an individual's response pattern. This article describes the strategy and the way it has been applied in a course at the University of Massachusetts entitled, "Education of the Self." The strategy consists of the following parts: (1) Confrontation—Generation of Data, (2) Unique and Common Response—Inventorying, (3) Recognizing Patterns, (4) Owning patterns, (5) Consequences, (6) Allowing alternatives, (7) Evaluation and choice.

Weinstein, Gerald. "Self-Science Education: The Trumpet." *Personnel and Guidance Journal,* 51:600–606, May 1973.

Self-science education involves programs for training learners in those skills, concepts, and attitudes that will expand their own unique style for being in this world. The trumpet is a process tool developed by Weinstein to provide the self-scientist with a cognitive map or sequence in working through a set of personal observations. The article elucidates the model by presenting a case study of a counseling situation with a sample set of responses and then draws implications from the trumpet model.

Yeomans, Thomas. "Search for a Working Model: Gestalt, Psychosynthesis, and Confluent Education." *Occasional Paper No. 22,* 1972. Available from DRICE. University of California, Santa Barbara.

The author first defines confluence and then, using the personality theories of Gestalt and Psychosynthesis, formulates a model for personal growth. This is followed by a discussion of the implications for education.

### III. Chapters in Books and Reports: Articles in Encyclopedias

American School Health Association Committee on Mental Health in the Classroom. "Suggested Areas for Guidance in Teaching Mental Health in the Classroom." In Lifton, W. (ed.) *Educating for Tomorrow; The Role of Media, Career Development, and Society.* New York: Wiley & Sons, Inc., 1970. 212-229.

Listing of Tables for Kindergarten through Grade 14 giving concepts, learning experiences and materials available for classroom use for each specific grade. Topics under consideration include: 1) Personality structure and development; 2) Interaction of an individual with others; 3) Socioeconomic status; and 4) Emotional climate in home and classroom.

Biber, Barbara. "Integration of Mental Health Principles in the School Setting," in Gerald Caplan (ed.) *Prevention of Mental Disorders in Children,* Chapter XV. New York: Basic Books Inc. 1961. 323–352.

The author "defines a position concerning the integration of mental health principles in the school setting, then describes a rationale and practice of education by which such a position can be and is enacted to varying degrees in various school settings, and finally indicates the structure and content of research activities designed to explore, test, and differentiate assumptions implicit in the translation of this theory into practice."

Biber, Barbara. "A Learning-Teaching Paradigm Integrating Intellectual and Affective Processes," in Eli M. Bower and William G. Hollister (eds.) *Behavioral Science Frontiers in Education.* New York: John Wiley & Sons, Inc., 1967. pp. 115–155.

Biber suggests that the present concentration on intellectual excellence has its assets and liabilities. She commends our moving ahead in upgrading the nature and variety of cognitive experiences for children, but she frowns on our blindness to the associated emotional processes in learning. First she presents what she sees as the goal of educational instruction, then the method by which the goal might be achieved, the rationale for doing it this way, and the associated processes of learning and development in the instructional method.

Bower, Eli. "Primary Prevention in a School Setting," in Gerald Caplan (ed.) *Prevention of Mental Disorders in Children.* Chapter XVI. New York: Basic Books, Inc., 1961. 353–377.

This discussion in this article centers around two main subjects. In the first section entitled "The School as a Social Institution," Bower discusses education as primary prevention as well as resistive factors, cultural conflicts and difficulties in preventative action. The second part entitled "A Research Program in Primary Prevention," discusses the research findings and program possibilities in primary prevention.

Dinkmeyer, Don. "Developing Understanding of Self and Others Is Central to the Educational Process." In G. J. Williams and S. Gordon, eds., *Clinical Child Psychology: Current Practices and Future Perspectives.* New York, N.Y.: Behavioral Publications, 1974, xiv, 545p.

"Discusses the need for systematic education programs which facilitate the child's development by being involved with his total being: his intellect, feelings, attitudes, values, behavior, and relationships with others. Several recent books are reviewed, and the author's 'C group' process which increases the teacher's self-understanding and thereby facilitates the child's growth is briefly described."

Kohlberg, Lawrence and Turiel, Elliot. "Moral Development and Moral Education," in Gerald S. Lesser (ed.) *Psychology and Educational Practice,* Chapter 15. Illinois: Scott, Foresman and Co., 1971. 410-465.

In this article the authors "attempt to demonstrate that moral education can be free from the charge of ethical relativity and arbitrary indoctrination which inhibits (the) teacher when she talks about (such ideas as) cheating. (They) present research findings which indicate that much of the failure of communication results not from value differences or value relativity, but from discrepancies of developmental level between the words or ideas of the teacher and those of children. (They) then suggest means by which the teacher can deal with this problem in a way which may raise the child's level of thinking. Finally (they) consider some ways of dealing with the child's actions, consistent with this approach."

Roen, S. R. "Primary Prevention in the Classroom Through a Teaching Program in the Behavioral Sciences," in E. L. Cowen, E. A. Gardner, and M. Zaz (eds.) *Emergent Approaches to Mental Health Problems.* New York: Appleton-Century-Crafts, 1967. 252-270.

This article gives an overview of what is being done in this area. Two programs sustained for over twenty-five years are discussed in detail: 1) the total school atmosphere emphasis which stems from the work of Barbara Biber and the Bank Street College of Education, and 2) the improved curriculum emphasis of Ojemann. Another program which is discussed extensively is the behavioral science curriculum course sponsored by the South Shore Mental Health Center in Boston. Roen discusses the rationale for the program, its history, its applications to classes, and its subsequent extension into residential treatment. He describes a controlled evaluation of the effectiveness of the program and the development of a seminar for teachers which has grown out of it.

Roen, Sheldon R. "Teaching of Behavioral Sciences." *The Encyclopedia of Education,* 1971, Vol. 1. 446-449.

Overview summary of past and recent trends in implementing behavioral science curriculums on the elementary and junior high school level. Mentioned is the 1963 experimental program in the South Shores suburbs of Boston where selected elementary schools offer classes in the behavioral sciences. Special teacher training for these classes was provided by Lesley College of Cambridge, Massachusetts. In 1969 Barbara Long conducted a special program at Webster College with sixth graders. For this program, specially invented games were used to teach behavioral science and mental health concepts.

Sanford, Nevitt. "The Development of Cognitive-Affective Processes Through Education," in Eli M. Bower and William G. Hollister *Behavioral Science Frontiers in Education.* New York: Wiley & Sons, Inc. 1967. 73–87.

The author explains the importance of the cognitive processes in education for the personality development of an individual. Education expands the major areas of a person, makes him also capable of responding to more aspects of the world, and enables him to do more kinds of things. Every child should be taught to enjoy reading, enjoy making up stories and enjoy imaginative work. The author discusses theories of development, education as intervention, the development of imagination, the importance of reading, and ego development and education.

Schmuck, Richard A.; Luszki, Margaret B.; Epperson, David C. "Interpersonal Relations and Mental Health in the Classroom," in Donald H. Clark and Gerald S. Lesser, *Emotional Disturbance and School Learning: A Book of Readings.* Chicago: Science Research Associates, 1965. 81–93.

This paper deals with the following four elements of mental health: 1) the pupil's attitudes toward himself, 2) the pupil's perception of reality, 3) the pupil's mastery of his environment, and 4) the pupil's actualization of his potential. This study attempts to clarify the nature of the relationship between classroom interpersonal relations on the one hand and mental health and academic learning on the other. Several implications for improving the classroom learning environment are drawn.

### IV. Whole Issues

American School Health Association Committee on Mental Health in the Classroom. "Mental Health in the Classroom." *Journal of School Health,* 38, Revised May 1968, No. 5., whole issue.

This report consists of tables of materials on teaching mental health concepts in the classroom from Kindergarten through Grade 14. For each grade the following topics are covered: 1) personality structure and development, 2) interaction of an individual with others, 3) socioeconomic status and its influence on mental health, and 4) emotional climate in home and classroom. These four topics are then presented under three headings: a) objectives, or concepts, b) learning experiences, and c) learning materials, such as books and films, which can be used to achieve the objective. No conclusions are presented. This report serves merely as a reservoir of suggestions on which teaching personnel may draw. An extensive bibliography on books and films is appended.

Bardon, Jack I. (ed.) "Teaching Psychology and the Behavioral Sciences in Schools." *Journal of School Psychology,* 5:167-251, Spring 1967.

Entire issue is devoted to this topic. Most articles deal with it at secondary level although there are several at the elementary level. Contains articles by Ojemann, Roen, Limbacher, and Bower, among others.

*Journal of School Psychology.* "Teaching Psychology and the Behavioral Sciences in the Schools." Vol. 5, Spring 1967, entire issue.

Special issue devoted to the topic of teaching psychology in the schools. "The first four articles by Engle, Noland, Thornton and Colver, and Scheel emphasize the teaching of psychology at the secondary level. These authors review the past, survey the present, and make some suggestions for the future. Ojemann, Roen, Burnes, and Limbacher describe various ways in which psychological concepts can be taught at the elementary school level. Peck, Bower, and Trow offer position papers concerning the teaching of psychology and the behavioral sciences in the schools. Snellgrove presents an overview of APA activities concerning the teaching of psychology in the schools and suggests ways in which readers may receive materials and ideas for development of curricula." Book reviews and an extensive bibliography conclude this issue.

*National Elementary Principal.* Special Issue on "Values and American Education." 42:6-44, November 1962.

Of particular interest to teachers concerned with humanistic education are: Lee, "Education and Cultural Values," which discusses human qualities through an autobiographical sketch of another culture, the Dakota Indians; Dahlke, "The Value Tangle and Educational Malaise," in which the author sketches five general value systems, one of which is the humanistic; Gordon, "Values in the Classroom," which states that the full expression of a person's nature is as important to his functioning as meeting his physical needs; Rath, "Clarifying Children's Values," which points out that values are learned, and that this learning is a personal and private operation; Long, "The Child and his Values," which recognizes the influence of the peer group for value development.

"Psychological Humanistic Education." *Educational Opportunity Forum.* Number 4, Vol. 1. Fall 1969.

This whole issue devoted to humanistic education contains articles by Alfred Alschuler, George I. Brown, Norman Newberg, and Gerald Weinstein, among others. Includes an extensive bibliography.

"Regeneration of the Humanities." *Theory Into Practice.* Vol. X. June 1971.

This whole issue is devoted to humanistic education and contains articles by Maslow, Stenhouse, McDonald, G. I. Brown, and Weinstein, among others.

"Special Feature on Psychological Education." *School Counselor,* 20:332-361, May 1973.

Fiedeman, D. "Guidance in Learning: An Examination of Roles in Self-Centering During 'Thinking.'" p. 334–39. Posits that counselors must learn to be tutors. Major goal of guidance in learning should continue to be the student's comprehension of his capacity for purposeful action.

Cottingham. "Psychological Education, the Guidance Function and the School Counselor." p. 340–45. School counselors face challenges in implementation of the guidance function through psychological education and must be innovative for more out-reach activities in the school and community.

Aubrey, C. "Organizational Victimization of School Counselors, p. 346–54. Describes programs where guidance can take place in the classroom. Model 1: Decentralized guidance department, divided into teams, systematically involved counselors by means of groups and teaching activities. Model 2: Place guidance in pivotal role by assigning leadership and development in that department.

Carroll, M. "The Regeneration of Guidance," p. 355–60. The separation in counselling must change and to do this there needs to be a broader approach to the training of counsellors. In some cases retraining may be necessary. Flexible time blocks within the curriculum is a possibility. In this way students can become counsellors. The community is a resource for counselling help. Counsellors must face the responsibility for change.

*The Personnel and Guidance Journal.* "Psychological Education: A Prime Function of the Counselor." 51, May 1973.

This whole issue is devoted to psychological, affective, and humanistic education. Allen E. Ivey and Alfred S. Alschuler, professors in the School of Education of the University of Massachusetts, give an introduction to the area of humanistic education which is followed by a variety of articles in this field under the major headings of techniques, programmatic approaches, and social applications. Also included is a list of readings and aids for someone who is interested in beginning in this field.

## V. Reports

ED 054053

Brown, George I. *Affectivity, Classroom Climate and Teaching.* American Federation of Teachers, Washington, D.C., 1971.

This paper defines "confluent education" as the integration of the affective and cognitive elements and discusses the complications of over-emphasizing either the affective or cognitive aspect to the detriment of the other. The author presents an overview of techniques in affective learning and suggests ways to integrate such techniques into conventional classroom practice and content.

ED 088 041

Hillman, Aaron. "Concepts and Elements of Confluent Education (Life Is Possibilities, Not Probabilities)." DRICE Monograph No. 3. Development and Research in Confluent Education, Santa Barbara, Calif. Ford Foundation, New York, N.Y. February 1973.

This project sought to find ways in which emotional learning could be brought to a level commensurate with intellectual learning. Confluent education refers to the concept of teaching a person through both cognitive and affective processes. Nine elements must be present in the teaching situation in order for confluent education to exist; responsibility—the ability to respond creatively and positively to any situation; convergency—relating and experiencing what is done or what is happening to the self; connectedness —a sense of positive affiliation with others; divergency—relating and experiencing what is happening in the world to the educational experience; power—a sense of personal control over what is happening or will happen; gestalt—gaining closure (satisfaction) through positive frustration and explication; identity—a feeling of self-worth, self-esteem, and ego identity; context-learning to understand communications through general semantics and environment; and evaluation—eliciting individuals' opinions concerning values. (LL)

Hillman, Aaron W. *An Introduction to Confluent Education.* Occasional Paper No. 24. 1973. Available from DRICE, University of Calif., Santa Barbara.

Hillman first explains what is meant by cognitive and affective domains and then proceeds to explain the merging of the two domains in confluent education which will result in the integrated man.

ED 042666

Hills, James L. *A Synthesis of Cognitive and Affective Processes in Social Studies Instruction.* American Educational Research Assoc., Washington, D.C. 1969.

A model is presented and developed to alert teachers to the place of the affective components in social studies instruction. It can be a useful tool in sequencing learning to assure experiences in the affective and cognitive realm.

ED 048023

"Knowledge Processes and Values in the New Social Studies." Wisconsin State Department of Public Instruction, Madison, Wisconsin, 1970.

This guide devotes one-half of its length to the teaching of values. This guide outlines teaching strategies and has as its objective the integration of the social sciences, rational, skills and knowledge to arrive at values which will be meaningful in the life of the student.

ED 070614

Knapp, Clifford E. *Teaching Environmental Education with a Focus on Values.* Southern Illinois University Carbondale. Dept. of Conservation and Outdoor Recreation, 1972.

Utilizes a variety of teaching strategies to help students develop their own environmental values and internalize the valuing process.

ED 056977

Mascagnoni, Virginia M. *Social Dimensions of the Self as an Open System: A Curriculum Design. Strategies for Implementation.* Florida Educational Research and Development Council. Gainesville. 1969.

Presents a strategy in three parts aimed at developing the individual as a social being who can build and enhance his social properties. Part one defines the seven social properties. Part two delineates the conceptualization process in which the student is to engage to build the seven social properties. Part three is concerned with the role of the teacher in the process.

ED 064091

Ojemann, Ralph H. *New Insights in Health Behavior.* Educational Research Council of America. Cleveland, Ohio. 1969.

Designed for teachers, administrators, and other specialized educational personnel, this professional paper describes new insights for putting health knowledge into action. It explores reasons for the discrepancy between knowledge and behavior and suggests asking two questions: 1) What basic problem is the individual trying to solve through his behavior? and 2) How does he happen to choose a particular method? Fundamentals about the dynamics of behavior are reviewed with an analysis of how behavior can be changed. Examples specifically related to health concerns illustrate the components of behavior-motivating force, resources, immediate physical settings, and show how they interact as well as cause changes in behavior. A conclusion is drawn that putting knowledge into action requires understanding the underlying causes of discrepant behavior and building a plan for action based on this understanding.

Raths, L. *Sociological Knowledge and Needed Curriculum Research.* Paper presented at the Edward A. and Rosa Uhrig Memorial Lectures, Milwaukee, Wisconsin, May 1960.

Raths states that the school curriculum should contain many more opportunities for the clarification of values and thinking. Raths further suggests that certain types of student behaviors are linked with a lack of value development. He identifies those behaviors and explains how a process of values clarification can add zeal, purpose, and direction to the lives of these children. The paper concludes with an extensive discussion of how thinking skills may be clarified. Many examples are described and a way of coding student work is presented.

Rest, James. "Developmental Psychology As a Guide to Value Education: A Review of 'Kohlbergian' Programs." *Review of Educational Research.* 44: 241-59, Spring 1974.

Rest first discusses the fundamental ideas upon which "Kohlbergian" programs are based: structural organization, developmental sequences, and interactionism. He next reviews the following "Kohlbergian" programs: the Blatt studies, the prison studies of Hickey, Sprinthall and Mosher's "Deliberate Psychological Education" program, and other projects. As he himself states, "The gist of this review is that 'Kohlbergian' value education programs are based on ideas that have been around for some time; the programs integrate and 'concretize' these basic ideas in new ways, although many further developments are necessary before one can claim to have successfully developed a distinctively new kind of educational program." Finally, some future steps in program development are suggested.

## 4. REPORTS OF RESEARCH

a. *Effects of Curriculum on Students*

### II. Magazines and Journals

Alschuler, Alfred. "Toward a Self Renewing School (A Case Study) VIII." *The Journal of Applied Behavioral Science,* #5. (September/October 1972). 577-600.

This case study describes the uses of OD (Organizational Development) strategies to introduce psychological curricula in a community college. The author hypothesizes that the success of the intervention was because of the combination of three factors: favorable historical antecedents, the nature of the intervention, and continuous leadership by key administrators before and after the intervention. The interdependence of these three factors is analyzed. Adapted from *Motivating Achievement in High School Students: Education for Human Growth* by Alfred Alschuler. Englewood Cliffs, New Jersey: Educational Technology Publication, 1972.

Barman, C. R. "Integrating Value Clarification with High School Biology." *American Biology Teacher,* 37:150-3, March 1975.

A lesson is presented which effectively integrates values clarification and high school biology. Then the author details a research experiment in which a control group of students not taught with value clarification and an experimental group taught using these techniques were compared to see if value clarification would affect student attitudes toward science and biology and would improve achievement in a BSCS Yellow Version Biology course. Results showed that the achievement of the experimental group was significantly greater even though there were no significant differences in attitudes toward science and biology between the two groups.

Biber, Barbara. *Schooling as an Influence in Developing Healthy Personality.*

IV. Ruth Kotinsky and Helen L. Witmer (eds.) "Community Programs for Mental Health; Theory, Practice, Evaluation," Cambridge, Massachusetts: Harvard University Press, 1955. 158–221.

"The introductory pages of this paper present a conception of the school's role in nurturing healthy personality and describe certain teaching principles and practices implicit in this general aim." Then analyses of three school projects conducted in 1950-51 are given. These are a citizen education project about better emotional adjustment of children, an intergroup education project designed to prevent prejudice, and a teacher education project.

Burgess, Evangeline. *Values in Early Childhood Education.* 2nd ed. Washington, D.C.: National Education Association, 1965.

"This report summarizes the research evidence of the values in early childhood education with emphasis on nursery school education. Included in the discussion are a) all the studies reported in accessible sources which provide evidence of the effects of nursery school experience on children's development in the areas of social, personal, and emotional development; intellectual growth; and later school achievement and b) a selection of studies which had the primary objective of understanding fundamental processes of child development in these areas." Of interest to psychologists and educators of young children.

Carkhuff, Robert R. "The Development of Effective Courses of Action for Ghetto School Children." *Psychology in the Schools,* 7:272-77, July 1970.

Relates result of study in developing systematic courses of action to achieve desired goals which can be effective in helping ghetto children with school problems. Shows evidence that trained specialists in this area are the most effective in giving help.

Cowen, Emory, *et al.* "A Preventive Mental Health Program in the School Setting: Description and Evaluation." *Journal of Psychology,* 56:307-356, October 1963.

Authors describe preventive mental health program in primary grades in Rochester, New York, from inception in 1959 to date of paper. The single broad basic hypothesis underlying this work was that such a program in the schools would produce measurable positive effects on its targets.

Two control schools were selected at the beginning of the project to parallel the experimental school as closely as possible in the socioeconomic background and the intellectual level of the students.

Eldridge, M. S. and others. "Effects of DUSO on the Self-Concepts of Second Grade Students and Others." *Elementary School Guidance and Counseling,* 7:256-60, May 1973.

Describes the results of a study of DUSO (Developing Understanding of

Self and Others) in two second grade classes. In each elementary school there was a control and an experimental group. One pre-test and three post-tests were administered. The conclusion was that there was a significant difference in the self-concept of students using the DUSO program. Teacher agreed. The study was small and further research is recommended.

France, Norman and Wiseman, Stephen. "An Educational Guidance Programme for the Primary School." *British Journal of Educational Psychology,* 36: 210-226, June 1966.

Shows success of a program designed for primary school children. Describes the testing of the France-Wiseman Educational Guidance Programme in the spring of 1964 and the standardization of it in November of 1964. The results of the testing of the untimed program of tasks as part of the children's normal classwork showed that they can produce a satisfactory discrimination over most of the ability range.

Gribbons, Warren D. "Evaluation of an Eighth Grade Group Guidance Program." *Personnel and Guidance Journal,* 37:740-745, May 1960.

Test results showed that after participating in a group guidance program pupils were helped to make accurate appraisals of their abilities, values and interest, and integrate this with information about educational and occupational job opportunities.

Griggs, Joe W. and Bonney, Merl E. "Relationship Between 'Causal' Orientation and Acceptance of Others, 'Self-Ideal Self' Congruency and Mental Health Changes for Fourth and Fifth Grade Children," *Journal of Educational Research,* 63:471-477, July/August 1970.

"Three hypotheses were tested in a program designed to teach 'causal' understandings to fourth- and fifth-grade pupils in two separate school systems. The experimental and control groups tended to be similar on the variables of mean IQ scores and socioeconomic backgrounds. At the end of the experiment a t-test comparison was made between pre- and post-tests in both the experimental and control groups." Results showed that there was a highly significant gain in acceptance of others.

Hefele, Thomas J. "The Effects of Systematic Human Relations Training Upon Student Achievement." *Journal of Research and Development in Education,* 5:52-69, Winter 1971.

Summarizes research to date in the area of the effects of systematic human relations training upon student achievement. Outlines method and results of a research project on this subject designed to clarify further important variables, to investigate their role in the preparation of teachers and to verify their relationship to pupil achievement. Results showed that 1) participants would experience more significant gains in their ability to discriminate teaching situations and to communicate effectively with their classes, 2) quality of interpersonal processes to which teacher-trainees were exposed would relate positively to their own interpersonal functioning, and 3) that quality of interpersonal processes occurring in the classroom would relate positively to pupil achievement.

Kolb, David A. "Achievement Motivation Training for Underachieving High School Boys." *Journal of Personality and Social Psychology,* 783–792, December 1965.

In a 1.5 year follow-up on a study involving two groups of underachieving high school boys, those who had received achievement motivation training showed significant improvement in grades correlated with participation variables.

Koval, Calista B. and Hales, Loyde W. "The Effects of the DUSO Guidance Program on the Self-Concepts of Primary School Children." *Child Study Journal.* 2:57–61, 1972.

"The purpose of the study was to investigate the effects of the DUSO Guidance Program on the self-concepts of Appalachian primary school children. This program was designed to aid children in the development of adequate self-concepts, the discovery of personal strengths, and the acceptance of limited success in some endeavors. A series of guided, group experiences (including stories, art, music, role-playing, discussion, and puppetry) are used to meet these objectives." A statistical analysis of the results of the study is presented.

Koval, Calista Bartha. "Effects of a Selected Guidance Program on the Self-Concepts of Appalachian Primary School Children." *Dissertation Abstracts International,* Vol. 32 (11-A), (May 1972). 6132.

Koval, Calista B. and Hales, Loyde W. "The Effects of the DUSO Guidance Program on the Self-Concepts of Primary School Children." *Child Study Journal,* 2:57–61, 1972.

This is a description and evaluation of a program designed to aid Appalachian children in the development of self-concept and discovery of personal strengths.

Long, Barbara Ellis. "Behavioral Science for Elementary School Pupils." *Elementary School Journal,* 70:253–260, February 1970.

A study of eighteen children from the middle and upper socioeconomic levels at the Webster College Experimental School in St. Louis to examine the feasibility of conducting a course in the behavioral sciences with children. It was found the children responded with interest and enthusiasm to a plan that allowed them to try out experiments or games on various topics from the field of psychology. Among the topics covered were aspects of perception, learning, emotions, child development, and personality.

Long, Barbara Ellis. "A Model for Elementary School Behavioral Science as an Agent of Primary Prevention." *American Psychologist,* 25:571-574, June 1970.

Assuming that the development of behavior is dependent on social learning, the author conducted a pilot study of eighteen children of the fourth through sixth grades. The curriculum in the behavioral sciences focused on role playing, experimentation, and class discussions on matters of personal concern and interest to the children. The curriculum was suited to the children, rather than the children to the course. General topics in the behavioral sciences, such as personality, learning, and even mob behavior, were deemed relevant to the study. In conclusion, the author stated that opportunities for enhancing ego development and psychological comfort appear good via this model for a behavioral science curriculum.

Long, Barbara Ellis. "To Teach About Human Behavior." *Educational Leadership,* 27:683-685, April 1970.

Author reports on successful studies in St. Louis of providing a curriculum of mental health education within the school program in the intermediate grades. "The children in the studies so far attempted have demonstrated again that the study of human behavior has real meaning at the visceral level for children of any age. Some of the impressions gained in these studies indicating a method of presentation for lessons concerned with human behavior" are outlined.

McClelland, D. C. "What is the Effect of Achievement Motivation Training in the Schools?" *Teachers College Record,* 74:129-45, December 1972.

Shows evidence that achievement motivation raises skill test scores and works better with boys than girls. In training teachers in this area the structure, climate and technique were studied and evaluated through multimedia approach. N Ach means that achievement planning, consciousness and thinking are raised, rather than school performance.

Mantz, Genelle. "A Mental Health Unit for Fourth and Fifth Grades." *Journal of School Health,* 39:658-661, November 1969.

Describes experimental classes in mental health at the fourth and fifth grade level in Illinois. The program was endorsed by students, teachers, and parents alike. At the end of the school year the teachers recommended that mental health be taught in a graduated fashion from kindergarten through eighth grade.

Mehta, Prayag. "Achievement Motivation Training for Educational Development." *Indian Educational Review,* 3:46-74, January 1968.

Describes an experiment in achievement motivation training in five schools, 290 boys in Class 9 in India. After training a statistically significant gain was shown in academic performance of the control group. There was also a gain in N Ach.

Miles, Matthew B. "Human Relations Training: Processes and Outcomes." *Journal of Counseling Psychology,* 7:301-306, Winter 1960.

Report on a two-week training laboratory at Bethel, Maine, in 1958 attended by thirty-four persons, mostly elementary school principals. The human relations laboratory strived to show that participants would show improvement on three variables: sensitivity, diagnostic ability, and action skill. The author gives some background research data on prior human relations studies, and supplies findings on the present study.

Morgan, Mildred I. and Ojemann, Ralph H. "The Effect of a Learning Program Designed to Assist Youth in an Understanding of Behavior and its Development." *Child Development,* 13:181-194, September 1942.

"In this study a learning program designed to develop an understanding of behavior in marriage, family and social relationships was administered to two experimental groups of young people. Each experimental group was paralleled by a matched control group. Measurements of conflict and selected attitudes were obtained before and following the administration of the learning program."

Mullins, R. F. "Increased Self-Actualization as a Result of an Intensive One Semester Academic Program." *Journal of Educational Research,* 66:210-14, June 1973.

Thirty-four college undergrads, not majoring in science, participated in an innovative program in biological sciences. The program stressed applications of biology to social problems, and emphasized emotional as well as intellectual growth. Students took part in discussions, field trips, projects in the community, and encounter-type process groups. At the end of the program, participants showed significant increases on nine of the twelve scales of the Personal Orientation Inventory, a measure of self-actualization. Greatest changes occurred in inner directedness and acceptance of their own aggression. The results indicate that the program met a broad spectrum of student needs, and support the efforts of those who are trying to include all aspects of personal growth in higher education.

Muuss, Rolf E. "The Effects of a One- and Two-Year Causal-Learning Program. *Journal of Personality,* 28:479-491, December 1960.

"The purpose of this study was to investigate the extent to which students who had participated in an experimental learning program designed to develop self-understanding and an appreciation of the dynamics of human behavior differ from control students on measures of causality and mental health. In general the findings support the hypothesis that experimental students show more knowledge of causality and they respond more in line with mental-health criteria."

Ojemann, Ralph H.; Nugent, Anne; Corry, Martha. "Study of Human Behavior in the Social Science Program." *Social Education,* 11:25-29, January 1949.

Ninth-graders studied the analytical approach to human behavior in their social studies class. Tests given at the beginning and at the end of the learning program indicate that the subjects made significant gains both in their understanding of behavior and in their attitude toward the use of the analytical approach. It was found that the concepts of human behavior learned by the students were so basic to social problems that these concepts could subsequently be applied to the study of such topics as the family, school, community relations, and government functions.

Ojemann, Ralph H.; Maxey, E. James; Snider, Bill C. F. "The Effect of a Program of Guided Learning Experience in Developing Probability Concepts at the Third Grade Level." *Journal of Experimental Education,* 33:321-330, Summer 1965.

"A program of guided learning experiences was devised for developing several aspects of the concept of probability. In constructing the program, use was made of an analysis of the psychological nature of the learning task and of the nature of the learners. The program was administered to equated experimental and control classes at the third-grade level. Four tests were used to measure the effect of the program."

Ojemann, Ralph H. "Investigations on the Effects of Teaching an Understanding and Appreciation of Behavior Dynamics." *Prevention of Mental Disorders in Children,* Chapter XVII., Gerald Caplan (Ed.) New York: Basic Books Inc., 1961. 378-397.

This chapter describes the causal approach to behavior, looks at changes in course content and teacher training that a causal approach would engender, and examines research on the effects of increasing an individual's understanding and appreciation of the dynamic nature of behavior.

Ojemann, Ralph H. and Snider, Bill C. "The Effect of a Teaching Program in Behavioral Science on Changes in Causal Behavior Scores." *Journal of Educational Research,* 57:255-260, January 1964.

"The purpose of this paper is to describe the changes in the observed daily behavior of the child that appeared following the administration of a teaching program in behavioral science. One of the aims of this program is to develop a sequence of learning experiences beginning in the earliest years to help the child acquire an understanding and appreciation of the dynamic nature of human behavior. The investigation involved the development of a method for making and scoring the observations of the child's daily behavior and its use with experimental and control groups."

Ojemann, Ralph H., and Campbell, Alexander. "The Development of Moral

Judgments—I." *Journal of Experimental Education,* 42:65-73, Spring 1974.

"This paper begins with an analysis of factors involved in the study of moral judgments, including motivating forces, methods the individual uses for working them out, examining alternative methods as to consequences, and the role of a goal or purpose in life. A learning program based on this analysis was developed for the elementary school. Two investigations of the effects of the program are reported—one with 5th grade subjects in a low socio-economic area and one with 6th grade students in a middle class suburb. Comparison of results from experimental and control groups indicated that significant growth in the dimensions tested were made by both groups. The process of making moral judgments can be influenced by planned learning experiences."

Purkey, William Watson. "Project Self-Discovery: Its Effect on Bright But Underachieving High School Students." *Gifted Child Quarterly,* 13:242-6, Winter 1969.

Discusses a study done with bright underachieving high school students called Project Self-Discovery. Evidence suggests project had a positive effect. It did not have highly positive hoped for effect, but counselors at high schools where it was tried were very enthusiastic about it.

Rosenthal, Sheldon. "A Fifth Grade Classroom Experiment in Fostering Mental Health." *Journal of Child Psychiatry,* 2:302-29, 1952.

An experimental study to ascertain benefits derived from a classroom program planned to foster mental health. The author provides background information on past experiments of others in the field and discusses in detail the classroom techniques and thirteen lesson plans used in his experiment. The subjects of the experiment were fifth grade Negro children from Harlem of low socioeconomic levels and low I.Q. averages. To evaluate the outcome of the experiment, three criteria were used: the sociogram, a modification of the social distance scale, and the California Test of Personality. Following the experiment some positive results were obtained in the mental health of the class in spite of adverse environmental and behavioral conditions. In Appendix II of the paper, the author lists written reactions of the children to the formal lessons.

7930
Schulman, Jerome L., Ford, Radin C., and Busk, Patricia. "A Classroom Program to Improve Self-Concept." *Psychology in the Schools,* 10:481-7, October 1973.

Describes the development of a self-concept unit for a mental health program. Subjects were 6th, 7th, and 8th graders in five suburban school districts. Coopersmith procedures were used to evaluate the results of the program. It is concluded that the unit of instruction affected the students' self-esteem and self-concept. An appendix contains the self-concept unit lesson plans.

Seamons, Terry R. "An Individualized Learning Unit Approach for Teaching Empathy as a Necessary Element in Effective Interpersonal Relationships." *Diss. Abstracts International,* Vol. 33 (6-A) (December 1972), 2775.

This study shows that a well-developed unit designed to teach empathetic understanding was effective. It has direct applications for classroom use.

Slobetz, Frank and Lund, Alice. "Some Effects of a Personal Developmental Program at the Fifth Grade Level." *Journal of Educational Research,* 49: 373-378, January 1956.

To determine some effects of a program geared to personal development of children at the fifth-grade level, a study was made of two groups of students who were similar in mental ages, intelligence quotients, and occupational status of fathers. In the experimental group, an organized program in personal development was provided, while no such program was given the control group. Some significant positive personality changes were noted in the experimental group in the area of self-adjustment as well as social adjustment.

Smith, Bryan. "Values Clarification in Drug Education: A Comparative Study." *Journal of Drug Education,* 3:369-76, Winter 1973.

Measured the relative effectiveness of two methods of teaching drug education to 63 preservice elementary school teachers. The methods compared were the traditional teacher-confined approach, and the value clarification group-centered process. In the latter technique the teacher acts as moderator in student-initiated discussions, and grades are determined by both student and teacher. Evaluation of the results shows that members of the values clarification group read more independently, achieved greater gain scores in affective and cognitive testing, and developed a sense of community that brought them together to solve problems.

6300

Sprinthall, Norman A., and Erickson, V. Lois. "Learning Psychology by Doing Psychology: Guidance Through the Curriculum." *Personnel and Guidance Journal,* 52:396-405, February 1974.

Describes two experimental high school courses dealing with the content and process of counseling psychology. Results are evaluated in terms of the development of student skills and the students' psychological maturation. It is concluded that creation of a comprehensive behavioral science curriculum is both promising and possible.

Stanford, Gene. "Psychological Education in the Classroom." *Personnel and Guidance Journal,* 50:585-92, March 1972.

A study of 8 groups of approximately 10 high school students each who were enrolled in seminars, 4 of which followed a customary English program and 4 of which not only followed the program but also spent half of their time in psychological education activities. Examples of such activities are described through excerpts from a student's notebook. Effects of the activities were measured by direct observation of seminar and by questionnaires. It is concluded that deliberate attention to social and emotional development in the classroom can have an important positive effect on students.

Stetter, Richard. "A Group Guidance Technique for the Classroom Teacher." *The School Counselor,* 16:179-184, January 1969.

A group guidance technique is used on ninth-graders in a controlled experiment designed to test the hypothesis: "The anxiety level of students will be lowered when they learn that others their age have personal-social problems similar to their own." A problem checklist was used to allow students to reveal their personal problems to each other while remaining anonymous. Subjective results of the experiment were presented through a description of class behavior, while the objective analysis of the results was based on the scores of anxiety tests.

Stiles, Frances Smythe. "Developing an Understanding of Human Behavior at the Elementary School Level." *Journal of Educational Research,* 43:516-524, March 1950.

This study observed the changes in the social behavior of elementary school children in the fourth through sixth grades as a result of a learning program especially designed for them. The following procedures were applied: 1) designing a learning program to analyze certain behavior patterns in children, 2) presenting the program to the children through stories and discussions, and 3) measuring the program for its effectiveness.

EJ 099 043

Swanson, Jon Colby. "Junior High Student Evaluations of Drug Education by Values and Traditionally Oriented Teachers." *Journal of Drug Education,* 4:43-50, Spring 1974.

Student perceptions of teacher qualities show significant differences between those teachers trained by values clarification techniques and those trained by traditional techniques. Courses taught by these teachers were also perceived differently by students who took them. A combination of lecture-discussion methods and values clarification techniques seem most appropriate.

Van Koughnett, B. C. and Smith, Merle E. "Enhancing the Self-Concept in School." *Educational Leadership,* 27:253-255, December 1969.

Pilot program in one elementary school in Pontiac, Michigan, in which teachers, by employing a positive approach and providing positive reinforcement, were able to enhance the self-concepts of students. Because there were many black children in the school, students were constantly reminded of the contributions made by the black man in America. An inservice education program for teachers was conducted throughout the school year to reinforce positive attitudes of the teachers. An evaluation of the project revealed schools can evolve a program that serves to make students regard themselves positively.

### III. Chapters in Books and Reports; Articles in Encyclopedias

Quinn, R. E. "Evaluation of a technique for clarifying environmental values with high school sophomores." *Dissertation Abstracts International,* April 1974, 34(10), 6371A.

The author of this research study developed 31 packets of student materials called value sheets. These value sheets contained many environmental topics including: air and water pollution, land use, wild life, etc. Twenty 10th grade classes were selected to participate in the 10 week study using the value sheets twice a week. Final testing indicated no significant difference from initial testing scores on the environmental attitudes of the students.

### V. Reports

Barr, Robert D. (Ed.) *Values and Youth.* "Teaching Social Studies in an Age of Crisis." No. 2. Washington, D.C.: National Council for the Social Studies, 1971.

This book consists of a series of articles by various authors which focus on the dilemmas of youth, the concerns of our society, and how social studies courses can become more responsive to the significant issues of our time. Part 1, "The World of Youth: Cultural Alternatives and Value Options," looks at misconceptions about youth, multiplicity of value options, forces creating cultural alternatives and value options, and value education in the social studies. In Part II, "Voices of Youth: Source for Teachers," a variety of youthful authors present their reactions to life around them. Part III, "Values in the Classroom: Instructional Guidelines for Teachers," outlines practical aids for teachers who wish to make education more relevant. Finally, an Appendix lists music that is relevant to young people, appropriate films, and a selected bibliography. This book is valuable as a practical resource for teachers who wish to make their teaching relevant.

ED 085 175

Chamberlain, Virginia May. "A Description of the Use of a Value Clarification Approach in the Teaching of Earth Science Classes." Ph.D. Dissertation, Michigan State University, 1971.

Reported is a descriptive study in which a value clarification approach—based on the work of Raths, Harmin, and Simon, as reported in the book, *Values and Teaching*—was used for a three-month period in the author's instruction of four earth science classes in a medium-sized rural school. Two major concerns were of interest: (1) the value of science as a meaningful part of daily life, and (2) the integration of cognitive and affective objectives rather than emphasis upon one area at the expense of the other. Evaluation of the strategies used was based upon observation and upon opinionnaire data collected by means of instruments designed by the researcher. The following findings were included: (1) girls increased in their perception of relationships between the study of science and the problems of their daily lives; (2) the perception of positive relationships was at the same level for both boys and girls at the experiment's conclusion; (3) boys showed an increase in action activities related to science, e.g. voluntary science demonstrations and participation in ecological issues arising within the local community, and (4) analysis of the experimental and initiatory use of a value clarification approach led the researcher to be concerned about the effects of teaching strategies as being measurable in terms of changed student behaviors as a criteria of success. (Author/EB)

ED 045461

Hanley, Janey P. and Others. *Curiosity, Competence, Community: An Evaluation of Man: A Course of Study,* 1970.

Describes objectives of MACOS and evaluation instruments used. An attempt was made to find evaluation instruments which were congruent with the objectives of MACOS. Data was organized in relation to several questions and consideration is given to the process of teacher education for MACOS. Reported success of MACOS in various areas by transcripts of student interviews and interpretations.

ED 070250 and 070251

Kuhlman, Charles and Wiley, William. "The Inside/Out Evaluation: The First Five Programs." Part I and II. (July 1972). 67 pp.

Summary of results obtained from testing done on the Inside/Out affective education curriculum in 1972 in 155 3rd and 4th grade classrooms. Testing methods used are as follows: "Specially designed classroom observation system for measuring relevant categories of teacher and student discussion following the program, viewing, teacher and observer questionnaires dealing with teacher and student reaction to programs and discussions; in-depth interviews with small groups of school children who had viewed programs in the series, but not participated in classroom discussions." Contains a wealth of evaluative information about this program including how it could be improved.

ED 098 557

Pracejus, Eleanor L. "The Effect of Value Clarification on Reading Comprehension." Ph.D. Dissertation, University of Pittsburgh. (Available from University Microfilms, P.O. Box 1764, Ann Arbor, Michigan 48106. 143p., 1974.

This study was designed to determine what effect knowledge of value
clarification would have on the reading comprehension of eighth graders. The
use of value clarification involves students in decision making, identification
with characters or situations, evaluative judgments, appreciations, and so
forth. In this study reading comprehension was defined as the understanding
and interpretation of the meanings embodied in printed symbols. Value
clarification was defined as a process whereby individuals are led in a systematic way without persuasion, to understand their own aspirations, purposes, and feelings, thus establishing goals and levels of achievement. There
were fourteen weekly sessions of 45 minutes each with two sessions used
for pre- and post-testing. The experimental group read stories and discussed
them using a value clarification approach. The comprehension group read the
same stories but used the approach suggested by the publisher. A control
group received only pre- and post-testing. Two major conclusions can be
made from the findings: (1) exposure to value clarification does seem to result in an increase in reading comprehension; (2) there are strong indications
of a positive relationship between knowledge of value clarification and reading comprehension. (Author/TO)

ED 033091

Preuss, William J. *The Initiation and Evaluation of a Human Relations Program
Conducted by Teacher Training Students in an Elementary School.* Concordia
Teachers College, Seward, Nebraska, Office of Education, Washington, D.C.,
1969.

Describes an experimental human relations program in which teacher
training students developed a one-to-one relationship with an elementary
school child. Object was to develop an acceptance of self, acceptance of
others, and acceptance by others in trainee and child. This report describes
the experiment and the results, which were not statistically significant but
did show that positive attitudinal and behavioral change can be transmitted
from instructor to student to child by using this approach.

ED 021928

Purkey, William Watson. *Project Self-Discovery: Its Effect on Bright Underachievers at Nine Florida High Schools,* February 1968.

This project was aimed at promoting social and personal development
of bright underachieving students. Statistical evidence showed "modest"
evidence that the program had a positive effect.

ED 060487

Spahn, Lee P. *Developmental Group Counseling in the Elementary School.*

May 1971.

This study tried to determine whether group counseling would improve peer relations in the elementary school classroom. Favorable results were found.

b. *Teacher-Training Programs.*

### II. Magazines and Journals

Aspy, David. "Better Self-Concepts Through Success." *Journal of Negro Education,* 40:369-72, Fall 1971.

Presents a scale for teacher self-evaluation of class performance. When teachers used the scale to evaluate video and audio recordings of teaching performances, the self-concept of the students improved at the same time.

Banmen, John and Capelle, Ron. "Human-Relations Training in Three Rural Manitoba High Schools: A Three Month Follow-Up." *Canadian Counselor,* 6:260-72, October 1972.

This study supports other studies which indicate that human-relations training results in lasting rather than temporary personal growth.

EJ 035777

Berenson, David H. "The Effects of Systematic Human Relations Training Upon Classroom Performance of Elementary School Teachers." *Journal of Research and Development in Education,* 4:70-85, Winter 1971.

Summarizes reseach in the area of the mental health and counseling aspects of classroom teaching. Details the method and results of a study of the effects of an integrated didactic and experimental human relations training program on the classroom performance of elementary school student-teachers. Results showed 1) that the student-teacher's level of interpersonal functioning appears to be highly correlated with several desirable outcomes of teacher training, and 2) that if it is desirable that teachers be capable of offering appropriately high levels of the conditions of empathy, regard, concreteness, etc., then learning the communication of these conditions must be included in their professional preparation.

Gulutsan, M. "Teachers' Reactions to Procedures in Teaching Human Relations." *Alberta Journal of Educational Research,* 11:154–65, 1965.

Study of twenty-one elementary school teachers using the Social Maturity Scale of the Vassar College Attitude Inventory showed significant differences between high and low scorers in use of unstructured permissive group discussion with rankings of expression of feelings, discussion of the dynamics of human behavior, and psychodrama.

EJ 082 258

Hartzell, Richard E., et al. "Comparative Effectiveness of Human Relations

Training for Elementary School Teachers." *Journal of Educational Research,* 66:457-61, July-August 1973.

The present study was designed to determine the effectiveness of a short (20 hours) training program in human relations skill for elementary student teachers.

Levitt, Eugene E. "Effect of a 'Causal' Teacher Training Program on Authoritarianism and Responsibility in Grade School Children." *Psychological Reports,* 1:449-458, December 1955.

"This study is a secondary follow-up of three intermediate level grade school classes whose teachers had been subjected to a 'causal' training program during the period June 1954 to April 1955. Various teaching materials based on the causal approach to curricular content were provided for the teachers. The purpose of the present study was to investigate the effects of the causal teacher training program on authoritarianism and responsibility of the children in their classes."

EJ 105 579

Lotecka, Lynn. "A Project Advocating Humanistic Education: An Evaluation of its Effect on Public School Teachers." *Journal of Drug Education,* 4:141-149, Summer 1974.

The philosophy and characteristics of a project for preventing drug abuse is described. A partial history of its ongoing evaluation is presented. The results show that participating teachers gained significantly in drug knowledge. There were also significant changes in attitudes concerning drug abuse, child development, and pedagogy.

Ojemann, R. J. *et al.* "The Effect of a 'Causal' Teacher Training Program and Certain Curricular Changes on Grade School Children." *Journal of Experimental Education,* 24:95-114, December 1955.

Four classroom teachers participated in a program designed to increase their understanding and appreciation of child behavior, to provide opportunity for growth in personal adjustment and to develop methods for teaching causally oriented curricular content. Results show this can bring significant differences in the child's growth.

3940

Osman, Jack D. "The Use of Selected Value—Clarifying Strategies in Health Education." *Journal of School Health,* Vol. 44:21-25, January 1974.

Explored the feasibility of using selected value—clarifying strategies in a health education course for future teachers. Students were instructed in the usual course content but with a focus on the levels of valuing as defined by Louis Raths. Strategies to assist students in valuing included the value sheet, a provocative, often controversial statement designed to stir up strong feelings. Other techniques are also described. A scale was administered to evaluate the program.

EJ 090 918
Smith, Bryan C. "Values Clarification in Drug Education: A Comparative Study." *Journal of Drug Education,* 3:369–75, Winter 1973.

The purpose of this study was to measure the relative effectiveness of two methods of teaching drug education to preservice elementary school teachers. The methods compared were the traditional teacher confined approach, and the value clarification group-centered process. The latter approach was found to be superior in all ways measured.

8558
Williams, John D. "Classroom implementation of self-enhancing education." *Psychological Reports,* 34:137–138, February 1974.

"Twenty-three teachers involved in a week-long self-enhancing education workshop and employed in 1 of 2 project schools for at least 1 year were compared on 11 measures of interaction analysis with 26 teachers who served as controls. Significant differences were found on 6 measures, showing that the project teachers had been successful in implementing the self-enhancing education process at the classroom level."

Withall, John. "Mental Health in the Classroom" *Journal of Teacher Education,* 15:193–199, June 1964.

Describes U.S. research to improve mental health through the classroom experience, including University of Wisconsin, Bank Street College of Education, San Francisco State College Project and University of Texas Study. Includes an overview of the University of Wisconsin's mental health-teacher education research project also.

## V. Reports

ED 039596
Anandem, Kamala, and others. *Feelings: To Fear or to Free.* 1970.

This report tells about a pilot study designed to test the effectiveness of two affective teaching methods. In one group of third graders, the teacher reinforced verbalization of feelings. In the other group, the class discussed and role-played feelings. The feelings class seemed to promote a more open atmosphere. •

ED 052478
Bannen, John and Capelle, Ron. *Human Relations Training in Three Rural Manitoba High Schools.* Manitoba Department of Youth and Education, Winnipeg, 1971.

It is assumed that too few principals, teachers and counselors possess the necessary personal characteristics which facilitate the growth of self-actualization of students. This study investigates whether these qualities could be developed, using a model of human relations training.

ED 038188

Bemis, Kathryn A. and Liberty, Paul G. *Southwestern Cooperative Educational Laboratory Interaction Observation: A System for Analyzing Teacher-Pupil Interaction in the Affective Domain.* SWREL. Albuquerque, New Mexico, 2 March 1970.

Classification of student behavior was based on Krathwohl's theory of the three lowest levels of the affective domain. Classification of teacher behavior was based on Sullivan's social-psychological theory of personality. Instructions are given on how to record behaviors. A copy of the observation schedule is included.

Bingman, William S. "An Investigation Into the Effects of a Humanistic Training Method on the Perceptions of Elementary Teachers-in-Training." Paper presented at the Annual Meeting of the American Educational Research Association, New Orleans, Louisiana, February 1973. 13p.

This study compares the effects of a 2-week humanistic training program, a 4-week participation observation experience, and a 7-week special methods program on the perceptions of prospective elementary school teachers from West Virginia University and elementary teachers from Monogalis County, West Virginia. Sixty-six subjects took part. The research tested the hypotheses that these programs would not affect the teachers' perceptions concerning (a) self concept, (b) personal beliefs, (c) degree of openmindedness, (d) classroom practices, (e) student relationship, and (f) reaction to classroom situations. All subjects were pretested with the Personal Orientation Inventory (POI), Relationship Inventory (RI), Personal Beliefs Inventory (PBI), Teacher Practices Inventory (TPI), Dogmatism Scale (DS), Teacher Situation Reaction Test (TSRT), and the Tennessee Self Concept (TSC). The experimental group of teachers completed the DS, PBI, TSRT, and the TPI. The following implications emerged: (a) efforts should be made to determine the individual needs of prospective teachers, and assignments should be made to individual programs; (b) sequential humanistic programs should be implemented early in the college program with emphasis on course presentation; and (c) future programs should be designed with frequent public school experiences early in the college program. (Eight references are included.) (BRB)

ED 002880

Bowers, Norman D. and Soar, Robert S. *Studies of Human Relations in the Teacher-Learning Process.* 1961.

The focus of this research project was the education of teachers in the methods and techniques of effective group membership. Evaluation studies were done using laboratory training experiments in the area of human relations. Sixty teachers participated, divided into an experimental group for laboratory workshops and a control group. Steps of pre-training, laboratory training for the former groups, and post-training were used for collecting pertinent data. Innovative action was represented by this project from the following standpoints: 1) in the measurement of teacher effectiveness in the areas of social-emotional climate of the classroom and the social skills of the children, 2) in the application of a method of learning which could upgrade these teacher skills, 3) in predicting which teachers could most likely profit from this type of learning experience, and 4) in increasing understanding of the nature of effective teaching. The report concluded that the results of the project could add significantly to many different aspects of education.

ED 090 109
DeMarte, Patrick J., Sorgman, Margo I. *A Pilot Study to Investigate the Effects of Courses in Humanistic Education on the Self-Perceptions of Preservice Teachers.* Paper presented at the Annual Meeting of the National Council for Social Studies (San Francisco, California, November 21, 1973).

The lack of empirical data on teacher self-perception led to this study of the effects of selected courses in humanistic education on the self-perceptions of preservice teachers. Changes in self perception of students in three courses—Values Clarification, Discovering Your Teaching Self, and Transactional Analysis—and differences in those taking these courses and student teachers who did not were assessed by a seven point semantic differential rating scale. Factor analysis and factor similarity provided data shown in tabular form for each of the concepts of Real Self, Ideal Self, and Teaching Self. Results for those in humanistic education courses showed that Real Self perceptions were lower in self-esteem and a sense of personal well-being but Ideal Self was viewed more positively in terms of capability, intelligence and leadership. Students completing the courses perceived their Teaching Self as better adjusted to its environment and more capable of doing something about it. A summary of questions evolving from the findings and recommendations for further investigation conclude the report. (Author/KSM)

ED 002418
Hough, John B. *The Dogmatism Factor in Human Relations Training of Preservice Teachers.* 1965.

Report presents research designed to study the effectiveness of programmed human relations training in improving the human relations skills of preservice teachers and to study the efforts of dogmatism on the learning of human relations skills. Subjects were 230 preservice teachers. Matched study groups were tested both before and after instruction to assess human relations skills.

It was concluded that the Human Development Institute General Relationship Improvement Program can teach human relations skills to preservice teachers, especially when instructional sessions are spaced one week apart, and that highly dogmatic subjects with relatively closed belief-disbelief systems make less gain in human relations skills than others, particularly in the area of empathetic understanding. This paper was presented at the Annual Meeting of the American Educational Research Association, Chicago, February 1965.

ED 045573

Khanna, J. L. *A Humanistic Approach to Inservice Education for Teachers.* Final Evaluation Report. Project Upper Cumberland, Livingston, Tennessee. Bureau of Elementary and Secondary Education, Washington, D.C. 1970.

This document evaluates a human relations training program for teachers. It describes evaluation techniques used and final results. A bibliography of evaluation techniques is included.

ED 066373

Long, Barbara Ellis. *Implications of a Teacher Training Program Developed For a Curriculum in Psychology Elementary Level.* July 1971.

This is a report of an in-service teacher training program conducted in St. Louis in 1970–71. The program was based on a curriculum in psychology and method of presentation designed for sixth grade students. Two hypotheses were tested: 1) that unselected teachers can learn and use the materials and method of the present curriculum without extensive prior training in psychology; 2) that sixth grade students can learn the content and method of this field and profit in terms of general psychological comfort, increased motivation and performance in the general school curricula, and increased self-concept. Findings from classroom observations, teachers' meetings and test results with children are presented. Implication for teacher training are discussed as well as possibilities for prevention of emotional disturbances in children and difficulties of communication.

Runquist, Merrell P.; Pinkerton, Rolffs S.; Martin, Paul L. "Evaluating a Mental Health Workshop for Teachers." *Hospital and Community Psychiatry.* 23: 379–81, December 1972.

This study was about an in-service training program for teachers on mental health concepts applied to the classroom. It was effective in changing teachers' attitudes about mental health in the classroom.

c. *Surveys of Student and Teacher Attitudes*

### I. Books

Byler, Ruth V.; Lewis, Gertrude M.; Totman, Ruth J. *Teach Us What We Want to Know; Report of a Survey on Health Interests, Concerns and Problems of 5,000 Students in Selected Schools From Kindergarten Through Grade Twelve.* New York: Mental Health Materials Center, 1969.

A sampling of what some 5,000 students in Connecticut have to say about their interests and concerns about mental health, social-emotional development, society, and in secondary school, about sex education. Chapters are divided by grade levels. A summary of comments is found at the end of each chapter. An analysis of all these summaries is given in Part 3 of the book.


## II. Magazines and Journals

Abrams, Alan M. and Stanley, Julian C. "Preparation of High School Psychology Teachers By Colleges." *American Psychologist,* 22:166–169, February 1967.

Report on the responses received from 1,000 chairmen of college psychology departments throughout the USA about the problem of a psychology teaching major or minor. The respondents viewed the problem along three primary dimensions: maturity-immaturity, supply-demand, and certification versus no certification. These are discussed by the author.

Anderson, Robert L. "Psychology in Michigan's High Schools." *American Psychologist,* 20:169, February 1965.

Survey of 57 high schools in 1963 in Michigan to determine the nature of psychology courses being offered, the characteristics of the students involved, and the qualifications of the teachers concerned. The nature of the course varies greatly, the course was usually offered to seniors and juniors in good academic standing, and credit hours earned by teachers of psychology range from five to forty-five.

Engle, T. L. "Objectives For And Subject Matter Stressed in High School Courses in Psychology." *American Psychologist,* 22:162–166, February 1967.

A nationwide survey of high school teachers of psychology in 1965 to determine nature of psychology courses being taught at that time. Of 257 queries, 130 responded. Psychology courses were generally taught for one semester as part of the social studies curriculum. Objectives for the course were listed as the study of personal problems, scientific knowledge, social relationships, philosophy of life, and family living. Subject areas stressed were mental health, individuality, motivation-emotions, and social behavior. Tables illustrate mean ranks by teachers and psychologists on objectives and subject areas for high school psychology courses.

Lewis, Gertrude M. "I Am—I Want—I Need." *Childhood Education,* 46:186–194, January 1970.

This is a partial report on a survey of health, interests, concerns, and problems of 5,000 Connecticut studnets in Kindergarten through grade twelve. Key passages were abstracted for the 10- to 13-year-old student showing that these students were very interested in learning more about themselves and others.

McFadden, Hugh B. and Pasewark, Richard A. "High School Psychology in the Rocky Mountain Region." *Journal of School Psychology,* 8:306–310, Summer 1970.

"While this study does not provide an overly gratifying view of high school psychology in the Mountain States, it does suggest that many students enrolled in introductory sections in college are probably repeating material already studied in high school. The authors therefore suggest that the field of psychology should concentrate considerable effort upon raising quality of instruction at the secondary school level, so that the student may pursue richer or more advanced work in college." Authors also suggest that better training for teachers of psychology be provided by the universities and the American Psychological Association.

McNiel, Bessie. "Development at the Youth Level of a Conception of the Causes of Behavior and the Effectiveness of a Learning Program in this Area." *Journal of Experimental Education,* 13:81-85, September 1944.

An experimental survey of 1,000 high school students to determine their understanding of behavior concepts. The first part of the study was to determine to what extent the concepts are operative in specified groups of adolescents, and the second part of the study was to determine how effective a learning program is in developing the concepts.

Noland, Robert L. "School Psychologists and Counselors View the Role of the High School Psychology Course." *Journal of School Psychology,* 5:177-184, Spring 1967.

"The inadequacy of properly defined objectives, course content and instructional materials available, and evidence regarding insufficiently trained teaching personnel led the author to attempt a clarification and assessment of overall isues relating to the role of psychology in high school. The article summarizes certain of the results of an investigation on the teaching of psychology as a secondary school subject in American schools, with special reference to the state of Ohio. The views of school psychologists and counselors are high-lighted."

Snellgrove, Louis. "Report on American Psychological Association Activities Concerning Teaching Psychology in the Schools." *Journal of School Psychology,* 5:250-251, Spring 1967.

Report by author of two committees of APA concerned with psychology in secondary schools. These committees are active in promoting high school psychology through a newsletter, a bibliography listing tapes, films, books, and other aids in teaching psychology; providing course outlines; encouraging universities to have summer institutes in psychology for teachers; and promoting the participation of high school students in science fairs.

Thornton, Bob M. and Colver, Robert M. "The Psychology Course in Secondary Schools." *Journal of School Psychology*, 5:185-190, Spring 1967.

Presents statistics of actual number of psychology courses taught in secondary schools in the United States in 1963. Tables present figures on number of high schools in each state teaching psychology and the corresponding number of students in these classes. This investigation showed that psychology as a separate course of instruction has notably increased since the previous national survey of 1950.

## V. Reports

ED 052119

*Education in Moral Values in Michigan: A Report on a Survey.* Lansing, Michigan: Michigan State Department of Education, 1968.

This report tells about a survey on the status of moral education in Michigan. Document includes questionnaire used, reasons for doing the survey, results of the survey, and implications for educators.

ED 002001

*Human Relations in the Classroom—A Challenge to Teacher Education,* 1965.

Reports on a survey of a representative sample of 1,075 secondary school teachers which shows that teachers are confronted daily in their classrooms wth a wide range of human relations problems and situations. Many examples are given as well as information which indicates that college courses tend to neglect the teaching of human relations information, values, and attitudes so that secondary school teachers are inadequately prepared to deal with situations that arise in the classroom. For this reason, inservice teacher education programs in human relations become an urgent necessity.

ED 002003

*Teacher Education for Human Relations in the Classroom—A Report From 1108 College Professors.* 1965.

The North Central Association of Colleges and Secondary Schools surveyed their member colleges to find what attitudes prevailed and what educational opportunities were offered in human relations. Although there is a large amount of agreement among the respondents that information about and understanding of human relations in general are important, about half are not sure of their importance for both the full personal or professional development of the individual. Less emphasis is given to the problem of intergroup relations than interpersonal relations. Most of the respondents avoid controversial topics in their courses. The results of this study convinced the committee that administrators should challenge their faculties to consider the questions of teaching intergroup relations. The gathering of information about the college courses should reveal omissions. Investigations of student attitudes and of values in human relations should be conducted. To complete the campus self-evaluation, textbooks, materials, activities, and organizations should be considered in light of effectiveness in developing human relations. Good practices used in various colleges and universities for developing human relations skills are faculty conferences, student seminars, a human relations center summer workshops, and field experiences for preservice teacher.

d.  *Relevant Psychological Research into Attitudes and Beliefs*

**I. Books**

Combs, Arthur W. *Flordia Studies in the Helping Professions.* Gainesville: University of Florida Press, 1969.

A series of studies attempting to discover the principles governing the nature and effective practice of helping relationships based upon humanistic, perceptual approaches to psychological thought. Experimentally, a program of hypotheses was tested in a series of research studies with teachers, students, counselors, college professors, nurses, and priests. This monograph brings these studies together. Part One deals with the background of the studies. Part Two presents in capsule form each of the researches. Part Three presents an overview and interpretation of the studies. Of interest to psychologists and educators.

Flepan, Dorothy. *Children's Understanding of Social Interaction.* New York: Teacher's College Press, 1968.

"The purpose of this study was to investigate children's ability to describe and make inferences about feelings, thoughts, and intentions that occur in interpersonal relationships and their ability to account for the sequences of behavior that occur. The initial problem of finding an appropriate technique was resolved by using sound films portraying episodes of social interaction suitable for presentation to children at various age levels and for eliciting children's own accounts of what had happened and their responses to a series of specific questions."

Knoblock, Peter and Goldstein, Arnold P. *The Lonely Teacher.* Boston: Allyn and Bacon, 1971.

The authors attempt to capture the perceptions of a group of teachers reporting the quality of their interpersonal relationships with children. A small group process approach was developed in which these teachers explore their feelings, concerns, and interactions with children and with other school staff members. These were teachers of troubled children functioning within the framework of Special Education. The book is divided into four parts and

includes an appendix, which briefly reports the results of psychological testing during the course of the group's development. Part I explores the theme
of teacher loneliness, part II discusses the utilization of group approaches
to facilitate communication between staff members, part III describes the actual group process in which these teachers participated, while part IV analyzes the quality of individual teacher-pupil relationships. Of interest to
psychologists and teachers in special education.

Laurendeau, Monique and Pinard, Adrien. *Causal Thinking in the Child: A
Genetic and Experimental Approach.* New York: International Universities
Press, 1962.

A scientific, technical study of 500 children based on Piaget's theory of
pre-causal thinking. The authors conducted an experiment to clarify and to
draw conclusions on objections raised against Piaget's thesis. The immediate
objectives of the experiment were 1) the verification of the existence of pre-
causal thinking, 2) the control of the sequence of the stages described by
Piaget, 3) and the determination of the age at which each stage is reached.
Children participating in the experiment ranged from four to twelve years
of age.

Minuchin, Patricia; Biber, Barbara; Shapiro, Edna; Zimules, Herbert. *The Psychological Impact of School Experience.* New York: Basic Books, Inc., 1969.

This is a report of a study by the Bank Street College of Education under
the auspices of the National Institute for Mental Health which explored the
basic question: "Does a school, perceived in its particularity as a life environment, affect the psychological development of children—their thinking prow-
ess and style, self-knowledge, interpersonal perception, and emerging value
systems—in predictable ways?" The study was carried out in four schools—
two which exemplified modern educational values and two which were
relatively unaffected by modern trends. Results of the study showed that
when modern ideology was integrated into the total functioning of the
school, it did support elements of healthy personality as self-knowledge and
self-connectedness, a sense of personal autonomy, and involvement. All
facets of the study are presented together with research instruments used.
This extremely valuable piece of research must be read by all who are concerned with the effects of schooling on children.

Simpson, Elizabeth L. *Democracy's Stepchildren: A Study of Need and Belief.*
San Francisco: Jossey-Bass, 1971.

An empirical study of the democratic beliefs of secondary students, this
is an attempt to find significant relationships between the basic human needs
described by Maslow (survival, safety, belongingness, self-esteem) and the
values embedded in American ideology. Evidence supported the conclusion
that satisfaction of these needs is an important factor in learning these humane values. The book also discusses each of these needs at some length, as

well as the nature of the democratic personality. It concludes with a suggested program for the schools which would facilitate democratic socialization.

## II. Magazines and Journals

Anderson, R. C. "Can First Graders Learn an Advanced Problem-Solving Skill?" *Journal of Educational Psychology,* 56:283-284, December 1965.

A training procedure employing programmed-instruction techniques was used to teach high IQ first graders to solve problems by varying each factor in succession while holding all other factors constant. Results showed that children can acquire, retain and transfer rather complex and "advanced" problem-solving skills when presented with suitable training.

Bovard, Everett W., Jr. "The Psychology of Classroom Interaction." *Journal of Educational Research,* 45:215-224, November 1951.

A study to show that the amount of social interaction in the classroom will influence the individual student's perception, feelings, and interpersonal relations, and perhaps even his personality development. The research contrasts the effects of two teaching procedures: the group-centered where student-to-student verbal interaction is encouraged, and the leader-centered where verbal interaction is channeled between teacher and student.

Bower, Eli M. "Mental Health in Education." *Review of Educational Research,* 32:441-54, December 1962.

Review of research concerning aspects of mental health in education. Attention is given to the following: a) concepts of mental health and of education, b) ego development in educational processes, c) mental health factors in school achievement, d) early identification of children with developing mental health problems, and e) psychoeducational approaches to the education of emotionally handicapped children.

Bower, Eli M. "Mental Health in Education." *Review of Educational Research* 38:447-59, December 1968.

This article reviews trends up to 1968 for five topics: concepts and research on mental health in education including their interrelationships, ego development in educational processes, mental health factors in school achievement, early identification of children with developing mental health problems, and approaches to the mental health and education of emotionally handicapped children. After the summary of trends to 1968, the author identifies major trends and directions in content and methodology in each of the five areas.

Brookover, W. B.; Shailer, Thomas; Patterson, Ann. "Self-Concept of Ability and School Achievement." *Sociology of Education,* 37:271-78, Spring 1964.

Three hypotheses about self-concept were tested using a sample of 1,050 seventh grade students and a selected subsample of 110 over- and under-achieving students. A significant positive relationship was found between self-concept of ability and grade point average. This relationship persisted even when measured intelligence was controlled. Specific self-concepts of ability related to specific areas of academic achievement were found. In some areas these were better predictors of achievement in the subject than general self-concept of ability. Self-concept was significantly and positively related to the perceived evaluation of significant others. A direction for further research is indicated.

Brown, G. "An Experiment in the Teaching of Creativity," *School Review,* 72:437–450, Winter 1964.

Study involves an attempt to teach creativity and to measure whether or not as a consequence significant change takes place. Creativity is defined as not only uniqueness originality, and statistically infrequent response, but also response that is adaptive to reality. Results show some increase in creativity on the Barron-Welsh Art Scale.

Bruce, Paul. "Relationship of Self-Acceptance to Other Variables With Sixth Grade Children Oriented in Self-Understanding." *Journal of Educational Psychology,* 48:229-238, October 1958.

"The purpose of this study was to investigate with sixth grade children some of the relationships between a measure of self-acceptance and other personality variables. The relationships were studied in two groups of students: one consisting of pupils who had taken part in a learning program designed to develop a more understanding and analytical approach to their own and others behavior (the experimental group) and one group consisting of pupils who had not undertaken such a program (the control group)."

Combs, C. F. "Perception and Self: Scholastic Underachievement in the Academically Capable." *Personnel and Guidance Journal,* 43:47-51, September 1964.

Study explored differences in how underachievers and achievers perceive themselves and their relationships to the world around them. Underachievers showed significant and consistent differences from achievers in that they a) saw themselves as less adequate, b) saw themselves as less acceptable to others, c) saw their peers as less acceptable, d) saw adults as less acceptable, e) showed an inefficient and less effective approach to problems, f) showed less freedom and adequacy of emotional expressions. Suggestions are made for certain factors that may produce underachievement and certain possible directions for future research.

Lewis, William A.; Lovell, John T.; Jessee, B. E. "Interpersonal Relationship and Pupil Progress." *Personnel and Guidance Journal,* 44:396–401, December 1965.

The hypothesis that students who perceive a relationship with the teacher that is in the direction of an ideal psychotherapeutic relationship will make greater academic gains that those students who perceive a non-therapeutic relationship with their teacher was confirmed with eighty-six sixth-grade students but not with seventy-six ninth-grade students.

Lichtenberg, Philip. "Emotional Maturity as Manifested in Ideational Interaction." *Journal of Abnormal and Social Psychology,* 51:298-301, September 1955.

This paper proposes "that emotional maturity is manifest in strivings for mutual satisfaction in groups and that immaturity involves efforts toward exclusive gratification. The theory was tested on six pairs of men of differential maturity in a discussion group."

Long, Barbara Ellis. "A Climate for Learning." *Today's Education,* 61:50-52, September 1972.

A survey of sixth grade students to find out why they act up when they have a substitute teacher. Students explained they were uncomfortable with teacher until they got to know him and how he operated. Getting to know the teacher and being understood by him for the purpose of reasonable prediction of behavior led to mutual trust. This mutual trust leads to a successful climate for learning. Children want to learn how to live, and this learning includes the prediction and understanding of human behavior.

Murray, Eloise. "Students' Perceptions of Self-Actualizing and Non-Self Actualizing Teachers." *Journal of Teacher Education,* 23:383-387, Fall 1972.

This study showed that students perceived self-actualizing teachers as more concerned than non-self actualizing teachers and thus has important implications for improving and maintaining productive learning situations which would lead to teacher and student growth.

Perkins, Hugh V. "Clarifying Feelings Through Peer Interaction." *Childhood Education,* 45:379-380, March 1969.

Author stresses importance of children relating with peers to provide them with opportunities for clarifying feelings about self and others and increasing self-esteem. Studies show that those children who are highly involved in the classroom peer group are better liked, make greater use of their academic abilities, and express more positive attitudes toward self and school.

Ripple, R. F. "Affective Factors Influence Classroom Learning." *Educational Leadership,* 22:476-80+, April 1965.

Review of some research on the influence of affective factors on classroom learning. Presents frame of reference, review of research on teacher-learner affective characteristics and interactions, concluding remarks. Affective qualities of teachers and classrooms are characterized by a) feeling of warmth, b) tolerance of moderate expressions of emotion, c) democratic group decision-making, d) use of nonpunitive control techniques, e) reduced frustration and anxiety, f) shifting states of order.

Rogers, Carl R. "Mental-Health Findings in Three Elementary Schools." *Educational Research Bulletin,* 21:69-79, 86, January 1942.

An early study of approximately 1500 children in Ohio to find the maladjusted child and to determine causes of this maladjustment. Findings revealed that problems of mental health existed in a large portion of the school population. Preventive policies and remedial policies in the mental health program were needed. Also changes in school administration, school personnel, and educational policy were needed if schools were to meet the problems brought to light in this study.

Whiteman, Martin. "Children's Conceptions of Psychological Causality." *Child Development,* 38:143-155, March 1967.

The general aim of this study was to explore the feasibility of using interviews with children at two age levels, the 5-6 year range and the 8-9 year range, to study developing conceptions of psychological causality. All children were Negro or Puerto Rican from schools in Harlem, New York. The interviews were conducted by the author in one testing situation, and by graduate students of the Columbia University School of Social Work in the second phase of the study. Story-telling was used to derive answers from the children.

Zirkel, Perry A. "Enhancing the Self-Concept of Disadvantaged Students." *California Journal of Educational Research,* 23:125-37, May 1972.

This article investigates and evaluates several efforts to improve the self-concepts of disadvantaged students: utilization of selected language arts materials in the regular curriculum, tutoring, "the significant other" and compensatory self-concept programs.


### III. Chapters in Books and Reports: Articles in Encyclopedias

Bower, Eli. "Mental Health" in R. L. Ebel (Ed.) *Encyclopedia of Educational Research.* Fourth Edition, New York: Macmillan Co., 1969, 811-828.

Presents an overview of research findings about mental health. Discusses the following: the monograph of Jahoda on the concept of positive mental health in 1958; present-day concepts of mental health; mental health problems among children; mental health problems of the population at large; man's past relationship with mental health and mental illness; achievement, stress, and mental health; preventative approaches to children's mental health problems; psychoeducational and psychotherapeutic approaches; and mental health and the teacher. Includes an extensive bibliography.

Gordon, Ira J. "Social and Emotional Development" in R. L. Ebel (Ed.) *Encyclopedia of Educational Research,* Fourth Edition. New York: Macmillan Co., 1969. 1221–1230.

Presentation of research findings on social and emotional development. Covers the following areas: emotions and their development, intergroup relations, moral development, cognitive style, development of the self-concept, and implications for education. Has an extensive bibliography.

Ojemann, Ralph. "Behavior Problems" in R. L. Ebel (Ed.) *Encyclopedia of Educational Research,* Fourth Edition. New York: Macmillan Co., 1969. 98–105.

Broad overview of research on behavior problems. Covers such areas as the following: kinds of incidence, causes, and prevention and control. Article concludes with an extensive bibliography.

Schmuck, Richard A. "Group Processes" in R. L. Ebel (Ed.) *Encyclopedia of Educational Research,* Fourth Edition. New York: Macmillan Co., 1969. 551–559.

Broad overview of results of research on group processes. Discusses such areas as the following: ways of categorizing groups, leadership, and dynamics of groups. Contains an extensive bibliography.

Wilson, Frances M. "Mental-Health Practices in the Intermediate Grades," in *Mental Health in Education,* 54th Yearbook of the National Society for the Study of Education, Part II, 1955. 195–215.

An investigation of the characteristics, thoughts and feelings of intermediate grade children was conducted. Material was gathered through interviews with children, parents, and teachers, through records of daily schedules kept by 2000 boys and girls, through class observations, and through teacher reports. Basic to helping children in the mental health area is knowledge and understanding of these children. The two most valuable techniques for the classroom teacher are observation and the interview. The author explores various devices available to teachers in promoting the mental health of students.

## V. Reports

ED 050336

Combs, Arthur W., and others. *Helping Relationships; Basic Concepts For the Helping Professions,* 1971.

Written for people who are entering or who are already engaged in some form of the helping professions, this book attempts to answer the following questions: "What ideas about human behavior have special value for understanding the helping relationship?" "What do these imply for effective practice in the helping professions?" Concepts discussed are what is a professional helper, two ways of looking at behavior, self-concept: product and producer of experience, a humanistic view of motive, the crucial character of meaning, learning as meaning change, the limits of man's becoming, freedom and self-actualization, goals and purposes of helping, developing understanding, establishing helping relationships, aiding the search for new meaning, communication, varied rules of helpers, and the helper as person and citizen. Selected readings, related to the topics in a chapter, are listed at the end of each chapter.

ED 036822

Combs, Arthur W., and others. *Florida Studies in the Helping Professions.* University of Florida Monographs Social Sciences, No. 37, 12 February 1969.

The monograph presents principles governing the nature and effective practice of helping professions. It is presented in three parts: 1) background of the studies and evaluation of the hypothesis, 2) research reports completed to date, 3) interpretation of the research and future directions. The research deals with perceptual organization of effective counselors, teachers, Episcopal pastors, person-oriented and task-oriented student nurses and college teacher. The report concludes that the perceptual approach provides greater understanding of professionals, but the major difficulty lies in measurement techniques of perceptual psychology.

Jasik, Marilyn S. "Exploring Efforts to Improve Self-Concepts of Pre-Kindergarten Children in School." *Dissertation Abstracts International,* Vol. 33 (6-A) (December 1972), 2765.

This dissertation explored the possibility of teachers and aides to improve the self-concept of pre-kindergarten children in school and resulted in important findings to support the hypothesis and implications for future studies and programs in this area.

Ralph, Sara J. "The Effects of Positive Value Statements on Self-Esteem." *Dissertation Abstracts International,* Vol. 33 (7-A) (January 1973), 3402-3.

Utilizing community college students, a course was designed to use positive value statements to increase self-esteem. Measurement of results showed that self-esteem increased significantly for the control group.

## 5. DESCRIPTIONS OF CLASSROOM ACTIVITIES

### I. Books

Belka, Marion F. (Ed.). *Being and Becoming; An Action Approach to Group Guidance.* Milwaukee: Bruce Publishing. 1966.

Designed to encourage the junior high school student to think for himself and to discuss with others some of the challenges encountered in four important aspects of life: education, family, vocation, and personal-social relationships. Included in the discussions are topics such as satisfying emotional needs, satisfying social needs, and self-concept. Easy reading for young people who want to learn more about themselves.

Bullis, H. Edmund. *Human Relations in the Classroom; Course I, II, III.* Wilmington: Delaware State Society for Mental Hygiene. 3 vols., 1947–1951.

Each volume contains 30 lesson plans for teachers aiding them to teach classes in human relations in the sixth, seventh and eighth grades. The author originally conducted similar classes in the Delaware schools. The present volumes are intended for use throughout the United States. The volumes supplement one another. Topics of interest covered are: personality growth, making and keeping friends, knowing ourselves, and emotional stresses and strains. An excellent guidebook for teachers. Note: First volume only is coauthored by Emily E. O'Malley.

Davis, David C. L. *Model for Humanistic Education: The Danish Folk High School.* Ohio: Charles E. Merrill, 1971.

One in the Studies of the Person series edited by Carl Rogers, this book describes how some of today's "new ideas" in education worked out a century ago in Denmark. Folk high schools in Denmark are boarding schools for people of eighteen or older concerned with cultural and social problems of universal interest. The courses reflect the interests and concerns of the student. The book describes the history and development of the folk high schools and draws implications for education in the U.S. The whole experiment is set against the backdrop of humanistic psychology as it exists today. By way of comparison, Davis offers some interesting insights into education in the United States.

*Dimensions of Personality.* Pflaum/Standard. Dayton, Ohio, 1970.

This is a complete program in affective education for elementary, junior high, and high school students. Basically it is a group-centered, experientially-oriented program of prevention designed to help the teacher assist children on their journey towards emotional maturity.

Primary-grade student materials are packaged in kits to serve four students. Each kit consists of four student work texts and a set of seven activity sheets which provide the group of four students with fourteen activities. The annotated teacher's text for each grade includes small reproductions of the activity sheets.

Grade One—*Now I'm Ready*—Helps reassure the first-grader that he is ready for school and the new challenges which formal learning can provide.

Grade Two—*I Can Do It*—Taking an experiential approach, the book explores the child's developing potential with regard to his physical, emotional and scholastic competencies.

Grade Three—*What About Me*—Fischer. This book explores the areas of emotions with the child. Devoting two units to the troublesome feelings of fear and anger, the work text concludes with a section on the child's feelings about himself.

Intermediate grade materials consist of student texts for each grade level. As a conclusion to each chapter the student texts include a number of discussion questions which incorporate concepts derived from the class experiences and from the reading matter. The annotated teacher's text for each level stresses affective experiences as basic to the introduction of the themes developed in the student texts. Detailed suggestions for these class activities precede each chapter in the teacher's text.

Grade Four—*Here I Am*—Limbacher. This book takes the student on a journey of self-exploration. He will learn about various factors which influence his personality development, inherited traits, environmental circumstances, acceptance of feelings and the consequent influence on the child's concept of himself.

Grade Five—*I'm Not Alone*—Limbacher. In this book the student is encouraged to explore his human environment: family, friends and classmates. His participation and interaction in these various groups and the influence they exert on him are discussed along with his need to recognize his own individuality and uniqueness as a person.

Grade Six—*Becoming Myself*—Limbacher. The preadolescent may already have begun to experience some of the changes that will transform him in the next few years. This book will help him prepare for these changes by encouraging the student to become better acquainted with his emotional life. The physical, intellectual, and interpersonal aspects of his life are also explored. They increase the student's realization that all these varied potentials must develop in harmony with one another if the person is to achieve a sense of inner peace.

Junior High—*Search for Meaning*—Carefully structured units present a variety of group-activity lessons that help students clarify their values and their understanding of their individuality. Flexible lessons are open-ended and non-judgmental. They include one-to-one, one-to-group activities. Materials cover these topical themes in thirty-six lessons: The power structure, rules, organizations, pressure, rewards/punishments, capability, flexibility, growth, responsibility, family, friends, maturing relationships.

High School—*Search for Values*—The seven carefully structured yet flexible units present 44 lessons to cover these pertinent topics: competition, authority, time, personal space, images, relationships and commitments. The procedure in using the materials is similar to keeping a diary. Over a period of time the diary is distributed in single sheets by the instructor as the lessons are introduced and developed. A detailed description of procedures for developing these group activities is included in the instructor's text.

Harmin, Merrill; Kerschenbaum, Howard; Simon, Sidney B. *Clarifying Values Through Subject Matter. Applications for the Classroom.* Minneapolis, Minnesota: Winston Press, Inc., 1973.

The authors explain three levels of teaching: facts, concepts, and values. After explaining the goals of values-clarification, they give examples of values—level teaching in all of the different subject areas of the curriculum. They also outline values strategies to use with subject matter. A bibliography is appended. Valuable for teachers who are looking for ways to incorporate values education into the curriculum.

*Life Skills Course.* Saskatoon, Saskatchewan, Canada: Saskatchewan New Start Inc., 1973.

Life Skills training provides disadvantaged adults with the knowledge and skills to demonstrate competence in human relations and in areas of life responsibilities. Life skills means problem-solving behaviors responsibly and appropriately used in the management of personal affairs. A sequence of planned experiences helps adult students to implement a program of personal development in each of the following areas: 1) developing oneself and relating to others, 2) coping with home and family responsibilities, 3) using leisure time purposefully, 4) exercising rights and responsibilities in the community, and 5) making responsible decisions for work future. Life Skills education is an activity program. Program consists of Life Skills Series: *Life Skills Coaching Manual, The Problems and Needed Life Skills of Adolescents, The Dynamics of Life Skills Coaching, Life Skills Course for Corrections,* and *Readings in Life Skills.*

Malamud, Daniel I. and Machover, Soloman. *Toward Self-Understanding; Group Techniques in Self-Confrontation.* Springfield, Illinois: Thomas, 1965.

The purpose of this book is to describe the Workshop in Self-Understanding, which was offered at New York University's Division of General Education as a non-credit course. "Part I includes an account of how the clinic Workshops were set up, narrative summaries of all the Workshop sessions, critical commentaries on each session, and an evaluation of the impact of the Workshops on the members. Part II deals with matters of principle and technique in Workshop methodology based on accumulated experience. Part II also includes recommended experiments, a comparison of the Workshop and psychotherapy, and a brief review of related approaches." Of interest to those in mental health education who wish a deeper insight into the Workshop approach which employs methods that stimulate intense, personal-emotional involvement.

ED 086 582

Simon, Sidney B. *I Am Loveable and Capable. A Modern Allegory of the Classical Put-Down.* Argus Communications, Chicago, Ill., 1973. (Available from Argus Communications, 7440 Natchez Avenue, Niles, Illinois 60648.)

    The IALAC (I Am Loveable and Capable) story presents one day in the life of 14 year old Randy, who puts on his IALAC sign each morning and sets out to face the world. As "put-downs" occur at home and at school little pieces of his sign are torn away; by the end of the day very little of the sign remains. This allegory is a tool for humanistic education which can be used by a teacher, clergyman, student, or any group leader who is concerned with making people feel loveable and capable. It deals with the "put-down," an American idiosyncrasy, which inhibits humanistic values. The content of the IALAC story can be modified to fit specific groups or dramatized for student participation. (JH)

## II. Magazines and Journals

Abramovitz, A. B. and Burnham, Elaine. "Exploring Potentials for Mental Health in the Classroom." *Mental Hygiene,* 43-253-259, April 1959.

    Shows an experimental mental health course from the viewpoint of three clinical psychologists who planned and taught it to classroom teachers.

Abrams, Richard S.; Vanecko, Michael; Abrams, Irving. "A Suggested School Mental Health Program." *Journal of School Health,* 42:137-141, March 1972.

    Discusses the mental health situation as it exists in Chicago, the needs of children and personnel within the school, the various components of the program and the cost of the program.

Barman, C. R. "Value Clarification and Biology." *The American Biology Teacher,* 36:241-42, April 1974.

    The need for classroom science teachers to include controversial and value laden issues in their teaching is presented. The issue of mercy killing is discussed briefly. Other examples from science education are mentioned to assist teachers in moving their teaching emphasis from the fact and concept levels to the individual value level.

Bessell, Harold. "The Content is the Medium: The Confidence is the Message." *Psychology Today,* 1:32-35,61, January 1968.

    A Human Development Program for nursery and kindergarten children was developed by the author and first introduced at a nursery school in California, in 1964. A curriculum was developed which explains personality development in simple terms, describes the most common defense maneuvers, suggests constructive interventions for maladaptive behavior, and gives semi-structured, daily plans for classroom use. The teacher becomes the facilitator of the small, modified encounter group. His course book is the HDP manual. Article fully describes program as it is used with the children. This program for building healthy egos is used now in more than fifty kindergartens, nursery schools, and other classes in Calfiornia and in Australia.

Betof, Edward H., and Kirschenbaum, Howard. "A Valuing Approach." *School Health Review,* 5:13-14, January/February 1974.

Using two illustrations the authors show how to make teaching more interesting and relevant by utilizing a three level approach learning—facts, concepts, and values.

Borton, Terry. "What Turns Kids On?" *Saturday Review,* 50:72-74, 80, April 15, 1967.

A report of a six-week pilot project in 1965 of a summer program for intermediate and secondary school students in Philadelphia. The curriculum was centered around student concerns. The major concern was one of self-identity. Students studied this concern through class discussions, drama improvisations, urban-affairs classes, art, and communications classes. The curriculum was based on a series of questions designed to explore this concern from a generalized concern about man's identity to the personal sense of identity. The student body was selected to represent an ethnic, racial, social, and economic cross-section of the city. Attendance was voluntary, and no grades were given.

Bracey, Bonnie. "Freedom to Think in Elementary School." *School Health Review,* 5:31-33, January/February 1974.

Author tells of her classroom experiences in using Inside-Out, a series of approximately 30 programs, developed by National Instructional Television to deal with the day-to-day problems and emotions of children from their point of view.

Bullis, H. Edmund. "How The Human Relations Class Works." *Understanding the Child,* 10, 5-10, October 1941.

Paper probes into the experimental mental hygiene program conducted by the Delaware schools for seventh and eighth graders. Movie excerpts, stories, plays, panel discussions, and personal anecdotes were used as stimuli for class discussions. A better understanding of one's own personal behavior actions often resulted, and it was found that the act of talking to and with a group is in itself the greatest stimulus of interest. The teachers also showed a growing interest in the personality development of their students.

Cernik, Helen C., Mueller, Nancy J.; Williams, Herman J. "Purpose of Your Life." *Character Potential,* 6:27-39, April 1972. (Union College, Character Research Project, Schenectady, New York).

This is a description of a project called "Purpose for Your Life" which focuses on self-assessment and future development.

Derell, G. Remy. "A Human Relations Class in the Middle School." *The School Counselor,* 17:384-387, May 1970.

A human relations course for eighth-graders at Wagner Middle School at Clark Air Base, Philippines, is discussed. The class on human relations is an important adjunct of the guidance program in this school. During the class the following guidance services are performed: 1) personal problems are discussed, 2) educational programs are planned, 3) vocational information is distributed, 4) interest inventories are administered, 5) sociodrama is used to gain insight into common teenage problems. The course outline is given in detail. A list of recommended book and films for teenagers is also given.

Dickenson, Walter A.; Foster, Car M.; Walker, Newman J.; Yeager, Frank. "A Humanistic Program for Change in a Large City School System." Journal of Humanistic Psychology, 10:111-120, Fall 1970.

This paper describes a series of new projects initiated by the Louisville Public Schools which had the second highest dropout rate among large U.S. cities in 1963. The self-contained classroom with one teacher and thirty or more students was abandoned for an open learning environment organized around groups of students assigned to teaching teams. The program is keyed to flexibility, individualized instruction, self-directed humanistic learning, processes, and daily team critiquing and planning. The traditional role of teacher as an authoritative manipulator of students' learning is to be replaced by a new role of teacher as a helping or facilitating person. Six areas of personal growth for the kind of humanistically oriented teacher the project wants to develop are awareness, identity, commitment, involvement, meaning, and becoming. Another innovation of the project is that the control of the schools is being turned over to administrative councils composed of parents, teachers, and students.

Dinkmeyer, Don. "Top Priority: Understanding Self and Others." *Elementary School Journal,* 72:62-71, November 1971.

Positive feelings that accompany learning result in lasting gains, negative feelings result in withdrawal. Planned experiences that personalize and humanize the educational experience are essential. Developing Understanding of Self and Others (DUSO) is an educational program that focuses on the development of purposeful behavior that is significant and satisfying. Giving priority to individuals emphasizes development of a fully functioning human being.

Dinkmeyer, Don. "C-Group: Focus on Self as Instrument." *Phi Delta Kappan,* 52:617-19, June 1971.

Relates how teacher can develop self effectively to help others. Effective teachers with healthy self-concepts have characteristics of perception and ability to identify with others. Suggests number one priority should be to develop these qualities. C-group approach to this development is called thus because components are collaboration, consultation, clarification, confidential, confrontation, communication, concern and commitment. Group has five or six members. Leader who clarifies purposes must be trained in group dynamics, group counseling and psychodynamics. Has been piloted in the student teaching department at Northeastern College in Chicago.

Dinkmeyer, Don. "Developing Understanding of Self and Others: Central to the Educational Process." *People Watching,* 1:12-16, Spring 1972.

Presents the rationale for a program in developing understanding of self and others (DUSO). This program helps the child become more aware of himself, others, and the nature of human development.

Dinkmeyer, Don. "Developmental Group Counseling." *Elementary School Guidance and Counseling,* 4:267-272, May 1970.

Describes a model for group guidance using group interaction and discussion about feelings, attitudes, values and problems to assist in dealing with developmental tasks.

"Feelings and Learning; Symposium." *Grade Teacher,* 88:32-6+, November 1970.

Contains a description of Project Insight, a human relations program which deals with self and one's relation to others. Two class meetings which utilized the program are transcribed in detail and there is a list of films which teachers can use to stimulate discussions.

Fowle, Carolyn M. "Elementary Guidance and Counseling Program." *Thrust for Educational Leadership,* 2:4-5, February 1973.

This model elementary guidance and counseling program in the Lodi Unified School District is concerned with correcting the offsetting negative effects of a hidden curriculum. It also describes the effects of lack of formal mechanism for the deliberate development of positive psychological growth for all children in the school. It includes a description of the program. How it differentiates itself from the secondary guidance counsellor is explained.

EJ 087 194
Fraenkel, Jack R. "Strategies for Developing Values." *Today's Education,* 62:49-55, November 1973.

Article suggests ideas that might aid the teacher in assisting students to understand and acquire values, which will make students develop their own decision making abilities.

Fritz, John O. "Humanization of Learning: A Mission in Embryo." *Alberta Journal of Educational Research,* 17:275-88, December 1971.

"The Humanization of Learning Mission is directed toward developing program alternatives which would accept as critical priorities for schooling the development of self-awareness, empathetic understanding, and the enhancement of social responsibility."

Glasser, William. "The Effect of School Failure on the Life of a Child." *National Elementary Principal,* 49:8-18, September 1969.

Glasser believes that school failure serves only to reinforce a failure identity. The way to motivate students is to get them involved. In this article he outlines seven steps to follow to help the students become involved and successful.

Goshko, Robert. "Self-Determined Behavior Change." *Personnel and Guidance Journal,* 51:629-632, May 1974.

Describes method and techniques by which children can learn the language of behavior modification, identify their own behaviors, and determine the type of behavior change they want to happen.

Harrelson, O. A. "Affective Approach; Television Series Called Inside/Out." *Instructor,* 82:69-71, October 1972.

Reports on a TV series called Inside/Out designed to help children identify expressions of love. Provides children with story of concerns of children waiting to be adopted. Children discuss film when it is over. Part of a growing body of books, pamphlets, films, tapes, filmstrips and records designed for use at elementary level for teachers. Teachers arrange class so children feel free to express feelings. Many activities possible for follow through. Fifteen films will be available in January 1973. A National Instructional Television Center production.

Hedlund, D. F. "Preparation for Student Personnel: Implications of Humanistic Education." *Journal of College Student Personnel.* 12:324-8, September 1971.

Describes a two-year graduate program which deals in humanistic education. Students in the program become committed to its objectives (behavioral, as well as broader knowledge) and have had behavior changes.

Howe, Leland W., et al. "Values Clarification: Strategies." *Law in American Society,* 2:38-9, May 1973.

Two strategies listed here—Values Voting Strategy and Rank Order Strategy—provided children with worthwhile experiences in making choices and decisions. These strategies came from the book, *Values Clarification, A Handbook of Practical Strategies for Teachers and Students.*

Howell, Margaret H. "Discovering a Vision for Your Life: A Sequential Guidance Program in a Junior High School." *Character Potential, A Record of Research,* 6:45-60, January 1973.

This article describes a guidance program for junior high students (seventh, eighth, and ninth grades) aimed at discovering "Life purpose."

Huggins, K. B. "Alternatives in Values Clarification." *National Elementary Principal,* 54:76-9, November 1974.

There are three difficulties in generating alternatives when using the values clarification approach: (1) the alternatives must be real and feasible to the students, (2) students who have not been exposed to alternative behavior need additional help, and (3) there is a cognitive element in understanding alternatives that students . . . may not have achieved. Some strategies that might be used for generating alternatives are the coat of arms, role playing, questions, and public interviews. In the cognitive area of study, the teacher should use a conceptual, rather than a factual, approach. The teacher must also look at the areas of confusion and conflict that are most important to the age level of the student. Since valuing is something that schools must teach, and since alternatives are necessary to this process, schools must look for ways to generate alternatives.

Kasschau, Richard A. "Curriculum Development for a High School." *People Watching,* 2:40-44, Spring 1973.

Describes a project to develop procedures for training high school psychology teachers and to develop some prototypic curriculum units. Discusses reasons underlying the method used, some components of materials that were developed, and results of a pilot study of the units.

Kennedy, Daniel A. and Seidman, Stanley B. "Contingency Management and Human Relations Workshops: A School Intervention Program." *Journal of School Psychology,* 10:69-75, March 1973.

This article presents a preventative and positive mental health program designed to be used by teachers in the Florida school system because of the shortage of school psychological personnel.

Koile, Earl A. and Gallessich, June. "A New Edge on Education: The Dallas Human Relations Labs." *Junior College Journal,* 41:31-37, March 1971.

Experimental human relations labs in which administrators, faculty, and staff of the Dallas County Junior College District were invited to participate. Through working together in intensive group experiences, participants "sought to improve interpersonal relationships, to reduce stereotyping, to build better understanding of individual and group behavior, and to create a climate for learning in which individual differences, trust, mutual sharing, and directness were valued."

Lafferty, J. Clayton; Dennerll, Donald; Rettich, Peter. "A Creative School Mental Health Program." *National Elementary Principal,* 43:28-35, April 1964.

Describes a project designed to explore how the school can more effectively help children develop an adequate self-concept. Discusses the theoretical background which was based on the work of Ojemann, Prescott, Ellis, McClelland, and Atkinson. An adequate approach to a school mental health program must be based on the classroom and must encompass the style of classroom management, method of instruction, and instructional content. The program was directed at increasing teacher competency as well as job satisfaction. Teachers were asked to test the ideas of McClelland, Atkinson, Ojemann, and Ellis. Finally there is a summary of some of the basic concepts of the project which may help readers see possible applications to other situations.

Langhorst and Sullivan, J. L. "Hey That's Me! A Relevant Course." *Clearing House,* 43:203-5, December 1968.
Describes an experimental course developed as a senior elective course in psychology. Content of the course was human conduct of self and others. A variety of methods were utilized in teaching the class, and this together with the content proved the course to be very relevant to the student.

Laufer, H. "Hey! I'm Important!" *Instructor,* 82:112, April 1973.
Describes philosophy of education in Florida. Every child is important—let's do all we can to let him know that he is. Every teacher gives three honest messages to each child each day that he's important. Can be a smile, positive comment or a compliment. Each child has responsibility, private time with teacher. Parents are encouraged to participate.

Limbacher, Walter J. "An Approach to Elementary Training in Mental Health." *Journal of School Psychology,* 5:225-234, Spring 1967.
Discussion by the author of his mental health training project conducted in the Denver diocesan school district in 1966–67. Participating in the project were thirty-three schools and approximately 1500 fifth-grade children. The stated objective of the course offered was to enable the child to lead a happy, useful life. The course provided "a systematic, direct, organized presentation of mental health principles aimed at giving the child insights into the causes and purposes of his behavior and the means to directly affect his own mental health."

Lombardo, Arthur. "A Mental Health Curriculum for the Lower Grades." *Mental Hygiene,* 52:570-6, October 1968.
The author attempts to show how a mental health curriculum can fit into the social studies curriculum for Kindergarten through Grade 4. The objectives to be attained, the materials, and the techniques to be used are described for each grade level. The psychological areas dealt with in this curriculum were: Kindergarten—separation from mother and home, First Grade—delay of gratification; Second Grade—rational expression of hostility,

Third grade—acceptance by the group and Fourth Grade—gaining independence.

Long, Barbara Ellis. "Behavioral Science for Elementary School Pupils." *Elementary School Journal,* 70:253-60, Feb. 1970.

Describes the development of a curriculum in the behavioral sciences as a mental health education program at the Webster College Experimental School in St. Louis. Presents results of the pilot study, the emergence of a teaching method, and problems that lie ahead.

MacDonald, Barry. "The Evaluation of the Humanities Curriculum Project: A Holistic Approach." *Theory Into Practice,* 10:163-7, June 1971.

Gives a brief overview of the origin, content, and history of the Humanities Curriculum Project. Discusses evaluation of work in progress and plans for future evaluation.

Maddock, James W. "Morality and Individual Development: A Basis For Value Education." *Family Coordinator,* 21:291-302, July 1972.

The author presents a program of value education which has particular application to sex and family life education.

Moon, Linda Lee. "Search for Self—The Counselor in the Classroom." *The School Counselor,* 22:121-3, Nov. 1974.

Describes a 9 week course called "Search for Self" in which a teacher and a counselor collaborated to humanize education in the classroom.

Mosher, Ralph L. and Sprinthall, Norman A. "Psychological Education: A New Form For Personal Development and Human Growth." *People Watching,* 1:6-11, Spring 1972.

A description of a curriculum development project currently under way at the Harvard Graduate School of Education and the Newton Public School System titled, "Psychological Education." By creating a series of laboratories in aspects of psychology, the objectives were focused toward psychology as a mean of educating the pupils in their own personal/psychological development.

Mosher, Ralph L. and Sprinthall, Norman A. "Psychological Education in Secondary Schools, A Program to Promote Individual and Human Development."*American Psychologist,* 25:911-24, October 1970.

This excellent article outlines the need for psychological education, the background of the work in "psychological education" at Harvard, the underlying assumption of their work in this area, and then gives the history of the program and the personnel doing work in this field. The latter part of the paper describes the curriculum in personal and human development that was developed, the resources used, the projected development of the program, and conclusions.

Mosher, Ralph L. and Sprinthall, Norman A. "Psychological Education in Secondary Schools: A Program to Promote Individual and Human Development." *American Psychologist,* 25:911-24, Sept. 1970.

Authors suggest that although adolescence is a time of change, it is also an excellent time to promote personal and social competence through the educational process. The adolescent can learn principles of psychological growth through a variety of ways ranging from relatively formal instruction to individualized and enactive learning in the laboratories. Improvisational drama, counseling and self-analytic labs, and direct use of personal resources in tutoring younger children are ways to make concrete relatively abstract principles of human behavior.

Mukerji, Rose. "Why Not Feelings and Values in Instructional Television?" *Young Children,* 26:273-81, May 1971.

Discussion of television shows produced especially for young children. A series produced by Northern Virginia Educational Television Association entitled, "Ripples" makes a special point of the importance of including the affective domain. Each program takes the child beyond the classroom so that he can have an encounter with interesting people with important ideas, and with challenging events as in real life. The series will help him to develop values and to deepen and to express his feelings. It will increase his knowledge about himself in relation to other people and to a changing environment.

Newberg, Norman. "Education for Student Concerns: Courses in Communications and Urban Affairs." *Educational Opportunity Forum,* 1:17-36, Fall 1969.

Describes the Affective Education Research Project in Philadelphia. A lesson entitled "Junk Man" demonstrates how the ability to SENSE is increased by learning the process of *perceiving and giving meaning.* The thrust of such lessons is to deal with feelings, attitudes, values, interpersonal relationships, and the capacity to give and to receive. Discusses the goals and contents of two courses in affective education developed as part of the project: communications course and urban affairs course. These goals include developing self-identity, relatedness, and potency. Includes a description of a process curriculum and an information processing model and then describes a lesson which includes the three parts of the model: sensing, transforming, and acting. Concludes with description of effects of the project upon education in Philadelphia.

Ojemann, Ralph H. "Basic Approaches to Mental Health: The Human Relation Program at the State University of Iowa." *Personnel and Guidance Journal,* 37:198-206, November 1958.

Outlining his concept of the causal approach to behavior, Ojemann describes his program of preventative mental health for teachers and students.

He discusses examples of curricular experiences, attitudes of participating teachers, the role of causal orientation in mental health, and assumptions underlying the program.

"OK Classroom: Transactional Analysis." *Instructor*, 82:33-40, May 1973.

Defines terms from Thomas Harris' book *I'm OK—You're OK* and applies techniques to development in the classroom. Initial step is how to make yourself OK so your classroom can be OK. Second step is helping children learn to be OK so they and your classroom can be OK. Gives suggestions about how to further study techniques and where to get materials.

"Operation Turn On." *Today's Education,* 61:12-14, December 1972.

School program in Fairfield, Connecticut high school where students are taken outside the classroom on hiking and biking trips to permit them opportunities to gain new perceptions about themselves and participate in real experiences which ultimately will teach them important lessons about growing up. The program was so well-received that the founder Robert Gillette, received a large grant of financial aid from the New England Program of Teacher Education to support its continuation. Robert Gillette was given the decision-making role in the expenditure of monies for the program. Operation Turn On places students in situations and environments which allow them to mature.

Osman, Jack D. "Value growth through drug education." *School Health Review,* 5:25-30, Jan./Feb. 1974.

Traditionally drug education has emphasized content. To be more effective teacher must assume role of facilitator. Several strategies taken from the work of Raths, Harmin, and Simon can help: (1) values sheets, (2) value ranking, (3) the drugs I use.

Palomares, U. H. "Communication Begins With Attitude." *National Elementary Principal,* 50:47-9, Nov. 1970.

This is an explanation of the Human Development Program which utilizes the "magic circle" to promote personal effectiveness and communication skills in children. Teacher preparation is also described and research data is given which shows gains in cognitive and affective areas after use of the program.

Patti, Joseph B. "Elementary Psychology for Eighth Graders?" *American Psychologist,* 11:194-6, April 1956.

The author, as teacher of an eighth grade class in psychology, reports on the enthusiastic acceptance of his class by students and parents alike. Topics studied included personality types, superstitions, psychology of advertising boy-girl relationships, and family relations. The emphasis in the subject matter was to try to explain human behavior within the framework of psychology through research, analysis, and discussion.

Perrin, D. and Wolfran, J. "Humanizing Instruction: From Mark Hopkins to Mediated Teacher Instructional Packages." *American Annals of the Deaf,* 117:538-44, October 1972.

Discusses need for teachers of the deaf to develop instructional packages (IPs) through use of the materials and techniques already at hand. This will better serve individual needs in the classroom. IPs will include 1) introduction, 2) behavioral objectives, 3) pre-test (optional), 4) content instruction, 5) post-test.

Pietrofesa, J. "Psychology in the High School; a Course Designed to Increase Self-Understanding." *Journal of Secondary Education,* 44:51-4, February 1969.

"Increasing pressures within the American society are requiring new ways to deal with mental health problems. Yet, the school has not effectively adjusted curricula to meet these problems. This article presents an outline for a course in high school psychology which logically should be available to all adolescents."

Pietrofesa, J. J. "High School Psychology: A Course in Personal Adjustment." *Catholic School Journal,* 68:66-67, September 1968.

There is a need to include in the high school social studies program an approach to healthy personal adjustment. Offers a course description as a guideline.

EJ 088 575
Poetker, Joel. "A Strategy for Value Clarification." *Social Science Record,* 11: 3-5, Autumn 1973.

A sequential, problem-solving approach is offered as a strategy for the classroom teacher who wants to help the student increase his skills of inquiry, conceptual learning, and value clarification.

Prince, George. "Leadership for Creativity and Synectics Meetings." *Educational Opportunity Forum,* 1:125-37, Fall 1969.

Identifies and describes leadership principles which will help groups become more creative and effective: rotate leadership, listen well to group members, encourage analogic ways of thinking, enforce the spectrum policy, don't permit anyone to be put on the defensive, never compete with the group members, and keep the energy level high. Develops a sequence of procedures to help groups find creative solutions, define the problem, reach an unusual perspective, and derive a creative solution.

Rees, F. D. "Teaching values through health education." *School Health Review,* 3:2-4, March/April 1972.

Rees notes the growing need in our society for clarifying values. He feels that schools must begin to deal with ideas rather than be content with the teaching of facts. He explains how values education must go beyond the modeling and imposing of values. The author describes the values clarification process through health education as a meaningful way of helping students construct their own set of values. In addition, the author touches on other related issues: establishing psychologically permissive learning environments, health curriculum areas where value teaching can occur, and value education in teacher preparation programs.

Ruben, Ann G. "Humanizing School Principles." *NASSP Bulletin,* 56:20-5, December 1972.

This article describes materials used, issues raised, and experiences shared in a problem-solving workshop for principals led by the author.

Ruckhaber, Charles J. "An Elementary School Mental Health Program: The Stark School Model." *Journal of School Psychology,* 8:197-201, Spring 1970.

"The development of a model elementary school mental health program is described. The outline is intended to serve as an effective guide for school psychologists interested in providing leadership in the formation of such programs within their schools. The Stark School Mental Health Program developed through five stages: 1) staff readiness, 2) in-service training, 3) application, 4) development of a mental health committee, and 5) development of innovative practices."

Samler, Joseph. "Basic Approaches to Mental Health: An Attempt at Synthesis." *Personnel Guidance Journal,* 37:639-431, May 1959.

Summarizes the major characteristics of six mental health programs described in previous issues of this journal and elucidates common aims as well as differences of approach among the programs.

Sanders, Norris M. and Tanck, Marlin L. "A Critical Appraisal of Twenty-six National Social Studies Projects: 18- Michigan Elementary Social Science Education Program." *Social Education,* 34:431-32, April 1970.

Program developed by a team of educators and social scientists at the University of Michigan Institute for Social Research and field-tested in Michigan schools. The staff sought to involve students in investigating human behavior and values. The program is broken down into seven units of study, each unit requiring about four to six weeks to teach. Hypothetical cases of social interactions are presented either as a reading, as a recording, as an episode role-played by students in class, or as descriptions or pictures in the project booklet for each unit. The program also provides a teacher's guide, which contains an overview and sequence of activities for each unit. The program is essentially an intellectual endeavor, and so no attempt at an evaluation of goals achieved is made.

Schlaadt, Richard G. "Implementing the values clarification process." *School Health Review,* 5:10-12, January/February 1974.

The author briefly explains the value clarification process à la Raths, Harmin, and Simon, and then gives directions for five strategies: Values Grid, Values Continuing, Success Versus Failure Value Sheet, Personal Coat of Arms, and Tied Down.

Seeley, John R. "The Forest Hill Village Project." *Understanding the Child,* 23:104-110, October 1954.

An experimental project in an upper and middle class community to study its way of life with emphasis on child-rearing procedures and their bearing on the mental health of the children. A child guidance clinic and counselling team composed of teachers, school psychologist, one of the project staff, plus one or more of the project's teachers in training were provided. In addition, children were encouraged to freely participate in group discussions on any subject they chose with minimal interference from an adult. A large part of the program was to prepare a selected group of teachers to function more effectively in the school situation in psychological and mental health matters. One of the purposes of the project was to study the psychological fate of the child in the social matrix of today's society.

Seeley, John R. "Basic Approaches to Mental Health: The Forest Hill Village 'Human Relations Classes.'" *Personnel and Guidance Journal,* 37:424-34, February 1959.

Describes a human relations project in Canada developed to do the following: 1) perform an operation with, in, and upon a community, more particularly its children, 2) train a first cadre of educators drawn from all over Canada, and thereby both to reform education to some degree from within and develop a differentiated and thus to some degree new profession, 3) extract, both from the experience itself and by means of the opportunities to which it gave rise, a body of "scientific" information that would have utility for behavior theory and relatively immediate practical implications.

Shannon, John R. "Help Students Identify Their Values." *Business Education Forum,* 29:26-7, November 1974.

Perhaps basic business teachers have been afraid of values in the past. It is their responsibility to help sutdents think through their values. Shannon challenges teachers to stimulate a higher level of value-related thought in students (as set forth by Kohlberg), to teach students to identify values implied in a controversial statement, and to use learning activities effective for developing values. He also gives several suggested activities.

Sharp, Billy. "Contract Learning and Humanistic Education." *Educational Technology,* 11:28-30, June 1971.

Written by the president of the Combined Motivation Education Systems,

Inc., this article describes a program which combines contract learning and affective education goals. Discusses principles of the program, ways to initiate the program in a school, and personal observation on humanizing thru Contract Learning.

Simon, Sidney. "Values Clarification: A Tool For Counselors." *Personnel and Guidance Journal,* 51:614-18, May 1973.

Lists and explains six strategies for clarifying values which counselors can use with teachers and/or students.

Simon, S. B., and Bohn, M. B. "What Schools Should Be Doing About Values Clarification." *National Association of Secondary School Principals Bulletin,* 58:54-60, February 1974.

A student self-evaluation process is described in this article. Its purpose is to aid students in finding the answers to the questions of who they are and where they are going. Seven strategies that can be used to help a student in self-evaluation are described: (1) name tag strategy, (2) twenty things I love to do, (3) "I learned" statements, (4) brown bag, (5) weekly reaction sheets, (6) proud whip, and (7) planning for living.

Simon, Sidney B., and O'Rourke, Robert. "Getting to Know You." *Educational Leadership,* 32:524-26, May 1975.

The authors stress that the basis for effective learning lies in the willingness and ability of the classroom teacher to make him/herself known to his students and for the students to make themselves known to their teacher. As a result, mutual needs can be brought to an awareness level and, hopefully, reciprocally met. The article illustrates four values clarification strategies which could assist teachers and students in revealing themselves to each other in a healthy and positive manner.

Simon, Sidney, and Sadker, Myra and David. "Where Do They Stand?" *Instructor,* 84:110, Aug. 1974.

Values continuum, values voting, rank orders, unfinished sentences, and diaries are examples of values clarification strategies which can be used to help students explore their beliefs about sexism.

Sparks, Troy M. Jr. "How Human Relations is Taught (and Practiced) in Fort Worth." *American School Board Journal,* 160:44-5, April 1973.

A human relations course for teachers and principals of the Fort Worth, Texas, school district. The course consists of ten, three-hour sessions. Groups are limited to fifteen people. Topics covered are: 1) basic communication skills, 2) group interaction designed to give teachers a review of the basic concepts in group dynamics and to increase participants' personal interaction within the group, 3) interpersonal skills focusing on teacher-pupil interaction, biases, and cultural differences, and 4) professional problems designed to expose participants to the complex and often delicate relationship existing between personal and professional behavior. A survey of teachers who had completed the course revealed they were better able to respond to different individuals and situations in a classroom.

Stenhouse, Lawrence. "The Humanities Curriculum Project: The Rationale." *Theory into Practice,* 10:154-62, June 1971.

The Humanities Curriculum Project has been exploring the problems of teaching in the area of controversial issues with students aged fourteen to sixteen, concentrating particularly on students who are expected to leave school as early as they can. Article presents value positions underlying the curriculum, a pattern of teaching, discussion of materials, and problems of motivation. The object is that the pupil should come to understand the nature and implications of his point of view, and grow to adult responsibility by adopting it in his own person and assuming accountability for it. Whether the pupil changes his point of view is not significant for the attainment of understanding.

Stronck, David R. "The Affective Domain in Environmental Education." *American Biology Teacher,* 36:107-9, February 1974.

Author lists the levels of the affective domain according to Krathwohl et al. and gives examples of questions at different levels. He suggests ways to seek affective goals and gives illustrations of projects that might be utilized to stimulate students to operate at higher levels of this domain.

Tec, Leon. "Preventative Child Psychiatry Through Work With School." *Psychotherapy and Psychosomatics,* 15:66, 1967.

Describes a program in which psychiatrists teach guidance personnel who in turn work with the teachers and students directly.

EJ 089 974
Van Camp, Sarah S. "A Human Relations Curriculum." *Childhood Education,* 50:73-6, November 1973.

Suggested activities to increase children's awareness of themselves, their families, human emotions, conflicts, and cooperation.

Warren, Carrie Lee. "Value Strategies in Mental Health." *School Health Review,* 5:22-4, January/February 1974.

Values strategies can clarify and expand instruction, help students gain insight and understandings, and serve as a dramatic change in class routine. The public interview, public voting, IALAC, and twenty loves are examples of strategies.

Wills, Vernon L. "A Practical Attempt at Humanizing Education." *Contemporary Education,* 43:28-29, October 1971.

A description of the Living/Learning Program at Northern Illinois University which attempts to reduce the impersonality of university and dormitory life through programs within the setting of the student dormitory.

Author explains the learning environment of his class entitled, "Human Development and Learning," which is a required course for students in secondary education. The author points out that the nucleus of learning may not be the teacher. Rather, the prime factor may be the living and learning environment present at the time.

Zide, Michéle Moran. "Group Dynamics Techniques." *Personnel and Guidance Journal.* 51:620-22, May 1973.

Lists and explains twelve techniques of group interaction which can be integrated into virtually any content course or meeting to reorient processes toward psychological goals that facilitate existing classroom or group objectives.

## V. Reports

ED 099 300

Allen, Rodney F. *But the Earth Abideth Forever: Values in Environmental Education.* 37p.

This document describes how environmental educators can incorporate values education into their classrooms. After analyzing Kohlberg's stages of moral development, the first section of the paper stresses that the environmental educator needs to facilitate student dialogue and reasoning appropriate to the student's moral stage and to encourage progress to the next level. Seven values objectives are provided for the teacher that include the development of equality, empathy, factual knowledge, social ethical principles, personal ethical principles, moral judgments and resolutions, and action. Ten specific teaching processes for guiding the classroom teachers in developing questions for student reflection are presented. The first three instructional models set forth processes for teaching basic skills for ethical analysis and reasoning. The three processes which follow stress an empathetic mode for understanding others' values and feelings. The next two processes involve contemplating, stressing, introspection, and shaping of one's own ethos and worldview. The last two are analytic, demanding the student to set forth the reason and principles which warrant his particular judgment and then defend these reasons in ways appropriate to his moral development. (Author/DE)

ED 014753

Bolman, William M. and Westman, Jack C. *Prevention of Mental Disorder—An Overview of Current Problems.* American Psychiatric Association, Washington, D.C., 1967.

Programs discussed include those which are oriented toward the child in school and others.

ED 097 263

Casteel, J. Doyle, et al. *Value Clarification in the Social Studies: Six Formats of the Values Sheet.* Research Bulletin. Florida Educational Research and Development Council. Gainesville, July 1974, 59p.

ED 023211

Cowen, Emory L. (Ed.) and Others. *Emergent Approaches to Mental Health Programs.* The Century Psychology Series, 1967.

Describes innovative approaches to mental health problems. Consists of a series of articles grouped under three headings: conceptualizations, community programs and new sources of manpower, and new approaches in the schools. Has extensive bibliography.

ED 033173

*The Development and Evaluation of a Television Workshop in Human Relations.* Far West Laboratory for Educational Research and Development. Berkeley, California, April 1969.

In this pilot project audio-visual dramatizations of human relations problems were developed and tested. This report describes the development of the videotapes, the five programs, the discussion leaders' and viewers' guides, and various other points. An evaluation and recommendations are also given.

ED 055933

Fox, Robert S. and Lippitt, Ronald. *The Human Relations School.* University of Michigan, Ann Arbor, Michigan, 1968.

As an expansion of ED 026320, the model for a human relations school is sketched in this document. Seven goals are identified and developed: 1) to achieve involvement and collaboration; 2) to develop and maintain continuing inservice educational programs; 3) to recruit, develop and utilize a great variety of human resources; 4) to mobilize and utilize creatively resources of technology, time, and space in such ways as to foster human relations goals and values; 5) to develop and maintain an open and supportive system of communication horizontally and vertically; 6) to develop and implement a curriculum in human relations knowledge, values, and skills; and 7) to achieve community-wide involvement in procedures for continuous evaluation and review of the educational program.

ED 051041

Gibson, John S. and Kenosian, Elizabeth M. *Development of Curriculum in American Civilization for the General Student: Case Study Approach. Final Report.* Lincoln Filing System for Citizenship and Public Affairs.

Report outlines case studies on intolerance, protest and dissent, and idealism which are used to help the student's focus on similar problems today.

ED 058167

Gibson, John S. *The Intergroup Relations Curriculum: a Program for Elementary School Education,* Vol. I, 1969.

"This report deals with the research and development of a curriculum which seeks to advance democratic intergroup relations through educational processes in elementary schools. Volume I describes the background research and development."

ED 058168

Gibson, John S. *The Intergroup Relations Curriculum: A Program for Elementary School Education,* Vol. II, 1969.

Designed to promote democratic intergroup relations, this report contains the curriculum of the project. It includes the conceptual framework, the methodological tools, teaching methods, learning activities, and instructional resources.

ED 027311

Goldstein, Miriam B. and Martin, Edward C. *Humanistic Education for the General Student: A Progress Report. The English Leaflet,* Vol. 63, No. 3, Fall 1964, 8–30.

Article reports on progress of a humanities curriculum being developed at Newton High School in New England. Combining history and English, the project emphasizes humanistic content with a special weight on man's development within a society and his use of language. The objective of the course is to develop the self awareness of the students.

ED 049134

Greydanus, Samuel and Oosterman, Gordon. *Curriculum Components in History/Social Studies for Christian High Schools,* 1971.

This is a curriculum guide which promotes creative growth, intellectual growth, spiritual growth, and identification of modern problems. One objective is to develop competence in the expression of thoughts, feelings, convictions, and the development of responsible citizenship. There is a wide range of options including sections on contemporary problems, value teaching and curriculum analysis. Pages 59–106 list a wide variety of materials on many subjects and in many formats for use in the curriculum described.

ED 001052

*Group Guidance for High School.* Board of Education, Chicago, Illinois, 1964.

Program is designed to help students develop realistic ideas about himself and within this context to make plans for himself. Units include the following: 1) "Getting the Most Out of High School," 2) "Developing Myself for the Future," 3) "Taking a Long Look Ahead," and 4) "Living in an Adult World." Bibliographies are provided for each unit.

ED 002160

*Group Guidance for Upper Elementary Grades: Seven and Eight.* Board of Education. City of Chicago, 1963.

Contains four units entitled: "Getting the Most Out of School", "Getting to Know Ourselves and Others". "Discovering More About Ourselves", and "Discovering Opportunities for Self-Development". Each unit lists materials, procedures, and a bibliography.

Describes a program to rekindle enthusiasm for learning in underachievers. A variety of units, curriculum materials, and techniques are used to encourage self-acceptance and to help students discover their style, aptitudes, and good potentialities.

ED 073010
Henrie, Samuel N. *Human Development Program.* Program Report, 1972.
The human relations unit, focusing on the affective domain, is designed for grades pre-kindergarten through fourth but is applicable to junior high grades. Objectives are to help children develop self-confidence, self-awareness, and social interaction skills. Teaching/learning strategies emphasize interaction among teacher and student, and group communication. A unique feature of the program is the "Magic Circle" discussion and activity session which encourages two-way communication and deals constructively with emotions. Topics and activities of these sessions are fairly structured, presented in a given sequence, and enforce certain rules. The content of the program involves the children's own experiences. Basic information on the program is provided in five sections: 1) goals and objectives; 2) content and materials; 3) classroom action, which includes a typical lesson, evaluation of students, and role of classroom personnel; 4) implementation requirements and costs; and 5) program development and evaluation.

ED 067344
*Human Relations.* Date County Public Schools, Miami, Florida, 1971.
This is a presentation of human relations units for teachers of secondary grades. Emphasis is upon social interaction in an attempt to help students realize their own potential and respond to the needs of others. Each of the four units includes a discussion of focus, broad goals, generalizations, instructional objectives, and learning activities. Unit 1 examines the development of personality while Unit II focuses on the students understanding and perceiving themselves and others. Problems and conflicts among individuals and groups is discussed in Unit III and effectiveness of communication is stressed in Unit IV. A resource list of books, articles, and films as well as appendices providing worksheets, charts, and cartoons are included.

ED 045557
*A Human Relations Curriculum Development Project.* Created by the Pace Association Program for Action by Citizens in Education, Cleveland, Ohio, 1970.
This is a short description of materials and lessons contained in a human

relations program in Ohio. Major emphases of the program are given but no attempt is made to describe the lesson in detail.

ED 065430

*Humanities I: Man and Evolution.* John Dickinson High School, Wilmington, Delaware, 1972.

This report describes a humanities program which deals with real social, ethical, and educational problems while retaining the essential skills of the traditional courses in English and social studies. Each unit contains objectives and activities appropriate for the unit. Subjects dealt with are man's need to know himself, how communication has helped man become more human, the interaction of biological and social factors on the evolution of man in becoming human, man's struggle within his environment, and man's struggle to master himself.

ED 065431

*Humanities III. The Future of Man.* John Dickinson High School, Wilmington, Delaware, 1971.

Objectives for the unit are as follows: create an understanding of communication and its impact on human activity, explore some problem solving techniques and philosophies and their possible impact on human direction, show relationships which determine formation of values with a view toward value planning for the future, discover major problems which man must successfully contend with in order to survive, and reveal that the positive approach to a problem is dealing with it squarely.

ED 059944

*Junior High School Curriculum, Guide for Social Studies.* Alberta Dept. of Education, 1971.

Provides value-oriented, broad framework, incorporating behavioral objectives defined by Alberta's Department of Education for educators planning a sequential program for junior high school social studies programs. Emphasis is on value issues with an interdisciplinary approach. Theme of course is "Man, Culture, and Technology," in pre-industrial Afro-Asian and Western Societies. Flexible outline.

ED 090 128

Kingman, Barry. *The Development of Value Clarification Skills: Initial Efforts in an Eighth Grade Social Studies Class.* Occasional Paper 74-3. State University of New York, Stony Brook. American Historical Association Education Project. 1974.

Most materials on value clarification techniques have been written by professionals working at university schools of education. To examine value clarification from another view, to see what difficulties teachers are having in translating new techniques into classroom realities, an eighth grade social studies teacher relates his classroom experiences while developing techniques discussed by Louis Raths and his co-authors in "Values and Teaching." Raths approaches value clarification with a seven-part valuing process which encourages children to prize one's beliefs and behaviors, to choose one's beliefs and behaviors, and to act on one's beliefs. Methods for implementing these steps emphasize the clarifying response and value sheets. The teacher's experiences with both of these techniques reflect several problems and pitfalls of their use in the classroom situation. A basic problem confronted in using the techniques is the extent of neutrality or direction on the part of the teacher. Student-teacher relations as affected by the techniques are considered. Systematic measure of the effects in the classroom are closely considered and means for accomplishing meaningful record-keeping are suggested and developed. (Author/KSM)

ED 080 317

Kuhn, David J. *Value Education in the Sciences: The Step Beyond Concepts and Processes.* Paper presented at the annual meeting of the National Science Teachers Association (21st, Detroit, Michigan, March 1973).

This paper is concerned with one question on how the value systems of individuals may be clarified and applied in the science classroom and in the real world outside. Science teaching is considered as occurring on three levels: the fact level, the concepts-process level, and the values level. The fact level was often stressed prior to the 1960's, the concepts-process level received added attention during the 1960's, and the values level will gain increasing importance in science teaching during the 1970's. Value education in the sciences must be built on the sound understanding of science concepts and processes. It will require innovative strategies, a new perspective on science education, and different roles for teachers. A number of strategies, including simulations, role playing, sensitivity modules, values continuums, and the use of attitudinal surveys are described. Appropriate teacher behaviors in the classroom (e.g., asking evaluative questions and promoting a classroom climate conducive to value exploration) are also examined. Science education must make the exploration of value systems paramount in order to produce a scientifically literate and aware citizenry capable of making proper decisions on such questions as population control, radioactive fallout, pesticide usage, and industrial effluents. (August/JR)

ED 069576

Prince, Gerald and Others. *Toward the Human Element. Beginning Handbook for Change,* Volume I, 1972. (Available from Bell Junior High School, Jefferson County, Golden, Colorado 80401).

This handbook is aimed at encouraging growth and renewal of "human element" in schools. Four fundamental processes are necessary to achieve this change in schools: problem-solving, shared decision making, open communication, and accountability. These skills are discussed and a variety of techniques, activities and resources are described which will help to achieve the skills.

ED 048080

Project Essay. *Teacher's Resource Guide for the Nature of Man and His Conflicts.* Grade 7, 1970.

Focuses on the individual and his conflicts. Objectives of the course are as follows: developing an understanding of the physical self and appropriate behavior in a social context, and understanding that each individual perceives his environment differently because of his unique biological, physiological, and sociological configuration. Also lists skill and attitudinal objectives. There are guides for each unit containing objectives, learning activities, and a bibliography.

ED 034999

Randolph, Norma, and Others. *Self-Enhancing Education: Communication Techniques and Processes that Enhance. A Training Manual.* Cuppertino Union High School District, California. Office of Education, Washington, D.C., 1968.

This training manual is designed to be used with the text Self-Enhancing Education by Randolph & Howe. Manual is divided into ten units which outline the contents of the unit and appropriate supplementary materials.

ED 010891

Schmidt, Wesley I. *Group Guidance in the Elementary School.* Illinois State Office Superintendent Public Instruction, Springfield, Illinois, 1966.

Objectives of group guidance at this level are to strengthen students' knowledge about self-concept, the world of work and education, and the relationship between self and the world. Report also mentions activities and programs which will aid in group guidance.

ED 059943

*Senior High School Curriculum Guide for Social Studies.* Alberta Dept. of Education, 1971.

An attempt to provide a value-oriented, broad framework, incorporating behavioral objectives defined by Alberta's Department of Education for educators planning a sequential program for senior high school social studies programs. Aims of the guide are: 1) emphasizes affective and cognitive objectives using an inquiry and interdisciplinary approach toward knowledge of social studies concepts; 2) elucidates values, skills, and knowledge parts of the curriculum; 3) provides a sequential program for grades 10, 11, and 12. Grade 10 program speaks to concerns of contemporary Canadian society while Grades 11 and 12 deal with world problems. One-third of the time is to be devoted to study of current interest topics. Valuable list of teaching aids and reference books.

## 6. DESCRIPTIONS OF PROGRAMS AND CURRICULA

### I. Books

Carter, Ronald D. *Help! These Kids Are Driving Me Crazy*. Champaign, Illinois: Research Press, 1972.

Booklet designed to illustrate workable techniques to modify behavior in elementary school children in the classroom. Authors provides examples and gives techniques for coping with various behavior problems in the classroom. Short analyses and explanations of how to establish desirable behavior in the child and how to weaken undesirable behaviors. Of some interest to the elementary school teacher.

Castillo, Gloria A. *Left-Handed Teaching*. New York: Praeger Publishers, 1974.

After outlining "a personal approach to confluent education," the author offers a variety of lessons in affective education which will help students enhance their imagination, sharpen sensory awareness, diminish aggression, and learn to let off interpersonal steam.

ED 098 224

Curwin, Richard L., Fuhrmann, Barbara Schneider. *Discovering Your Teaching Self; Humanistic Approaches to Effective Teaching*. 1975. (Available from Prentice-Hall, Inc., Englewood Cliffs, New Jersey 07632. (1)

This book offers a program of self-improvement for teachers and prospective teachers that grows out of humanistic criteria. The book is a collection of activities designed to increase the reader's potential as a teacher. There is an introduction entitled "Discovering Your Teaching Self." The remaining two sections are devoted to activities. "Awareness of Your Teaching Self," chapter 2, deals with the reader's awareness of himself as a teacher—his ideals, beliefs, attitudes, values, and goals. The activities are internally focused; extensive use is made in this section of fictional logs, such as conversations in which the reader is asked to take part, worksheets, and other assignments which center on discussion of a teacher's role and teacher behavior. The activities in chapter two are designed to help the reader become aware of the teacher he is now and the teacher he would like to become. Chapter 3, "Examining Your Teaching Self," deals with the collection and interpretation of significant data about teaching. These activities are externally focused and are meant to make the reader's classroom behavior congruent with his ideals. Assignments in this section are related to the reader's actual classroom teaching. (JA)

DeMille, Richard. *Put Your Mother on the Ceiling. Children's Imagination Games*. New York: The Viking Press, 1955.

Acting on the beliefs that conscious and unconscious mental processes are just as real as overt behavior, and imagining can change behavior as effectively as reasoning, willing, or remembering, the author has written a book filled with imagination games which can be used by teachers, parents, and anyone who works with children. These games can be used in a variety of ways to help children stimulate their imaginative abilities, and to help teachers focus on the students' concerns and feelings.

Grainger, A. J. *The Bullring. A Classroom Experiment in Moral Education.* Oxford: Pergamon Press, 1970.

The Bullring refers to a safe area in the classroom in which young adolescents can find out for themselves what sort of persons they and their friends and their enemies are in relation to one another. It thus extends the principle of free discovery into the realm of personal relationships, to help children to discover themselves and to discover a morality by which to live. Since the Bullring was an experience of personal relationships and not merely a discussion about them, it follows that the children and the teachers were in an unusual sense "at risk." The contents of the book consist of two Bullrings and an analysis of what was going on. The author also discusses the background of the idea, the rules and the setting, group dynamics, authority and anxiety, moral education, and the bullring and the school community. This experiment, which took place in Britain should be read by anyone who is seeking ways to teach meaningful moral education.

Hall, Brian P. *Value Clarification as Learning Process. A Guidebook.* New York, N.Y.: Paulist Press, 1973.

The book is divided into four sections. "Part I is an introduction in which we give a definition of value and value-ranking, and value indicators. Part II is a treatment of value techniques in six areas, the importance of primary values and the dimensions of the process involved in using a value education approach. Part III explains and gives several conference designs. Part IV contains simple classroom techniques that correlate with the sourcebook."

Hall, Brian P. *Value Clarification as Learning Process. A Sourcebook.* New York, N.Y.: Paulist Press, 1973.

This book raises questions about values and then tries to suggest approaches to answers. In Part I the author states that values are the underlying principles that guide the human person in relationship to himself, to others close to him, and to society. He defends values clarification and looks at the values we live by and the question of value ranking. He explores the interrelationships of values within any individual. Part II deals in greater detail wth particular aspects of man in relation to time and space with their value implications. It deals with values more in the area of priorities rather than individual value, focusing mainly on value ranking. Guilt is discussed in relation to the past. Anxiety is evident when we look to the future. In the final chapter the author deals with the present as it relates to the past and the future. It is in the present that values are acted out, lived, and affirmed.

ED 044416

Heyer, Robert and Meyer, Anthony. *Discovery in Film.* New Jersey: Paulist/ Newman Press, 1969.

Seventy-eight "classic" short films are arranged into six categories: communication, freedom, love, peace, happiness, and the underground. The critique for each film includes content and style of the film, questions designed to elicit discussion, and other resource materials. Appendices offer a brief discussion of three major propaganda films, a selection of feature films classified into the six categories, an essay on "teaching the film," and an alphabetical index to the films discussed.

Johnson, David W. *Reaching Out.* New Jersey: Prentice-Hall, 1972.

This book seeks to provide the theory and experiences necessary to develop effective interpersonal skills. Much of the material was developed for a youth project of the Youth Research Center, Minneapolis, Minn. "Project Youth was founded to answer the question, 'Can a portion of our nation's youth be trained to help those who seem to be headed for a life of unhappiness, delinquency, and general tragedy?' " Among the subjects discussed and illustrated by exercises are the following: (1) development and maintenance of trust, (2) increasing communication skills, (3) verbal expression of feelings, (4) nonverbal expression of feelings, (5) listening and responding, (6) acceptance of self and others, (7) constructive confrontation, (8) reinforcing interpersonal skills, (9) modeling interpersonal skills, (10) solving interpersonal problems, and (11) resolving interpersonal conflicts. This is an effective handbook for those seeking to enlarge their interpersonal effectiveness.

Mattox, Beverly A. *Getting It Together.* San Diego, California: Pennant Press, 1975.

This book is meant to be a primer for teachers who wish to understand the Kohlberg approach to values and moral education and would like to know how to use it in the classroom. Kohlberg's theory is explicated, the teacher's task is outlined, and many dilemmas are presented for teachers to use in the classroom as diagnostic and growth tools to reveal the stage at which the student is currently functioning and to help students advance to thinking at the next higher stage.

Pfeiffer, J. William and Jones, John E. *A Handbook of Structured Experiences for Human Relations Training.* Vol. I. Iowa: University Associates Press, 1969.

This handbook contains three types of structured experiences: unadapted "classic" experiences, highly adapted experiences, and innovative experiences. Intended to be used by facilitators of groups, some of whom may only have limited experience.

Shrank, Jeffrey. *Media in Value Education: A Critical Guide.* Chicago: Argus Communications, 19701.

A good reference volume for teachers doing work in humanistic education, with particular emphasis on value clarification. Provides a comprehensive summary of approximately one hundred films which could be used in value education along with suggested questions for discussion. The emphasis on discussion and the failure to present other possible activities weakens the book's practical value and the section on records is likely to be dated rapidly. Still, the book is useful in helping the teacher decide which films to order.

Shrank, Jeffrey. *Teaching Human Beings: 101 Subversive Activities for the Classroom.* Boston: Beacon Press, 1972.

Because he felt that many teenagers have "learned" that they are not important, that their feelings cannot be trusted, that adults usually know better, and that they must become what others want them to be, Jeffrey Shrank wrote this book to help them unlearn this knowledge. He offers a wide variety of classroom activities to help students grow and learn for themselves. Among the topics covered are sense education, hidden assumptions, violence, prejudice, drug education, and death. Two appendices list extensive sources of films and simulation games.

Simon, Sidney B. *Meeting Yourself Halfway: Thirty-one Values Clarification Strategies for Daily Living.* Illinois: Argus Communications, 1974.

After an introduction which outlines the values clarification process and a list of instructions on how to use the book, Simon lists 31 strategies to "help you locate, sort out, and build a set of values."

Simon, Sidney B., and Clark, Jay. *More Values Clarification.* San Diego, Calif. Pennant Press, 1975.

After giving some viewpoints on values clarification, the authors describe the basic framework used in applying values clarification, include guidelines helpful in working with students, examine some factors involved in using values clarification with groups, and outline processes of values clarification. Next they outline techniques for teachers to personally apply values clarification to their own lives. Finally, the bulk of the book is devoted to strategies to use with students in helping them clarify their values.

Simon, Sidney B.; Howe, Leland W.; Kirschenbaum, Howard. *Values Clarification.* New York: Hart Publishing Co., 1972.

This book answers the question, "How do we teach young people about values?" Rather than relying on moralizing, *laissez-faire* attitudes, or modeling, the authors outline the values clarification approach which focuses on prizing one's beliefs and behaviors, choosing one's beliefs and behaviors, and acting on one's beliefs. The book contains a wealth of strategies designed to help the student become aware of what values they prize and what the alternative modes of thinking and acting are.

Sugarman, Daniel A. and Hochstein, Rolaine A. *Seven Stories for Growth.* New York: Pitman, 1965.

This book contains seven stories for primary-school children to help children identify feelings, learn about emotion, and to apply some aspects of the material to their own lives. Each story is preceded by explanatory material to aid teachers in understanding the mental health goals of each presentation. At the end of each story are questions for discussion and a list of projects that would further illumine the concepts learned from the story. Topics presented are accepting feelings, accepting ourselves, talking about our problems, doing things for others, replacing worry with work and planning, learning to live with change, enjoying the little things in life. Recommended for teachers of primary grades and prospective teachers of these grades.

## II. Magazines and Journals

Adams, Lavarn B. "The Classroom Council: A Method for Improvement of Interpersonal Classroom Relationships." *Elementary School Guidance and Counseling,* 7:244-7, March 1973.

This discussion of a method for improvement of interpersonal classroom relationships provides a vehicle by which a peer group and a teacher can work together toward solution of common concerns.

Alschuler, Alfred S. and Ivey, Allen E. "Getting into Psychological Education." *Personnel and Guidance Journal,* 51:682-691, May 1973.

Authors discuss materials to use to learn more about psychological education under the following headings: activities and exercises, programs in psychological education, transmitting counseling skills to people, community and societal backgrounds, and general background.

Arnaud, Elie E. "Can the Schools Affect Character Education?" *Texas Personnel and Guidance Association Journal,* 2:39-42, March 1973.

The Character Education Project of San Antonio, Texas, is producing a curriculum for character development beginning at age three and extending into adulthood. The materials, seen as closely related to the counseling program, are being given extensive field testing in several areas of the country.

Brown, Stanley B. and Brown, L. Barbara. "Look—I See Me." *Childhood Education,* 47:84-85, November 1970.

Choosing real-life situations for role-playing by primary school children is a technique by which children can learn to understand their own behavior as well as the behavior of others. Authors present several examples of actual role-playing situations which can be used in the classroom.

Buffie, Edward, and Others. "Human Relations—One Dimension of Teaching." *Viewpoints,* 46:81-104, November 1970.

Describes a simulation package developed at Indiana University and provides the evaluation component of the multi-media package.

Cheney, Ruth. "Youth, sexuality and values clarification." *Findings,* Fall 1970, pp. 14–16.

The complexities of growing up in our pluralistic society are noted. Specific reference is made to the conflicting values and standards young people must face in the area of human sexuality. The author favors the values clarification approach for helping young people to make responsible decisions in their relationships with members of the opposite sex. In addition to describing the theory of values clarification and listing some useful resources, the article relates the experiences of using the values clarification process with a group of high school students during a summer religious retreat.

Colby, Anne. "Book Reviews." *Harvard Educational Review,* 45:134-143, February 1975.

The author reviews two books dealing with the theory and practice of values clarification. In addition, a comprehensive comparison of the values clarification theory and Kohlberg's theory of moral development is made. Although the article concludes that in many ways the moral development and values clarification approaches do conflict, it is possible to use them in a complimentary way without being inconsistent.

Curwin, Geri, and Curwin, Richard L. "Building trust: A Starting Point for Clarifying Values." *Learning,* 3:30-33, 36, February 1975.

This article, excerpted from the book *Developing Individual Values in the Classroom,* describes how the values clarification process helps student meet their need to find meaning and order in their social environment. The authors describe a three stage process for building trust. The major portion of the article is devoted to describing nine new strategies as a beginning for clarifying values and building trust among students.

DeLara, Lane E. "Cigar Box to Personality Box," *Mental Hygiene,* 52:577-581, October 1968.

Technique used by art teacher in junior high school to get students to identify with feelings of classmates and express these feelings through art. In this project an empty cigar box represents a personality box, an extension of outer and inner personalities. Each student picks a paper written by a classmate in which that person disclosed his inner feelings and thoughts. No names are used. Then each student decorates his cigar box to reflect the personality or feelings of that student. Through this technique students come to understand themselves and their classmates better.

Dinkmeyer, Don and Owens, Karen. "Guidance and Instruction: Complementary for the Educative Process." *Elementary School Guidance and Counseling,* 3:260-8, May 1969.

Presents a teacher's view of classroom guidance. Incorporates an individual student-teacher conference program done in conjunction with an independent study project to accomplish objectives which will produce significant learning. Describes in detail how the program operated and its results in the classroom.

Elliot, Jane. "Discrimination Day." *People Watching,* 2:17-21, Spring 1973.

Relates an experience in moral education for elementary students and adults. After dividing the group into blue-eyed and brown-eyed sections, the author led the group through a series of experiences in discrimination.

Frankel, J. R. "Strategies for Developing Values." *Today's Education,* 62:49-55, Dec./Nov. 1973.

For the secondary teacher, it develops some strategies which can be used to help students discover their own values among conflicting ones through discussion techniques, empathy, and clear definition of words. Emphasizes that a value judgment is not a factual judgment.

Gollub, Wendy and Graff, Karen. "What—So What—Now What: Teaching People Watching." *People Watching,* 1:18-23, Spring 1972.

Presents a format teachers can use to generate sequences of classroom activity that promote 1) recognition of an experience ("What"), 2) contemplation and analysis ("So What"), and 3) application and practice in personally relevant situations ("Now What"). The three phases correspond to three broad educational goals.

Grainger, A. J. "The Teacher in the Building." *People Watching,* 1:72-75, Spring 1972.

Describes a free discussion lesson involving children between the ages of thirteen and fourteen. This method developed tolerance and understanding of interpersonal relationships among the children.

Grambs, Jean. "Two Open-End Stories to Teach Intergroup Understanding." *Grade Teacher,* 86:122-123, April 1969.

Two open-ended stories on Negro school children are related. These can be used in the classroom as a basis for group discussion to promote intergroup relationships and understanding.

Greer, Donald. "Instructional Media for Teaching About Values." *Social Education.* 35:911-15, December 1971.

First the author discusses the two main theories on values acquisition. Next he outlines the value teaching-value processing issue and finally he discusses seven curriculum units which teach values.

Greer, Margaret. "Affective Growth Through Reading." *Reading Teacher,* 25:336-41, January 1972.

In this article Greer suggests many ideas and techniques to use in order to make reading an affective experience.

Grossman, Bruce D. "Enhancing the Self." *Exceptional Children.* 38:248-54, November 1971.

This article gives specific classroom activities designed to develop the self including body image, kinesthetic self, and the psychological self.

Gum, Moy F., Tamminen, Armas W., Smaby, Marlowe H. "Developmental Guidance Experiences." *Personnel and Guidance Journal,* 51:647-52, May 1973.

DGE's are structured experiences based on Havighurst's developmental tasks and are designed to promote healthy sociopsychological development. Author explains methods and three examples showing developmental guidance in education.

Harmin, Merrill and Simon, Sidney B. "How to Help Students Learn to Think ... About Themselves." *High School Journal,* 55:256-64, March 1972.

Article suggests methods of teaching so that the student not only learns how to think, but learns how to think about life itself, especially himself.

Harmin, Merrill; Kirschenbaum, Howard; Simon, Sidney B. "Teaching Science With a Focus on Values." *Science Teacher,* 37:16-20, January 1970.

Discusses subject matter on three levels: factual, conceptual, and value. Presentation of topics of discussion and projects associated with them. Teaching science with responsibility and a willingness to grapple with the complexities of social issues is needed in today's world. An example of the three levels of teaching sciences would be Newton's Laws of Motion: 1) Factual— What Are Newton's laws? 2) Conceptual—Demonstrate, via certain laboratory experiments, that you know these laws, 3) Values—How, if at all, have these laws touched your own life?"

Hawley, Robert C. "Values and Decision Making." *The Independent School Bulletin,* 32:19-23, October 1972.

The author notes the growing complexities and confusion of values that characterize modern day living. A three step process to stimulate more openness, more acceptance, and more thoughtfullness is presented with the hope of helping individuals move toward a more comprehensive level of valuing. The majority of this "paper workshop" article is devoted to offering teachers seven strategies and ideas that might be useful in helping students with their valuing process.

"Human Relations in the Classroom." *Today's Education,* 62:30-43+, January 1973.

Suggests a variety of ways by the teacher can eliminate causes of prejudice and improve intergroup relations in school. One must begin by examining his attitudes and involve the community. Describes a number of class and individual activities which can be done by the class.

"Interaction Briefs." *Today's Education,* Vol. 57: (September 1968), 28-29; (October 1968), 67; (November 1968), 68; (December 1968), 79-80; Vol. 58: (January 1969), 67; (February 1969), 55; (March 1969), 68; (September 1969), 64; (October 1969), 57; (December 1969), 59. Vol. 59: (January 1970), 70; (February 1970), 68; (April 1970), 12; (September 1970); 76.

Vol. 57 (September 1968), 28-29. "The Fishbowl: Design for Discussion" helps spread participation in a group discussion and makes each student more aware of the part he plays. (October 1968), 67. "Accent on Listening" helps students become aware of the various aspects of listening. (November 1968), 68. "Brainstorming" teaches ways to produce ideas. (December 1968), 79-80. "Diagnosing a Classroom Problem" helps students to focus on a problem as a prelude to solving it.

Vol. 58 (January 1969), 67. "Role Playing" teaches how to role play for greater understanding. (February 1969), 55. "Lost on the Moon: A Decision-Making Problem" teaches the problems and potentials of working in groups. (March 1969), 68. "Stop Action" is a technique of interrupting work on a task to examine the way we are working. (September 1969), 64. "An Experiment in Communication" teaches two-way communication thereby encouraging students to ask pertinent questions and become better communicators. (October 1969), 57. "An Experiment in Cooperation" helps students become more sensitive to how their behavior may help or hinder joint problem solving. (December 1969), 59. "Team Learning" helps children learn how to work in groups.

Vol. 59 (January 1970), 70. "Looking at Leadership" helps students focus on what makes a good leader. (February 1970), 68. "The Bean Jar Problem" helps students clarify problems and find inventive ways to solve them. (April 1970), 12. "Learning About Behavior Styles" helps children become aware of their own behavior styles and sensitive to the work styles of others. (September 1970), 76. "Teaching Tact and Timing" helps children develop greater insight and skill in human interaction.

Kirschenbaum, H. and Simon, S. "Teaching English With a Focus on Values." *English Journal.* 58:1071-1076, October 1969.

Describes use of values sheets in introducing new topics or books in English teaching. A values sheet is a ditto upon which is written a provocative, value-laden statement. Questions are then asked which call for an opinion about the values sheet statement from the student.

Levine, Esther. "Affective Education: Lessons in Ego Development." *Psychology in the Schools,* 10:147-50, April 1973.

This cursory outline of the Human Development Program has been given as one example of affective curricula available for classroom use. While it is not within the scope of this paper to describe fully the mechanics of the Program, some mention is made of selection and preparation procedures.

Long, Barbara Ellis. "Unit 1: Who Am I?" *Grade Teacher,* 89:119-122, September 1971.

Outlines contents of a lesson designed to help children focus on self-identity. Helps them to see the self as a legitimate part of the school program.

Long, Barbara Ellis. "More About Us." *Grade Teacher,* 89:20-28, October 1971.

Outlines three short classroom experiments which illustrate some of the various areas of study in the behavioral sciences. Helps children realize that human behavior can be studied objectively and illustrates a method used in studying behavior.

Long, Barbara Ellis. "Identity Auction." *Grade Teacher,* 89:56-58, 78+, November 1971.

This game which is outlined in detail helps children to realize that we choose among alternatives in our life styles. We become what we are by a series of choices according to what we think of ourselves and what we hope others will think of us.

Long, Barbara Ellis. "Getting the Message." *Grade Teacher,* 89:44-47, December, 1971.

Describes a series of activities which classroom teachers can use to show students how they communicate themselves to others and how they respond to the signals others send to them.

Long, Barbara Ellis, with Moore, Ronald. "When Confusion Reigns." *Grade Teacher,* 89:43-46, 93+, January 1972.

This article describes a model for open-ended discussions which teachers can use to encourage better communication and help children learn how to deal with stress.

Long, Barbara Ellis. "The Milk Bottle Game." *Grade Teacher,* 89:38-41, 72+, Feb. 1972.

Outlines a human relations game which teachers can use to help children focus on perception, learning, personality, and small-group process.

Long, Barbara Ellis, with Litz, Bret. "Decision, Decisions." *Grade Teacher,* 89:20-33, March 1972.

Long utilizes a lesson on ethical dilemmas designed by a sixth grader to help children focus on the process of values and decision making.

Long, Barbara Ellis. "Why Words?" *Grade Teacher,* 89:21-28, April 1972.
This is a unit that deals with the age-old concern of philosophers—Is verbal communication the thing that makes us human or is it the other way around?

Long, Barbara Ellis. "Why Do People Do What They Do?" *Grade Teacher,* 89: 70-76, May/June 1972.

This lesson asks children to speculate about behavior and reasons behind it. In the process there is much learning about attitudes and feelings.

"Magic Circles Lead to Understanding Self and Others." *Illinois Education,* 61:38, 1972-73.
Describes a 20-minute daily period in classrooms in Park Forest in which the children have experiences in three areas: 1) self-awareness, 2) mastery, and 3) social interaction. Program is also beginning at the junior high level.

Mastrude, Peggy. "Terra II—A Spaceship Earth Simulation for the Middle Grades," *Intercom,* 13–58, 1972.
This unit of study consists of four lessons based on the concept that the earth is a large system made up of many small systems (air, food, water, man, etc.). Complete procedures are included to study the environment, examine developing countries, determine interaction between peoples and nations. The problem-solving exercises use an inquiry approach to values.

Myrick, R. D. "Helping Humanize Education." *Elementary School Guidnace and Counseling,* 7:295-9, May 1973.
Describes a teaching technique called "one-way glasses" to help children get in touch with various attitudes and how they color thinking. Gives four lessons which can be used and describes what happened to children who had this experience in subsequent weeks. Technique developed by Gerald Weinstein.

Ohlsen, M. M. "Increasing Youth's Self-Understanding," *Educational Leadership,* 22:239-41+, January 1965.
Gives principles which should be considered by those who give youngsters information about themselves. Let them know you know them, give sources of information, use resources you are qualified to use, respect pupils' perception of themselves, be sensitive to cues which suggest that the pupil does not comprehend, be wary less perceptions color objective data.

EJ 090 937
Osman, Jack D. "A Rationale for Using Value Clarification in Health Education." *Journal of School Health,* 43:621-3, December 1973.

This paper discusses a value clarification model for health education as an alternative to a purely factual approach which is becoming inadequate in the face of ever increasing amounts of information. This hierarchial model consists of three levels: (1) the information level providing the factual basis; (2) the conceptual level, centering on the relationships between facts; and (3) the values level which personalizes the information.

Owen Carolyn M. "The Practice of Humanistic Teaching-Learning." *American Journal of Occupational Therapy,* 28:222-5, April 1974.

Describes the application of basic principles of humanistic theory to an undergraduate course in adolescent development. In a standard lecture course of approximately 50 students, methods of providing a sense of physical well being, belonging, esteem, and self-actualization were developed from A. Maslow's hierarchy of needs. Psychomotor, affective, and cognitive areas were emphasized in a series of relaxation exercises, personal exchanges of feelings between students and instructors, small group process techniques, and a contract plan which enabled students to choose the amount and kind of learning they need. A review of student responses to the course and suggested revisions based on class feedback are presented.

Palomares, Uvaldo H. and Rubini, Terri. "Human Development in the Classroom." *Personnel and Guidance Journal,* 51:653-7, May 1973.

Discusses the method and theory of the Human Development Program which focuses on three main themes: a) awareness (knowing our feelings, thoughts, and actions); b) mastery (self-confidence); c) social interaction (knowing other people). Also describes applications of the program and things to keep in mind when implementing the program.

Palomares, Uvaldo H., and Rubini, Terri. "Magic Circle: Key to Understanding Self and Others." *Educational Leadership,* 32:19-21, October 1974.

Explicates the magic circle which is a key concept in the Human Development Program designed by Palomares and Bessell to develop self-awareness, positive self-concept, and supportive interaction in children using cues and follow-up activities suggested by the curriculum.

Peatling, John H. and Glasson, Mary C. "Vision Finder." (Union College, Character Research Project, Schenectady, New York). *Character Potential,* 6:19-26, April 1972.

This article describes "Vision Finder" an instrument which makes it possible to select among some possible futures. After the initial selection, a process of exploration and long-range planning begins. This process demonstrates the importance of dominating purpose to a psychologically healthy life for children.

Perry, Cereta E. "Can Human Relations Be Taught Through a Formalized Program?" *Educational Leadership,* 32:27-30, October 1974.

Discusses a program developed by Moustakis and Perry to humanize learning in the public schools. This program stimulated growth in self awareness
through academic program and through communication between student and
teacher.

Reddin, Louise. "Gestalt Techniques Applied in Art Classes." *People Watching,*
2:22-25, Spring 1973.

Purpose of the lessons presented was to show that artistic activity can be
combined effectively with affective, personal, Gestalt experiences. Results
showed that the children flourished in this atmosphere because they were
encouraged to give their own personal interpretation of their emotional and
intellectual experience.

Schulman, Jerome L. "Mental Health in the Schools." *Elementary School Journal,* 74:48-56, October 1973.

The concern of this article is with mental health programs that are directed at primary prevention of emotional difficulties. Three types of programs and examples of each are outlined: (1) those directed toward children
such as the Ojemann program, (2) those directed toward teachers and administrators as examplified by the studies at the University of Michigan and
the Technical Assistance Program developed by Newman in Washington, D.C.,
and (3) finally those directed toward children, teachers, administrators, and
parents, the St. Louis Health Dept. mental health program, and the program
developed by the University of Rochester and the public schools of Rochester, N.Y. The author then lists basic requirements for a mental health program
and outlines the contents of a program which meets these requirements:
Person-to-Person: A Classroom Program.

Shreve, Robert E. and Tanenbaum, Sarah. "Do Your Students Need a Psychology Lab?" *School Management.* 11:110-16, March 1967.

Through the active support of administrators and students, two psychology teachers were able to provide for their students a challenging do-it-your-
self laboratory course in experimental psychology. Much of the equipment
for the laboratory was built by the students themselves. Dividends realized
from the laboratory were: new interests in statistics generated by the psychology laboratory and keen interest in library research, and perhaps the
greatest benefit was that students learned to understand why people act and
react as they do.

Simon, Sidney. "The Teacher Educator in Value Development" *Phi Delta Kappan,* 53:649-51, June 1972.

Six strategies for clarifying values are outlined. Author is concerned with
bringing into teacher education an emphasis on values clarification so that
teachers in turn can help their students clarify values.

Simon, Sidney and Massey, Sara. "Value Clarification." *Educational Leadership,* 30: 738-9, May 1973.

Students explore the "Who Am I?" by making their own value questionnaires and trading them with each other.

Smith, Lester V., and Ojemann, Ralph H. "A Decision-Making Model." *School Health Review,* 5:6-9 Jan./Feb. 1974.

This article sets forth the Ojemann model for decision making. "Step One—Examine what motivating forces seem to be operating in a given situation. ... Step Two—Devise and examine the probable intermediate and remote effects of possible alternative ways of satisfying these motivations. ... Step Three—Apply one's personal standard to the proposed course of action to determine if the effects of the action and the standards are compatible. ... Step Four—Decide either for or against the selected behavior at their point in time."

Sprinthall, Normal A. (U. Minnesota) "The Adolescent as a Psychologist: An application of Kohlberg to a high school curriculum." *School Psychology Digest,* 1:8-14, Summer 1972.

Describes a program designed to promote ego development in teenagers through regular classroom learning experiences. A series of high school classes in psychology, including a seminar and practicum, were based on the stage theories of Kohlberg and Piaget. An attempt was made to expand social role participation and provide a broadened experience, focusing on both the meaning of "self" and the understanding of others. It is suggested that this approach provides a new framework for intervention through programs and classes in psychological and moral education.—J. McCowin.

EJ 081 061

Stager, Mary; Hill, Jane, "The Moral Education Project." *Orbit,* 4:11-14, April 1973.

This article defines moral education, gives current examples of classroom experiences in moral education and literature, program materials available, and lists some problems the idea is encountering.

Stanford, G. and Stanford, B. "Affective Approaches to Literature." *English Journal,* 62:64-8, January 1973.

Teacher who sees the importance of dealing with students' feelings can draw on the following types of activities: open-ended discussion, improvisation, simulations and simulation games, experiences beyond the classroom. Describes activities in each area which can be implemented in the classroom.

Taylor, B. L., and McKean, R. C. "Values Curriculum Being Developed." *Educational Leadership,* 32:238, December 1974.

This brief article describes a three year values education project in Aurora, Illinois. The project includes curriculum development, instructional manuals, teacher in-service education, and evaluation, and is relying heavily on the work of Raths, Simon, Harmin, Kirschenbaum, Kohlberg, and Rokeach.

"Unfinished Story." *Today's Education.*

This is a regular monthly feature of this magazine. Each story is designed to stimulate discussion about incidents which have no "right" solution. In the process, children become aware of their values in relation to other members of the group.

Wass, Kannelore; Combs, Arthur W. "Humanizing the Education of Teachers." *Theory Into Practice,* 13:123-9, April 1974.

A brief description of the University of Florida's Childhood Education Program, which aims to produce teachers who have learned to use themselves effectively as instruments to carry out their educational functions. The research on which the developments of the program is based is also reviewed.

Wilkinson, C. "Value Learning Replaces School Religious Classes." *The Calgary Herald,* September 14, 1974, p. 38.

The author reports that the values clarification movement initiated in the United States is spreading and growing throughout Canada. Interest and support for values education has been so strong that an amendment to the Consolidated Education Act was passed by the Canadian government to officially endorse the teaching of values education in schools. Wilkinson further notes that the work of Simon, Howe, and Kirschenbaum have directly assisted Canadian educators in providing an effective, challenging, and meaningful program of values clarification in their classrooms. Examples of classroom strategies are outlined and discussed.

Wullschleger, Karl R. "Facing Up to Emotions; Some Tested Methods for Primary Teachers." *Today's Education,* 62:57-58, February 1973.

Presents a few techniques elementary school teachers can use in their classroom in helping children understand and deal with emotions. Among the techniques described are role-playing, puppets, and stories where groups of children express happy, sad, or angry feelings appropriate to the story. Teachers should accept children's feelings and help them to cope with and express them.

Zeitz, F. F. "Emotion Box." *Instructor,* 82:117, August 1972.

The emotion box was placed in the classroom by the teacher for them to record feelings, negative, positive or neutral. Teacher read them daily, found that most were signed, and that he was aware of feelings in the classroom only one-third of the time.

Zeitz, F. F. "Lessons in Awareness." *Instructor,* Vol. 82 (August 1972), 117; (October 1972), 86; (November 1972), 84; (December 1972), 34; (January 1972), 92; (February 1973), 38; (March 1973), 42; (April 1973), 39; (June 1973), 20.

> Monthly feature in *Instructor;* not in every issue. Every lesson has suggestions for classroom activities which will increase awareness in children. April 1973 describes a class which learned awareness through partnering off, listening to what each other had to say; and complimenting each other. June/July 1973 class had value auction and discussed results as a follow-up.

### III. Chapters in Books and Reports; Articles in Encyclopedias

Malamud, D. I. and Machover, S. "The Workshop in Self-Understanding: A New Approach to Mental Health Education," in Abt, Laurence E. and Riess, Bernard F. (eds.) *Progress in Clinical Psychology.* New York: Grune, 1964, 200–8.

> "The authors have developed a series of carefully planned experimental classroom situations in which students are given the opportunity to experience such concepts as that 1) all behavior is caused, 2) unconscious phenomena are real and meaningful, 3) childhood experiences have a crucial bearing on personality, 4) trivial things can be significant, 5) a coherent and understandable style of reacting may be discerned in one's life, and 6) the self is an active agent in one's development. Many experiments follow which must meet the following requirements: 1) simple enough so that all can participate, 2) sufficiently novel and disarming that stereotyped responses cannot be used, 3) able to evoke a wide variety of individual responses and provoke students to wonder whether their reactions were as inevitable as they thought they were."

Weinberg, Carl. "Social science and humanistic education" in the *Seventy-third Yearbook of the National Society for the Study of Education,* Part II, 1974, Chicago, Ill., National Society for Study of Education, pp. 100–122.

> This paper is about a contemporary version of education which will be referred to as "humanistic," its roots in the society, and the role that social science and social scientists have played in the development of humanism in education.
> The new humanism in education must be seen primarily as a school version of the liberation movements throughout the society. It contains its distinct pedagogical strategies which differentiates it from some of the strategies used by humanistic psychologists or political radicals, for example; but the goals are the same. The main goal appears to be the shifting emphasis from institution to individual. Subgoals include increased personal awareness and decreased self-estrangement. Specifically, the task is to integrate persons into

their institutional life by permitting them control over the institutions in which they must exist.

## VI. Whole Issues

*A Teaching Program for Education in Human Behavior,* Developed by Ralph Ojemann, Educational Research Council of America, Rockefeller Building, Cleveland, Ohio 44113.

Based on the idea of "causal" behavior, this program helps children focus on reasons for behavior and alternative ways of responding to the feelings aroused by that behavior. They also learn ways of expressing feelings implicit in their own behavior. Children examine the reasons for their behavior and that of other people in their lives. There is a teacher's manual for each grade level in the elementary school which discusses the theory of causal behavior, lessons to use, and ways to integrate this program into other subject areas. Essentially it is based on a class discussion approach, although other activities are suggested.

Bessell, Harold and Palomares, Uvaldo. *Methods in Human Development. Theory Manual.* San Diego, California: Human Development Training Institute, 1973.

This manual contains principles and practices for teachers who are using the Human Development Program in their classrooms. Part One focuses on the theory of the program and practical techniques to use when initiating the program. Part Two is an explanation of the three main themes of the program: 1) awareness (of feelings and thoughts), 2) mastery (knowing your abilities and how to use them), and 3) social interaction (relating constructively to other people).

*Developing Understanding of Self and Others (DUSO).* American Guidance Service, Inc. Publishers' Building, Circle Pines, Minnesota 55014.

Developed by Don Dinkmeyer for children of preschool age through grade three, DUSO enables a teacher to accentuate the positive in the classroom and guide students to a healthy self-image, an understanding of how to get along with others, a tolerance for those who are "different" and a development of purposeful behavior. Designed for daily use in the classroom, each DUSO unit includes an introductory story and song to focus attention on the unit theme. Following the introductory activities, each unit is divided into cycles including a story to be followed by a discussion, a problem situation to be discussed, a role-playing activity, a puppet activity, several supplementary activities, and recommended reading. There are 8 units, designed to be taught for four or five weeks each.

*Human Development Program.* Institute for Personal Effectiveness in Children, P.O. Box 20233, San Diego, California 92120.

Developed by Harold Bessell and Uvaldo Palomares, this is a curriculum for preschool and elementary children based on widely accepted personality development theories. The program provides a technique and subject matter for the teacher to lead small group discussions for 20–40 minutes a day. These focus on the students' feelings and thoughts in three areas: awareness (of feelings and thoughts), mastery (knowing your abilities and how to use them), and social interaction (relating constructively to other people). The discussions are intended to develop self-confidence, self-control, empathy, tolerance, and leadership. The discussions are structured by the teacher using the lesson guides, but they are open-ended and build on cumulative experiences. They do not involve confrontations as in some encounter-group and sensitivity training techniques. By fostering emotional growth, the KDP intends to "improve communication between teacher and students and to improve motivation and achievement."

The daily lesson occurs in a small group of students who sit in a circular arrangement, the "magic circle," conducive to verbal and nonverbal communication with the teacher or a pupil volunteer as leader. There is a teachers' manual of lessons and activities for each grade level in the elementary school and skills and activities are cumulative. The theory and methods of the program are outlined in a manual entitled *Methods in Human Development: Theory Manual* by Bessell and Palomares.

## V. Reports

ED 025784

Barnes, Don. *Teaching Strategies for the Clarification of Values. Guidelines,* Paper VI, Northview Public Schools, Grand Rapids, Michigan, 1968.

Important emphasis in the study of values are 1) building self-appreciation, 2) working with parents and community, 3) finding models, 4) using generalization to stimulate discussion, 5) examining issues, 6) building on interests, 7) introducing children to life's paradoxes, and 8) determining personal goals and their symbolic representations. These emphases are discussed with supporting classroom activities.

ED 013166

Borota, Nicholas H. *Attitudes, A Guidance Unit for the Learning Laboratory of Booker T. Washington Junior-Senior High School of Miami, Florida,* 1967.

Objectives for the course are described. Sections to be covered are written in outline form: 1) personal outlook, 2) the egocentric, 3) the altruist, 4) attitudes within the group, and 5) attitude maturity. Three attitude inventories are included as well as suggested activities.

Brown, Jeannette A. and MacDougall, Mary A. "Simulated Social Skill-Training for Elementary School Children" *Elementary School Guidance Counseling.* 6:175–179, 1972.

An instructional method is described which can be used in teaching children to be better problem-solvers in social skills.

ED 053051

Busselle, Tish. *Conflict Resolution Unit.* Denver University, Colorado, Graduate School of International Studies, 1971.

This seven-day unit for secondary students focuses on conflict resolution between individuals, groups and nations. Objectives are given and specific lesson plans for each day as well as materials used are included.

ED 053789

Camp, Janet and Wilkerson, Peggy. *All About Me.* Unit 1, Curriculum Guide, 1970.

This curriculum guide presents a two- or three-week unit concerned with the individual child and his relationship with members of the classroom social group. A listing and explanation of each of the skills to be developed is accompanied by suggested instructional activities.

ED 093 725

*Education for Student Concerns. Affective Education Research Project.* Philadelphia School District, Pa., Office of Curriculum and Instruction. 1968. 213p.

This book, designed to supplement and enrich the standard secondary curriculum, educates students in the area of feelings, values, and group interaction. Students learn particular logical and psychological processes with which to gain greater conscious control over themselves, their inter-personal relations, and their environment. A theoretical section briefly suggests why a period of drastic social change demands a curriculum more relevant to the concerns of students and presents an information processing model of man as the basis on which to develop such a curriculum. A rationale for teaching particular processes, as opposed to specific content, is developed and a model sequence is outlined, as is a model for teaching a particular lesson. Two courses built on these models are described in detailed course outlines and lesson plans. A communications course concentrates on processes most important for personal and interpersonal growth. The content centers around the study of media—print, films, sculpture, and music—and the study of group interaction. An urban affairs course concentrates on processes most important for social growth, with content focusing on the student's own neighborhood as a microcosm of his city. A self-evaluation survey and a bibliography on affective education are included. (Author/KSM)

ED 044320

Fraenkel, Jack. *Teaching Strategies for Value Education in Social Studies: A Theoretical Position.* San Francisco State College, California, 1968.

Demonstrates a teaching strategy that develops empathy for and identification with individuals placed in a conflict situation and a strategy that promotes sensitivity to the feelings and needs of others.

ED 064738
Hargraves, Richard B. *Values: Language Arts,* 1971.

This course outline focuses on nine areas which are designed to develop student awareness and development of a personal value system. Activities are based on a study of literature and there is a fourteen-page listing of resource materials.

ED 062247
Hiles, Dorothy, and Others. *Social Studies. Teenage Living: Home and Family Education.* Dade County Public Schools, Miami, Florida, 1971.

This junior high social studies program focuses on factors influencing the attitudes, behavior, and interrelationships of teenagers. A major objective is for the teenager to examine his values and those of his peers in a way that will help him obtain and set goals for himself. Approach of the unit is on the guidance/human relations method.

ED 061115
*Howard County Public School's Social Studies Curriculum Units. Middle School Human Relations.* Howard County Board of Education, Clarksville, Maryland, 1970.

This unit is based on three objectives for the student: to better understand and accept himself as an individual and member of a group, become aware of the responsibilities of being a pre-adolescent and react to conflicts and problems arising from this, demonstrate by examples and discussion that knowledge should result in action. All materials necessary for the unit are contained in the document.

ED 041841
*Human Relations Education: A Guidebook to Learning Activities.* Buffalo Public Schools, New York. Human Relations Project of Western New York. Office of Education, Washington, D.C., 1969.

A product of ESEA Title III funds, this guidebook is intended to acquaint teachers with human relations classroom materials, extra-curricular activities, and an in-service approach to self-evaluation. Objectives and lessons are presented for primary grades, intermediate grades, English classes (7–12), and social studies classes (7–12). Lessons include attitude and behavioral objectives. Many of the lessons deal directly with feelings.

ED 081 062
Keepes, Bruce D. *A School Without Failure: A Description of the Glasser Approach in the Palo Alto Unified School District.* 1973. Paper presented at American Educational Research Association Annual Meeting (28th, New Orleans, Louisiana, February 25–March 1, 1973).

Glasser builds his alternative, a "School Without Failure," on an analysis of what children need to achieve a successful identity and on an examination of the ways in which schools affect children to teach them failure. The author discusses the Glasser approach and describes an attempt to implement the approach in a Palo Alto elementary school. The author observes that, after four years of operating on the Glasser plan, the school staff is noticeably committed to creating a success-oriented experience for students as evidenced by the warm teacher-pupil relationship, the emphasis on individualized instruction, the absence of arbitrary universal standards, the problem-solving approach to discipline, and the general sense of joint effort observable both within the classroom and within the school as a whole. (Author/JF)

ED 092 467

Kuhmerker, Lisa. *We Don't Call It Moral Education: American Children Learn About Values.* 1973.

Values education has become an important theme in social studies education in recent years. Although long ignored, moral education, as the British call it, is being emphasized as the pressures on and needs of children in a fast-paced society have become evident. Professional organizations have conducted workshops on the topic of values education. On the "how to" level, the Americans have produced a variety of programs, curriculum materials, and teacher guides that are of use to the social studies teacher. Sources of such materials include the Social Science Education Consortium's "Data Book" and the November 1973 issue of "Social Education" A variety of books in education dealing with increasing options in teaching are relevant to moral educators. Projects such as "Man: A Course of Study" include extensive teacher training programs. As values education gains a legitimate place in the curriculum, teachers will feel increasingly free about incorporating a value orientation into other parts of their regular curriculum. (JH)

ED 036526

LeSueur, Virginia T. *The Discovery Route to Values, Via Literature: "To Kill a Mockingbird" and the Importance of Individuals,* 1968.

"The main section of this tenth-grade unit . . . consists primarily of sample dialogue, between the teacher and students, which attempts to lead the students to think critically about values."

ED 036527

LeSueur, Virginia T. *The Discovery Route to Values, Via Literature: "Abe Lincoln in Illinois" and Commitment,* 1968.

Tenth-grade teaching unit focuses on an awareness of the character development of Lincoln and a discovery of values through sample student-teacher dialogue.

ED 036528

LeSueur, Virginia T. *The Discovery Route to Value, Via Literature: "Richard Cory" and Success,* 1968.

Sample student-teacher dialogue leads students to think about values.

ED 070687

Miller, Harry G. and Vinocur, Samuel M. *A Method for Clarifying Value Statements in the Social Studies Classroom: A Self Instructional Program,* 1972.

Includes in the self-instructional program ways of identifying value statements, ways of clarifying value statement, ways to promote value judgments in the classroom, and simulation techniques.

ED 010626

Sherman, Vivian S. *Guidance Curriculum for Increased Self-Understanding, and Motivation for Career Planning. Planning and Development of Research Programs in Selected Areas of Vocational Education,* Vol. III, Appendix. American Institute for Research in Behavioral Sciences, 1966.

Contains materials to help students explore themselves, their attitudes and personal values, achievements, abilities, and career possibilities.

ED 062261

*Sixth Grade Interdisciplinary Packet: Science-Social Studies.* Madison Public Schools, Wisconsin, 1972.

This curriculum guide . . . focuses upon "Who Is Man?", "Who Am I?" and "Man Needs Man" in an interdisciplinary sequence.

Ed 070994

*Strand III—Mental Health for Grades K-3. Special Edition for Evaluation and Discussion.* New York State Education Department, Albany Bureau of Elementary Curriculum Department, 1970.

Contents of this curriculum cover the family, understanding the life cycle, and human growth and development. Each unit includes specific objectives, teaching aids, and learning activities.

ED 072377

*Strand III—Mental Health: Health Curriculum Materials for Grades 4, 5, 6.* New York State Educational Dept., Albany Bureau Elementary Curriculum Development, 1970.

Curriculum content areas covered are family as a social unit, role arrangements in family life, and the construction of personality. Curriculum includes specific objectives, teaching aids, and learning activities.

ED 084 209

Todd, Karen; Rohne Pritchett. *Promoting Mental Health in the Classroom, A Handbook for Teachers.* Argonne National Lab, Ill. 1974. (Available from Superintendent of Documents, U.S. Government Printing Office, Washington, D.C. 20402 ($1.25).

This handbook is a course of study to teach teachers at all grade levels to understand, implement, and teach to their students the causal approach to human behavior. Although the major portion of the handbook is based on the concepts of Ralph H. Ojemann's causal approach to behavior, and the curricular materials are presented to explain this approach, it is contrasted with and supplemented by the approaches of Berman, Raths, Torrance, and others. Provided are thirteen guide units designed to help teachers (1) recognize the need for promoting mental health in the classroom, (2) understand the causes and effects of behavior, (3) change behavior in the classroom, (4) teach students the causal approach to behavior in different curriculum areas, (5) develop curricular materials for the classroom that will promote mental health, (6) promote individualization and self-directed in learning, (7) understand group dynamics and intergroup relationships. Included in each unit are objectives, purpose statements, group activities, and suggested readings for the exercises, reading assignments and discussions. (Author/RM)

ED 065407
*Unit on Human Feelings and Relations, Wellesley Public Schools.* Massachusetts: Abt Associates, Inc., 1970.

The human relations units, intended especially for the benefit of slow learners but also valuable for other children, help students become more aware of the dynamics of intra- and interpersonal relations. Emphasis is upon involving all class members in participation at their own level. Discussion of all common concerns is a primary technique involved in the units stimulated by pictures, stories, and role plays. Students discuss feelings, types of circumstances, how to deal with circumstances, and how our feelings affect other people. Three units, each of which combines a dramatic picture, an incomplete story, and a role play are presented. Units can be given in a single day or over a period of weeks, and may be used in a sequential manner or altered by the teacher.

ED 073990
Williams, Elmer. *Values and the Valuing Process. Social Studies for the Elementary School.* Georgia University, Athens, Department of Social Science Education, 1972.

This article's purpose is to help teachers develop awareness of the affective domain and competency in using teaching strategies designed to help children clarify their values. Article contains many activities and a bibliography.

ED 076472
*You Are Unique.* Cedar Rapids Community School District, Iowa, 1971.

This report describes a social studies unit which is intended to build better understanding between teacher and pupils and between pupils themselves. It focuses on differences and similarities between all human beings.

## 7. INSTRUCTIONAL TECHNOLOGY, PROGRAMMED LEARNING, AND MEDIA

### II. Magazines and Journals

Canfield, John T. "Dear Machine: Don't Call Us, We'll Call You!" *Educational Technology*, 11:23-6, June 1971.

In an issue devoted to humanizing education through technology, Canfield describes some of the basic programs and research being done in affective education. Ends with a description of a program designed by combined Motivation Education Systems to provide learning environments which will respond to student needs at any given time in any sequence in which they may arise.

Ray, Henry. "Media and Affective Learning." *American Annals of the Deaf*, 117:545-9, October 1972.

This article presents suggestions for utilizing the visual media in developing teaching strategies and designing learning resources for affective learning.

Ray, H. "Media and Affective Learning." *American Annals of the Deaf*, 117:-545-9, October 1972.

Expresses a need for the man of the future to learn how to learn. Describes activities using light, color and sound which are nonverbal and yet stimulate thought and learning. Some practical suggestions as a means to an affective dimension in the learning experience.

Theagarin, S. "Affective Objectives, Deaf Learners and the Programming Process." *American Annals of the Deaf*, 117:512-18, October 1972.

Offers practical suggestions on the use of the programming process for developing instructional packages that help deaf learners attain affective objectives. Programmed learning offers prespecification, modification and validation. Steps are task analysis, design, editing, developmental testing, validation testing. Approaches for individuals include systematic desensitization and behavior modification as programmed instruction.

Withrow, F. "Humanistic Education and Technology." *American Annals of the Deaf*. 117:531-7, October 1972.

Posits that families and educators of the deaf must change traditional methods of education. Technology and flexibility toward education can lead to an enriched life for the children. Differences should be more important than conformity.

### IV. Whole Issues

*American Annals of the Deaf*, Vol. 117, No. 5, October 1972.

This whole issue is devoted to media and humanistic education. Contains articles such as "The Affective Domain of Instructional Technology," "Media and the Affective Domain of Minority Deaf Children," "The Affective Domain: A Challenge to ITV," "The Child in the Process: Affecting His Potential Through Life," "Humanistic Education in Technology," and "Media and Affective Learning."

"Humanizing Education Through Technology: Symposium." *Educational Technology.* 11:9-33, June 1971.

Landers, R. R. "An Approach to Humanizing Education Through Technology," p. 9-11—Describes three primary elements under consideration: humanizing, education and technology. Identifies two types of humanizing, "soft" and "hard." Major thesis: education can be humanized through technology as long as the failure modes, defects and hazards in the revised educational system are identified, analyzed and eliminated or controlled.

Goshen, C. E. "The Humanizing Process," p. 12-14. Proposes that it is incorrect to look at technology in education as either humanizing or dehumanizing. Humanizing environment is one in which human relationships appear, develop or prosper. Technology for teachers can serve a humanizing influence if it frees the teacher from monotonous routine tasks which can then provide more time for personal interaction with students.

Martin, J. H. "Self-Growth and Self-Enhancement Through Technology." Needed: a technology that can respond affirmatively to such criteria as: 1) does it involve many senses?, 2) does it permit the learner to get into the curriculum?, 3) does it make possible the braided trilogy of sound, text and pictures?, 4) does it bring freedom to the act of learning in the unique random style of each and every learner?

Persselin, L. E., "Humanizing Education Through Technology: The View from an Ivory Fox Hole," p. 18-20—Educational technology may be defined in terms of three component elements: 1) Programmed Learning, 2) Mediated Instruction, 3) Educational Accountability in Effective Technology, Product and Process are Inseparable.

Barnes, D. E. "Humane Benefits for Education: Some Directions in Technology," p. 21-23—Advances proposal that technology will exert increasing influence on instruction and may do so with humane results. Two forces operating are rising costs and limited resources and the capability of technologists to improve cost-effectiveness in many instructional situations.

Canfield, J. T. "Dear Machine, Don't Call Us, We'll Call You!" p. 23-26. Describes some programs designed to teach in the affective domain. Key factor in the growth of a teacher's development is his attitude toward his pupils. There is need to train teachers to develop nuturing capability.

Williamson, M., "Some Reservations About Humanizing Education Through Technology," p. 26-29—Should make sure that in developing the humanizing process, undesirable elements are taken out. Teachers can be identified as positive or negative models in teaching. Should make list of actions and attitudes that "de-humanize" people.

Sharp, B. B., "Contract Learning and Humanistic Education," To humanize education through technology, the goal must be to educate toward human differences. Such a goal requires a reallocation of both human and technological resources which enables machines to produce sameness and humans to produce differences.

Kranzberg, M., "The New Role of the Humanities and Social Sciences," p. 31–3. States that 21st century will be characterized by accelerating social changes and be even more technologically based. Defines "interface" as where science and technology meet with humanistic and social concerns. Should educate future citizens to understand the social forces accompanying technological change.

### V. Reports

Betts, George T. "An Audiovisual Presentation to Facilitate a Heightened Awareness of Emotion and Feelings." *Dissertation Abstracts International,* Vol. 33 (7-A) (January 1973), 3367.

## 8. TEACHER TRAINING

### I. Books

Association For Student Teaching. *Mental Health and Teacher Education.* Forty-Sixth Yearbook. Dubuque, Iowa: Wm. C. Brown Co., Inc., 1967.

The task of this yearbook was to present an up-to-date, comprehensive report on mental health and teacher education. It includes four basic parts. In Part I the meaning of mental health is defined and related to teacher education. Part II presents a theoretical position in teacher education and mental health. Part III explains four projects in teacher education sponsored by the National Institute of Mental Health. Interpretations of their findings for the improvement of teacher education are also described. Finally, Part IV offers a comprehensive review of research in mental health and teacher education and implications of the yearbook for teacher education. The book also includes several bibliographies on mental health and teacher education. This book is an extremely valuable overview of the relationship between mental health and teacher education.

Casteel, J. Doyle, and Stahl, Robert J. *Value Clarification in the Classroom: A Primer.* Pacific Palisades, California: Goodyear Publishing Co., Inc., 1975.

This book is specifically designed to be used in teacher education programs. After giving a rationale for value clarification and an approach to value clarification, they explicate thoroughly their specific value clarification strategy which is the value sheet. They identify and give many examples of different kinds of value sheets: (1) the standard format, (2) the forced-choice format, (3) the affirmative format, (4) the rank-order format, (5) the classification format, and (6) the criterion format. Appendices contain checklists for constructing different formats of the value sheets and verbal categories of inquiry.

Combs, A. W. *The Professional Education of Teachers: A Perceptual View of Teacher Preparation.* Boston, Massachusetts; Allyn, Bacon & Co., 1965.

Combs has attempted in this book to look at the professional aspects of undergraduate, preservice teacher education through a new set of glasses provided by modern thinking in perceptual-existential psychology. After defining the effective teacher as "a unique human being who has learned to use himself effectively and efficiently to carry out his own and society's purposes in the education of theirs," he builds a frame of reference about the nature of behavior and learning on which to base our thinking about teacher education. Finally, he takes a precise look at the "self instrument" concept of good teaching. This pioneer who has helped apply the principles of third force psychology to education has written an excellent book for all who are involved in the professional education of teachers. Revised in 1974 by Combs and others to include an account of the teacher training program at the University of Florida which is based on the perceptual model.

Clark, Donald H. and Kadis, Asya L. *Humanistic Teaching.* Ohio: Charles E. Merrill Publishing Co., 1971.

Designed and written for teachers, this engaging book sets forth two people's vision of what life in the classroom can be like. It is a "helping hand to the teacher who wants to remember and respect" the individual students in her classroom. The first chapter contains a personal letter of introduction from each author. The main body describes the orientation of the authors for dealing with human problems, describes the group approach to classroom living, and contains many examples of ways to handle specific common problems. Finally, the authors describe where a school best fits into the human community. Excellent for beginning and more experienced teachers.

Cummings, Susan N. *Communication for Education.* Scranton, Pennsylvania: Intext Educational Publishers, 1971.

"This book brings together subject matter which will lead to an understanding of the individual, particularly as his behavior is affected by language and by other people. This manuscript has been written for the purpose of facilitating communication, particularly oral communication, and more specifically, discussion. All of the topics suggested have been used previously in discussion groups. This book is aimed primarily at the teacher and, more importantly, the teacher trainee."

Curwin, Richard L., Curwin, Geri, with the editors of *Learning* magazine. *Developing Values in the Classroom.* Palo Alto, California: Education Today Co., Inc., 1974.

This is a practical handbook for teachers who want activities to use for developing values in the classroom. After a brief introduction to values clarification, the authors list and explain strategies under the following headings: (1) building trust, (2) helping children discover their true self, (3) integrating values and curriculum areas. The final sections deal with ways to create activities for the classroom, methods of evaluating, record keeping and processing, and a bibliography of resources.

Fraenkel, Jack R. *Helping Students to Think and Value, Strategies for Teaching.* Englewood Cliffs, N.J.: Prentice Hall, 1973.

Fraenkel presents a cognitive view of teaching the social studies with a focus on thinking and valuing. A large portion of the book is devoted to an explanation of the author's model. Curriculum suggestions are included to augment the theoretical framework.

Gordon, Thomas. *Teacher Effectiveness Training.* New York: Wyden, 1974.

Applying the same successful methods as *Parent Effectiveness Training,* this book embodies the principles of the training program for teachers devised by Dr. Gordon eight years earlier. After setting forth his model of effective teacher-student relationships, Dr. Gordon discusses such topics as helping students with problems, verbal communication, active listening, classroom environment, classroom conflict, and value collisions. This book is filled with practical workable ideas to help teachers become more effective teachers rather than disciplinarians.

**II. Magazines and Journals**

Adamson, William C. "A School Mental Health Program: Development and Design." *Community Mental Health Journal.* 4:454-460, December 1968.

"This paper describes the development of an educational-clinical mental health team model that has been effective on all levels of a medium-sized public school system. Essentially the program served to reinforce the generic role of teachers in the classroom with a team-oriented opinion. While the team approach often served to reinforce what was already taking place in the classroom, it also helped to make such classroom experiences both more psychologically intelligible and more consistently constructive within an ego-building frame of reference."

Arnstine, D. "Knowledge Nobody Wants: The Humanistic Foundations in Teacher Education." *Educational Theory,* 23:3-15, Winter 1973.

Surveys status of humanistic foundations as currently taught in teacher preparation courses and examines criticisms of such teaching. Low priority is often given to humanistic foundations in teacher training. Main thrust of responsible criticism of humanistic foundations has been to deplore the diversity in their approaches and to admit their potential, while denying their necessity.

Aspy, David N. "Maslow and Teachers in Training." *Journal of Teacher Education.* 20:303-9, Fall, 1969.

Aspy relates Maslow's hierarchy of needs to the teacher-training process and asserts that during the teacher-training period survival rather than competence in teaching is the immediate concern of the student teachers. Author feels that if teacher training is to be successful in improving the teaching competency of the student teacher, his survival needs must be met before teacher training begins.

Avila, Donald L. "The Florida Experimental Program in Elementary Education." *Improving College and University Teaching,* 20:148-49, Spring 1972.

Purpose of article is to inform the reader of the existence of an experimental program in the training of elementary school teachers. Basic principles on which it is based: 1) one learns best when learning is made personally meaningful and relevant, 2) one learns best when learning is adjusted to the rate and need of the individual, 3) one learns best when there is a great deal of self direction, 4) one learns best when there is a close relationship between theory and practice.

Biber, Barbara; Gilkeson, Elizabeth; Winsor, Charlotte, "Basic Approaches to Mental Health: Teacher Education at Bank Street College." *Personnel and Guidance Journal,* 37:558-568, April 1959.

After stating what they consider to be basic propositions which are useful in understanding psychological constancies in the educational process, the authors discuss the role of the teacher in the elementary school, preparation for teaching which is essentially a program for knowledge and self-knowledge, preparation for teaching which is integration for the student, and the findings of research studies.

Blume, Robert. "Humanizing Teacher Education." *Phi Delta Kappan,* 52: 411-14, March 1971.

Blume discusses the teacher education program at the University of Florida, a humanistic educational program to produce humanistic teachers. He outlines principles basic to the program which arose out of the research of Combs and gives an overview of the Florida New Elementary Program.

Brickman, William W. "Emotional Emphasis in Education; Laboratory for Confluent Education and the Center for Humanistic Education." *School and Society,* 99:78, February 1971.

Describes the projected development of humanistic education at University of California, Santa Barbara, and University of Massachusetts utilizing grants from the Ford Foundation. (Part of "Opinion:Newer Concepts of Academic Freedom.")

Brown, George I. "An Introduction to Humanistic Education: A Weekend Workshop for Educators." *Educational Opportunity Forum,* 136–153, Fall 1969.
Describes in detail the experiences at a weekend workshop designed to communicate discoveries of the staff, encourage interest in affective education, establish models for teacher training in affective education techniques, demonstrate ways of integrating affective and cognitive learning, and to stimulate possible development of other programs in affective education. Concludes with an evaluation of the results of the weekend.

Combs, A. W. "Some Basic Concepts for Teacher Education." *The Journal of Teacher Education,* 23:286-90, Fall 1972.
In this article Combs lists and explains seven basic concepts which emerged during his studies of the differences between effective and ineffective practitioners in the helping programs. These basic concepts have formed the foundation of a new program of teacher education at the University of Florida: helping students to become teachers rather than teaching students about teaching.

Combs, A. W. "Personal Approach to Good Teaching." *Educational Leadership,* 21:369-77, March 1964.
Goes into discoveries in the area of effective teaching and personality traits of good teachers. Applies hypotheses on what makes a good teacher to teacher education programs. Advocates personal tailoring of methods to suit the individual teacher's personality.

Combs, A. W. "Personal Approach to Good Teaching." *Educational Leadership,* 21:535+, May 1964.
Letter to the editor about the title article. It describes a San Francisco State College Teacher Education Project which worked from a similar basis. Letter written by Fred T. Wilhelms, Associate Secretary, National Association of Secondary School Principal.

Dales, Gus T., and Strasser, Ben B. "The starting point for values education." *School Health Review,* 5:2-5 Jan./Feb. 1974.
This opening article of an issue devoted to values clarification focuses the reader's attention upon what a value is, how value development takes place, and how we can reinforce or modify values. The last part of the article sets forth a teaching strategy to build values awareness which has been developed by the authors.

DeWitt, Gerald. "How to Identify Humanistic Teachers." *National Association for Secondary School Principals Bulletin.* 57:19-25, December 1973.

Affective skills are too often overlooked when sizing up a potential teacher. Five helpful interview techniques are outlined here that can clarify an applicant's attitudes toward both himself and children: (1) breaking barriers, (2) rank ordering, (3) use of continuums, (4) "I Like" list, and (5) autobiographical questions.

EJ 096 006
Farrell, Edmund J. "Choosing Values and Valuing Choices." *Association of Departments of English Bulletin,* No. 40, pp. 51-56, March 1974.

Discusses the role of teaching and of teachers in determining and asserting our values and in the exploration of alternatives and in their consequences.

Flanders, John N. and Norman, Douglas. "Inservice Training for Teachers of Rural Appalachian Mountain Children: A Humanistic Approach." *Journal of Humanistic Psychology,* 10:21-29, Spring 1970.

Summarizes three-year humanistically oriented teacher training program in Tennessee and shows a positive change in teacher attitudes as a result of human relations training.

Gazda, George M. "Systematic Human Relations Training in Teacher Preparation and Inservice Education." *Journal of Research and Development in Education,* 4:47-51, Winter 1971.

The "whole" teacher or educator must be qualified in both matter skills *and* in human relations. Systematic Human Relations Training provides the model for training educators in these areas. A brief outline is given for training teacher educators, prospective teachers, and practicing teacher/ educators in human relations skills. Systematic training of these groups insures that all those educators who are in positions which affect student learning and behavior affect them positively by serving as good models.

EJ 090 876
Gerler, Edwin R., Jr. "The Magic Circle Program: How to Involve Teachers." *Elementary School Guidance and Counseling,* 8:86-91, December 1973.

The Magic Circle program, consisting of a small group of children seated in a circular arrangement with an adult leader, aims to facilitate growth in three areas: awareness of feelings, self-confidence, and social interaction.

EJ 085 747
Goldfarb, Sidney; Lee, Mildred K., "Humanistic Education: New Design for Counselors." *Elementary School Guidance and Counseling,* 8:12-17, October 1973.

After explaining reasons necessitating changes in counselor roles, the authors describe their implementation of a counselor training program in humanistic education in District 8 of the Bronx of New York. A short description of the ways in which the counselors then used the techniques they had learned in interacting with the teachers and students is also included.

Gutsch, Kenneth Urial. "Education: In Search For a Better Academic Tomorrow." *Southern Journal of Educational Research,* 5:131-4, July 1971.
Article explores the idea of viewing the teacher as his own technique and modifying the training process to include more emphasis on human relations.

Iannone, R. V. and Carline, J. L. "Humanistic Approach to Teacher Education." *Journal of Teacher Education,* 11:429-33, Winter 1971.
States belief that a major problem in education today is lack of teacher training in meeting human needs of today's youth. Describes a program for a humanistic teacher training program consisting of three blocks of learning experiences: 1) human encounter with self; 2) human encounter with basic teaching skills, and 3) human encounter with real teaching. This program is designed to develop qualities such as spontaneity, acceptance, creativity, and self-realization, and is presently in use at West Virginia University.

Ivey, Allen E. and Rollin, Stephen A. "A Behavioral Objectives Curriculum in Human Relations: A Commitment to Intentionality." *Journal of Teacher Education,* 23:161-5, Summer 1972.
Object of the article is to show that a behavioral objectives curriculum in human relations can foster the exercise of free choice in the participant. Considers a curriculum in human relations, with a behavioral frame of reference, whose primary objective is the development of teachers who can act freely and spontaneously with intentionality. Describes in detail one of the hierarchies of a behavioral objectives curriculum.

Kneer, Marian E. "How Human Are You? Exercises in Awareness." *Journal of Health and Physical Education Recreation,* 45:32-4, June 1974.
To become a more humanistic educator one must become more self-aware. The author gives examples of several inventories to help teachers and students become more self-aware. A list of references is provided to help physical educators become better acquainted with their expressed belief in humanizing education to humanize their own teaching performance.

Lawrence, Gordon. "A Place for Sensitivity Training in Education?" *Educational Sciences: An International Journal,* 4:73-9, September 1970.
Discusses the aims and objectives of sensitivity training. It sees identity and authority as two major concerns of sensitivity training which are also concerns of educators. Therefore, sensitivity training is relevant to educators

who need to learn diagnostic and action skills necessary for social situations in which they will exercise authority and responsibility.

Link, Frances R. "Man: A Course of Study: Getting Innovative Curricula into The Bloodstream of American Education." *Theory Into Practice,* 10:178-84, June 1971.

    Calls for teacher development programs to be made a part of curriculum innovation and development and gives examples from the implementation of *Man: A Course of Study.*

McCarty, F. H. "Awareness Experiences for Elementary Teachers." *Journal of Teacher Education,* 23:457-60, Winter 1972.

    Lists thirty activities for student teachers and elementary teachers to try in seeking awareness of themselves and their profession. Intended to serve as stimuli for new ones keyed specifically to each individual. Example: observe a class with earplugs, watch for non-verbal clues to what is being communicated.

Mantz, Genelle K. "Can Mental Health Be Taught?" *Journal of School Health,* 42:398-99, September 1972.

    The author suggests ways to help teachers teach mental health from kindergarten on.

Moustakas, Clark. "Basic Approaches to Mental Health: A Human Relations Seminar at the Merrill-Palmer School." *Personnel and Guidance Journal,* 37:342-49, January 1959.

    This article records the experience of teachers in a two-semester Seminar in Interpersonal Relations which seeks to help the individual teacher express and explore the values, meanings, and dynamics of personal and professional experience, to achieve self-awareness, and to develop sensitive, understanding, responsive attitudes in relations with children and parents.

Nash, Paul. "Integrated Feeling, Thinking and Acting in Teacher Education." *AACTE Bulletin,* 24:7-8, April 1971.

    Author presents a brief analysis of the purposes of humanistic and behavioral studies in teacher education, under the following three rubrics. 1) Feelings are part of the human personality. They are important determinants of human thoughts, values, and decisions, and they can be appropriately included in a program of teacher education. 2) Students need to learn how to think. Learning how to think should involve growing confidence in one's own intellectual processes, in one's own intuitions, reflections, findings, personal knowledge, and commitments. 3) It is necessary to relate the affective, cognitive, and conative in an integrated way in the educational process.

Neil, Hugh M. "Humanization: A Learning Experience." *Journal of Creative Behavior,* (Spring 1970). 77–84.

Describes preparation course for art teachers taught by author at State University College at Buffalo in which students are personally involved in learning experiences through drama. Author describes several drama situations in which his students participate to learn about themselves and others. Learning and development go together in education, and emerge from a system of interaction and mutuality between teacher and students. "Learning is change, and just as most people experience apprehensions, anxieties and fears in the face of change, so do they react emotionally to learning."

Patterson, C. H. "Preparation of Humanistic Teachers; Exerpts from *Humanistic Education." Intellect,* 101:195–200+, December 1972.

Book review. Deals with preparation of humanistic teachers. A major defect in the psychological preparation of teachers is that they are not provided with a systematic theoretical approach to human behavior. The importance of a humanistic atmosphere in teacher education is emphasized in addition to the didactic aspect of teacher education. An experiential aspect is necessary. A further aspect of the experiential curriculum is a group experience, which should exist in addition to a continuing seminar, to integrate the total educational experience of the teacher education student. It appears that the most effective place to begin to work toward a more humanistic society is with the education of teachers.

Pine, Gerald J. "Let's Give Away School Counseling." *The School Counselor,* 22:94-99, November 1974.

Author discusses research to support his contention that school counseling can be done by lay people. He outlines materials available to teach helping skills to the lay person. He then discusses changes in school counseling, implication for counselor education programs and counselors, and concludes with some cautions. An extensive bibliography is included.

EJ 107964

Rowe, Mary Budd. "A Humanistic Intent: The Program of Preservice Elementary Education at the University of Florida." *Science Education,* 58:369–76, July/September 1974.

The major purpose of this article is to elaborate on some of the philosophical, psychological, and evaluational questions that arise in an intentionally humanistic venture such as the preservice elementary program at the University of Florida, Gainesville.

Schell, John S. "Curriculum for Teacher Preparation for Teachers of Elementary and High School Psychology Courses. *Journal of School Psychology,* 5:191-194 Spring 1967.

The author feels that existing teachers of psychology in the elementary and secondary school levels are not competent to teach the subject. The author suggests that more electives in psychology be made available by universities for the elementary school teacher. Another recommendation is to develop a "minor" in psychology available to students in teacher education. Recommended competencies for three groups—school psychologists, guidance counselors, and certified teachers of psychology—who may reasonably be considered for the role of psychology teacher are discussed.

Schneider, D. "Time is Ripe for Affective Education." *Clearing House.* 49: 103-6, October 1972.

Describes movement toward affective education and teacher workshops in which four basic things were done: 1) increase self-awareness, 2) increase interpersonal sensitivity, 3) train teachers in group dynamics and group leadership, and 4) equip them with a repertoire of affective techniques for classroom use.

Shapiro, Barbara. "Training The Emotional Educator." *Journal of Emotional Education,* 9:28-32, Winter 1969.

"Describes a new teacher-training program at the Gramercy Hill Institute which attempts to develop teachers who will be able to remain totally flexible within a minimally structured environment.

Victoria, James. "A Language for Affective Education." *Theory Into Practice,* 10:300-4, October 1971.

Describes the function of nonverbal gestural behavior as a qualitative aspect of teacher communication in teaching-learning situations. Qualitative nonverbal behavior may provide an additional body of knowledge that can be investigated by teachers and that may condition how they see themselves in their interpersonal relations with students.

Wolfe, D. E. "Student Teaching: Toward a Confluent Approach." *Modern Language Journal,* 57:113-19, March 1973.

Discusses how to help student teachers become more aware of themselves and comfortable in the classroom during their student teacher experience. Describes need for confluent teacher training programs. Techniques are present to help supervisors, teacher trainers, and cooperating teachers.

## III. CHAPTERS IN BOOKS AND REPORTS; ARTICLES IN ENCYCLOPEDIAS

Bernard, Viola W. "Teacher Education in Mental Health (From the Point of View of the Psychiatrist)", in Morris Krugman, (ed.) *Orthopsychiatry and the School.* New York: American Orthopsychiatry Association, 1958, 184-203.

The author discusses the psychiatrist's role in teacher training, consideration of the meaning of personality appraisal of teachers, and the psychiatrist's role in the school setting. The author points out that the assimilation of relevant mental health principles into general educational theory and practice entails a close working rapport between the psychiatrist and the educator.

Biber, Barbara. "Teacher Education in Mental Health (From the Point of View of the Educator)", in Morris Krugman, (ed.) *Orthopsychiatry and the School.* New York: American Orthopsychiatry Association, 1958, 169-183.

The author discusses the teacher's role, selection, and preservice preparation in connection with the school's function to promote mental health in the classroom. The author draws on her own research and teaching experience in teacher education programs for the nursery, primary, and elementary levels. Biber indicates how psychiatric concepts are reflected in teacher training.

Brown, George I. "The Training of Teachers for Affective Role," in the *Seventy-fourth Yearbook of the National Society for the Study of Education.* 1975, Chicago, Ill. NSSE, pp. 173-203.

Brown does an admirable job of providing a brief historical context after which a number of major constructs are considered, including humanistic education, affective education, psychological education, self-science education, and confluent education, with relationships and differences between these constructs described. There follows an examination of the affective domain as it relates to teachers and students in a classroom context. Teacher training in the affective domain is then described both in terms of exemplar academic programs and projects in the field. Finally, related research is explored, accompanied by comments on valuation, research needed, and directions for the future.

### V. Reports

ED 073081

Andrew, Michael C. *Teachers Should Be Human Too.* Washington, D.C.: Association of Teacher Educators, 1972.

Andrew sketches a model for humanizing teacher education. Four areas are emphasized: developing knowledge and skill in characteristically human ways of knowledge acquisition and means of self-expression, developing positive identity as a teacher, developing skill in interpersonal communication and effective group process, and developing a personal knowledge of children. Outlines changes necessary in teacher education programs to create more humanistic teachers.

ED 096 581

*Beyond the Three R's. Training Teachers for Affective Education.* Southern Regional Education Board, Atlanta, Ga. Spons. Agency—National Institute on Drug Abuse (D-HEW/PHS), Rockville, Maryland, June 1974, 89p.

The report takes a look at teacher training in affective education. It defines vague concepts such as affective education and interpersonal skills, develops a rationale for needed changes in the school system, and outlines specific strategies in teacher training as one way to begin to bring about change. The manual was developed in response to past unsatisfactory approaches to drug education. If schools are going to meet the increased demands of a rapidly changing society then teachers must be better equipped to handle new responsibilities more effectively. The publication is divided into several parts which focus on definitions and rationale, the training process itself, recommendations for schools of education, school systems, and teachers, special concerns such as working with special populations or in special settings, and resources. Author/PC)

Christopher, Lochie B., and Harrelson, Orvis A., eds., *Inside Out; A Guide for Teachers.* National Instructional Television Center, Bloomington, Ind., Spons Agency—EXXON Corp., New York, N.Y. 1973. 89p. (Available from National Instructional Television Center, Box A, Bloomington, Indiana 47401).

Material is provided to help teachers plan creatively to meet the challenges of affective teaching which are presented by "Inside/Out." "Inside/Out" is a series of thirty 15 minute color films designed to help 3rd, 4th, and 5th graders to achieve and maintain well-being. In a feelings approach to health education, it emphasizes communication skills, learner involvement and interpersonal relations and relies upon student valuing and decision making. For each of the 30 films in the series the guidebook provides the teacher with a brief synopsis of the program, a statement of the film's purpose, lists of important points to consider, and a guide to possible activities to enhance additional learning. Special notes are also included for some of the films when they are deemed appropriate.

ED 067566
Doll, Henry C. and Harding, Ronald. *A Human Relations Learning Experience Program for Action By Citizens in Education,* Cleveland, Ohio, 1971.

This program has three objectives: to train teachers in human relations methods and techniques, to help teachers develop their own human relations curricula, and to support teachers in their classroom efforts.

ED 092 525
Forsyth, Alfred S., Jr., and .Gammel, J. D. *Toward Affective Education: A Guide to Developing Affective Learning Objectives.* Battelle Memorial Institute, Columbus, Ohio, Center for Improved Education, 1973, 67p.

This guide was designed to assist the educator in designing and implementing a program in affective education by introducing him to affective education, attempting to make him feel comfortable with it, and enabling him to improve his skills in the affective domain. The first chapter introduces the affective domain, discusses its importance, and presents a brief history of the approaches to affective education culminating with the Battelle Project/Alpha approach. A model of the "effective human being," the goal of all education, is presented in the second chapter. In the third chapter, a hierarchy of objectives is presented with methods of determining attainment of objectives in the affective domain. The fourth chapter discusses activities in affective education and their interrelation with objectives. The final chapter focuses on the educator or facilitator and concludes with a general presentation on how to proceed in the structuring of a program in affective education from start to finish. (HMD)

ED 051113
Ivey, Allen E., and Others. *Human Interaction: A Behavioral Objectives Curriculum in Human Relations.* Massachusetts University, Amherst School of Education, 1970.

"The University of Massachusetts School of Education has developed a curriculum in human relations—Human Interaction—written from a behavioral frame of reference, whose primary objective is the development of teachers who can act freely and spontaneously with intentionality." This report describes the curriculum.

ED 090 064
Johnson, James M., ed. *Instruction Strategies and Curricula for Secondary Behavioral Sciences.* State University of New York, Plattsburgh College at Plattsburgh, Spons. Agency—National Science Foundation, Washington, D.C., 1973, 209p. Report of a workshop supported by NSF Project on Undergraduate Pre-Service Teacher Education. (Available from James M. Johnson, Department of Psychology, State University of New York, Plattsburgh, New York 12901 ($3.00)

As a result of rapid growth in student interest and enrollments at the secondary level, a workshop was designed to bring together teachers and teacher-trainees of high school behavioral sciences to explore current methods of classroom operation and to review specific areas of curriculum. Results of the workshop are seen in the first two sections of this manual. The first and longest section presents teaching strategies and methods for four approaches—humanistic, programmed learning, inquiry, and Rogerian. Emphasis is given to the humanistic approach through a composit of eleven educational games or units. The second section, on classroom aspects, consists of short discussions on the basic classroom issues of grading, exposure to controversial issues, and independent study and self-pacing. A third section, developed by workshop participants on the basis of previous experiences, offers a variety of approaches to numerous curriculum units which may be incorporated into the teaching of the behavioral sciences. The unit topics are: language and communication, nonverbal communication, study of small groups; development of a community classroom, experiential sociology—the city as a resource, micro-scoiety, operant conditioning, and esthetics. (Author/KSM)

Ed 034747

Johnson, Mel. *Model Program for Teacher Inservice-Training Emphasizing The Affective Dimension.* Elk Grove Training and Development Center, Office of Education, Washington, D.C., 1969.

This teacher training program was designed to combat the growing threat to teachers and students from the impersonalization and isolation of many crowded classrooms today. Report describes the objectives of the program and the methods used to implement them. Objectives were to help teachers focus on their behavior and its effect on the classroom group, to help teachers view students as individuals, and to help teachers assess their own behavior.

ED 055965

Jones, Donald W. *Human Relations in Teacher Education,* 1970.

The material in this report comes from a cooperative project in which eighteen teacher education institutions took part. There are two major groups of reports. The theme group reports include: 1) "Direct Experiences and Program Designed to Better Prepare Prospective Teachers in Terms of Human Relations Skills and Understandings;" 2) "Human Relations in Pre-Student Teaching Experiences;" 3) "Human Relations, a Broad Perspective;" 4) "The Need for Human Relations in the School and with the Community;" 5) "Human Relations in the Selection of Students in Teacher Education;" 6) "The Culturally Disadvantaged Students; the Administration, the Teacher;" and 7) "Building Better Relationships Between the College and Public School." The individual studies include: 1) "Interpersonal Relationships in Learning;" 2) "Toward Improving Human Relations in the Supervision of Student Teachers;" 3) "A Program for the Preparation of Teachers in Early Childhood Education;" 4) "The Design and Trial Runs of Instruments for Analyzing Seminars: Affective Domain;" 5) "Building Better Relationships Between the College and Public School;" 6) "I am an Indian;" 7) "Human Relations in the Selection of Students in Teacher Education;" 8) "Human Relations in the Student Teaching Field;" and 9) "The Responsibility of Teacher Education in Preparing the Candidate Teacher to Cope With Human Relations Problems." Each report has its own bibliography.

ED 070682

Mosher, Ralph L. *Objectives of Training Programs for Secondary School Teachers of Psychology,* 1971.

Two arguments for teaching psychology in the secondary school are to teach students the scientific method and to familiarize students about how students develop and behave, in the long run upgrading human potential.

Suggests offering elective courses rather than a survey course. Training of secondary school teachers of psychology should not only equip them academically but should prepare them to help students apply and personalize the principles of psychology; to train teachers in pedagogical skills, to educate teachers in the knowledge of adolescent growth and behavior so they will be sensitive to personal concerns of students; and to develop and evaluate psychology curricula. Most important psychology should have an educational effect on the adolescent.

ED 024087

Pietrofesa, John L. *Teaching Practices Designed to Foster Self-Understanding.* Detroit, Michigan: Wayne State University, Detroit Public Schools, 1968.

Describes a workshop designed to help youngsters to improve their self-concepts by sensitizing teachers to implications of various elements of self-theory. Workshop consisted of lectures, small group discussion, and sessions to develop classroom materials. Topics covered included self-concept, mechanisms that distort reality, and healthy personality.

ED 078 203

Ruud, Josephine Bartow. *Teaching for Changed Attitudes and Values.* Home Economics Education Association, Washington, D.C., August 1971, 44p. (Available from Home Economics Education Association, 1201 16th Street, N.W., Washington, D.C. 20036 (Stock #265-08378).

This publication has been prepared to help home economics teachers present the intangibles of attitudes and values to students. Definitions and a discussion of the dimensions of values and attitudes are included, along with information pertaining to teaching for changed values and attitudes. In addition, numerous techniques for helping students recognize their own values and attitudes and become more accepting of the values and attitudes of others are described, and sample teaching materials are provided. (SB)

## 9. EVALUATION AND MEASUREMENT

### I. Books

Beatty, Walcott H. *Improving Educational Assessment and an Inventory of Measures of Affective Behavior.* Association for Supervision and Curriculum Development, NEA, Washington, D.C., 1969.

The first part of this book contains four papers which analyze the system we have for collecting and using data—and which propose extensions of the system to catch new purposes and new dimensions. Ralph Tyler talks about "The Purposes of Assessment," Robert Stake discusses "Language, Rationality and Assessment," and Daniel Stufflebeam writes about "Evaluation as Enlightenment for Decision Making." Finally, Warren H. Beatty offers a treatment of the affective domain in "Emotion: The Missing Link in Education."

The second section is a comprehensive, well annotated resource list of devices already developed or under development which will help to assess and measure affective behavior. This book has much to contribute in an area very often neglected. Valuable for curriculum planners particularly.

Popham, James. *Evaluating Instruction.* Englewood Cliffs: Prentice-Hall, 1973.
Popham defines evaluation as assessment of merit and makes distinctions between *formative* and *summative* evaluation, as well as *product* and *process* criteria. He sees many evaluators as suppliers of information to which no judgments to aid in decision-making. Accountability is seen as *personal, collegial,* or *public.* A clear, basic book.

Weiss, Joel (Ed.). *Curriculum Evaluation: Potentiality and Reality.* Curriculum Theory Network Monograph Supplement. The Ontario Institute for Studies in Education.
Considerations, models, methodology, and potentiality are considered. Most applicable to confluent education are Rippey's chapter ("Can Evaluation Research be Integral to Innovation?") and Scriven's ("General Strategies in Evaluation.")

## II. Magazines and Journals

Borich, Gary D. "Accountability in the Affective Domain." *Journal of Research and Development in Education,* 5:87-96, February 1971.
Many of the testing problems of performance contracting are rooted in the use of a single measure of criterion performance. By securing a network of variables related to cognitive outcomes, we may emphasize important behaviors that are adjuncts to learning and mitigate measurement problems of the performance contract. To place the performance contract in parity with the objectives of the school, parent, teacher and the community, we must measure affective as well as cognitive behavior with both obtrusive and unobtrusive methods. Describes how the teacher may test the effectiveness of the performance contract by the use of a network of variables. If the performance contract is to meet the objectives of the school, parent, teacher and community, both affective and cognitive behavior must be measured.

Carswell, F. M. "To Become Through Behaving." *Instructor,* 82:18, February 1973.
Discusses the place of behavioral objectives in humanizing education. What can be done: 1) reexamine goals and select those few which can be reached by all children, being sure they are unique to schools, 2) practice writing and evaluating behavioral objectives until those which can be used to meet the needs of individual students can be discovered, 3) make frequent efforts to re—deploy people, materials, facilities, and time in ways that will enable all children to reach their behavioral goals.

Combs, A. W. "Can We Measure Good Teaching Objectively?" *National Educational Association Journal,* 53, 34–36, January 1964.

Presents an argument that good teaching cannot be measured objectively. Improved study in teacher effectiveness must rest on competent interdisciplinary teams, and massive financial support over a long period of time. There is a need for continued refinement of systematic observation tools, and systematic study of the relationship between the patterns of teachers' classroom behavior and the corresponding changes in pupils.

Greenberg, J. S. "Behavior Modification and Values Clarification and Their Research Implications." *Journal of School Health,* 45:91-5, February 1975.

"In this article, behavior modification and values clarification are discussed. In particular, each of these methodologies (i.e., behavior modification and values clarification) are defined, conditions under which they are best conducted are described, contrasts and similarities between the two methods are drawn, and potential for research pertaining to behavior modification and values clarification is mentioned."

Harbeck, M. B. "Instructional Objectives in the Affective Domain." *Educational Technology,* 10:49-52, January 1970.

Writers of performance objectives in the affective domain have identified several areas needing more discussions and work: 1) a rigid list of desirable behaviors in the affective domain does not seem possible, 2) objectives in the affective domain may have to be more open and specify only acceptable types of behavior to be expected in a given situation, 3) if less restrictive objectives are prepared, then elevation will be less precise, 4) major problem to be dealt with is the credibility gap between the desired objective and the student behavior that will be accepted as evidence that the objective has been achieved. Perhaps technology will help find breakthrough.

Kapfer, Philip G. "Behavioral Objectives in the Cognitive and Affective Domains." *Educational Technology,* 8:11-13, June 1968.

"The purpose of this article is to report approaches to the cognitive and affective domains currently being developed and used with students as part of a Title III PACE project at Ruby S. Thomas Elementary School in Las Vegas, Nevada. The approach reported in this article should prove useful to teachers and curriculum developers as an initial step in assisting a student to learn a behavior and to evaluate his own attainment of that behavior."

Kelley, E. C. "New Approaches to Educational Outcomes." *Educational Leadership,* 24:112-14, November 1966.

Article points up the resistance to change in testing procedures of school systems and how results are misinterpreted. A modification of assessment procedures in test scores and new uses of the results are suggested.

Ojemann, Ralph H. "Research in Planned Learning Programs and the Science of Behavior." *Journal of Educational Research,* 42:96-104, October 1968.

"In this paper three infrequently recognized ways have been described in which the use of planned learning programs can contribute to our conception of behavior. In each case critical tests of hypotheses relative to human behavior and development are possible. Furthermore, behavior which represents the next steps in the development of man's imagination can be dealt with."

Ojemann, Ralph H. "Should Educational Objectives Be Stated in Behavioral Terms?, Part II." *Elementary School Journal,* 69:229-35.

Second paper on objectives, now asks questions. 1) What have been the results of using behavioral referents where they have been employed with understanding to solve the problem of meaning? 2) How can the full potential of this procedure be realized? 3) Are there other methods for solving the problem of "meaningful communication? 4) If so, what are they? 5) What are their potentials? 6) Their limitations?

Ojemann, Ralph H. "Should Educational Objectives Be Stated in Behavioral Terms?, Part III." *Elementary School Journal,* 70:271-8, February, 1970.

Explains how the observations of overt behavior can be used as an indicator of knowledge of concepts or other internal changes in learning.

Renne, Carl H. "Criteria for Evaluating Curriculum Materials in Human Relations." *Educational Leadership,* 32:37-40, October 1974.

"If human relations materials are intended to accomplish their purpose, they must meet certain standards. Six criteria for judging their potential effectiveness are suggested here."

### III. Chapters in Books and Reports: Articles in Encyclopedias

"Human Relations Appendix," in *Model Elementary Teacher Education Program.* Final Report, University of Massachusetts. Washington, D.C.: Department of Health, Education, and Welfare, 1968, 181–261.

A presentation of tests and measurements meaningful for teacher trainees in the area of personal change. Measurement of this change occurs at several levels, and individual tasks are each associated with a technique for assessing performance. The appendix is in four parts. These are performance criteria for human relations, intrapersonal system skills, physiological and non-verbal skills, and interpersonal system.

## V. Reports

ED 075920
Brandes, Barbara J. *Problems in the Evaluation of Affective Education: A Case Study,* 1973.
Describes problems and also presents "procedures being used for formative evaluation of an elementary school program in achievement behavior."

ED 050173
Campbell, Paul B. and Beers, Joan S. *Definition and Measurement in the Affective Domain. Appreciation of Human Accomplishments.* Pennsylvania State Department of Education, Harrisburg, 1971.
Describes the development and analyzes the reliability of two inventories—the Pennsylvania Inventory of Cultural Appreciations for 11th graders and Things People Do for 5th graders. These are based on the first three levels of the taxonomy in the affective domain. Inferences and implications are discussed.

ED 067381
Combs, Arthur W. *Educational Accountability. Beyond Behavioral Objectives.* Association for Supervision and Curriculum Development, Washington, D.C., 1972.
Combs speaks to the problem of educational accountability. He first analyzes what lies behind "behavioral objectives" and "accountability." He then redefines accountability in human professional terms. Presents a plea for balance of humanistic and behavioral objectives for education.

ED 028101
Eiss, Albert F. and Harbeck, Mary Blatt. *Behavioral Objectives in the Affective Domain.* National Science Supervisors Association, Washington, D.C., 1969.
Investigates problem of stating objectives of affective domain in behavioral terms and preparing a means of evaluating achievement of stated objectives. Useful appendices include examples of affective goals in behavioral terms, test items in the affective domain, and evaluation instruments.

ED 069663
Geisert, Paul. *The Dimensions of Measurement of the Affective Domain.* Wyoming University, Laramie College of Education, 1972.
Outlines seven-step plan for implementing an educational program in the affective domain and points to the self report, the record, and observational data as the means of measurement.

ED 050578
Kapfer, Miriam B. *Behavioral Objectives in Curriculum Development; Selected Readings,* 1971.
Among the eight sections into which the readings are organized is a section

on the adaptability of the behavioral approach to the teaching of values and influencing affective behavior in general. At the end of each section is a bibliography of additional materials.

ED 099 394

Tyler, Ralph W. *Assessing Educational Achievement in the Affective Domain.* National Council on Measurement in Education. Vol. 4, No. 3, Spring 1973, 8p. (Available from NCME, Office of Evaluation Services, Michigan State Univ., East Lansing, Michigan 48823.)

Both cognitive and affective components in interests, attitudes, values, and appreciations are identified as well as problems in selecting objectives for the affective domain. The suggestions offered on how to best assess feelings draw on a variety of measurement techniques. The possibilities and problems involved in assessing student achievement of objectives in the affective domain are illustrated. The problems lie not only in the difficulty of appraising emotional responses that are often covert but also in selecting and defining objectives that are proper goals for the public schools. This means affective behavior that is of constructive value to the individual, that can be developed through school experience, that is not sectarian or politically partisan and is not an unwarranted invasion of privacy. When objectives meeting these conditions are identified and defined, it is possible to assess, at least crudely, the student's achievement of these behavior patterns.

ED 069731

Wight, Albert R. and Doxsey, James R. *Measurement in Support of Affective Education.* Interstate Educational Resource Service Center, Salt Lake City, Utah, 1972.

"General concerns and considerations regarding measurement in affective education, primarily measurement to support the student in his learning program and the teacher as a facilitator of learning, are explored."

## 10. GENERAL

### I. Books

American Council on Education. *Elementary Curriculum in Intergroup Relations; Case Studies in Instruction.* Washington, D.C., 1950.

This book reports on school programs throughout the United States concerned with training elementary school children in all areas of interpersonal relationships. Each chapter tells chronologically how teachers arrived at their plans, how they proceeded in teaching, and what problems they met. Detailed reports of plans and classroom activities are described. This book is intended for teachers and curriculum planners who see a need for a sound, systematic program in intergroup relations.

Association for Supervision and Curriculum Development. *To Nurture Humaneness; Commitment for the '70's.* Association for Supervision and Curriculum Development 1970 Yearbook Committee, Washington, D.C., 1970.

The concern about the kind of human being a child will become is the pervasive theme of this book. Twenty-two papers are presented on the subject. Of particular interest to teachers and administrators are the following: 1) Nystrand and Cunningham, "Organizing Schools to Develop Humane Capabilities," 2) Foshay, "Curriculum Development and the Humane Qualities," 3) Combs, "An Educational Imperative: The Humane Dimension," 4) Graham, "Toward a Humane School." If schools are to meet the new challenge of preparing students to learn to cope more effectively with their environment, school curriculums must provide students with the opportunities to reach their potential for humaneness which ideally includes both rational and humane behavior. An excellent source of readings on the subject for teachers and administrators.

Berman, L. *New Priorities for the Curriculum.* New York: Merrill Press, 1968.

This carefully documented book should be read and studied by curriculum workers, teachers, and administrators. Knowing that we need both process and content and that we have been overbalanced in favor of content, she discusses such processes as perceiving, communicating, loving, knowing, decision making, patterning, creating, and valuing. Berman pools the resources of many writers in these areas and has set forth a state-of-the-art discussion of them. "This book expands the philosophy of Peirce and Dewey—of experiencing, knowing, valuing, growing, living, and learning."

Combs, Arthur W. and Syngg, Donald. *Individual Behavior: A Perceptual Approach to Behavior.* Revised Edition. New York: Harper & Row, Publishers, 1959.

The perceptual approach to behavior seeks to understand behavior by observing behavior from the point of view of the behaver himself. After explicating the perceptual view of behavior and the needs of people, the authors describe several factors which influence behavior: the physical organism, time, opportunity, the effect of need, goals and values, the phenomenal self, and the restriction of the field. They then proceed to elucidate the nature of capacities, emotion, feeling, the adequate personality, and the inadequate personality. Part II concerns itself with applications of the perceptual approach. Topics covered include the following: general implications, the individual and his society, how people can help themselves, goals and purposes of education, the teaching relationship, the personal approach to treatments, and the exploration of meaning. Comprehensive bibliography appended. Useful as a reference tool for people who are doing research in humanistic education. Lays a basic framework for affective education.

Henry, Nelson B. (ed.) *Mental Health in Modern Education.* The Fifty-fourth

Yearbook of the National Society for the Study of Education. Part II. Illinois: University of Chicago Press, 1955.

This book is an in-depth look at the field of mental health in education. Five major areas are covered: "History and Present Status of the Mental-Health Movement," "Conditions Affecting Mental Health in the Classroom," "Problems and Practices Related to Mental Health at Different Educational Levels," "Personal and Professional Development of the Teacher," and "Mental Health for Today and Tomorrow." Although dated, this book is an excellent overview of the important work and thought in the area of mental health up to 1955.

Hamilton, Norman K. and Saylor, J. Galen. *Humanizing the Secondary School.* Washington, D.C.: Association for Supervision and Curriculum Development, 1969.

The essays in this book grew out of two conferences sponsored by the Secondary Education Council of ASCD which attempted to look at new directions for secondary schools. The book opens with a discussion of alternatives in values toward which secondary schools can move in the Monez and Bussiere chapter, "The High School in Human Terms." Herbert A. Thelen's chapter, "The Humane Person Defined," is a discussion of the range of values of the humane person and how he sustains and extends his humaneness. In MacDonald's "The High School in Human Terms: Curriculum Design," we find a discussion of curriculum design, not so much from the standpoint of curriculum content as from conditions under which curriculum should be selected and the humanizing goals it should achieve. A summary of the steadily accumulating research evidence which supports the argument for an open learning environment is presented by Robert Soar in "Achieving Humaneness: Supporting Research." Dwight Allen in "A Technology and Performance Curriculum" points out alternative strategies for the development and use of educational applications of technology while Lloyd Michael in "Alternative Modes of Organizing Secondary Schools" analyzes the essential elements of a secondary school by examining methods of managing time, space, and human and material resources as a means of achieving the humanizing goals of secondary education. In "Building Leadership Skills," John Wallen helps us look frankly at ourselves as secondary leaders in terms of role expectation and personal qualities which equip us to be effective. Finally, J. Galen Saylor in a summary chapter draws inferences from the various points of view and suggests the characteristics of a truly humane secondary school. This book is important for educators and curriculum planners because it analyzes issues and points out alternatives for those who select the goals toward which the secondary school should be directed.

Jarrett, James L. *The Humanities and Humanistic Education.* Menlo Park, California: Addison-Wesley, 1973.

This book is a serious, if tentative, attempt to follow the tradition of humanistic studies to contemporary humanistic education. While the orientation remains classical and the approach to the presentation is middleweight academic (and therefore still not humanistic education for universal, or even mass, education) the trip is thought-provoking indeed.

The Joint Commission on Mental Health of Children. *Mental Health From Infancy Through Adolescence: Reports of Task Forces I, II, and III and the Committees on Education and Religion.* 512p. ISBN 0-06-012228-5. LC 78-123939.

The Joint Commission on Mental Health of Children. *The Mental Health of Children—Services, Research, and Manpower: Reports of Task Forces IV and V and the Report of the Committee on Clinical Issues.* 576p. ISBN 0-06-012227-7. LC 72-123940. ea. col: index, Harper, April 1973.

These well-written volumes, parts four and five of a series of six by the Joint Commission (see LJ, July 1970 and LJ, April 15, 1972), result from the commission's continuing effort to enlighten the public on contemporary needs of children and youth through studies produced by the intensive research of distinguished experts in the fields of education, medicine, psychology, and sociology. *Mental Health From Infancy Through Adolescence* is divided into five sections, corresponding to the work of two committees (one on education and mental health, and the other on religion and mental health) and three task forces (covering children from infancy to age five, from kindergarten through eighth grade, and from adolescence through age 24). *The Mental Health of Children—Services, Research and Manpower* comprises three parts, corresponding to reports by a committee on clinical issues and by two task forces (one on programs of prevention and issues related to research, manpower, rehabilitation, and treatment, and the other on the organization administration, and financing of services for emotionally disturbed children).

All in all, these books present a scathing indictment of our nation's failure to provide a propitious milieu for the development of human potential and its failure to meet minimal requirements for adequate health services for children and youth. The contributors support their position with statistics on such indicators as the incidence of emotional disturbance in our population, poverty, infant mortality, unwanted children, mental retardation, learning disability, delinquency, and suicide among youth. Most important, these volumes contain carefully conceived recommendations for improvement, touching on topics from birth control and teacher-training programs to a comprehensive system for coping with the manifold mental health needs of children and youth. Innovative suggestions for research and useful, up-to-date references appear throughout both pioneering tomes.—Shelby Ruth Cohen, Department of Special Education, Newark State College, N.J.

Leeper, Robert R. (ed.) *Humanizing Education: The Person in the Process.* Washington, D.C.: Association for Supervision and Curriculum Development, NEA, 1967.

A compilation of the addresses given at the 22nd ASCD Annual Conference, these papers affirm the importance of the person in the educational process. Carl Rogers discusses the importance of an interpersonal relationship in developing self-starting, self-initiating learners while Fred Wilhelms looks at humanization via the curriculum. Some of the other articles expand upon such topics as actualization alientation, automation, the teacher, foundations, government, and civil rights. All of these are related to humanization. Arthur Combs has a beautiful article entitled "The Person in the Process" in which he makes an eloquent plea for humanistic education to counteract the growing alienating and dehumanizing forces at work in the world today. Finally Galen Saylor reports on the progress of a movement toward national assessment of the current status of education as of March 1967. This book sounds a clarion call for a re-emphasis on the affective domain in education. Excellent for anyone involved in the field of education today.

Richards, Fred and Welch, I. David (eds.). *Sightings: Essays in Humanistic Psychology.* Colorado: Shields Publishing, Inc., 228p., 1973.

"This book consists, in part, of presentations given at the Second Annual Conference on Humanistic Psychology held at the University of Northern Colorado (January 1972)." It relates humanistic psychology to such topics as education, science, the black revolution, the family, and the new image of man.

Samples, Bob and Wohlford, Bob. *Openings; A Primer for Self-Actualization.* Massachusetts: Addison-Wesley Publishing Co., 1973.

This book is a happening. Replete with dazzling graphics, it is a book about living and learning—how to live more open, actualizing lives. It speaks about personal openness, about our values and prejudices, and about our meadowland of creativity. How can we become more self-actualized? What is the content of the actualizing environment? What happens when one does become more self-actualized? All of these questions race by, lively and lightweight.

Torrance, E. Paul and Strom, Robert D. *Mental Health and Achievement; Increasing Potential and Reducing School Dropout.* New York: Wiley & Sons, Inc., 1965.

A collection of readings on child development and mental health. The book is divided into three parts: Part One—Home and Community: Influence and Responsibility, Part Two—the Changing School, Part Three—Curriculum Learning and Evaluation. Among the papers presented are: 1) R. Jones, "Peer Influence on Personal and Academic Success," 2) P. Jackson, *et al.,* "Psychological Health and Cognitive Functioning in Adolescence," 3) R.

Armstrong, "Improving the Mental Health of School Personnel," 4) G. Allport, "Psychological Models for Guidance," 5) R. Strom, "School Evaluation and Mental Health." The book is of interest to administrators, teachers, counselors, and psychologists.

## II. Magazines and Journals

Borton, Terry. "Reach, Touch, and Teach." *Saturday Review,* 52:56-58, January 18, 1969.

This article discusses the issues involved in implementing a program of education aimed at affective or humanistic goals. The author outlines several programs now in existence and critically discusses their effectiveness and their impact on the curriculum.

Borton, Terry. "Reaching the Culturally Deprived." *Saturday Review,* 49: 77-78, 104–105, February 19, 1966.

Author uses books written in a realistic manner to help low-ability children broaden their understanding of the literature and themselves. Tape recordings of the books and short written assignments lead to discussions on the material. Good literature speaks about things important to students, and provides for them a perspective for their own feelings. Good literature can broaden students' perspective on their own lives, and will give them reasons to acquire better reading and writing skills.

Carter, John. "Trends in the Teaching of Values." *Contemporary Education,* 44:295-7, April 1973.

This paper describes three ways values are presently taught in public education—the traditional, the scientific, and the process approach—and presents an alternative approach.

Combs, Arthur W. "Administration and the Adequate Personality." *Colorado Journal of Educational Research,* 12:24:27, Fall 1972.

This article is concerned with the administrator and his interrelationships with other people on the job. To establish a climate of openness and trust requires honesty and integrity of the administrator. The author discusses two general approaches to the problems of dealing with other people and with the question of leadership. These approaches to human relationships are the stockyard approach, which uses force and coercion in dealing with other people and the facilitating in which the leader's job is asisting or facilitating a group in its work. The author points out that the administrator as the adequate or healthy personality is one who sees himself and others as worthy, wanted, and able. Only then can a climate be created characterized by mutual concern and respect for the perceptions and needs of all those involved.

Combs, Arthur W. "Can Education Be Relevant?" *Colorado Journal of Educational Research,* 9:2-8, Spring 1970.

Combs offers the following ten suggestions as ways to make education more relevant: 1) change our way of approaching the problem of curriculum change, 2) avoid trying to follow industrial models in creating educational change, 3) be willing to begin where people are, 4) find ways of creating needs to know in students, 5) work for greater self-direction and responsibility in the students, 6) avoid worrying about mistakes, 7) deal with the importance of children's self-concepts, 8) get rid of the grading system, 9) eliminate competition, and 10) break out of the grade level myth.

Combs, Arthur W. "The Human Aspect of Administration." *Educational Leadership,* 28:197-205, November 1970.

The importance of performing supervisory responsibilities with an eye toward their beneficial effects on those under one's control is discussed.

Combs, Arthur W. "The Human Aspect of Administration." *Colorado Journal of Educational Research,* 9:9-15, Spring 1970.

The problems of the educational administrator in solving crises arising in his school and within his students and ways to meet these crises are discussed in detail.

Combs, Arthur W. "Can Education Be Relevant?" *Colorado Journal of Educational Research,* 9:2-8, Spring 1970.

Some ways to make education more relevant to the students of today are presented and discussed in depth.

Combs, Arthur. "An Intellectual Conversion." *Theory Into Practice,* 8:298-9, December 1969.

This brief article describes the manner in which Arthur Combs developed his view of psychology and its impact on learning which led to the publication of *Individual Behavior.*

Cooper, Saul and Seckler, Donald. "Behavioral Science in Primary Education: A Rationale." *People Watching,* 2:37-9, Spring 1973.

Describes the efforts of the South Shore Mental Health Center near Boston to create a behavioral science curriculum. Defines issues and activities involved in such a process.

Coopersmith, Stanley and Silverman, Jan. "How to Enhance Pupil Self-Esteem." *Today's Education,* 58:28-29, April 1969.

A teacher can enhance a child's self-esteem by being interested in and concerned about him as an individual. The teacher needs to set up realistic class standards that are clear and definite, but which permit the child freedom to act within reasonable limits. A child's work should be challenging so that he achieves success by stretching his abilities. The task of building self-esteem in the child is important for it is crucial to the development of every child.

Doll, Henry C. "These Districts Teach Human Relations Painlessly, Not Aimlessly." *American School Board Journal,* 158:24-25, June 1971.

Article describes a human relations program in Cuyahoga County, Ohio which utilizes films and an occasional game to stimulate thinking, encourage inductive thinking, concentrate on feelings and reactions rather than on facts, and to promote the exchange of ideas between students. The program is sponsored by PACE (Program for Action by Citizens in Education).

Dow, Peter B. "Man: A Course of Study in Retrospect: A Primer for Curriculum in the 70's." *Theory Into Practice,* 10:168-177, June 1971.

Summarizes Bruner's ideas in *The Process of Education,* the *Development of Man: A Course of Study,* and the critique of the program by Jones in *Fantasy and Feelings in Education.* Also expounds philosophy of Paulo Freire and possible implications for *Man: A Course of Study.* Finally, it offers some guidelines for future curriculum development.

*Edvance.* Combined Motivation Education Systems, 6300 River Road, Rosemont, Illinois 60018.

This is a newsletter on affective/humanistic education which presents articles, curriculum materials, newsnotes, and practical classroom suggestions to help teachers provide meaningful affective experiences in the classroom.

Engle, T. L. "Teaching Psychology at the Secondary School Level: Past, Present, Possible Future." *Journal of School Psychology,* 5:168-176, Spring 1967.

A brief historical overview of psychology being taught at the secondary level since 1831 and the current dilemma that not much progress has been made in incorporating psychology into the high school curriculum. The need for teacher training in the field, the need for more relevant textbooks in psychology, the need for schools to offer basic courses in psychology, and APA's role in promoting the teaching of psychology are presented. High school psychology may have a bright future if psychologists are willing to give it their enthusiastic support.

Farson, Richard E. "Emotional Barriers to Education." *Psychology Today,* 1:32-35, October 1967.

Author probes into education for the 21st century, which he feels will be designed to expand and enrich all aspects of human experience-sensory, emotional, and esthetic, as well as intellectual- and to liberate creativity in all these realms. Among the new social technology available for social and educational change are systems engineering to help analyze what people really need, the use of the small human-relations group to promote personal growth, and classroom use of simulations to help students learn such nonacademic skills as decision-making and communication. Author discusses a few emotional barriers to change in education, such as our allegiance to the accustomed, fear of emotional involvement with others, and the notion that non-cognitive and non-verbal skills are not academically respectable.

Hamilton, Vernon. "Comments on the Report of the Working Party on the Teaching of Psychology in Schools." *British Psychological Society Bulletin,* 23:41-42, January 1970.

Recommendations by the Working Party of the BPS to encourage and support the program of teaching psychology in the schools. Four propositions raised were: 1) psychology must be able to compete successfully for more students by permitting students to evaluate subject on par with traditional subjects, 2) need for firm basis for a science of behavior, 3) find ways to obtain funds for academic and research development, and 4) the development of tightly formulated and valid laws governing behavior as a question for species survival.

Hollister, William G. "An Overview of School Mental Health Activities." *Journal of School Health,* 36:114-117, March 1966.

The author presents an overview of what was being done in 1966 to promote the cause of school mental health. Among the accomplishments mentioned were 1) publication by the College of Education at San Francisco State College of their five-year study of the Mental Health Training of the Teacher, 2) behavioral science training of the school administrator, 3) Project Headstart, 4) the use of teacher aids in the classroom, as well as the VISTA youth program to work with delinquent, handicapped, or deprived school children, 5) the increase of guidance workers in the schools, and 6) the growth in the field of special education of the emotionally disturbed and mentally retarded children.

Hollister, William C. "Current Trends in Mental Health Programming in the Classroom." *Journal of Social Issues,* 15:50-58, 1959.

The author describes trends affecting mental health programming in the classroom. The trends discussed are 1) increased use of the consultation process to strengthen classroom guidance of behavior, 2) wider employment of group methods of behavior guidance, 3) greater emphasis on teacher-parent cooperation, 4) more orientation to personality dynamics and relationship process in teacher preparation for classroom work, 5) wider interest in the evaluation process, and 6) increased emphasis on behavior and human relationships education in the curriculum.

Kandel, I. L. "Character Formation: A Historical Perspective." *The Educational Forum,* 7:307-316, March 1961.

This is an historical view of character education. Today character formation is more difficult with the declining influence of religious institutions, with the change in the nature of family life, with the mechanization of industrial occupations and with the extension of mass media of communications. The old notions—the customs, traditions, and value on which the hopes and ambitions of a collective society are built and which form the common currency of social intercourse—have not changed, although the sanctions may have shifted.

Kuhmerker, Lisa. "An Aesthetic Approach to Moral Education" *Humanist,* 32:22-3, Nov./Dec. 1972.

The author visited moral education programs in four countries and describes here one in Milan, the Centro Coscienza, which uses an aesthetic rather than a rational or psychological approach.

Kuhmerker, Lisa R. "Values Are Our Curriculum: An Investigation of Moral Education in Europe." *People Watching,* Vol. 2, No. 2 (Spring 1973), 26-31.

Reports on the status of moral education in Britain, Holland, Belgium, and Italy. Gives an explanation of the program efforts in these countries.

McAllister, J. E. "Affective Climate and the Disadvantaged." *Educational Leadership,* 22:481-531, April 1965.

Story of work with a sampling of Mississippi principals, teachers and students from many high schools. Elements of learning and teaching include: a) attitude biases from home life, and b) biases of college. Worked on personal security as a means of dealing with segregation.

Miller, Wesley. "Roots of the Revolution: A New Image of Man." *Educational Leadership,* 30:13-5, October 1972.

There exist today two groups, each seeing the world through different eyes—one cool, detached, rational; the other passionate, involved, visceral. Thus the conflict has developed between those who wish to experience the environment and those who wish to control it.

Noland, Robert L. "A Century of Psychology in American Secondary Schools." *Journal of Secondary Education,* 41:247-254, October 1966.

"The purpose of this article is to trace the history of the teaching of psychology in American high schools in an attempt to assess the proper present and future role of this subject in the high school curriculum. Author presents view that the presentation of a psychology course on the high school level is in keeping with the objectives of contemporary secondary education and equal in importance to the youth of today to many courses now included in the high school curriculum." The main reason cited for more schools not instituting courses in psychology was the lack of properly trained teachers.

Author outlines some specific courses in educational psychology appropriate for the prospective secondary psychology teacher.

Seif, Elliot. "Toward a Humanistic Elementary Social Studies Education." *Pennsylvania Social Studies News and Views,* 17:16-22, Spring 1971.
Suggest how teachers can develop more "humanistic" education by focusing on human experiences and basic human concerns in the education process.

Southworth, Warren H. "Health Education from Kindergarten through College." *Journal of School Health,* 38:193-202, April 1968.
Author is concerned about lack of health instruction in the schools. As evidence of this lack he cites findings reported in the "Summary Report" of the School Health Education Study of 1961–63. Examples of problems related to health education in schools were ineffectiveness of instruction methods, inadequate professional preparation of staff, indifference toward and hence lack of support for health education on the part of teachers, parents, and administrators, and inadequate facilities and instructional materials. The author points out that there is little communication and cooperation among the various professional organizations of health educators. Therefore, there is a need to unite the profession of health education into a single organization if proper health instruction in the schools is ever to be realized.

Trow, William Clark. "Psychology and the Behavioral Sciences in the Schools." *Journal of School Psychology,* 5:241-249, Spring 1967.
Author's recommendation's to bring the teaching of psychology into the classroom at the secondary school level. Three possibilities are recommended: 1) course in psychology as a discipline, 2) fit psychological content at various points into the present science and social studies programs, and 3) to assume the leadership in promoting an area-study curriculum. The author concludes the latter choice is the most satisfactory. It would present the world of interrelated phenomena as it is, and would help students see the various psychological, social, economic, political, and other forces in the situations which they study.

Walstedt, Joyce J. "Teaching Empathy." *Mental Hygiene,* 52:600-611, October 1968.
Author explores the possibility of introducing the concept of empathy into teaching programs for therapists. Author presents overview of findings of other research work in the field and provides some preliminary and tentative suggestions for a teaching program in empathy for mental health practitioners.

Winthrop, Henry. "Empathy and Self-Identity Versus Role Playing and Alienation." *Journal of Existentialism,* 5:37-50, Summer 1964.

An overview of the literature on the subject of empathy and self-identity and on the subject of empathy and alienation. Role-playing by persons in their daily lives is considered by the author to be unnecessary. It is a retreat for the thoughtless and insecure. A technologically advanced culture may require complexity of thought, but not of behavior. The author supports integrated education programs which can promote empathic consciousness through the curriculum. The impact of studies on the human person is just as important as the content of those same studies. A man who lacks self-knowledge and human understanding is simply not educated.

Wise, Charles N. "A Prolegomena to a Study of the Antecedents of Interpersonal Communication." *Today's Speech,* 20:59-64, Fall 1972.

"After describing the widespread popularity enjoyed by recently established courses in interpersonal communication, this article traces the genesis of such courses to humanistic trends in education, contemporary theories in psychotherapy developed by Carl Rogers and Abraham Maslow, and the concern for feelings expressed by students in the sixties."

## III. Chapters in Books and Reports; Articles in Encyclopedias

Shedd, Mark R.; Newberg, Norman A.; Delone, Richard H. "Yesterday's Curriculum/Today's World: Time to Reinvent the Wheel." *The Curriculum Retrospect and Prospect,* Chapter VII. The Seventeenth Yearbook of the National Society for the Study of Education. Part I (Ed. by Robert M. McClure, Illinois: University of Chicago Press, 1971, 153-184.

In a volume devoted to curriculum, the authors of this article discuss new ways of structuring educational goals. They analyze what they feel are errors in many attempts to "re-invent" the wheel, they suggest what the process of rethinking educational goals might mean in theory and in practice and then sketch what might be involved in changing the schools. There is a discussion of many contemporary educational efforts including a good analysis of the Philadelphia Affective Education Project.

## IV. Whole Issues

*New Directions in Teaching.* Department of Education, Bowling Green State University, Bowling Green, Ohio 43402.

Each issue contains articles with practical suggestions on humanizing teaching and learning.

*People Watching Curriculum and Techniques for Teaching the Behavioral Sciences in the Classroom.* Behavioral Publications, 2852 Broadway, New York, New York 10025.

"This quarterly publication features articles, techniques, reviews, and programs which deal with aspects of the behavioral sciences and their application in the curriculum."

*Periodically.* American Psychological Association, Clearinghouse on Precollege Psychology and Behavioral Science. Issued monthly May through September. Subscription free on request.

Excellent source and wealth of information for psychology teachers at the elementary and secondary levels. Current findings, institutes, graduate programs, new pamphlets, films, books, and book reviews all highlight this four-page newsletter.

## V. Reports

Ed 068405

*Association for Humanistic Psychology Newsletter,* Vol. 8, No. 6 Association for Humanistic Psychology, San Francisco, California, 1972.

Includes philosophies, viewpoints, activities, teaching approaches and resources on humanistic psychology.

ED 099 275

*Humanizing Education in the Seventies: Imperatives and Strategies.* National Education Association, Washington, D.C., 1974, 50p. Report on Civil and Human Rights in Education (12th, Washington, D.C., April 19-21, 1974). (Available from NEA Publications, Order Dept., The Academic Building, Saw Mill Road, West Haven Conn. 06516, #6659-6-00, $1.50.)

The National Education Association Council on Human Relations annual conference on civil and human rights in education provides a forum for teachers, principals, superintendents, and representatives of government agencies, civil rights organizations, and community groups to exchange views about controversial educational issues. The 1974 theme, humanizing education is discussed in the following speeches and reports: "Introduction" by George W. Jones; the keynote speech, "A Humane Environment: A Search for New Understandings" by Luvern L. Cunningham; "Reaction" by representatives of the NEA's Asian, Black, Chicano, First American, and Women's Caucuses; "Imperatives and Strategies for Organizing Schools to Serve Students Humanely" by Jean D. Grams; "Imperatives and Strategies for Organizing Schools to Serve Their Communities" by Herschell "Ace" Sahmaunt; "Imperatives and Strategies for Reforming High Education to Produce Humane Educators" by Tomas A. Arciniega; "Imperatives and Strategies for Committing Education Associations to Advocate Humanizing Education" by Charles Williams; "Being Humane, Teaching Humanely" by Marcia Gillespie; and "Forum and Caucus Reports In Wrap-Up", Helen D. Wise relates the concerns of the conference to the concerns of NEA as a politically effective organization. (Author/JH)

ED 063215

Roberts, Thomas B. *Seven Major Foci of Affective Experiences: A Typology for Educational Design, Planning, Analysis, and Research.* Dekalb, Illinois: Northern Illinois University, 1972.

Roberts offers a valuable aid to educators, researchers, and administrators who wish to understand and analyze what is happening in affective education, and to design their own learning experiences. Affective education is divided into seven major types and eight subtypes: personal awareness, creative behavior, interpersonal awareness, subject orientation, specific content (affective and cognitive), affective styles of teaching/learning and teacher, administrator, and other educators. Using these criteria, the designer can assess the value of the learning experience. There is a short bibliography.

## 11. BIBLIOGRAPHIES

### II. Magazines and Journals

Borton, Terry. "Teaching for Personal Growth: An Introduction to New Materials." *Mental Hygiene,* 53:594-599, October 1969.

The author makes available to school personnel an annotated listing of books and films that would aid them in encouraging students to express their feelings and attitudes in the classroom: The importance of these factors—feelings, motives, interpersonal relations, and attitudes—to academic achievement, personal growth, and mental health were revealed in recent studies, and have encouraged educators and psychologists to develop new approaches to the emotional and personal lives of students within the school.

ED 054471

Breed, George and Jourard, Sidney M. *Research in Self-Disclosure: An Annotated Bibliography.* Florida University, Gainesville; South Dakota University, Vermillion, 1970.

Compilation of abstracts of research as they relate to self-disclosure. Of particular interest among the many content areas included are achievement, attitude, group cohesiveness, learning, locus of control, person perception, personal values, self-actualizers, self-concept, and self-esteem.

Breed, George and Jourard, Sidney M. *Research in Self-Disclosure.*

An annotated bibliography of research studies covering self-disclosure and related areas.

Canfield, John T. and Phillips, Mark. "Humanisticography." *Media and Methods,* 8:41-56, September 1971.

An annotated bibliography of books, films, tapes simulations, classroom exercises, curricula, journals, organizations, and growth centers which relate to humanistic education.

Jeffries, Doris and Schraffino, Kathy. "Group Counseling With Children: An Annotated Bibliography." *Educational Technology,* 13:48-49, January 1973.

Selected articles and research are briefly outlined in order to assist those interested in working with children in groups to be aware of possible resources. Various theories and practices are represented in the sample.

Noland, Robert L. and Bardon, Jack I. "Supplementary Bibliography of Teaching Psychology and the Behavioral Sciences in the Schools." *Journal of School Psychology,* 5:257-260, Spring 1967.

A special bibliography compiled to supplement those references cited by authors in the special issue of the *Journal of School Psychology* entitled "Teaching Psychology and the Behavioral Sciences in the Schools." The bibliography includes articles, books, monographs, and dissertations relevant to the subject. About 126 titles are listed.

### IV. Whole Issues

EJ 095 419

"Education and Mental Health." *Educational Documentation and Information Bulletin* of the International Bureau of Education, Vol. 47, No. 188 1189, pp. 1-190, 3rd/4th Quarter 1973.

This bibliography on education and mental health covers the following topics: social change, factors affecting children, parent roles, preschool children, factors affecting learning readiness, pedagogic methods, curriculum, special problems, adolescence, integration and needs of special group, developing countries, and general references and bibliographies.

### V. Reports

ED 091 637

"An Annotated Bibliography on Mental Health in the Schools 1970-1973." National Institute of Mental Health (DHEW), Bethesda, Md. 1973.

This selected bibliography of 200 references provides a guide to the professional literature relevant to school mental health published between the years 1970 and 1973. The annotations which accompany each reference are intended to be factual summaries of the author's methodology and results and are not evaluative or critical. The list is arranged by subject with selected cross references and is intended to serve as a background and/or reference source for professional and paraprofessional mental health personnel, school administrators, teachers, and community action groups. In addition, it contains prototypes for the various school systems that are planning or evaluating mental health programs. The majority of the references are in the areas of (1) school mental health and related programs, (2) mental health personnel, including teachers, nonprofessionals, peers, and parents, and (3) prevention and intervention. Though items on treatment in the form of behavior modification are included, material on other types of treatment or other kinds of therapy has been omitted. (Author)

ED 061689

*Board of Cooperative Educational Services,* Jericho, New York. "Biblio-therapy: An Annotated Bibliography Dealing with Physical and Self-Image Handicaps." 1971, 26p.

Bibliography of books ranging from primary to senior high levels relating to such handicaps as the following: deaf, deaf-blind, blind, limited vision, orthopedic handicaps, chronic disease, and self-image handicap. Coded to reveal age level and type of handicap.

ED 078 617

Bolen, Jackie. *A Bibliography of Affective Materials for the Adolescent Years* University of Southern California, Los Angeles, Instructional Materials Center for Special Education. Spons Agency—Bureau of Education for the Handicapped (DHEW/OE), Washington, D.C., June 1973. (Available from Jackie Bolen, Instructional Materials Center, Special Education, 1031 South Broadway, Suite 623, University of Southern California, Los Angeles, California 90015.)

The annotated bibliography lists approximately 146 instructional materials and books useful to teachers who deal with normal and abnormal adolescent affective behavior in junior and senior high schools. An explanation sheet gives instructions for correlating publisher with a specific material, and for finding items according to topic categories. A list of 21 publishers includes addresses. Topic areas of related materials are the following (total of items for each are in parentheses): social awareness (53), moral decisions (12), interpersonal relationships (51), self understanding (58), and cultural awareness (14), A short evaluative description, playing time, number of pages, purchase or rental price, or other pertinent features accompany each item listing. Some of the subjects materials or books cover are teen-parent relationships, sex education, alcoholism, running away, cheating, maturation and growth, Afro-American history, or American Indian studies. Items by media compose the following (quantity noted in parentheses); filmstrips with records, cassettes or guides (73), films (16mm, 8mm, filmloops, and 8mm sound (40), transparencies (2), simulation games (4), records (3), books and booklets (24), cassettes (1), professional material (1), and study prints (1).

Bolen, Jackie. *The Growing Years: A Bibliography of Affective Materials for the Preschool Child.* University of Southern California Los Angeles. Instructional Materials Center for Special Education. Spons Agency—Bureau of Education for the Handicapped (DHEW/OE), Washington, D.C., June 1972,

38p. (Available from Jackie Bolen, SEMC, 1031 South Broadway, Suite 623, University of Southern California, Los Angeles, California 90015.)

This annotated bibliography lists approximately 90 instructional materials useful in developing affective behavior in normal and abnormal preschool children. An explanation sheet gives instructions for correcting problems with a specific material, and for finding items according to topic categories. A list of 24 publishers includes addresses. Materials are indexed according to 24 topic areas, such as feelings, right and wrong, senses, racial understanding, recognizing individual differences, understanding self, truth, respect, friendship and relating to the environment. A short evaluative description, playing time, number of pages, price, or other pertinent features accompany each item. Items by media comprise the following (numbers in parentheses refer to quantity of individual items, sets, or series): professional materials (4), picture story sets (3), transparencies (1), film loops (1), instructional material (4), mixed media kits (6), records (9), children's books (10), films (9), cassettes (1), filmstrips (2), and filmstrips with records, cassettes, or tapes (6). A section on newer news lists more recent items, and is subject to updating. (For related information, see EC 052 158). (MC)

ED 049118

Burgess, Bonita. *A Bibliography* (Compiled for a Human Development Curriculum), 1969.

This is a bibliography compiled for a Human Development Curriculum. Materials are included for teachers and students, children and adults. Categories of materials include printed works, films, filmstrips, photographs, records, and centers which produce instructional materials. There is an extensive annotated bibliography of childrens' books that relate to the following areas of the curriculum: man's curiosity about his world, search for meaning in life, man's feelings about himself, man's concern for others, man's generations and their relationships, the world of work, and social roles.

ED 067356

Canfield, John T. and Phillips, Mark. *A Guide to Humanistic Education, Paper Dragon,* No. 4, 1970.

Bibliography covers all types of material related to humanistic education. Designed for people who are introducing new courses and activities to enhance positive self-concept, increase achievement motivation, promote creative thinking and behavior, and promote better human relations.

ED 032587

Clovinsky, Sanford J. *Bibliography of Guidance and Guidance Related Materials.* Wayne County Intermediate School District, Detroit, Michigan, 1969.

Bibliography includes listings of audio-visual materials, books and booklet series grouped under the following topics: general education, guidance, psychology-mental health, sociological grouping, testing materials, and vocational occupational information.

ED 067358
*Curriculum Projects and Materials in Elementary School Behavioral Sciences.*
American Psychological Association, Washington, D.C. Clearinghouse on Precollege Psychology, 1972.
     Purpose of the document is to inform educators about materials which focus on human behavior. Each description includes title, director or author, publishers, education level, list of materials, and a short annotation.

ED 014016
Durham, Lewis E., and Others. *A Bibliography of Research. Explorations, Human Relations Training and Research,* No. 2, National Training Labs., Washington, D.C., 1967.
     This bibliography contains two sections. The first contains research conducted between 1947 and 1960, some of which is annotated. The second section includes research since 1960. Again, some of it is annotated. Research topics covered include T-groups, group structure and dynamics, interpersonal relationship and competence, self-concept, personality change, behavior and attitude change, and organizational change.

ED 049817
Feldman, Ronald, Comp.; Coopersmith, Stanley, Comp. *A Resource and Reference Bibliography in Early Childhood Education and Development Psychology.* The Affective Domain. Office of Education, Washington, D.C., 1971.
     This is a comprehensive bibliography covering such categories as achievement motivation, aggression, anger and frustration, character and moral development, creativity, games, social behavior, etc. Contains books, anthologies, and papers and deals with theoretical treatments, specific research findings, teacher practices, and curricular material.

ED 044400
Harvey, Robert, Comp.; Denby, Robert W., Comp. *Human Relations in the Schools, Sensitivity Training, and Self-Image Enhancement: Abstracts of ERIC Documents.* National Council of Teachers of English, Champaign, Illinois. ERIC Clearinghouse on the Teaching of English Office of Education, Washington, D.C., September 1970.
     While concentrating heavily on interracial education, this bibliography of 115 citations does contain some abstracts of interest to those pursuing affective education.

ED 095 472
Hearn, D. Dwain, Ed., and Nicholson, Sandy. *Values, Feelings and Morals*

*Part 1: Research and Perspectives. Part 2: An Annotated Bibliography of Programs and Instructional Materials.* American Association of Elementary, Kindergarten, and Nursery Educators, 1201 16th Street, N.W., Washington, D.C. 20036, 1974.

This two-part document offers approaches and directions for school personnel in the development of childrens' values, feelings, and morals. Part 1 contains the presentations made at the 1973 National Research Committee Conference entitled "Children/Values, Feelings and Morals," each of which addresses a particular aspect of the overall topic. Presentations are (1) the development of moral thought in children, (2) children's understanding of morals, (3) mass media and moral development, (4) matching communication pace with children's cognitive styles, (5) primary level curriculum, cognitive developmental theory of moral reasoning, (6) Influencing children's values, feelings, and morals: program development and problems and (7) ethnic and social class attitudes and behaviors of children. Part 2 is an annotated bibliography of books for children and teachers, films and filmstrips, media materials, program guides, and catalogs—all dealing with the topic of developing values, feelings, and morals in children. (Author/PC)

ED 051315

Jayatilleke, Raja. *Human Relations in The Classroom: An Annotated Bibliography,* 1971.

This document covers printed materials relating to race relations, racial attitudes, racial recognition, self-concept, psychological identification, social influences, cultural differences, cross-cultural training, ethnic environment, human relations, intergroup relations, interpersonal relationships, student-teacher relationships, changing attitudes, teacher behavior, teacher attitudes, student attitudes, Negro attitudes, teacher education, teacher training institutes, activism, and violence.

ED 064417

Jayatilleke, Raja. *Human Relations in the Classroom, An Annotated Bibliography: Supplement 2:* ERIC-IRCD. Urban Disadvantaged Series, Number 33,

Citations cover such topics as race relations, racial recognition and attitudes, self-concept, and self-esteem, psychological identity, ethnic and Afro-American studies, social influences, cultural differences, cross-cultural training, curriculum development, classroom environment, intergroup and human relations, interpersonal and student-teacher relationships, teacher behavior and attitudes, changing attitudes, student attitudes, Negro attitudes, teacher education and training institutes, activism, and violence.

ED 079 437

Jayatilleke, Raja. *Human Relations in the Classroom, An Annotated Bibliography: Supplement 2.* ERIC-IRCD. Urban Disadvantaged Series, Number 33,

June 1973. Columbia Univ., New York, N.Y. ERIC Clearinghouse on the Urban Disadvantaged.

The second annual supplement to the bibliography series on human relations in the classroom covers the calendar year 1972 for items announced in RIE and also for journal articles cited. All of the published books and reports and unpublished documents listed are accompanied by ED numbers; their availability is clarified by a separate availability statement in one of the introductory pages of the bibliography. Journal articles mentioned are cited as not being available from the ERIC system but as being available in local libraries. Citations for items in the ERIC system are followed in each instance by a suitably edited abstract. Journal article citations are followed by appropriate descriptions, and in very many cases by brief annotations. As in the previous bibliographies, citations were searched for in the monthly issues of RIE and CIJE for 1972, using some 30 descriptors encompassing such issues and concepts related to human relations in the classroom as: classroom environment, race relations, psychological identity, social influences, cultural differences, curriculum development, changing attitudes, Negro attitudes, racial recognition and attitudes, self concept and esteem, cross cultural training, ethnic and Afro-American studies, intergroup and human relations, interpersonal and student-teacher relationships, teacher behavior and attitudes, teacher education and training institutes, and activism and violence. (RJ)

Kremer, Barbara. *Self-Concept Development: An Abstract Bibliography,* 1972, 28p.

This document is a compilation of resources in the ERIC file under "Research in Education" and "Current Index to Journals in Education" on the subject of self-concept as it relates to such topics as: early childhood education, racial activities, and programs which develop self-concept.

Kuhmerker, Lisa. *A Bibliography on Moral Development and the Learning of Values in Schools and Other Social Settings,* 1971, 45p.

Contains a listing of books on five major topics related to values: moral development, values in education, related to values in education, psychological approaches to learning of values, and cultural approaches to learning of values.

ED 013984

McGuire, Carson. *Research and Development Center for Teacher Education,* The University of Texas. Behavioral Science Memorandum, Number 13, Parts A and B, 1967.

This is an annotated bibliography for instructors in teacher education. It contains texts, books of readings, selected journal articles, various monographs, and recent books upon topics pertinent to teacher education. The references are relevant to the course "Behavioral Sciences in Education" offered at the University of Texas for both elementary and secondary education sections.

ED 097 269
"Moral and Values Education." *Bibliographies in Education,* No. 44 Canadian Teachers' Federation, Ottawa (Ontario). May 1972, 29p.

Sources consulted in preparing this bibliography of education material related to the teaching of moral or values education include the "Bibliographie de Quebec," "British Education Index," the "Canadian Education Index," the "Cumulative Book Index," the "Current Index to Journals in Education," the "Directory of Education Studies in Canada," the "Education Index," "Research in Education," and "Research Studies in Education." The period covered is approximately five years, from 1968 to 1973. The 414 citations are arranged alphabetically by author in three categories: books, articles, and theses. ERIC materials include ERIC document (ED) numbers and availability statements. Documents that are a part of the library of the Canadian Teachers' Federation are indicated by asterisks.

ED 056965
Pali, Rosario, Comp. *Humanities in the Classroom,* 1971.

This annotated bibliography contains sixty-four publications that deal with the humanities and humanizing formal instruction at all instructional levels.

ED 066411
Roen, Sheldon R. *References to Teaching Children About Human Behavior: Pre-High School,* 1970.

Lists approximately 400 publications on the teaching of behavioral sciences to elementary and intermediate grade children. Six major sections are as follows: directly relevant sources, other resources for teachers, selected curriculum and teaching materials, children's books and texts, high school psychology, and surveys of projects.

ED 052074
*Teaching of Psychology in the Secondary School: Research Studies 1964-1971; Teaching of the Behavioral Sciences in the Elementary School. Selected Bibliographies.* Washington, D.C.: American Psychological Association Clearinghouse on Precollege Psychology, 1971.

These two bibliographies give a total of 139 citations for books, journals, articles, research reports, newsletters, books, doctoral dissertations, and government publication on the teaching of the behavioral sciences at the elementary and secondary level.

ED 024064
Thomas, Walter L. *A Comprehensive Bibliography on the Value Concept.*

Northview Public Schools, Grand Rapids, Michigan, 1967.
Approximately 814 listings on the concept of value.

ED 038706
Zimpfer, David G. *Group Procedures in Guidance: A Bibliography*. Rochester University, New York, 1969.
Includes books, dissertations, unpublished documents and journal articles. Two major sections are topical and author listing. Covers materials up to 1968.

# About the Authors

Mother of three young adults, **Elizabeth Léonie Simpson** (Adjunct Associate Professor, University of Southern California) is a Ph.D. (University of California, Berkeley) who has taught there, as well as at USC and the University of California at Irvine. Besides her interest in humanistic education, she has researched and written on moral development and political socialization. Her published works include: *Democracy's Stepchildren: A Study of Need and Belief* (Jossey-Bass, 1971), a social science textbook series (Harcourt, Brace, Jovanovich), poetry and fiction, as well as many professional articles.

**Mary Anne Gray** grew up in Grand Rapids, Michigan. After graduating from Calvin College with an A.B. in English and education, she taught school in Chicago, Detroit, and West Germany. She has traveled extensively in Europe and recently returned to the University of Southern California where she received a master's degree in library science. At present she is director of the library at Buena Vista College in Storm Lake, Iowa.